EDITORS
PAUL ROSENZWEIG ★ TIMOTHY J. McNULTY
ELLEN SHEARER

NATIONAL SECURITY LAW IN THE NEWS

A GUIDE FOR JOURNALISTS, SCHOLARS, AND POLICYMAKERS

Cover by Elmarie Jara/ABA Publishing.

The materials contained herein represent the opinions of the authors and editors, and should not be construed to be the views or opinions of the law firms or companies with whom such persons are in partnership with, associated with, or employed by, nor of the American Bar Association or the Standing Committee on Law and National Security unless adopted pursuant to the bylaws of the Association.

Nothing contained in this book is to be considered as the rendering of legal advice for specific cases, and readers are responsible for obtaining such advice from their own legal counsel. This book is intended for educational and informational purposes only.

© 2012 American Bar Association. All rights reserved.

No part of this publication may be reproduced, stored in a retrieval system, or transmitted in any form or by any means, electronic, mechanical, photocopying, recording, or otherwise, without the prior written permission of the publisher. For permission, contact the ABA Copyrights and Contracts Department by e-mail at copyright@americanbar.org or fax at 312-988-6030, or complete the online request form at http://www.americanbar.org/utility/reprint.

Printed in the United States of America

16 15 14 13 12   5 4 3 2 1

Library of Congress Cataloging-in-Publication Data

National security law in the news : a guide for journalists, scholars, and policymakers / edited by Timothy J. McNulty, Paul Rosenzweig, and Ellen Shearer.—1st ed.
   p. cm.
   Includes bibliographical references and index.
   ISBN 978-1-61438-767-1 (print : alk. paper)
1. National security—Law and legislation—United States. I. McNulty, Timothy J. II. Rosenzweig, Paul, 1959– III. Shearer, Ellen, 1952–
   KF4850.N39 2012
   343.73'01—dc23

                                                            2012040522

Discounts are available for books ordered in bulk. Special consideration is given to state bars, CLE programs, and other bar-related organizations. Inquire at Book Publishing, ABA Publishing, American Bar Association, 321 North Clark Street, Chicago, Illinois 60654-7598.

www.ShopABA.org

To those who labor to protect American liberty by fighting
for it and by reporting on the fight.

Contents

Introduction	xi
Part I: Basic Issues of Constitutional and International Law	**1**
1 Separation of Powers and National Security	**3**
By Vijay M. Padmanabhan	
The Reality	4
Experts	11
Resources	12
2 The First Amendment and National Security	**13**
By Julia Atcherley and Lee Levine	
Setting the Stage: The Sedition Act and the Pentagon Papers	14
Criminal Prosecution of Journalists	16
Sources and Subpoenas: The Reporter's Privilege	18
Conclusion	21
Experts	21
Resources	22
3 U.S. Government Secrecy and Classification	**25**
By John R. Tunheim and Andrew M. Borene	
Classification in U.S. History	25
Executive Orders	27
The Current Executive Order Governing Classification	27
Modern Classification Categories	28
Sensitive Compartmented Information	29
Special Access Programs	30

CONTENTS

Ban on Use of Classification to Hide Embarrassing Information	31
Access to Classified Information	33
Unclassified but Protected—"For Official Use Only"	34
Sanctions: Legal Consequences for Violating Classification Rules	35
Experts	36
Resources	36
Appendix to Chapter 3	39

4 The Role of International Law in Domestic Courts   67
By Deborah Pearlstein

What Is International Law?	68
Treaties	68
Customary International Law	69
When Questions of International Law Arise before U.S. Courts	71
Conclusion	75
Experts	75
Resources	76

5 Defining Terrorism under International Law   79
By David Scharia

Introduction	79
Defining Terrorism at the United Nations	80
Resolutions Requiring Member States to Take Measures against Terrorism	86
Terrorism as an International Crime	88
Terrorism as a Crime under International Customary Law	90
Conclusion	91
Experts	92
Resources	92

Part II: The Laws of War and Military Operations   95

6 The Laws of War: Regulating the Use of Force   97
By Geoffrey S. Corn and Laurie R. Blank

The *Jus ad Bellum:* The International Legal Basis for the Use of Force	98
The *Jus in Bello:* Regulating the Conduct of Hostilities	105
Conclusion	118
Experts	119
Resources	120

7 Secret Operations: Covert Action and Military Activities   123
By Benjamin Powell

Military Activities under Title 10 of the U.S. Code	125
Covert Action under Title 50 of the U.S. Code	126
Traditional Military Activities and Covert Action	129

Experts	132
Resources	133

8 Piracy — 135
By Eugene Kontorovich

Background	135
Causes of Somali Piracy	137
Private Military Contractors and Rules of Engagement	138
Difficulties in Prosecution	140
Transfers for Trial	141
Experts	142
Resources	143

9 The United Nations Convention on the Law of the Sea — 145
By Glenn M. Sulmasy and Chris Tribolet

Introduction	145
Early Development of the Law of the Sea	146
Jurisdiction Creep Begins	147
The 1958 Conventions on the Law of the Sea	148
The Push for a Comprehensive Law of the Sea Treaty	148
The United Nations Convention on the Law of the Sea (UNCLOS III)	149
The Status of UNCLOS III in U.S. Law	158
Experts	159
Resources	159

10 Targeted Killings and the Law — 161
By Amos N. Guiora

Historical Background of Self-Defense	163
Differentiating Extrajudicial Killing from Targeted Killing	166
The Decision-Making Process	166
Conclusion	170
Experts	170
Resources	171

11 Military Commissions — 173
By David W. Glazier

Military Commission History	174
Bush Administration Military Commissions	177
Guantanamo Trials under the Military Commissions Act of 2009	178
Guantanamo Military Commission Issues	179
Conclusion	181
Experts	182
Resources	182

CONTENTS

12 Courts-Martial and Other Military Legal Proceedings   **183**
By Jim McPherson
Administrative Personnel Proceedings   183
Court-Martial Proceedings   186
Posttrial Proceedings   192
    Experts   193
    Resources   193

Part III: Domestic Law Enforcement and Counterterrorism   195

13 U.S.-Based Intelligence: The Law and Organizational Structure   **197**
By W. Renn Gade and Harvey Rishikof
"U.S.-Based Intelligence" Defined   200
Post-9/11 Changes and the Structure of the U.S.-Based Intelligence Enterprise   201
Department of Homeland Security   202
Director of National Intelligence   203
Department of Justice and the FBI   204
Department of Defense   207
Future Challenges with U.S.-Based Intelligence   208
    Experts   210
    Resources   210

14 National Security Investigations   **215**
By Todd Hinnen
The Historical Foundations of Modern National Security Investigations   216
The Emergence of a Legal Framework   218
Oversight of National Security Investigations   224
Conclusion   225
    Experts   226
    Resources   226

15 Electronic Surveillance and Cybersecurity   **227**
By James X. Dempsey
Constitutional Origins   227
Statutes Regulating Electronic Surveillance and Related Activities   231
Cybersecurity   241
    Experts   242
    Resources   242

16 Material Support of Terrorism: Tool for Public Safety or Recipe for Overreaching?   **243**
By Peter Margulies
A (Very) Short History of Conspiracy   245
History of the Material Support Laws   246
Prosecutions for Aiding Terrorist Activity under Section 2339A   247
Use of Informants   250

Material Support of Designated Organizations	250
Criticisms of the Material Support Law	256
Material Support beyond Criminal Law	257
Military Commissions	258
Immigration Impact	260
Experts	261
Resources	261

17 Extraterritorial Issues: Investigation and Prosecution of National Security Cases — 263
By Jennifer C. Daskal

Introduction	263
Jurisdiction for Extraterritorial Offenses	264
Investigations Abroad	268
Obtaining the Defendant	272
Posttrial	274
Conclusion	275
Experts	275
Resources	275

18 Data Mining: A Primer — 279
By Adam Isles

What Is Data Mining?	281
Historical Context	285
Understanding the Relationship of Technology to Policy	290
In the News	293
Experts	297
Resources	297

19 Exports of Surveillance Technology to Repressive Regimes — 299
By Michael T. Gershberg

Substantive Law—A Patchwork of Rules	301
Procedure—Vastly Differing Time Horizons between News and Investigation Cycles	306
Conclusion	308
Experts	308
Resources	309

Part IV: Homeland Security Issues — 311

20 The Use of the Military in the Homeland — 313
By Kurt Johnson

Military Roles in the Homeland	314
Civilian Control of the Military	315
Federal versus State Powers and the Tenth Amendment to the U.S. Constitution	315

CONTENTS

The "Military"	316
Unity of Command versus Unity of Effort and the Dual Status Commander	317
Who Is in Charge? The Civil Support/Homeland Defense Continuum	318
The Posse Comitatus Act and the Insurrection Act	320
Immediate Response Authority	323
Intelligence Oversight	323
Conclusion	325
Experts	326
Resources	326

21 Border Security and the Law   **329**
By Susan Ginsburg

Background	330
Border Security Intelligence Authorities	331
Use of Immigration Law in Counterterrorism	334
Traveler Screening and the Visa Process	340
Illegal Immigration and Border Security	342
Allocation of Federal, State, and Local Immigration Authority	345
Military Homeland Defense	347
Conclusion	348
Experts	349
Resources	350

22 Airport Screening and Scanning   **351**
By J. Bennet Waters and Paul Rosenzweig

Introduction	351
The Legal Environment	352
Advanced Imaging Technology: Understanding the Technology	354
Limitations and Concerns	355
Necessity and Justification: The Administrative Procedures Act	357
Experts	358
Resources	359

23 Responding to Biological Attacks   **361**
By Barry Kellman

Detection and Diagnosis	362
Medical Countermeasures	365
Response and Restoration of Order	368
Conclusion	371
Experts	371
Resources	372

About the Editors	**375**
About the Contributors	**379**
Index	**389**

Introduction

By Paul Rosenzweig, Timothy J. McNulty, and Ellen Shearer

Looking back with the perspective of more than a decade, we can see that the terrorist attacks on September 11, 2001, were an inflection point in American law and policy. Controversies continue, but many of the fundamental legal changes seem, at this distance, to have become an accepted part of our system of governance and, indeed, our way of life.

Before the 9/11 attacks, other dramatic events—such as the 1995 Oklahoma City bombing—occurred, and policy decisions were questioned in every administration. Sensational courts-martial, though rare, were convened and merited widespread media coverage. For the most part, though, journalists' interest in the legal evolution of national security law was minor unless it seemed to run smack into First Amendment speech issues.

Times have changed. One way of capturing that change is to survey journalists' use of some common phrases regarding national security law and policy.

Anecdotally, the changes are stunning. Mentions of "military commissions" in newspapers and wire services, for example, rose from just eight in 2000 to nearly 900 in 2011.[1] "Cybersecurity" merited only 144 mentions in 2000 compared with more than 3,000 in 2011. "Border security" similarly jumped from fewer than 300 mentions to more than 3,000. And "drones" were just a gleam in their designers' eyes with zero mentions in 2000 and more than 1,900 in 2011 (likewise "targeted killings" rose from four to over 400). The figures give substance to the fundamental premise of this book—that after September 11 the language of public discourse changed.

Not only has the language of our public policy changed, but so too has our collective experience. A list of high points and low points of the past decade would reflect a global and national reality that is significantly different from that of the

---

1. The data we present here are from a broad-based Lexis-Nexis search of major U.S. newspapers and wire services during the years in question. We thank John Odle, a student at Emory University School of Law, for his research assistance in collecting this data.

INTRODUCTION

turn of the century, including of course the 9/11 attacks themselves, the invasion of Iraq, and the war in Afghanistan.

Experiences like Transportation Safety Administration screenings at the airport have become shared reference points and part of popular culture. Guantanamo Bay, which had faded in American memory, returned to prominence. And perhaps most tellingly, obscure corners of law and policy now have a significant impact on American conversations that erupt over national security issues.

Almost everyone has an opinion about what is happening: The introduction of backscatter X-ray machines in 2010 as part of airport security prompted a spate of protests by some who saw them as an invasion of privacy. When President Barack Obama chose to commit American military forces to the NATO mission in Libya in 2011, the public argument over the wisdom of that course of action was vocal and widespread. Even as we write this, the same argument is recurring over the decision *not* to intervene militarily in Syria.

The level of public engagement in issues of national security concern has returned to levels not seen in America since the 1960s and 1970s. The discussion is at once invigorating, engaging, frustrating, and challenging. Journalists, as the voice of a free people, are at once responsible for reporting on that discourse and, to some degree, creating it.

This book is intended to help journalists reporting on those discussions understand the legal underpinnings so they can provide context and avoid factual missteps. Others in the public sphere likewise find the law obscure. Our thesis, amply substantiated by the essays in this volume, is that the United States is a country bound by the rule of law and, thus, that behind every policy question lurks a legal landscape. Obama's Libya decision was not only a policy issue but also an occasion for the discussion of the lawfulness of presidential war making without the benefit of congressional approval.

In short, the law matters. But because lawyers have a tendency to speak a foreign language—that is, "lawyer-ese"—and to cite earlier case histories in shorthand, the legal landscape is often inaccessible to those outside that profession. Journalists and others without legal training but eager to inform the general public often have difficulty making sense of the volumes of judicial decisions, administrative rulings, and other mandates in the legislative and judicial universe.

We aim to lift those clouds of obscurity—particularly for journalists who cover the national security beat, though it is our hope that any interested layman also will find clarity in these pages. We have asked legal experts with a wide breadth of experience to provide us with clear and precise summaries of significant areas of law that bear on national security and homeland security policy. Many are current or former national security officials who represent various administrations. Others are widely respected academics. All have given of their time for the pure joy of the effort, and they have our deepest thanks.

Each chapter contains a summary of legal and policy issues of significance and is accompanied by an annotated bibliography for further reading. In

Introduction

addition, and especially helpful for journalists new to the particular legal issue, each chapter also contains a list of experts to contact for additional background and information.

Part I begins, as it should, at the beginning. This section contains essays on aspects of the law that pervade all of the other subjects. It includes chapters on the scope of the president's authority, the meaning and effect of the First Amendment, and basic rules of classification and secrecy that bear on all of the domestic issues discussed. This section also covers the role of international law in American courts and the problems attending even the basic question of defining exactly what terrorism is.

Part II turns the focus to the military and explores questions about military organization and operations. These topics range from broad questions about the laws of armed conflict and the allocation of responsibility between the military and intelligence community, to narrower questions about the legality of targeted killing and the lawfulness of our responses to piracy. There is also a discussion of the controversial military commission system and the far more common system of courts-martial.

Part III looks at the world of domestic law enforcement and intelligence collection. This section begins by describing how this world of government activity is organized. We then turn to a series of chapters on how government operates—looking first at the legal authorities to conduct investigations broadly, and then at the narrower question of electronic surveillance. This section also has chapters on the material support provisions of law, the principal legal tools used to prosecute alleged terrorists and their supporters today, and the vexing question of how to apply U.S. law to acts outside our borders. We conclude with two of the hot-button issues of the day: the potential problems surrounding data mining (the collection and analysis of large quantities of personal data by the government) and the role of export controls in restricting access to technology.

Finally, in Part IV we turn to homeland security issues. Two of the topics in the section—border security and immigration, and the use of airport screening technology—will be familiar to almost everyone. The other two topics—the use of the military in the homeland and the scope of biological threats—will be less well known but will be of equal, if not greater, importance in the coming years.

Our goal is to demystify the law and how it developed. In doing so, our aim is to provide the necessary legal background and context for journalists and others who want to understand ongoing policy debates. Readers will have a better appreciation for the many legal and policy changes that have happened since September 11, how and why they came about, and whether they were overreactions or reasonable judgments. Our objective is to inform the discussion and, we hope, educate as well.

Part I

Basic Issues of Constitutional and International Law

Separation of Powers and National Security

By Vijay M. Padmanabhan

The allocation of wartime authority between the president and Congress, always hotly contested, has been the subject of much discussion during the last two administrations. President George W. Bush invoked his constitutional authority as commander in chief, among other authorities, to order the detention, interrogation, and trial of members of al-Qaida and the Taliban, as well as the warrantless wiretapping of suspected members of al-Qaida and their contacts in the United States.

President Barack Obama relied on his constitutional powers to use force in Libya without congressional authorization and to claim that some congressional restrictions on the transfer of detainees from Guantanamo are unconstitutional.

In each of these instances, critics of expansive use of presidential power argued that the president exceeded his constitutional authority and called upon Congress and the federal courts to take action to reset the constitutional balance. This chapter lays out the framework for understanding the constitutional allocation of national security powers among the branches as it is understood today.

The text of the U.S. Constitution grants many wartime authorities to Congress. Article I grants Congress the following relevant powers:

- to declare war
- to raise and appropriate funds for the national defense

- to define and punish war crimes and other violations of international law
- to regulate the conduct of the armed forces, including setting rules with respect to those captured on land and at sea[1]

Article II installs the president as commander in chief of the armed forces and also gives him the authority to negotiate treaties, subject to the advice and consent of the Senate. Article III provides the courts no particular national security powers, although they are empowered to hear cases and controversies arising under the U.S. Constitution, which frequently include national security questions.

There is scholarly debate surrounding the intention of the drafters of the Constitution with respect to the allocation of national security powers among the branches. Some believe the drafters were concerned about the aggregation of wartime powers in the hands of the executive branch in the aftermath of a revolution against monarchical rule. For these scholars, a strong congressional role in national security decisions is a popular check on executive predilections in favor of war.

A Justice Department official in the Bush administration, John Yoo, presents an opposing viewpoint, arguing that the Framers intended for a strong executive to lead during wartime, with the congressional role limited to the power of the purse.[2] From this perspective, many congressional restrictions imposed on the president's wartime decisions are unconstitutional.

THE REALITY

Regardless of which vision of the balance of powers between the branches is historically accurate, in practice the president has emerged as the central actor in responding to emergencies that require the use of force. The president, as a single powerful figure, has a greater capacity to respond to national security crises than the slow, deliberative, and diffuse Congress. Moreover, there is often a lack of political will in Congress to use appropriations and oversight authorities to force a change in presidential policy.[3] Democrats, who gained a majority in both houses of Congress in 2006 based in part on opposition to the war in Iraq, nevertheless were unable to force any major changes in Bush administration policy toward that war.

Consistent with this reality, the Office of Legal Counsel at the Department of Justice has concluded that the president has the power without the authorization of Congress to commit U.S. troops abroad and take military action short of war to

---

1. U.S. CONST. art. I, § 8.
2. John C. Yoo, *The Continuation of Politics by Other Means: The Original Understanding of War Powers*, 84 CAL. L. REV. 167 (1996).
3. *See* Harold H. Koh, *Why the President Almost Always Wins in Foreign Affairs: Lessons of the Iran-Contra Affair*, 97 YALE L.J. 1255 (1988).

Congress has declared war only five times:

- War of 1812
- Mexican-American War
- Spanish-American War
- World War I
- World War II

In recent years Congress has authorized the use of force without a formal declaration of war:

- Vietnam (Gulf of Tonkin Resolution, 1964)
- Iraq (1993)
- Afghanistan (2001)
- Iraq (2003)

But presidents have used force without any congressional authorization at all, including

- Somalia (1993)
- Haiti (1994)
- Bosnia (1995)
- Kosovo (1998)
- Haiti (2004)
- Libya (2011)

protect important national interests.[4] Even measures amounting to war may be undertaken without congressional action in an emergency to protect the country from foreign invasion or insurrection.[5] Presidents have time and again invoked their constitutional authority as justification for the use of force, both where they act without congressional authorization and even where there was arguably some congressional approval.

The president's constitutional authority is not without bounds, however. The Supreme Court has held consistently that the president must respect limits on the exercise of his commander-in-chief authority that have been imposed by Congress in the proper exercise of its constitutional powers. In the landmark decision *Youngstown Sheet & Tube Co. v. Sawyer (Steel Seizure Case)*,[6] the court struck

---

4. *See* Memorandum from Caroline D. Krass, Office of Legal Counsel, U.S. Dep't of Justice, to Att'y Gen. Eric Holder, Authority to Use Military Force in Libya (Apr. 1, 2011) (defending President Obama's decision to use airpower in Libya without congressional authorization).

5. *See* The Prize Cases, 67 U.S. 635 (1863) (upholding President Lincoln's blockade of the Confederate States in advance of congressional authorization on grounds of emergency authority to protect against foreign invasion or insurrection).

6. 343 U.S. 579 (1952).

down President Harry Truman's order nationalizing steel mills to prevent a strike that would have crippled steel production during the Korean War. In his famous concurring opinion, Justice Robert Jackson identified a three-category approach to presidential actions that is still used by the Supreme Court today:

Category 1: Where the president acts pursuant to congressional authorization, he acts with the authority of both branches. Such actions are permissible unless the federal government as a whole lacks authority to act.

Category 2: Where the president acts without any relevant congressional action, he is in a "zone of twilight," meaning there may be concurrent authority for the president and Congress to act. A long pattern of congressional inaction in the face of presidential action is treated as acquiescence to presidential authority.

Category 3: Where the president acts against the express or implied will of Congress, he acts illegally unless the congressional restrictions imposed are unconstitutional.[7]

Given this framework, presidents generally claim that their national security actions are pursuant to congressional authorization, which will almost always render them lawful. President Bush claimed that Congress granted him authority in the Authorization for Use of Military Force after the 9/11 attacks to conduct warrantless foreign intelligence surveillance within the United States. The program, called the Terrorist Surveillance Program or TSP, would have been on much firmer constitutional footing if it were more clearly authorized by Congress, since it would then be lawful provided that the government had authority to undertake the activity.

While courts have never opined on whether the TSP was authorized by Congress, they have on other occasions been circumspect in concluding that Congress authorized presidential action. In *Hamdan v. Rumsfeld*[8] the Supreme Court considered whether Bush had lawfully created military commissions to prosecute alien enemy combatants detained at Guantanamo Bay. Among other arguments, Bush argued that Congress had authorized the commissions in the Detainee Treatment Act (DTA) when it created federal court review procedures for military commission convictions. The Supreme Court rejected this argument, explaining that while the DTA recognized commissions, it did not authorize them.

Even without congressional authorization, presidential action may be lawful if Congress acquiesces to the president's actions. In *Dames & Moore v. Regan*,[9] the Supreme Court rejected President Jimmy Carter's argument that Congress had authorized him to dismiss claims against Iran pending in federal courts as part of

---

7. *Id.* at 635–38 (Jackson, J., concurring).
8. 548 U.S. 557 (2006).
9. 453 U.S. 654 (1981).

an agreement ending the Iran hostage crisis. The Court nevertheless upheld the president's actions because Congress had long allowed the executive authority to enter into claims settlement agreements. This long-standing pattern in effect constituted a form of approval of executive actions. The Justice Department Office of Legal Counsel has made similar arguments to justify presidential use of force short of war without congressional authorization.

The Supreme Court considers numerous factors when it reviews whether Congress has acquiesced to presidential action, including the consistency, density, frequency, duration, and normalcy of the practice.[10] In the *Steel Seizure Case*, Justice Felix Frankfurter's concurring opinion rejected Truman's argument that Congress had acquiesced to presidential authority to seize steel mills. Frankfurter found that there were just three isolated instances where the president had seized private property without congressional authorization or declaration of war, a level of activity insufficient to constitute acquiescence.[11]

In those instances where Congress does exercise its prerogative to restrict presidential authority in the national security area, those restrictions must be followed except where unconstitutional. For example, in *Hamdan* the Supreme Court found that Congress had specifically authorized the use of military commissions in the Uniform Code of Military Justice subject to several conditions.[12] The president was bound to follow these conditions because they were passed pursuant to Congress's war powers.

POST-9/11 U.S. SUPREME COURT NATIONAL SECURITY DECISIONS		
Case Name	Year	Holding
Ashcroft v. al-Kidd, 131 S. Ct. 2074	2011	Government does not violate the Fourth Amendment when it uses properly obtained material witness warrants for the purpose of detaining terrorism suspects.
Holder v. Humanitarian Law Project, 130 S. Ct. 2705	2010	Government does not violate the First Amendment when it criminalizes speech that is directed by or coordinated with a foreign terrorist organization.
Boumediene v. Bush, 553 U.S. 723	2008	Detainees held at Guantanamo Bay, Cuba, are protected by the Suspension Clause of the U.S. Constitution. The case-by-case review scheme created by Congress in the Detainee Treatment Act and Military Commissions Act constitutes an unconstitutional suspension of the writ of habeas corpus.

continued

---

10. *See* Michael J. Glennon, *The Use of Custom in Resolving Separation of Powers Disputes*, 64 B.U. L. Rev. 109 (1984) (providing factors).
11. 343 U.S. at 611 (Frankfurter, J., concurring).
12. 548 U.S. at 593.

SEPARATION OF POWERS AND NATIONAL SECURITY

Case Name	Year	Holding
Munaf v. Geren, 553 U.S. 674	2008	The federal courts have jurisdiction over the habeas claim of a U.S. citizen detained by U.S. forces acting as part of an international coalition overseas. The court will defer to the government's determination that a U.S. citizen will not be tortured after transfer to the custody of a foreign state.
Hamdan v. Rumsfeld, 548 U.S. 557	2006	The executive must abide by restrictions on his authority to convene military commissions imposed by Congress in the Uniform Code of Military Justice.
Hamdi v. Rumsfeld, 542 U.S. 507	2004	A U.S. citizen detained in the United States has a constitutional right to notice of the reasons for his detention and the ability to contest those reasons in front of a neutral fact finder with the assistance of counsel.

In rare instances, the Supreme Court has found that Congress exceeded its constitutional role by infringing on an enumerated presidential power. In *INS v. Chadha*[13] the Court struck down a provision of the Immigration and Naturalization Act that gave the House of Representatives the authority to override, by resolution, immigration determinations made by the attorney general. The Supreme Court held that the so-called legislative veto infringed upon the president's sole authority, found in the Presentment Clause, to decide whether to sign or veto legislation. While the courts have rarely found such infringements, this line of argument is frequently advanced by scholars and executive-branch lawyers to claim that restrictions imposed by Congress on the president's commander-in-chief power are unconstitutional.

The most extreme example of this argument was made by the Office of Legal Counsel at the Justice Department in the now infamous "torture memo."[14] That memo concluded that capture, detention, and interrogation of enemy combatants is a core function of the commander in chief, and therefore is not subject to regulation by Congress. As a consequence, the memo recognized the authority of the president to ignore the federal statute criminalizing torture by U.S. officials in conducting interrogations pursuant to his commander-in-chief authority.

The "torture memo" is inconsistent with the approach to separation of powers taken by the Supreme Court. The Court has found that while the Constitution prohibits infringements on enumerated presidential powers, it permits restrictions on implied or aggregated powers provided that any such restriction advances a congressional power and is proportionate to the aims sought.[15] The authority to

---

13. 462 U.S. 919 (1983).
14. Memorandum from Jay Bybee, Office of Legal Counsel, Dep't of Justice, to Alberto Gonzales, White House Counsel (2002).
15. *See* Pub. Citizen v. U.S. Dep't of Justice, 491 U.S. 440 (1989) (Kennedy, J., concurring) (describing distinction in Court approach to congressional restrictions on enumerated presidential powers compared to implied or aggregated powers).

interrogate enemy combatants is implied from the president's commander-in-chief authority. The criminal prohibition on torture was passed pursuant to enumerated congressional powers, including the power to define and punish offenses against the law of nations and to set rules for captures on land and at sea, and does not prevent the president from exercising his duties as commander in chief. The Office of Legal Counsel in the Justice Department subsequently withdrew the "torture memo" and accepted that the statute criminalizing torture is constitutional as applied to interrogations undertaken during armed conflict.[16]

Similar questions surround the TSP authorized by President Bush. The warrantless domestic wiretapping permitted by the order creating the program deviated from the Foreign Intelligence Surveillance Act (FISA), which requires warrants for domestic surveillance. While the Justice Department argued this program was authorized by Congress, as discussed above, it also contended that FISA would be unconstitutional if it did not permit the wiretapping at issue because it would prevent the president from carrying out core duties as commander in chief.[17]

This argument is extremely controversial. The Office of Legal Counsel memo portrayed surveillance operations as a core wartime tactic, which the commander in chief must be free to employ in a conflict authorized by Congress. It relied on historic practice predating FISA in which the president had engaged in similar activities to protect national security.

Critics responded that wiretapping is an implied presidential power subject to proportionate restrictions by Congress issued pursuant to its wartime powers. They defend the constitutionality of FISA because it was made pursuant to the power of Congress to make rules for the regulation of land and naval forces.[18] And they reject the relevance of pre-FISA practice because whatever inherent authority the president had to conduct surveillance before FISA, he must now follow restrictions imposed by Congress. No court has ever ruled on whether the presidential justification for the TSP was valid.

Despite the requirement that the president follow congressional restrictions on his emergency powers that are constitutional, courts are often unwilling to get involved in disputes regarding the exercise of wartime authority. Courts have used a variety of doctrines to refuse to adjudicate on the merits disputes regarding the exercise of wartime authority. Three are worth noting here.

First, courts will decline to hear cases that require the adjudication of a political question, meaning an issue that the Constitution assigns to the political

---

16. *See* Memorandum from Steven G. Bradbury, Office of Legal Counsel, Dep't of Justice, to File (2009) ("[T]he sweeping assertions . . . that the President's Commander in Chief authority categorically precludes Congress from enacting any legislation concerning the detention, interrogation, prosecution, and transfer of enemy combatants are not sustainable.").

17. U.S. Dep't of Justice, Legal Authorities Supporting the Activities of the National Security Agency Described by the President (Jan. 19, 2006).

18. *See* The National Security Agency's Domestic Spying Program: February 2, 2006 Letter from Scholars and Former Government Officials to Congressional Leadership in Response to Justice Department Whitepaper of January 19, 2006, 81 IND. L.J. 1415 (2005).

branches or that is a purely political dispute. In *Corrie v. Caterpillar*[19] the family of a woman killed by an Israeli bulldozer sued Caterpillar, alleging it aided and abetted Israel's violations of international law when it sold the bulldozer. Caterpillar did so as part of a U.S. government program aiding the sale of military equipment to allies including Israel. The Ninth Circuit Court of Appeals affirmed dismissal of the case on political question grounds. Holding Caterpillar liable for participation in a U.S. government program would require second-guessing the government's decision to authorize the sale, a discretionary decision best left in the hands of the government.

Second, plaintiffs must have alleged a concrete injury to themselves perpetrated by the government. In *ACLU v. National Security Agency*[20] the Sixth Circuit Court of Appeals upheld dismissal on standing grounds of claims by journalists, academics, and civil liberties groups alleging they had been the subjects of unlawful wiretapping as part of the TSP. Plaintiffs lacked standing because they could not demonstrate they had been the victims of wiretapping. The standing analysis was not affected by the fact that FISA prevented plaintiffs from learning whether they had been wiretapped. The Second Circuit Court of Appeals recently reached the opposite conclusion, and the Supreme Court has now agreed to resolve the matter.[21]

Third, courts will decline to hear cases that require disclosure of state secrets damaging to the country's national security. In *Mohamed v. Jeppesen Dataplan*[22] the Ninth Circuit affirmed dismissal of claims that the defendant had aided the Central Intelligence Agency in its program of extraordinary rendition, which moved terrorist suspects from one country to another, allegedly for the purpose of interrogation using torture. The court concluded that the nature of the claims and defenses raised required the exposure of secret information regarding the rendition program that would have damaged national security, thereby mandating dismissal.

To overcome some of these institutional and structural limitations on its role in regulating the use of force, Congress passed the War Powers Resolution (WPR) in the aftermath of the Vietnam War. The WPR attempts to enforce a role for Congress in the use of force by

- terminating the president's authority to use force within 60 days unless Congress authorizes the use of force, extends the 60-day period, or cannot meet due to armed attack upon the United States, and
- granting Congress the authority to terminate the use of force by concurrent resolution.

---

19. 503 F.3d 974 (9th Cir. 2007).
20. 493 F.3d 644 (6th Cir. 2007).
21. Amnesty Int'l USA v. Clapper, 638 F.3d 118 (2d Cir. 2011), *cert. granted*, No. 11-1025 (Sup. Ct. May 21, 2012). A decision is expected in the October 2012 Supreme Court term.
22. 614 F.3d 1070 (9th Cir. 2010) (en banc).

President Nixon vetoed the WPR, arguing that these provisions unconstitutionally restricted the president's commander-in-chief authority, but Congress overrode his veto. Subsequent presidents have maintained that aspects of the WPR are unconstitutional but have largely claimed they have acted consistently with its provisions.

The WPR is generally viewed as a failure in restricting the president's use of his emergency powers. Presidents have narrowly interpreted the 60-day-clock provision to claim that apparent uses of force did not start the 60-day window. Most recently, President Obama argued that his decision to commit U.S. airpower to the U.N.-authorized mission to protect civilians in Libya did not amount to introduction of armed forces into "hostilities or into situations where imminent involvement with hostilities is indicated by the circumstances," which triggers the clock. State Department legal adviser Harold Koh identified four features of the use of force in Libya, which he argued collectively precluded the 60-day clock from being triggered:

1. U.S. forces played a constrained and supporting role in the mission;
2. No U.S. casualties or substantial risk of U.S. casualties;
3. Limited risk of escalation;
4. Modest U.S. military engagement.[23]

While some scholars and members of Congress have been critical of this interpretation, the WPR fails to provide meaningful enforcement for its provisions. The federal courts have found that members of Congress lack standing to enforce the provisions of the WPR in court because they have legislative options to stop presidential action that violates the WPR.[24] But these steps—cutting off funding for military missions or even impeaching the president—were available to Congress prior to passage of the WPR, and their illusory nature was justification for passage of the WPR in the first place. Thus, whether WPR requirements are met becomes largely a discretionary decision for the president and therefore serves only as a limited check on his emergency powers.

EXPERTS

William C. Banks, Professor of Law and Director of the Institute for National Security and Counterterrorism, Syracuse University; (315) 443-3678; wcbanks@law.syr.edu

---

23. Press Release, U.S. Dep't of State, Harold H. Koh, Testimony Before the Senate Foreign Relations Committee (June 28, 2011), http://www.state.gov/s/l/releases/remarks/167250.htm.
24. See Campbell v. Clinton, 203 F.3d 19 (D.C. Cir. 2000) (holding that members of Congress lacked standing to bring a claim alleging a violation of the WPR).

David D. Cole, Professor of Law, Georgetown University; (202) 662-9078; cole@law.georgetown.edu

Jack L. Goldsmith, Henry Shattuck Professor of Law, Harvard University; (617) 384-8159; jgoldsmith@law.harvard.edu

Martin S. Lederman, Associate Professor of Law, Georgetown University; (202) 662-9421; msl46@law.georgetown.edu

Trevor W. Morrison, Isidor and Seville Sulzbacher Professor of Law and Co-Chair of the Hertog Program on Law and National Security, Columbia University; (212) 854-1997; tmorri@law.columbia.edu

John C. Yoo, Professor of Law, University of California, Berkeley; (510) 643-5089; yoo@law.berkeley.edu

RESOURCES

Memorandum from Steven G. Bradbury, Office of Legal Counsel, Dep't of Justice, to File (2009) (providing analysis of current Justice Department views on the ability of Congress to restrict the president's wartime authority).

Dep't of Justice, Legal Authorities Supporting the Activities of the National Security Agency Described by the President (Jan. 19, 2006) (Bush administration justification for the TSP).

The National Security Agency's Domestic Spying Program: February 2, 2006 Letter from Scholars and Former Government Officials to Congressional Leadership in Response to Justice Department Whitepaper of Jan. 19, 2006, 81 IND. L.J. 1415 (2005) (critical response to Bush administration justification of TSP program).

Press Release, U.S. Dep't of State, Harold H. Koh, Testimony Before the Senate Foreign Relations Committee (June 28, 2011), http://www.state.gov/s/l/releases/remarks/167250.htm (Obama administration justification for use of force in Libya without congressional authorization).

War Powers Resolution, 50 U.S.C. §§ 1541–1548 (2006).

John C. Yoo, *The Continuation of Politics by Other Means: The Original Understanding of War Powers*, 84 CAL. L. REV. 167 (1996).

Harold H. Koh, *Why the President (Almost) Always Wins in Foreign Affairs: Lessons of the Iran-Contra Affair*, 97 YALE L.J. 1255 (1988).

The First Amendment and National Security

By Julia Atcherley and Lee Levine

From its beginnings, U.S. law has grappled with the potential for conflict between the commands of the First Amendment to the Constitution—"Congress shall make no law . . . abridging the freedom of speech or of the press"—and the obligation of the federal government to ensure the security of its citizens. Both presidents and Supreme Court justices have long recognized that the Constitution is not a "suicide pact,"[1] and that the law may therefore properly place at least some limits on the scope of the First Amendment's protections to prevent substantial harm to the nation's security. The

---

1. Terminiello v. Chicago, 337 U.S. 1, 37 (1949) (Jackson, J., dissenting); *see also* Letter from Thomas Jefferson to John Colvin (Sept. 20, 1810), *reprinted in* 3 THE FOUNDERS' CONSTITUTION 127–128 (Philip Kurland & Ralph Lerner eds., 1987), *available at* http://press-pubs.uchicago.edu/founders/documents/a2_3s8.html ("A strict observance of the written laws is doubtless one of the high duties of a good citizen, but it is not the highest. The laws of necessity, of self-preservation, of saving our country when in danger, are of higher obligation. To lose our country by a scrupulous adherence to written law, would be to lose the law itself, with life, liberty, property and all those who are enjoying them with us; thus absurdly sacrificing the end to the means."); Abraham Lincoln, Proclamation 94—Suspending the Writ of Habeas Corpus, Sept. 24, 1862 (suspending habeas corpus during the Civil War); OFFICIAL OPINIONS OF THE ATTORNEY GENERAL OF THE UNITED STATES: ADVISING THE PRESIDENT AND HEADS OF DEPARTMENTS IN RELATION TO THEIR OFFICIAL DUTIES 81 (W.H. & O.H. Morrison, 1868) ("I am clearly of opinion that, in a time like the present, when the very existence of the nation is assailed, by a great and dangerous insurrection, the President has the lawful discretionary power to arrest and hold in custody persons known to have criminal intercourse with the insurgents, or persons against whom there is probable cause for suspicion of such criminal complicity").

legitimacy of governmental efforts to enact and enforce such laws has received considerable scrutiny following September 11, 2001, when the nature of the perceived threat was, as a practical matter, dramatically transformed.

This chapter provides a broad overview of the two most significant conflicts that have arisen since 9/11 in the context of the First Amendment and national security:

1. The potential criminal liability of journalists for receiving and reporting information that may endanger the nation's security, and
2. The ability of journalists to protect the identities of the confidential sources who provide such information.

To set the stage, it is important to note the historical backdrop against which these contemporary disputes are played out—namely, the debate over the constitutionality of the Sedition Act of 1798 and the government's efforts in 1971 to enjoin publication of the so-called Pentagon Papers.

SETTING THE STAGE: THE SEDITION ACT AND THE PENTAGON PAPERS

It did not take long for the new nation called the United States of America to face the inevitable conflict between the sweeping language of the First Amendment to its Constitution, guaranteeing the freedom of speech and press, and the perceived need of its elected representatives to protect the citizenry from foreign threat. Thus, with the prospect of another armed conflict at hand and the perception that internal dissent had weakened the government's ability to meet that threat, John Adams, the nation's second president, signed into law the Sedition Act of 1798, which had the practical effect of making it a crime to criticize the government during such perilous times. As Justice William J. Brennan recounted almost two centuries later in his landmark opinion announcing the Supreme Court's decision in *New York Times Co. v. Sullivan*,[2] at the time of its passage, "the Act was vigorously condemned as unconstitutional in an attack joined in by Jefferson and Madison," the latter the principal architect of the Constitution itself, and it expired by its terms in 1801, when the perceived external threat was thought to have passed. Still, it was not until 1964, and the Supreme Court's decision in *Sullivan*, that the justices authoritatively declared that "[a]lthough the Sedition Act was never tested in this Court, the attack upon its validity has carried the day in the court of history. Fines levied in its prosecution were repaid by Act of Congress on the ground that it was unconstitutional," and "Jefferson, as President, pardoned those who had been convicted and sentenced under the Act." Those actions, coupled with subsequent pronouncements by Supreme Court justices and scholars alike, Brennan

---

2. 376 U.S. 254 (1964).

Setting the Stage: The Sedition Act and the Pentagon Papers

wrote, "reflect a broad consensus that the Act, because of the restraint it imposed upon criticism of government and public officials, was inconsistent with the First Amendment." As a consequence of *Sullivan*, the notion that the government may prosecute in the name of national security those who criticize it has been entirely discredited.

Seven years after *Sullivan*, in *New York Times Co. v. United States*,[3] the Supreme Court considered, for the first time, the right of the government to prevent the press from publishing information that might endanger national security. In that case, President Richard Nixon sought to enjoin two newspapers, *The New York Times* and *The Washington Post*, from publishing the Pentagon Papers, a classified study of the United States' involvement in the Vietnam War, on the ground that public dissemination of the information would jeopardize the government's ability to conduct that war and would inevitably lead to the loss of American lives. For their part, the newspapers defended their right to publish by pointing to what had generally been acknowledged to be the historic meaning of the freedom of the press—the inability of the government to restrain speech in advance of its publication.[4] In an unsigned opinion speaking for six of its nine justices, the Supreme Court rejected the government's position, holding that "[a]ny system of prior restraints of expression comes to this Court bearing a heavy presumption against its constitutional validity." As Justice Hugo Black explained in his separate concurring opinion, "Both the history and language of the First Amendment support the view that the press must be left free to publish news, whatever the source, without censorship, injunctions, or prior restraints." In the wake of the Pentagon Papers case, the government's ability to secure a prior restraint against the press has been rendered largely theoretical.[5]

Because of *Sullivan* and the Pentagon Papers case, the basic freedoms enjoyed by journalists to report about national security matters are both substantial and firmly established. As a practical matter, in the name of protecting the nation from harm, the government may neither enjoin news reports in advance of their publication nor punish the press for publishing criticism of government and its officials. As a result, in the post-9/11 world, the predominant conflicts between the First Amendment and the national security concern whether the government can

- prosecute journalists and news organizations *after* they have published, not for criticizing public officials, but for disseminating classified

---

3. 403 U.S. 713 (1971).
4. WILLIAM BLACKSTONE, COMMENTARIES ON THE LAWS OF ENGLAND: OF OFFENSES AGAINST THE PUBLIC PEACE (1765).
5. In a case that tested the limits of the presumption of unconstitutionality attached to prior restraints, a Wisconsin federal judge granted an injunction against publication of an article titled "The H-Bomb Secret: How We Got It, Why We're Telling It"—essentially a how-to guide for manufacturing and assembling a hydrogen bomb—concluding that the perceived threat of "direct, immediate and irreparable injury" to national security warranted suppression in the narrow facts of that case. United States v. Progressive, Inc., 467 F. Supp. 990, 1000 (W.D. Wis. 1979).

government information that the government says may harm the nation's security, and
- compel journalists to disclose confidential sources of such information.

CRIMINAL PROSECUTION OF JOURNALISTS

Particularly in the national security context, a journalist may receive, and his or her news organization may publish, classified information acquired from a source, typically a government official, who may have unlawfully gained access to it or, even if authorized to possess it, may have unlawfully transmitted it to the journalist. In other contexts, not involving classified or other information affecting the national security, the Supreme Court has afforded journalists significant First Amendment rights to publish such information unlawfully acquired or transmitted by a source without fear of civil or criminal punishment. In *Bartnicki v. Vopper*,[6] the Supreme Court held that the First Amendment precludes the government from enacting laws that purport to punish the dissemination of accurate reports about matters of public concern in the absence of a governmental interest of the "highest order."[7] In *Bartnicki*, a radio station and talk show host were sued for disseminating the content of a telephone call about a controversial labor dispute unlawfully recorded by a third party. The Court declared that "a stranger's illegal conduct does not suffice to remove the First Amendment shield from speech about a matter of public concern."

The open question remains under what circumstances, if any, the government may prosecute a journalist for receiving and publishing classified or other information, unlawfully acquired or transmitted to the journalist by its source, when such publication allegedly jeopardizes national security—a governmental interest that, as the Supreme Court put it in *Bartnicki*, is unarguably of the "highest order." Although the Supreme Court has yet to address this issue, it has been considered indirectly by some lower federal courts in the context of criminal prosecutions brought under the Espionage Act of 1917, albeit not against journalists.

Although there are a number of statutory provisions peppered throughout the U.S. Code that may theoretically give rise to criminal liability for the publication of national security–related information by the press, the most likely source of such a prosecution is § 793 of the Espionage Act.[8] Specifically, § 793(e) prohibits the unlawful possession, retention (and failure to return), or communication of documents or other tangible materials, or any other information "relating to the national defense"—where the recipient has reason to believe that the document or information could be used to the injury of the United States

---

6. 532 U.S. 514 (2001).
7. *Id.* at 528 (quoting Smith v. Daily Mail Publ'g Co., 443 U.S. 97, 103 (1979)).
8. 18 U.S.C. § 793.

or to the advantage of any foreign nation. Indeed, although the only issue before the Supreme Court in the Pentagon Papers case was the government's asserted right to restrain publication in advance, six of the justices openly contemplated the possibility of postpublication criminal prosecution of the newspapers under § 793 of the Espionage Act.[9]

Following the Pentagon Papers case, the first and to date most influential judicial decision addressing the prospect of such a prosecution is *United States v. Morison*,[10] decided by the Fourth Circuit Court of Appeals in 1988. Morison, a government employee, was convicted under the Espionage Act[11] for providing classified photographs of a Soviet aircraft carrier to the British publication *Jane's Defence Weekly*. On appeal, the Fourth Circuit affirmed the conviction, holding that the relevant subsections of the Espionage Act (§ 793(d) and (e)) prohibit the willful transmittal of information to "one not entitled to receive it," and the press was not entitled "to receive" the photographs Morison had provided.[12] *Jane's*, however, was never charged, and two members of the three-judge appellate panel who heard the case wrote separately to express their serious doubts that the First Amendment would tolerate such a prosecution.[13] As Judge J. Harvie Wilkinson explained, "Morison as a source would raise newsgathering rights on behalf of press organizations that are not being, and probably could not be, prosecuted under the espionage statute."

More recently, in 2005, a federal grand jury indicted two private lobbyists, Steven J. Rosen and Keith Weissman, who worked for the American-Israel Public Affairs Committee, and charged them with conspiring unlawfully to receive classified information from a government official, Larry Franklin, and transmitting that information to the press and to others in violation of § 793(d) and (e) of the Espionage Act.[14] Through this prosecution, the Department of Justice sought, apparently for the first time, to impose criminal liability on private citizens for receiving and communicating information acquired from an individual who may have unlawfully obtained or disclosed the information—conduct journalists engage in routinely.

The defendants in *United States v. Rosen* thereafter moved to dismiss the indictments against them, arguing among other things that application of the Espionage Act to the conduct in which they allegedly had engaged—that is, receiving

---

9. *See* New York Times Co. v. United States, 403 U.S. 713, 727, 729 (1971) (Stewart J., concurring); *id.* at 730, 740 (White, J., concurring); *id.* at 740, 744 (Marshall, J., concurring); *id.* at 747, 751 (Burger, C.J., dissenting); *id.* at 752, 754 (Harlan, J., dissenting) (Justice Blackmun joined in this dissent).
10. 844 F.2d 1057 (4th Cir. 1988).
11. As well as under 18 U.S.C. § 641, which punishes the theft or conversion of government property or records for one's own use or the use of another.
12. *Morison*, 844 F.2d at 1063.
13. *Id.* at 1081, 1085 (Wilkinson, J., concurring); *id.* at 1086 (Phillips, J., concurring).
14. United States v. Rosen, 445 F. Supp. 2d 602 (E.D. Va. Aug. 9, 2006), *aff'd*, 557 F.3d 192 (4th Cir. 2009).

classified information from a source and publishing it—violated the First Amendment. Denying defendants' motion to dismiss, the trial judge held not only that § 793 extends to oral disclosures (in addition to the transmittal of documents and other tangible things) but that the prosecution of an ordinary citizen (as opposed to a public official who had agreed not to disclose classified information as a condition of receiving a security clearance) is both permitted by the statute and not forbidden entirely by the First Amendment. By the same token, Judge Thomas S. Ellis held that the statute could survive First Amendment scrutiny only if construed narrowly to require the government to prove that the defendants acted with a bad-faith purpose to undermine national security.[15] In the wake of this decision, following an unsuccessful effort to appeal Ellis's ruling, the government abandoned its prosecution of Rosen and Weissman, effectively conceding that it could not meet the heightened intent requirement the court had imposed. That said, although the Fourth Circuit held that it did not have jurisdiction to consider the government's appeal, it nevertheless expressed its "concern[]" that Ellis may have imposed "an additional burden on the prosecution not mandated by the governing statute."[16] Thus, following *Rosen*, the role of the First Amendment in limiting the theoretical prosecution of a journalist under the Espionage Act remains very much in dispute.

SOURCES AND SUBPOENAS: THE REPORTER'S PRIVILEGE

As the *Morison* and *Rosen* cases demonstrate, however, as a practical matter, the government has refrained from even attempting to prosecute journalists under the Espionage Act, or any other federal statute, for publishing classified or other information allegedly harmful to national security. Instead, the government has confined itself to attempting to identify and then prosecute those within its ranks who have leaked such information to the press. Grand jury investigations and subsequent criminal prosecutions of such sources have raised a different conflict between the First Amendment and national security: the right of a journalist to protect the identity of a confidential source in the context of such an investigation or prosecution.

Outside the national security context, American law has long afforded journalists a privilege (usually qualified) from compelled disclosure of their confidential news sources. Most states have enacted so-called shield laws providing such protection by statute, and most federal and state courts have recognized a "reporter's privilege" of some dimension, grounded either in the First Amendment or in the common law. Congress, however, has never passed a federal shield law, and the Supreme Court has never squarely addressed the issue of whether such a

---

15. 445 F. Supp. 2d at 626.
16. 557 F.3d at 199 n.8.

Sources and Subpoenas: The Reporter's Privilege

privilege exists under the First Amendment or otherwise. Thus, in the absence of a federal shield law, the ability of a journalist to protect a confidential source's identity in the context of a grand jury investigation of, or federal criminal prosecution for, alleged violations of the Espionage Act turns on judicial determinations of whether either the First Amendment or the common law affords such a privilege.

To date, the lower federal courts have struggled to answer these questions, largely because the only Supreme Court precedent to address them, *Branzburg v. Hayes*,[17] was decided by a sharply divided Court. Five of the nine justices held that no privilege protected the journalists in the four consolidated cases considered in *Branzburg* from testifying before a grand jury about unlawful conduct (unrelated to national security) they had allegedly observed;[18] however, one of those five, Justice Lewis Powell, wrote a separate concurring opinion indicating that each invocation of the asserted privilege "should be judged on its facts by the striking of a proper balance between freedom of the press and the obligation of all citizens to give relevant testimony."[19] For three decades following *Branzburg*, most federal courts held that Powell's concurring opinion, coupled with the dissenting opinion written for four justices by Justice Potter Stewart, require a case-by-case balancing of these competing interests when reporter's privilege is asserted.[20]

After the events of 9/11, however, grand juries investigating alleged crimes implicating national security have afforded several federal courts the opportunity to revisit *Branzburg* in that context. The most significant of these decisions was rendered in the so-called CIA leak case, a special prosecutor's investigation of crimes potentially committed by government officials who leaked the identity of CIA operative Valerie Plame to several news reporters, including Judith Miller of *The New York Times*. Although Miller never wrote an article regarding or identifying Plame, a grand jury issued subpoenas seeking her testimony about the identity of her source. She moved to quash the subpoenas, arguing that, following *Branzburg*, reporters have both First Amendment and common law–based privileges to maintain the confidentiality of their sources.

Denying Miller's motion, the district court ordered her to testify; when she refused, she was held to be in contempt of court.[21] The U.S. Court of Appeals for the D.C. Circuit unanimously affirmed the district court's decision, agreeing that *Branzburg* provided no First Amendment–based reporter's privilege in the grand jury context, at least when the government has undertaken its investigation in good

---

17. 408 U.S. 665 (1972).
18. Caldwell v. United States, 434 F.2d 1081 (9th Cir. 1970), *aff'd sub nom.* Branzburg v. Hayes, 408 U.S. 665 (1972); *In re* Pappas, 266 N.E.2d 297 (Mass. 1971), *aff'd sub nom.* Branzburg v. Hayes, 408 U.S. 665 (1972); Branzburg v. Pound, 461 S.W.2d 345 (Ky. 1970), *aff'd sub nom.* Branzburg v. Hayes, 408 U.S. 665 (1972); Branzburg v. Meigs, 503 S.W.2d 748 (Ky. 1971), *aff'd sub nom.* Branzburg v. Hayes, 408 U.S. 665 (1972).
19. *Branzburg*, 408 U.S. at 709 (Powell, J., concurring) (These "vital constitutional and societal interests" are to be balanced "on a case-by-case basis.").
20. *Id.* at 743 (Stewart, J., dissenting).
21. *In re* Special Counsel Investigation, 332 F. Supp. 2d 26 (D.D.C. 2004).

faith.²² After serving 85 days in prison for refusing to comply with the subpoena, Miller agreed to testify, but only after her source—Lewis "Scooter" Libby, then chief of staff to Vice President Richard Cheney—released her from her pledge of confidentiality. Libby was ultimately indicted and convicted, not for violating federal law by disclosing Plame's identity to journalists, but for obstructing the government's subsequent investigation by providing false information about his conduct to the grand jury.²³

Shortly after the *Miller* decision, in *New York Times Co. v. Gonzales*,²⁴ the Second Circuit Court of Appeals refused to apply a First Amendment–based privilege to invalidate a subpoena for the telephone records of two reporters. The subpoena in *Gonzales* was issued in the context of a grand jury's investigation of a leak to the newspaper of an imminent government search of the headquarters of two charities suspected of funding terrorist organizations. In both the *Miller* and *Gonzales* cases, however, the appellate courts stopped short of holding that journalists enjoyed no privilege to protect their confidential sources in the context of grand jury proceedings. Rather, both courts suggested that the common law, as opposed to the First Amendment, might afford such a privilege, but held that any such privilege had been overcome by the government's showing of compelling need on the facts presented in the individual cases.²⁵ Indeed, in his separate opinion in *Gonzales*, Judge Robert Sack observed that the "fundamental" importance of the court's holding was that it "reaffirms the role of federal courts" in balancing the competing interests of law enforcement and of the press in such cases and rejects an "unsupervised authority" of the executive branch to "police the limits of its own power under these circumstances."²⁶

Most recently, another federal court, this one a district court in Virginia, has had the opportunity to consider the intersection of the First Amendment and national security in the context of a journalist's efforts to safeguard the identity of a confidential source. In late 2010, former CIA officer Jeffrey Sterling was charged with violating the Espionage Act by disclosing classified information to author James Risen, which was allegedly published in Risen's book *State of War: The Secret History of the CIA and the Bush Administration*.²⁷ Risen moved to quash government-issued subpoenas that would have required him to testify both before the federal grand jury that subsequently indicted Sterling and, thereafter, at his criminal trial. Judge Leonie Brinkema quashed both subpoenas, holding that under the First Amendment–based privilege afforded journalists, Risen would not be compelled to disclose whether Sterling was his source, either to the grand jury or at Sterling's trial.

---

22. *See In re* Grand Jury Subpoena (Miller), 438 F.3d 1141, 1144–45 (D.C. Cir. 2006).
23. United States v. I. Lewis Libby, a/k/a "Scooter Libby," No. CRIM. 05-394 (D.D.C. Oct. 28, 2005).
24. 459 F.3d 160 (2d Cir. 2006).
25. *Gonzales*, 459 F.3d at 173; *Miller*, 438 F.3d at 1150.
26. *Gonzales*, 459 F.3d at 175–78 (Sack, J., dissenting).
27. United States v. Sterling, __ 818 F. Supp. 2d, 945, 950 (E.D. Va., 2011).

In her most recent opinion, rendered in the context of the government's subpoena to compel Risen to disclose the identity of his source at Sterling's trial, Brinkema articulated a robust privilege "that may be invoked when a subpoena either seeks information about confidential sources or is issued to harass or intimidate the journalist."[28] She explained that "[w]hen a reporter invokes the privilege, the court must balance the reporter's need to protect his or her sources against the legitimate need of prosecutors or civil litigants for the journalist's testimony to establish their case."[29] The government has delayed Sterling's trial in order to appeal Brinkema's ruling to the Fourth Circuit Court of Appeals, where a decision is expected in 2012.

CONCLUSION

As we have seen, the potential for conflict between the freedom of the press and the national security in the United States is as old as the nation itself and as new as ongoing litigated disputes in our post-9/11 world. For journalists reporting on matters affecting the national security, however, the path of the law remains dimly lit and the road itself leads to no certain answers.

EXPERTS

Julia C. Atcherley, Associate, Levine Sullivan Koch & Schulz, LLP; (212) 850-6111; jatcherley@lskslaw.com

Rachel L. Brand, Chief Counsel for Regulatory Litigation, National Chamber Litigation Center, U.S. Chamber of Commerce; Former Assistant Attorney General, Office of Legal Policy, Department of Justice; rbrand@law.gwu.edu

Lucy A. Dalglish, Dean of the Philip Merrill College of Journalism, University of Maryland; (301) 405-8806; dalglish@jmail.umd.edu

Randall D. Eliason, Professorial Lecturer in Law, George Washington University Law School; reliason@law.gwu.edu

Lee Levine, Partner, Levine Sullivan Koch & Schulz, LLP; (202) 508-1110; llevine@lskslaw.com

Gabriel Schoenfeld, Senior Fellow on Leave, Hudson Institute; schoenfeld.g @gmail.com, http://gabrielschoenfeld.com/

---

28. *Id.* at 951.
29. *Id.* at 959–60.

Jeffrey H. Smith, Partner, Arnold & Porter LLP; Former General Counsel, CIA; (202) 942-5115; jeffrey.smith@aporter.com

Geoffrey R. Stone, Edward H. Levi Distinguished Service Professor, University of Chicago Law School; (773) 702-4907; g-stone@uchicago.edu

RESOURCES

Legislation

Espionage Act, 18 U.S.C. §§ 792–799, 40 Stat. 217 (1917). Key provisions:

- 18 U.S.C. § 793 (prohibits the gathering, transmitting, or receipt of defense information with intent or reason to believe the information could be used against the United States or to benefit a foreign nation)
- 18 U.S.C. §§ 795, 797 (prohibits the unauthorized creation, publication, sale, or transfer of photographs or sketches of vital defense installations or equipment as designated by the president)
- 18 U.S.C. § 798 (punishes the knowing and willful disclosure of certain classified information by fine and/or imprisonment for not more than 10 years)

Intelligence Identities Protection Act, 50 U.S.C. §§ 421–426 (1982). Key provisions:

- 50 U.S.C. § 421 (prohibits the disclosure of information identifying a covert agent)
- 50 U.S.C. § 422 (provides defenses to § 421)
- 18 U.S.C. § 1030(a)(1) (prohibits the willful retention, communication, or transmission of classified information retrieved by knowingly accessing a computer without authorization, and with reason to believe the information will be used against the United States or to benefit a foreign nation)
- 18 U.S.C. § 641 (prohibits the theft or conversion of government property or records for one's own use or the use of another)
- 18 U.S.C. § 1924 (prohibits the unauthorized removal of classified material by government employees, contractors, and consultants who come into possession of the material by virtue of their employment by the government)

Publications

Lee Levine, Robert C. Lind, Seth D. Berlin & C. Thomas Dienes, Newsgathering and the Law (LEXIS Law, 4th ed. 2011). For further analysis of issues relevant to reporting on matters of national security, see §§ 1.06, 3.04(3), 11.02(3)(b), 15.03(2), 15.10(1). For an overview of the reporter's privilege generally, see §§ 16.01–19.01.

GARY ROSS, WHO WATCHES THE WATCHMEN? THE CONFLICT BETWEEN NATIONAL SECURITY AND FREEDOM OF THE PRESS (Nat'l Intelligence U., July 2011). Ross argues that the tension between maintaining national security secrets and the public's right to know cannot be solved, but can be better understood and more intelligently managed.

Harold Edgar & Benno C. Schmidt, Jr., *The Espionage Statutes and Publication of Defense Information*, 73 COLUM. L. REV. 929 (1973). Edgar and Schmidt present a thorough and widely cited overview of the Espionage Act.

Lee Levine, Nathan E. Siegel & Jeanette M. Bead, *Handcuffing the Press: First Amendment Limitations on the Reach of Criminal Statutes as Applied to the Media*, 55 N.Y.L. SCH. L. REV. 1015 (2011). Levine, Siegel, and Bead examine the First Amendment limitations on the permissible reach of criminal statutes as applied to the press, following publication of information allegedly received from a person who may have accessed or provided such information in violation of a criminal statute.

Monica Langley & Lee Levine, *Branzburg Revisited: Confidential Sources and First Amendment Values*, 57 GEO. WASH. L. REV. 13 (1988). Langley and Levine advocate robust First Amendment protection for journalists to keep their sources confidential.

Gabriel Schoenfeld, *Has* The New York Times *Violated the Espionage Act?* COMMENTARY, March 2006, http://www.commentarymagazine.com/article/has-the-%e2%80%9cnew-york-times%e2%80%9d-violated-the-espionage-act/. Schoenfeld argues for government prosecution of a number of reporters and editors at *The New York Times* under the Espionage Act after the newspaper reported on the National Security Agency's warrantless surveillance of people within the United States.

U.S. Government Secrecy and Classification

3

By John R. Tunheim and Andrew M. Borene*

Broadly speaking, classified information policy refers to a range of federal governmental practices that aim to restrict access to information or documents on the grounds of national security. The purpose in limiting access to this information is to prevent it from being used by persons, organizations or nations to inflict harm upon the United States.[1]

CLASSIFICATION IN U.S. HISTORY

The U.S. government has been protecting sensitive information from its founding. Typically, the information protected pertains to security, diplomacy, military, or intelligence operations.

During the American Revolution, officers in the Continental Army wrote "Secret" or "Confidential" on some strategic communications in an effort to control their dissemination. However, these early practices were informal. The first systematic classification scheme in the United States did not emerge until 1912,

---

*Andrew Borene would like to thank Jerrod Montoya, an attorney and graduate student in the University of Minnesota's Master's in Science and Security Technologies program, for his research assistance with this chapter.

1. KEVIN R. KOSAR, CONG. RESEARCH SERV., CLASSIFIED INFORMATION POLICY AND EXECUTIVE ORDER 13526 (December 10, 2010).

when the War Department set procedures for the protection of national defense information.[2]

The first evolution of what has become classification as we know it today began with President Franklin D. Roosevelt's Executive Order 8381 in 1940, which expanded upon an earlier statute related to the security of armed forces installations. In his order, Roosevelt defined "vital military and naval installations or equipment requiring protection against the general dissemination of information relative thereto."[3]

Since Roosevelt's issuance of Executive Order 8381, subsequent presidents have also set and revised the federal government's classification standards by executive order. Similar to Roosevelt's order, which relied on the 1938 military installations statute, current executive orders related to classification are based on both legislative and executive powers granted by the Constitution.[4]

While the Constitution does not explicitly grant the executive branch classification authority,[5] a number of Supreme Court cases have affirmed the president's authority to classify national security information.[6] Congress has codified the president's authority to designate material as classified in the Freedom of Information Act (FOIA) and in the Internal Security Act of 1950.[7] Additionally, the National Security Act of 1947 specified that the director of central intelligence was responsible for protecting intelligence sources and methods from unauthorized disclosures.

Ultimately, anyone seeking to understand the legal justification for and administration of the current U.S. classification system will need to understand the basics of executive orders.

Classified information is information designated by the executive branch as protected information because its unauthorized disclosure could imperil national security.

---

2. HAROLD C. RELYEA, CONG. RESEARCH SERV., SECURITY CLASSIFIED AND CONTROLLED INFORMATION: HISTORY, STATUS, AND EMERGING MANAGEMENT ISSUES (updated Feb. 11, 2008).

3. Exec. Order No. 8381, Defining Certain Vital Military and Naval Installations and Equipment, Mar. 22, 1940.

4. JENNIFER K. ELSEA, CONG. RESEARCH SERV., THE PROTECTION OF CLASSIFIED INFORMATION: THE LEGAL FRAMEWORK (Jan. 10, 2011).

5. ARVIN S. QUIST, SECURITY CLASSIFICATION OF INFORMATION VOLUME I: INTRODUCTION, HISTORY, AND ADVERSE IMPACTS (prepared for Oak Ridge Nat'l Lab., Sept. 20, 2002).

6. ELSEA, *supra* note 4.

7. QUIST, *supra* note 5.

EXECUTIVE ORDERS

Executive orders are official documents, numbered consecutively, through which the president of the United States manages the operations of the federal government.[8]

Every president since the founding of the United States has issued executive orders.[9]

No provision of the Constitution defines executive orders. The power of the president's executive order is derived from nonspecific clauses in the Constitution. Article II states that "the executive power shall be vested in a President of the United States," that "the President shall be Commander in Chief of the Army and Navy of the United States," and that the president "shall take Care that the Laws be faithfully executed."

Executive orders are written directives of the president to agencies and entities under his control as chief executive and commander in chief. They are considered to be validly enforceable written documents that have the force of law in court, yet they are subordinate to any contravening act of Congress. Typically executive orders are directed at, and control, specific government agencies and actions.

Only rarely do executive orders directly affect private citizens, and violations of executive orders typically do not constitute legal offenses. As a result, criminal liabilities for unauthorized disclosure of classified information are defined by statute. The Internal Security Act of 1950 authorized the criminal punishment of any federal official or employee who communicated classified information without authorization.[10]

Frequently, a new executive order repeals the classified information policies of previous executive orders.

THE CURRENT EXECUTIVE ORDER GOVERNING CLASSIFICATION

President Barack Obama issued Executive Order 13,526, titled Classified National Security Information, on Dec. 29, 2009. Its purpose was to create "a uniform system for classifying, safeguarding, and declassifying national security information, including information relating to defense against transnational terrorism."

---

8. U.S. Nat'l Archives & Records Admin., FAQ's About Executive Orders, *available at* http://www.archives.gov/federal-register/executive-orders/about.html.
9. VANESSA K. BURROWS, CONG. RESEARCH SERV., EXECUTIVE ORDERS: ISSUANCE AND REVOCATION (Mar. 25, 2010).
10. QUIST, *supra* note 5.

In the preamble to his order, Obama sought to balance a need for protecting information vital to national security with what he referred to as an equally important priority of "a commitment to open government."

> Our democratic principles require that the American people be informed of the activities of their Government. Also, our Nation's progress depends on the free flow of information both within the Government and to the American people. Nevertheless, throughout our history, the national defense has required that certain information be maintained in confidence in order to protect our citizens, our democratic institutions, our homeland security, and our interactions with foreign nations. Protecting information critical to our Nation's security and demonstrating our commitment to open Government through accurate and accountable application of classification standards and routine, secure, and effective declassification are equally important priorities.

Furthermore, in accord with this balancing principle between security and open government, the general provisions state that "nothing in this order limits the protection afforded any information by other provisions of law," including the Constitution, FOIA exemptions, the Privacy Act of 1974, and the National Security Act of 1947, as amended.

Generally speaking, U.S. government classification programs seek to protect sources and methods of intelligence collection and to prevent unauthorized access to military plans and secrets.

MODERN CLASSIFICATION CATEGORIES

Executive Order 13,526 maintains the three long-standing classification levels, and classification markings, of top secret, secret, and confidential. Each classification level corresponds with a different severity of damage[11] to national security if the information were compromised.

---

11. "Damage to the national security" means harm to the national defense or foreign relations of the United States from the unauthorized disclosure of information, taking into consideration such aspects of the information as the sensitivity, value, utility, and provenance of that information.

Sensitive Compartmented Information

CLASSIFICATION LEVEL	DEFINITION (EXECUTIVE ORDER 13,526)	MARKING
Top Secret	Information, the unauthorized disclosure of which reasonably could be expected to cause exceptionally grave damage to the national security that the original classification authority is able to identify or describe.	TS
Secret	Information, the unauthorized disclosure of which reasonably could be expected to cause serious damage to the national security that the original classification authority is able to identify or describe.	S
Confidential	Information, the unauthorized disclosure of which reasonably could be expected to cause damage to the national security that the original classification authority is able to identify or describe.	C

No information may be classified at any of the three levels unless (1) its disclosure could "reasonably be expected to cause identifiable or describable damage to the national security" and (2) the information pertains to one or more of the following specific subjects:

- military plans, weapons systems, or operations
- foreign government information
- intelligence activities (including covert action), intelligence sources or methods, or cryptology
- foreign relations or foreign activities of the United States, including confidential sources
- scientific, technological, or economic matters relating to the national security
- U.S. government programs for safeguarding nuclear materials or facilities
- vulnerabilities or capabilities of systems, installations, infrastructures, projects, plans, or protection services relating to national security
- the development, production, or use of weapons of mass destruction

If information is not classified into one of the three levels, it is deemed unclassified.

SENSITIVE COMPARTMENTED INFORMATION

Within the three core levels of classification, an additional set of controls, known as sensitive compartmented information (SCI) controls, may be employed. Information controlled within these SCI channels is handled with enhanced protection and secrecy protocols that include additional clearance investigation, adjudication, and security management. SCI security and access are managed by a special type of administrator known as a special security officer. Special security officers are also trained and prepared to supervise the administration of a specially accredited facility for the handling of such information known as a sensitive compartmented information facility (SCIF).

SPECIAL ACCESS PROGRAMS

In addition to the three classification levels, some government programs are deemed so sensitive that they are further categorized as special access programs—SAPs—with further restricted access. These special, sensitive programs are established only when "required by statute or upon a specific finding that: (1) the vulnerability of, or threat to, specific information is exceptional; and (2) the normal criteria for determining eligibility for access applicable to information classified at the same level are not deemed sufficient to protect the information from unauthorized disclosure."[12] These programs can be either acknowledged or unacknowledged.

In general, any program requiring additional security protection and information handling measures; special investigative, adjudicative, and clearance procedures; unique reporting procedures; or formal access lists could be considered a "special access" program. Some examples of instances when special access programs may be deemed necessary are the development of specific military technologies with strategic importance, highly sensitive intelligence collections sources, or technological methods.

Sometimes the government will "neither confirm nor deny" any media speculation on the existence of certain SAPs. For instance, although the aircraft had been in development for many years, the existence of a special access program for the F-117A Nighthawk "stealth fighter" was not officially acknowledged until the late 1980s. The B-2 Spirit bomber program is another historical example of a technology deemed so sensitive that special access treatment was justified.[13] Similar controls on information access can exist for other military technologies and intelligence collection methods.

Unless another individual is empowered to do so by the president, only the secretaries of State, Defense, Energy, and Homeland Security, the attorney general, and the director of national intelligence, or the principal deputy of each, may create a special access program. These specially designated officials are also mandated to "keep the number of these programs at an absolute minimum."[14]

---

12. Exec. Order No. 13,526. § 4.3(a), 75 Fed. Reg. 707 (January 5, 2010).
13. ALICE C. MARONI, CONG. RESEARCH SERV., SPECIAL ACCESS PROGRAMS AND THE DEFENSE BUDGET: UNDERSTANDING THE "BLACK BUDGET" (updated Oct. 24, 1989).
14. *Id.*

BAN ON USE OF CLASSIFICATION TO HIDE EMBARRASSING INFORMATION

Obama's executive order bans the use of classification as a means of protecting political or bureaucratic interests unrelated to national security. It states specifically that "[i]n no case shall information be classified, continue to be maintained as classified, or fail to be declassified in order to: (1) conceal violations of law, inefficiency, or administrative error; (2) prevent embarrassment to a person, organization, or agency; (3) restrain competition; or (4) prevent or delay the release of information that does not require protection in the interest of the national security." Additionally, "basic scientific research information not clearly related to the national security shall not be classified."

> ### *Classification Glossary*
>
> *Access:* The ability or opportunity to gain knowledge of classified information.
>
> *Classification:* The act or process by which information is determined to be classified information; a determination that information requires, in the interest of the national security, protection against unauthorized disclosure.
>
> *Classified national security information, Classified information:* Information that has been determined to require protection against unauthorized disclosure and is marked to indicate its classified status when in documentary form.
>
> *Clearance:* Adjudicated eligibility for access to classified information, in conjunction with a signed nondisclosure agreement and current training on safeguarding classified information.
>
> *Confidential source:* Any individual or organization that has provided, or that may reasonably be expected to provide, information to the United States on matters pertaining to the national security with the expectation that the information or relationship, or both, are to be held in confidence.
>
> *Damage to the national security:* Harm to the national defense or foreign relations of the United States from the unauthorized disclosure of information, taking into consideration such aspects of the information as the sensitivity, value, utility, and provenance of that information.
>
> *Declassification:* The authorized change in the status of information from classified information to unclassified information.
>
> *Document:* Any recorded information, regardless of the nature of the medium or the method or circumstances of recording.

"For official use only" (FOUO): A document designation, not a classification. This designation is used by a number of federal agencies to identify information or material that, although unclassified, may not be appropriate for public release under the Freedom of Information Act.

Information: Any knowledge that can be communicated or documentary material, regardless of its physical form or characteristics.

Intelligence activities: All activities that elements of the intelligence community are authorized to conduct pursuant to law or Executive Order 12,333, as amended, or a successor order.

Intelligence community: Includes any element or agency of the government identified in or designated pursuant to section 3(4) of the National Security Act of 1947, as amended, or section 3.5(h) of Executive Order 12,333, as amended.

National security: The national defense or foreign relations of the United States.

"Need to know": A determination within the executive branch in accordance with directives issued pursuant to this order that a prospective recipient requires access to specific classified information in order to perform or assist in a lawful and authorized governmental function.

Safeguarding: Measures and controls that are prescribed to protect classified information.

Security clearance: An administrative determination by competent authority that an individual is eligible, from a security standpoint, for access to classified information.

Security countermeasures: Actions, devices, procedures, and/or techniques to reduce security risks.

Security manager: Ensures that access to classified information is limited to appropriately cleared personnel with a "need to know" and is responsible for implementing an overall security program for classified material. The security manager shall remain cognizant of all information, personnel, and industrial security functions and ensure that local security programs are inclusive of all relevant policy requirements.

Sensitive compartmented information (SCI): A program established for a specific class of classified information that imposes safeguarding and access requirements that exceed those normally required for information at the same classification level.

Special access program (SAP): A sensitive program, approved in writing by a head of agency with original top secret classification authority, that imposes need-to-know and access controls beyond those normally provided for access to confidential, secret, or top secret information. The level of controls is based on the criticality of the program and the assessed hostile intelligence threat. The program may be an acquisition program, an intelligence program, or an operations and support program.

Special security officer (SSO): Responsible for the operation (security, control, use, etc.) of all command sensitive compartmented information facilities (SCIFs). All SCI matters shall be referred to the SSO. The SSO may be designated as security manager if the grade requirements for security manager are met; however, the security manager cannot function as an SSO unless specially designated as such.

Unauthorized disclosure: A communication or physical transfer of classified information to an unauthorized recipient.

U.S. entity: Includes (1) state, local, or tribal governments; (2) state, local, and tribal law enforcement and firefighting entities; (3) public health and medical entities; (4) regional, state, local, and tribal emergency management entities, including state adjutants general and other appropriate public safety entities; and (5) private sector entities serving as part of the nation's critical infrastructure/key resources.

Violation: (1) any knowing, willful, or negligent action that could reasonably be expected to result in an unauthorized disclosure of classified information; (2) any knowing, willful, or negligent action to classify or continue the classification of information contrary to the requirements of this order or its implementing directives; or (3) any knowing, willful, or negligent action to create or continue a special access program contrary to the requirements of this order.

ACCESS TO CLASSIFIED INFORMATION

A person who desires access to classified information must (1) be adjudicated as eligible for access by a specific agency, (2) have signed an approved U.S. government nondisclosure agreement (NDA), and (3) have a "need to know" for the specific information sought.

Eligibility + NDA + "Need to Know" = Access

What is frequently known as a government "security clearance" is a combination of an adjudicated eligibility based on an adequate background investigation, a signed nondisclosure agreement, and current training on safeguarding of classified information. So the equation above can be simplified to:

Appropriate Clearance + "Need to Know" = Access to Classified Information

Depending on the level of classification, different rules control the level of clearance needed to view the information and how the information must be stored, transmitted, and destroyed. Additionally, access is restricted on a "need to know" basis. Simply possessing a clearance does not automatically authorize the individual to view all material classified at or below that level. The individual must present a legitimate "need to know" in addition to the proper level of clearance.

UNCLASSIFIED BUT PROTECTED—"FOR OFFICIAL USE ONLY"

Some government information that has not been classified pursuant to Executive Order 13,526 may nonetheless warrant withholding from the public. U.S. government information in this category may be considered as "For Official Use Only" and will be marked "FOUO." To qualify for the protective FOUO marking, specific information must meet a special FOIA exemption. If information does not meet specialized exemption criteria, it cannot be withheld from public disclosure or marked FOUO. It is important to note that FOUO is not authorized as a form of classification to protect national security interests.

FOUO protections are employed by the Department of Defense, the intelligence community, the Department of Homeland Security, and some other federal agencies. Although each agency is individually responsible for determining how the FOUO caveat will be used, any information marked FOUO must be covered by one of nine limited exemptions from public release under FOIA, and a "legitimate government purpose" must be served by withholding it.

The nine categories that currently allow government exemption from mandatory release under FOIA are:

1. Information that is currently and properly classified.
2. Information that pertains solely to the internal rules and practices of the agency. This exemption has two profiles, "high" and "low." The "high" profile permits withholding of a document that, if released, would allow circumvention of an agency rule, policy, or statute, thereby impeding the agency in the conduct of its mission. The "low" profile permits withholding if there is no public interest in the document, and it would be an administrative burden to process the request.
3. Information specifically exempted by statute establishing particular criteria for withholding. The language of the statute must clearly state that the information will not be disclosed.
4. Information such as trade secrets and commercial or financial information obtained from a company on a privileged or confidential

Sanctions: Legal Consequences for Violating Classification Rules

basis that, if released, would result in competitive harm to the company or would impair the government's ability to obtain like information in the future or to protect its interest in compliance with program effectiveness.

5. Interagency memoranda that are deliberative in nature; this exemption is appropriate for internal documents that are part of the decision-making process and contain subjective evaluations, opinions, and recommendations.
6. Information the release of which could reasonably be expected to constitute a clearly unwarranted invasion of the personal privacy of individuals.
7. Records or information compiled for law enforcement purposes that (a) could reasonably be expected to interfere with law enforcement proceedings; (b) would deprive a person of a right to a fair trial or impartial adjudication; (c) could reasonably be expected to constitute an unwarranted invasion of the personal privacy of others; (d) would disclose the identity of a confidential source; (e) would disclose investigative techniques or procedures; or (f) could reasonably be expected to endanger the life or physical safety of any individual.
8. Certain records of agencies responsible for supervision of financial institutions.
9. Geological and geophysical information concerning wells.

SANCTIONS: LEGAL CONSEQUENCES FOR VIOLATING CLASSIFICATION RULES

According to Obama's order:

> Officers and employees of the United States Government, and its contractors, licensees, certificate holders, and grantees shall be subject to appropriate sanctions if they knowingly, willfully, or negligently:
>
> (1) Disclose to unauthorized persons information properly classified under this order or predecessor orders;
>
> (2) Classify or continue the classification of information in violation of this order or any implementing directive;
>
> (3) Create or continue a special access program contrary to the requirements of this order; or
>
> (4) Contravene any other provision of this order or its implementing directives.

As mentioned above, executive orders typically do not carry traditional criminal penalties. Executive Order 13,526 is no exception. Consequences for the behaviors above are generally restricted to reprimand, suspension without pay, removal, termination of classification authority, and loss or denial of access to classified information. Violators of classification rules can face much more serious legal consequences based on prosecutions of criminal statutes.

EXPERTS

Stewart Baker, Partner, Steptoe & Johnson; (202) 429-6402; sbaker@steptoe.com

Jamie Gorelick, Partner, WilmerHale; (202) 663-6500; jamie.gorelick @wilmerhale.com

Gen. (Ret.) Michael Hayden, former Director of the Central Intelligence Agency; Former Principal Deputy Director of National Intelligence; Former Director of the National Security Agency; (202) 552-5280

Ronald Kessler, investigative reporter; author of 19 books on intelligence and current affairs including, most recently, *The Secrets of the FBI*; KesslerRonald @gmail.com

Benjamin Powell, Partner, WilmerHale; (202) 663-6770; benjamin.powell @wilmerhale.com

Jeffrey H. Smith, Partner, Arnold & Porter LLP; (202) 942-5115; Jeffrey.Smith@aporter.com

RESOURCES

Defense Security Service oversees the protection of U.S. and foreign classified information in the hands of industry (http://www.dss.mil).

Office of the Director of National Intelligence Special Security Center. The SSC exists to assist the Director of National Intelligence in his dual role as head of the Intelligence Community and as the Security Executive Agent for U.S. Government security clearance programs (pursuant to Executive Order 13,467) (http://www.dni.gov/ssc/default.htm).

The Information Security Oversight Office is responsible to the president for policy and oversight of the government-wide security classification system and the National Industrial Security Program (http://www.archives.gov/isoo).

Office of the National Counterintelligence Executive (http://www.ncix.gov).

Resources

Office of Information Policy is responsible for encouraging agency compliance with the Freedom of Information Act (http://www.justice.gov/oip/).

FOIA.Gov is a Department of Justice website dedicated to providing general information about FOIA (http://www.foia.gov/).

Appendix to Chapter 3

PDF found on the Federal Investigative Services website at: http://www.opm.gov/investigate/resources/executive/index.aspx.

APPENDIX

Tuesday,
January 5, 2010

Part VII

The President

Executive Order 13526—Classified National Security Information
Memorandum of December 29, 2009—Implementation of the Executive Order "Classified National Security Information"
Order of December 29, 2009—Original Classification Authority

Appendix

Federal Register Vol. 75, No. 2 Tuesday, January 5, 2010	**Presidential Documents**

Title 3—	Executive Order 13526 of December 29, 2009
The President	**Classified National Security Information**

This order prescribes a uniform system for classifying, safeguarding, and declassifying national security information, including information relating to defense against transnational terrorism. Our democratic principles require that the American people be informed of the activities of their Government. Also, our Nation's progress depends on the free flow of information both within the Government and to the American people. Nevertheless, throughout our history, the national defense has required that certain information be maintained in confidence in order to protect our citizens, our democratic institutions, our homeland security, and our interactions with foreign nations. Protecting information critical to our Nation's security and demonstrating our commitment to open Government through accurate and accountable application of classification standards and routine, secure, and effective declassification are equally important priorities.

NOW, THEREFORE, I, BARACK OBAMA, by the authority vested in me as President by the Constitution and the laws of the United States of America, it is hereby ordered as follows:

PART 1—ORIGINAL CLASSIFICATION

Section 1.1. *Classification Standards.* (a) Information may be originally classified under the terms of this order only if all of the following conditions are met:

(1) an original classification authority is classifying the information;

(2) the information is owned by, produced by or for, or is under the control of the United States Government;

(3) the information falls within one or more of the categories of information listed in section 1.4 of this order; and

(4) the original classification authority determines that the unauthorized disclosure of the information reasonably could be expected to result in damage to the national security, which includes defense against transnational terrorism, and the original classification authority is able to identify or describe the damage.

(b) If there is significant doubt about the need to classify information, it shall not be classified. This provision does not:

(1) amplify or modify the substantive criteria or procedures for classification; or

(2) create any substantive or procedural rights subject to judicial review.

(c) Classified information shall not be declassified automatically as a result of any unauthorized disclosure of identical or similar information.

(d) The unauthorized disclosure of foreign government information is presumed to cause damage to the national security.

Sec. 1.2. *Classification Levels.* (a) Information may be classified at one of the following three levels:

(1) "Top Secret" shall be applied to information, the unauthorized disclosure of which reasonably could be expected to cause exceptionally grave damage to the national security that the original classification authority is able to identify or describe.

(2) "Secret" shall be applied to information, the unauthorized disclosure of which reasonably could be expected to cause serious damage to the

APPENDIX

national security that the original classification authority is able to identify or describe.

(3) "Confidential" shall be applied to information, the unauthorized disclosure of which reasonably could be expected to cause damage to the national security that the original classification authority is able to identify or describe.

(b) Except as otherwise provided by statute, no other terms shall be used to identify United States classified information.

(c) If there is significant doubt about the appropriate level of classification, it shall be classified at the lower level.

Sec. 1.3. *Classification Authority.* (a) The authority to classify information originally may be exercised only by:

(1) the President and the Vice President;

(2) agency heads and officials designated by the President; and

(3) United States Government officials delegated this authority pursuant to paragraph (c) of this section.

(b) Officials authorized to classify information at a specified level are also authorized to classify information at a lower level.

(c) Delegation of original classification authority.

(1) Delegations of original classification authority shall be limited to the minimum required to administer this order. Agency heads are responsible for ensuring that designated subordinate officials have a demonstrable and continuing need to exercise this authority.

(2) "Top Secret" original classification authority may be delegated only by the President, the Vice President, or an agency head or official designated pursuant to paragraph (a)(2) of this section.

(3) "Secret" or "Confidential" original classification authority may be delegated only by the President, the Vice President, an agency head or official designated pursuant to paragraph (a)(2) of this section, or the senior agency official designated under section 5.4(d) of this order, provided that official has been delegated "Top Secret" original classification authority by the agency head.

(4) Each delegation of original classification authority shall be in writing and the authority shall not be redelegated except as provided in this order. Each delegation shall identify the official by name or position.

(5) Delegations of original classification authority shall be reported or made available by name or position to the Director of the Information Security Oversight Office.

(d) All original classification authorities must receive training in proper classification (including the avoidance of over-classification) and declassification as provided in this order and its implementing directives at least once a calendar year. Such training must include instruction on the proper safeguarding of classified information and on the sanctions in section 5.5 of this order that may be brought against an individual who fails to classify information properly or protect classified information from unauthorized disclosure. Original classification authorities who do not receive such mandatory training at least once within a calendar year shall have their classification authority suspended by the agency head or the senior agency official designated under section 5.4(d) of this order until such training has taken place. A waiver may be granted by the agency head, the deputy agency head, or the senior agency official if an individual is unable to receive such training due to unavoidable circumstances. Whenever a waiver is granted, the individual shall receive such training as soon as practicable.

(e) Exceptional cases. When an employee, government contractor, licensee, certificate holder, or grantee of an agency who does not have original classification authority originates information believed by that person to require classification, the information shall be protected in a manner consistent

Appendix

with this order and its implementing directives. The information shall be transmitted promptly as provided under this order or its implementing directives to the agency that has appropriate subject matter interest and classification authority with respect to this information. That agency shall decide within 30 days whether to classify this information.

Sec. 1.4. *Classification Categories.* Information shall not be considered for classification unless its unauthorized disclosure could reasonably be expected to cause identifiable or describable damage to the national security in accordance with section 1.2 of this order, and it pertains to one or more of the following:

(a) military plans, weapons systems, or operations;

(b) foreign government information;

(c) intelligence activities (including covert action), intelligence sources or methods, or cryptology;

(d) foreign relations or foreign activities of the United States, including confidential sources;

(e) scientific, technological, or economic matters relating to the national security;

(f) United States Government programs for safeguarding nuclear materials or facilities;

(g) vulnerabilities or capabilities of systems, installations, infrastructures, projects, plans, or protection services relating to the national security; or

(h) the development, production, or use of weapons of mass destruction.

Sec. 1.5. *Duration of Classification.* (a) At the time of original classification, the original classification authority shall establish a specific date or event for declassification based on the duration of the national security sensitivity of the information. Upon reaching the date or event, the information shall be automatically declassified. Except for information that should clearly and demonstrably be expected to reveal the identity of a confidential human source or a human intelligence source or key design concepts of weapons of mass destruction, the date or event shall not exceed the time frame established in paragraph (b) of this section.

(b) If the original classification authority cannot determine an earlier specific date or event for declassification, information shall be marked for declassification 10 years from the date of the original decision, unless the original classification authority otherwise determines that the sensitivity of the information requires that it be marked for declassification for up to 25 years from the date of the original decision.

(c) An original classification authority may extend the duration of classification up to 25 years from the date of origin of the document, change the level of classification, or reclassify specific information only when the standards and procedures for classifying information under this order are followed.

(d) No information may remain classified indefinitely. Information marked for an indefinite duration of classification under predecessor orders, for example, marked as "Originating Agency's Determination Required," or classified information that contains incomplete declassification instructions or lacks declassification instructions shall be declassified in accordance with part 3 of this order.

Sec. 1.6. *Identification and Markings.* (a) At the time of original classification, the following shall be indicated in a manner that is immediately apparent:

(1) one of the three classification levels defined in section 1.2 of this order;

(2) the identity, by name and position, or by personal identifier, of the original classification authority;

(3) the agency and office of origin, if not otherwise evident;

(4) declassification instructions, which shall indicate one of the following:

(A) the date or event for declassification, as prescribed in section 1.5(a);

(B) the date that is 10 years from the date of original classification, as prescribed in section 1.5(b);

(C) the date that is up to 25 years from the date of original classification, as prescribed in section 1.5(b); or

(D) in the case of information that should clearly and demonstrably be expected to reveal the identity of a confidential human source or a human intelligence source or key design concepts of weapons of mass destruction, the marking prescribed in implementing directives issued pursuant to this order; and

(5) a concise reason for classification that, at a minimum, cites the applicable classification categories in section 1.4 of this order.

(b) Specific information required in paragraph (a) of this section may be excluded if it would reveal additional classified information.

(c) With respect to each classified document, the agency originating the document shall, by marking or other means, indicate which portions are classified, with the applicable classification level, and which portions are unclassified. In accordance with standards prescribed in directives issued under this order, the Director of the Information Security Oversight Office may grant and revoke temporary waivers of this requirement. The Director shall revoke any waiver upon a finding of abuse.

(d) Markings or other indicia implementing the provisions of this order, including abbreviations and requirements to safeguard classified working papers, shall conform to the standards prescribed in implementing directives issued pursuant to this order.

(e) Foreign government information shall retain its original classification markings or shall be assigned a U.S. classification that provides a degree of protection at least equivalent to that required by the entity that furnished the information. Foreign government information retaining its original classification markings need not be assigned a U.S. classification marking provided that the responsible agency determines that the foreign government markings are adequate to meet the purposes served by U.S. classification markings.

(f) Information assigned a level of classification under this or predecessor orders shall be considered as classified at that level of classification despite the omission of other required markings. Whenever such information is used in the derivative classification process or is reviewed for possible declassification, holders of such information shall coordinate with an appropriate classification authority for the application of omitted markings.

(g) The classification authority shall, whenever practicable, use a classified addendum whenever classified information constitutes a small portion of an otherwise unclassified document or prepare a product to allow for dissemination at the lowest level of classification possible or in unclassified form.

(h) Prior to public release, all declassified records shall be appropriately marked to reflect their declassification.

Sec. 1.7. *Classification Prohibitions and Limitations.* (a) In no case shall information be classified, continue to be maintained as classified, or fail to be declassified in order to:

(1) conceal violations of law, inefficiency, or administrative error;

(2) prevent embarrassment to a person, organization, or agency;

(3) restrain competition; or

(4) prevent or delay the release of information that does not require protection in the interest of the national security.

(b) Basic scientific research information not clearly related to the national security shall not be classified.

(c) Information may not be reclassified after declassification and release to the public under proper authority unless:

(1) the reclassification is personally approved in writing by the agency head based on a document-by-document determination by the agency that reclassification is required to prevent significant and demonstrable damage to the national security;

(2) the information may be reasonably recovered without bringing undue attention to the information;

(3) the reclassification action is reported promptly to the Assistant to the President for National Security Affairs (National Security Advisor) and the Director of the Information Security Oversight Office; and

(4) for documents in the physical and legal custody of the National Archives and Records Administration (National Archives) that have been available for public use, the agency head has, after making the determinations required by this paragraph, notified the Archivist of the United States (Archivist), who shall suspend public access pending approval of the reclassification action by the Director of the Information Security Oversight Office. Any such decision by the Director may be appealed by the agency head to the President through the National Security Advisor. Public access shall remain suspended pending a prompt decision on the appeal.

(d) Information that has not previously been disclosed to the public under proper authority may be classified or reclassified after an agency has received a request for it under the Freedom of Information Act (5 U.S.C. 552), the Presidential Records Act, 44 U.S.C. 2204(c)(1), the Privacy Act of 1974 (5 U.S.C. 552a), or the mandatory review provisions of section 3.5 of this order only if such classification meets the requirements of this order and is accomplished on a document-by-document basis with the personal participation or under the direction of the agency head, the deputy agency head, or the senior agency official designated under section 5.4 of this order. The requirements in this paragraph also apply to those situations in which information has been declassified in accordance with a specific date or event determined by an original classification authority in accordance with section 1.5 of this order.

(e) Compilations of items of information that are individually unclassified may be classified if the compiled information reveals an additional association or relationship that:

(1) meets the standards for classification under this order; and

(2) is not otherwise revealed in the individual items of information.

Sec. 1.8. *Classification Challenges.* (a) Authorized holders of information who, in good faith, believe that its classification status is improper are encouraged and expected to challenge the classification status of the information in accordance with agency procedures established under paragraph (b) of this section.

(b) In accordance with implementing directives issued pursuant to this order, an agency head or senior agency official shall establish procedures under which authorized holders of information, including authorized holders outside the classifying agency, are encouraged and expected to challenge the classification of information that they believe is improperly classified or unclassified. These procedures shall ensure that:

(1) individuals are not subject to retribution for bringing such actions;

(2) an opportunity is provided for review by an impartial official or panel; and

(3) individuals are advised of their right to appeal agency decisions to the Interagency Security Classification Appeals Panel (Panel) established by section 5.3 of this order.

(c) Documents required to be submitted for prepublication review or other administrative process pursuant to an approved nondisclosure agreement are not covered by this section.

Sec. 1.9. *Fundamental Classification Guidance Review.* (a) Agency heads shall complete on a periodic basis a comprehensive review of the agency's classification guidance, particularly classification guides, to ensure the guidance reflects current circumstances and to identify classified information that no longer requires protection and can be declassified. The initial fundamental classification guidance review shall be completed within 2 years of the effective date of this order.

(b) The classification guidance review shall include an evaluation of classified information to determine if it meets the standards for classification under section 1.4 of this order, taking into account an up-to-date assessment of likely damage as described under section 1.2 of this order.

(c) The classification guidance review shall include original classification authorities and agency subject matter experts to ensure a broad range of perspectives.

(d) Agency heads shall provide a report summarizing the results of the classification guidance review to the Director of the Information Security Oversight Office and shall release an unclassified version of this report to the public.

PART 2—DERIVATIVE CLASSIFICATION

Sec. 2.1. *Use of Derivative Classification.* (a) Persons who reproduce, extract, or summarize classified information, or who apply classification markings derived from source material or as directed by a classification guide, need not possess original classification authority.

(b) Persons who apply derivative classification markings shall:

(1) be identified by name and position, or by personal identifier, in a manner that is immediately apparent for each derivative classification action;

(2) observe and respect original classification decisions; and

(3) carry forward to any newly created documents the pertinent classification markings. For information derivatively classified based on multiple sources, the derivative classifier shall carry forward:

(A) the date or event for declassification that corresponds to the longest period of classification among the sources, or the marking established pursuant to section 1.6(a)(4)(D) of this order; and

(B) a listing of the source materials.

(c) Derivative classifiers shall, whenever practicable, use a classified addendum whenever classified information constitutes a small portion of an otherwise unclassified document or prepare a product to allow for dissemination at the lowest level of classification possible or in unclassified form.

(d) Persons who apply derivative classification markings shall receive training in the proper application of the derivative classification principles of the order, with an emphasis on avoiding over-classification, at least once every 2 years. Derivative classifiers who do not receive such training at least once every 2 years shall have their authority to apply derivative classification markings suspended until they have received such training. A waiver may be granted by the agency head, the deputy agency head, or the senior agency official if an individual is unable to receive such training due to unavoidable circumstances. Whenever a waiver is granted, the individual shall receive such training as soon as practicable.

Sec. 2.2. *Classification Guides.* (a) Agencies with original classification authority shall prepare classification guides to facilitate the proper and uniform derivative classification of information. These guides shall conform to standards contained in directives issued under this order.

(b) Each guide shall be approved personally and in writing by an official who:

(1) has program or supervisory responsibility over the information or is the senior agency official; and

Appendix

(2) is authorized to classify information originally at the highest level of classification prescribed in the guide.

(c) Agencies shall establish procedures to ensure that classification guides are reviewed and updated as provided in directives issued under this order.

(d) Agencies shall incorporate original classification decisions into classification guides on a timely basis and in accordance with directives issued under this order.

(e) Agencies may incorporate exemptions from automatic declassification approved pursuant to section 3.3(j) of this order into classification guides, provided that the Panel is notified of the intent to take such action for specific information in advance of approval and the information remains in active use.

(f) The duration of classification of a document classified by a derivative classifier using a classification guide shall not exceed 25 years from the date of the origin of the document, except for:

(1) information that should clearly and demonstrably be expected to reveal the identity of a confidential human source or a human intelligence source or key design concepts of weapons of mass destruction; and

(2) specific information incorporated into classification guides in accordance with section 2.2(e) of this order.

PART 3—DECLASSIFICATION AND DOWNGRADING

Sec. 3.1. *Authority for Declassification.* (a) Information shall be declassified as soon as it no longer meets the standards for classification under this order.

(b) Information shall be declassified or downgraded by:

(1) the official who authorized the original classification, if that official is still serving in the same position and has original classification authority;

(2) the originator's current successor in function, if that individual has original classification authority;

(3) a supervisory official of either the originator or his or her successor in function, if the supervisory official has original classification authority; or (4) officials delegated declassification authority in writing by the agency head or the senior agency official of the originating agency.

(c) The Director of National Intelligence (or, if delegated by the Director of National Intelligence, the Principal Deputy Director of National Intelligence) may, with respect to the Intelligence Community, after consultation with the head of the originating Intelligence Community element or department, declassify, downgrade, or direct the declassification or downgrading of information or intelligence relating to intelligence sources, methods, or activities.

(d) It is presumed that information that continues to meet the classification requirements under this order requires continued protection. In some exceptional cases, however, the need to protect such information may be outweighed by the public interest in disclosure of the information, and in these cases the information should be declassified. When such questions arise, they shall be referred to the agency head or the senior agency official. That official will determine, as an exercise of discretion, whether the public interest in disclosure outweighs the damage to the national security that might reasonably be expected from disclosure. This provision does not:

(1) amplify or modify the substantive criteria or procedures for classification; or

(2) create any substantive or procedural rights subject to judicial review.

(e) If the Director of the Information Security Oversight Office determines that information is classified in violation of this order, the Director may require the information to be declassified by the agency that originated the classification. Any such decision by the Director may be appealed to the President through the National Security Advisor. The information shall remain classified pending a prompt decision on the appeal.

APPENDIX

(f) The provisions of this section shall also apply to agencies that, under the terms of this order, do not have original classification authority, but had such authority under predecessor orders.

(g) No information may be excluded from declassification under section 3.3 of this order based solely on the type of document or record in which it is found. Rather, the classified information must be considered on the basis of its content.

(h) Classified nonrecord materials, including artifacts, shall be declassified as soon as they no longer meet the standards for classification under this order.

(i) When making decisions under sections 3.3, 3.4, and 3.5 of this order, agencies shall consider the final decisions of the Panel.

Sec. 3.2. *Transferred Records.*

(a) In the case of classified records transferred in conjunction with a transfer of functions, and not merely for storage purposes, the receiving agency shall be deemed to be the originating agency for purposes of this order.

(b) In the case of classified records that are not officially transferred as described in paragraph (a) of this section, but that originated in an agency that has ceased to exist and for which there is no successor agency, each agency in possession of such records shall be deemed to be the originating agency for purposes of this order. Such records may be declassified or downgraded by the agency in possession of the records after consultation with any other agency that has an interest in the subject matter of the records.

(c) Classified records accessioned into the National Archives shall be declassified or downgraded by the Archivist in accordance with this order, the directives issued pursuant to this order, agency declassification guides, and any existing procedural agreement between the Archivist and the relevant agency head.

(d) The originating agency shall take all reasonable steps to declassify classified information contained in records determined to have permanent historical value before they are accessioned into the National Archives. However, the Archivist may require that classified records be accessioned into the National Archives when necessary to comply with the provisions of the Federal Records Act. This provision does not apply to records transferred to the Archivist pursuant to section 2203 of title 44, United States Code, or records for which the National Archives serves as the custodian of the records of an agency or organization that has gone out of existence.

(e) To the extent practicable, agencies shall adopt a system of records management that will facilitate the public release of documents at the time such documents are declassified pursuant to the provisions for automatic declassification in section 3.3 of this order.

Sec. 3.3 *Automatic Declassification.*

(a) Subject to paragraphs (b)–(d) and (g)–(j) of this section, all classified records that (1) are more than 25 years old and (2) have been determined to have permanent historical value under title 44, United States Code, shall be automatically declassified whether or not the records have been reviewed. All classified records shall be automatically declassified on December 31 of the year that is 25 years from the date of origin, except as provided in paragraphs (b)–(d) and (g)–(j) of this section. If the date of origin of an individual record cannot be readily determined, the date of original classification shall be used instead.

(b) An agency head may exempt from automatic declassification under paragraph (a) of this section specific information, the release of which should clearly and demonstrably be expected to:

(1) reveal the identity of a confidential human source, a human intelligence source, a relationship with an intelligence or security service of a foreign

government or international organization, or a nonhuman intelligence source; or impair the effectiveness of an intelligence method currently in use, available for use, or under development;

(2) reveal information that would assist in the development, production, or use of weapons of mass destruction;

(3) reveal information that would impair U.S. cryptologic systems or activities;

(4) reveal information that would impair the application of state-of-the-art technology within a U.S. weapon system;

(5) reveal formally named or numbered U.S. military war plans that remain in effect, or reveal operational or tactical elements of prior plans that are contained in such active plans;

(6) reveal information, including foreign government information, that would cause serious harm to relations between the United States and a foreign government, or to ongoing diplomatic activities of the United States;

(7) reveal information that would impair the current ability of United States Government officials to protect the President, Vice President, and other protectees for whom protection services, in the interest of the national security, are authorized;

(8) reveal information that would seriously impair current national security emergency preparedness plans or reveal current vulnerabilities of systems, installations, or infrastructures relating to the national security; or

(9) violate a statute, treaty, or international agreement that does not permit the automatic or unilateral declassification of information at 25 years.

(c)(1) An agency head shall notify the Panel of any specific file series of records for which a review or assessment has determined that the information within that file series almost invariably falls within one or more of the exemption categories listed in paragraph (b) of this section and that the agency proposes to exempt from automatic declassification at 25 years.

(2) The notification shall include:

(A) a description of the file series;

(B) an explanation of why the information within the file series is almost invariably exempt from automatic declassification and why the information must remain classified for a longer period of time; and

(C) except when the information within the file series almost invariably identifies a confidential human source or a human intelligence source or key design concepts of weapons of mass destruction, a specific date or event for declassification of the information, not to exceed December 31 of the year that is 50 years from the date of origin of the records.

(3) The Panel may direct the agency not to exempt a designated file series or to declassify the information within that series at an earlier date than recommended. The agency head may appeal such a decision to the President through the National Security Advisor.

(4) File series exemptions approved by the President prior to December 31, 2008, shall remain valid without any additional agency action pending Panel review by the later of December 31, 2010, or December 31 of the year that is 10 years from the date of previous approval.

(d) The following provisions shall apply to the onset of automatic declassification:

(1) Classified records within an integral file block, as defined in this order, that are otherwise subject to automatic declassification under this section shall not be automatically declassified until December 31 of the year that is 25 years from the date of the most recent record within the file block.

APPENDIX

(2) After consultation with the Director of the National Declassification Center (the Center) established by section 3.7 of this order and before the records are subject to automatic declassification, an agency head or senior agency official may delay automatic declassification for up to five additional years for classified information contained in media that make a review for possible declassification exemptions more difficult or costly.

(3) Other than for records that are properly exempted from automatic declassification, records containing classified information that originated with other agencies or the disclosure of which would affect the interests or activities of other agencies with respect to the classified information and could reasonably be expected to fall under one or more of the exemptions in paragraph (b) of this section shall be identified prior to the onset of automatic declassification for later referral to those agencies.

(A) The information of concern shall be referred by the Center established by section 3.7 of this order, or by the centralized facilities referred to in section 3.7(e) of this order, in a prioritized and scheduled manner determined by the Center.

(B) If an agency fails to provide a final determination on a referral made by the Center within 1 year of referral, or by the centralized facilities referred to in section 3.7(e) of this order within 3 years of referral, its equities in the referred records shall be automatically declassified.

(C) If any disagreement arises between affected agencies and the Center regarding the referral review period, the Director of the Information Security Oversight Office shall determine the appropriate period of review of referred records.

(D) Referrals identified prior to the establishment of the Center by section 3.7 of this order shall be subject to automatic declassification only in accordance with subparagraphs (d)(3)(A)–(C) of this section.

(4) After consultation with the Director of the Information Security Oversight Office, an agency head may delay automatic declassification for up to 3 years from the date of discovery of classified records that were inadvertently not reviewed prior to the effective date of automatic declassification.

(e) Information exempted from automatic declassification under this section shall remain subject to the mandatory and systematic declassification review provisions of this order.

(f) The Secretary of State shall determine when the United States should commence negotiations with the appropriate officials of a foreign government or international organization of governments to modify any treaty or international agreement that requires the classification of information contained in records affected by this section for a period longer than 25 years from the date of its creation, unless the treaty or international agreement pertains to information that may otherwise remain classified beyond 25 years under this section.

(g) The Secretary of Energy shall determine when information concerning foreign nuclear programs that was removed from the Restricted Data category in order to carry out provisions of the National Security Act of 1947, as amended, may be declassified. Unless otherwise determined, such information shall be declassified when comparable information concerning the United States nuclear program is declassified.

(h) Not later than 3 years from the effective date of this order, all records exempted from automatic declassification under paragraphs (b) and (c) of this section shall be automatically declassified on December 31 of a year that is no more than 50 years from the date of origin, subject to the following:

(1) Records that contain information the release of which should clearly and demonstrably be expected to reveal the following are exempt from automatic declassification at 50 years:

Appendix

(A) the identity of a confidential human source or a human intelligence source; or

(B) key design concepts of weapons of mass destruction.

(2) In extraordinary cases, agency heads may, within 5 years of the onset of automatic declassification, propose to exempt additional specific information from declassification at 50 years.

(3) Records exempted from automatic declassification under this paragraph shall be automatically declassified on December 31 of a year that is no more than 75 years from the date of origin unless an agency head, within 5 years of that date, proposes to exempt specific information from declassification at 75 years and the proposal is formally approved by the Panel.

(i) Specific records exempted from automatic declassification prior to the establishment of the Center described in section 3.7 of this order shall be subject to the provisions of paragraph (h) of this section in a scheduled and prioritized manner determined by the Center.

(j) At least 1 year before information is subject to automatic declassification under this section, an agency head or senior agency official shall notify the Director of the Information Security Oversight Office, serving as Executive Secretary of the Panel, of any specific information that the agency proposes to exempt from automatic declassification under paragraphs (b) and (h) of this section.

(1) The notification shall include:

(A) a detailed description of the information, either by reference to information in specific records or in the form of a declassification guide;

(B) an explanation of why the information should be exempt from automatic declassification and must remain classified for a longer period of time; and

(C) a specific date or a specific and independently verifiable event for automatic declassification of specific records that contain the information proposed for exemption.

(2) The Panel may direct the agency not to exempt the information or to declassify it at an earlier date than recommended. An agency head may appeal such a decision to the President through the National Security Advisor. The information will remain classified while such an appeal is pending.

(k) For information in a file series of records determined not to have permanent historical value, the duration of classification beyond 25 years shall be the same as the disposition (destruction) date of those records in each Agency Records Control Schedule or General Records Schedule, although the duration of classification shall be extended if the record has been retained for business reasons beyond the scheduled disposition date.

Sec. 3.4. *Systematic Declassification Review.*

(a) Each agency that has originated classified information under this order or its predecessors shall establish and conduct a program for systematic declassification review for records of permanent historical value exempted from automatic declassification under section 3.3 of this order. Agencies shall prioritize their review of such records in accordance with priorities established by the Center.

(b) The Archivist shall conduct a systematic declassification review program for classified records:

(1) accessioned into the National Archives; (2) transferred to the Archivist pursuant to 44 U.S.C. 2203; and (3) for which the National Archives serves as the custodian for an agency or organization that has gone out of existence.

Sec. 3.5. *Mandatory Declassification Review.*

(a) Except as provided in paragraph (b) of this section, all information classified under this order or predecessor orders shall be subject to a review for declassification by the originating agency if:

APPENDIX

(1) the request for a review describes the document or material containing the information with sufficient specificity to enable the agency to locate it with a reasonable amount of effort;

(2) the document or material containing the information responsive to the request is not contained within an operational file exempted from search and review, publication, and disclosure under 5 U.S.C. 552 in accordance with law; and

(3) the information is not the subject of pending litigation.

(b) Information originated by the incumbent President or the incumbent Vice President; the incumbent President's White House Staff or the incumbent Vice President's Staff; committees, commissions, or boards appointed by the incumbent President; or other entities within the Executive Office of the President that solely advise and assist the incumbent President is exempted from the provisions of paragraph (a) of this section. However, the Archivist shall have the authority to review, downgrade, and declassify papers or records of former Presidents and Vice Presidents under the control of the Archivist pursuant to 44 U.S.C. 2107, 2111, 2111 note, or 2203. Review procedures developed by the Archivist shall provide for consultation with agencies having primary subject matter interest and shall be consistent with the provisions of applicable laws or lawful agreements that pertain to the respective Presidential papers or records. Agencies with primary subject matter interest shall be notified promptly of the Archivist's decision. Any final decision by the Archivist may be appealed by the requester or an agency to the Panel. The information shall remain classified pending a prompt decision on the appeal.

(c) Agencies conducting a mandatory review for declassification shall declassify information that no longer meets the standards for classification under this order. They shall release this information unless withholding is otherwise authorized and warranted under applicable law.

(d) If an agency has reviewed the requested information for declassification within the past 2 years, the agency need not conduct another review and may instead inform the requester of this fact and the prior review decision and advise the requester of appeal rights provided under subsection (e) of this section.

(e) In accordance with directives issued pursuant to this order, agency heads shall develop procedures to process requests for the mandatory review of classified information. These procedures shall apply to information classified under this or predecessor orders. They also shall provide a means for administratively appealing a denial of a mandatory review request, and for notifying the requester of the right to appeal a final agency decision to the Panel.

(f) After consultation with affected agencies, the Secretary of Defense shall develop special procedures for the review of cryptologic information; the Director of National Intelligence shall develop special procedures for the review of information pertaining to intelligence sources, methods, and activities; and the Archivist shall develop special procedures for the review of information accessioned into the National Archives.

(g) Documents required to be submitted for prepublication review or other administrative process pursuant to an approved nondisclosure agreement are not covered by this section.

(h) This section shall not apply to any request for a review made to an element of the Intelligence Community that is made by a person other than an individual as that term is defined by 5 U.S.C. 552a(a)(2), or by a foreign government entity or any representative thereof.

Sec. 3.6. *Processing Requests and Reviews.* Notwithstanding section 4.1(i) of this order, in response to a request for information under the Freedom of Information Act, the Presidential Records Act, the Privacy Act of 1974, or the mandatory review provisions of this order:

Appendix

(a) An agency may refuse to confirm or deny the existence or nonexistence of requested records whenever the fact of their existence or nonexistence is itself classified under this order or its predecessors.

(b) When an agency receives any request for documents in its custody that contain classified information that originated with other agencies or the disclosure of which would affect the interests or activities of other agencies with respect to the classified information, or identifies such documents in the process of implementing sections 3.3 or 3.4 of this order, it shall refer copies of any request and the pertinent documents to the originating agency for processing and may, after consultation with the originating agency, inform any requester of the referral unless such association is itself classified under this order or its predecessors. In cases in which the originating agency determines in writing that a response under paragraph (a) of this section is required, the referring agency shall respond to the requester in accordance with that paragraph.

(c) Agencies may extend the classification of information in records determined not to have permanent historical value or nonrecord materials, including artifacts, beyond the time frames established in sections 1.5(b) and 2.2(f) of this order, provided:

(1) the specific information has been approved pursuant to section 3.3(j) of this order for exemption from automatic declassification; and

(2) the extension does not exceed the date established in section 3.3(j) of this order.

Sec. 3.7. *National Declassification Center.* (a) There is established within the National Archives a National Declassification Center to streamline declassification processes, facilitate quality-assurance measures, and implement standardized training regarding the declassification of records determined to have permanent historical value. There shall be a Director of the Center who shall be appointed or removed by the Archivist in consultation with the Secretaries of State, Defense, Energy, and Homeland Security, the Attorney General, and the Director of National Intelligence.

(b) Under the administration of the Director, the Center shall coordinate:

(1) timely and appropriate processing of referrals in accordance with section 3.3(d)(3) of this order for accessioned Federal records and transferred presidential records.

(2) general interagency declassification activities necessary to fulfill the requirements of sections 3.3 and 3.4 of this order;

(3) the exchange among agencies of detailed declassification guidance to enable the referral of records in accordance with section 3.3(d)(3) of this order;

(4) the development of effective, transparent, and standard declassification work processes, training, and quality assurance measures;

(5) the development of solutions to declassification challenges posed by electronic records, special media, and emerging technologies;

(6) the linkage and effective utilization of existing agency databases and the use of new technologies to document and make public declassification review decisions and support declassification activities under the purview of the Center; and

(7) storage and related services, on a reimbursable basis, for Federal records containing classified national security information.

(c) Agency heads shall fully cooperate with the Archivist in the activities of the Center and shall:

(1) provide the Director with adequate and current declassification guidance to enable the referral of records in accordance with section 3.3(d)(3) of this order; and

(2) upon request of the Archivist, assign agency personnel to the Center who shall be delegated authority by the agency head to review and exempt

APPENDIX

or declassify information originated by their agency contained in records accessioned into the National Archives, after consultation with subject-matter experts as necessary.

(d) The Archivist, in consultation with representatives of the participants in the Center and after input from the general public, shall develop priorities for declassification activities under the purview of the Center that take into account the degree of researcher interest and the likelihood of declassification.

(e) Agency heads may establish such centralized facilities and internal operations to conduct internal declassification reviews as appropriate to achieve optimized records management and declassification business processes. Once established, all referral processing of accessioned records shall take place at the Center, and such agency facilities and operations shall be coordinated with the Center to ensure the maximum degree of consistency in policies and procedures that relate to records determined to have permanent historical value.

(f) Agency heads may exempt from automatic declassification or continue the classification of their own originally classified information under section 3.3(a) of this order except that in the case of the Director of National Intelligence, the Director shall also retain such authority with respect to the Intelligence Community.

(g) The Archivist shall, in consultation with the Secretaries of State, Defense, Energy, and Homeland Security, the Attorney General, the Director of National Intelligence, the Director of the Central Intelligence Agency, and the Director of the Information Security Oversight Office, provide the National Security Advisor with a detailed concept of operations for the Center and a proposed implementing directive under section 5.1 of this order that reflects the coordinated views of the aforementioned agencies.

PART 4—SAFEGUARDING

Sec. 4.1. *General Restrictions on Access.*

(a) A person may have access to classified information provided that:

(1) a favorable determination of eligibility for access has been made by an agency head or the agency head's designee;

(2) the person has signed an approved nondisclosure agreement; and

(3) the person has a need-to-know the information.

(b) Every person who has met the standards for access to classified information in paragraph (a) of this section shall receive contemporaneous training on the proper safeguarding of classified information and on the criminal, civil, and administrative sanctions that may be imposed on an individual who fails to protect classified information from unauthorized disclosure.

(c) An official or employee leaving agency service may not remove classified information from the agency's control or direct that information be declassified in order to remove it from agency control.

(d) Classified information may not be removed from official premises without proper authorization.

(e) Persons authorized to disseminate classified information outside the executive branch shall ensure the protection of the information in a manner equivalent to that provided within the executive branch.

(f) Consistent with law, executive orders, directives, and regulations, an agency head or senior agency official or, with respect to the Intelligence Community, the Director of National Intelligence, shall establish uniform procedures to ensure that automated information systems, including networks and telecommunications systems, that collect, create, communicate, compute, disseminate, process, or store classified information:

(1) prevent access by unauthorized persons;

(2) ensure the integrity of the information; and

Appendix

(3) to the maximum extent practicable, use:

(A) common information technology standards, protocols, and interfaces that maximize the availability of, and access to, the information in a form and manner that facilitates its authorized use; and

(B) standardized electronic formats to maximize the accessibility of information to persons who meet the criteria set forth in section 4.1(a) of this order.

(g) Consistent with law, executive orders, directives, and regulations, each agency head or senior agency official, or with respect to the Intelligence Community, the Director of National Intelligence, shall establish controls to ensure that classified information is used, processed, stored, reproduced, transmitted, and destroyed under conditions that provide adequate protection and prevent access by unauthorized persons.

(h) Consistent with directives issued pursuant to this order, an agency shall safeguard foreign government information under standards that provide a degree of protection at least equivalent to that required by the government or international organization of governments that furnished the information. When adequate to achieve equivalency, these standards may be less restrictive than the safeguarding standards that ordinarily apply to U.S. "Confidential" information, including modified handling and transmission and allowing access to individuals with a need-to-know who have not otherwise been cleared for access to classified information or executed an approved non-disclosure agreement.

(i)(1) Classified information originating in one agency may be disseminated to another agency or U.S. entity by any agency to which it has been made available without the consent of the originating agency, as long as the criteria for access under section 4.1(a) of this order are met, unless the originating agency has determined that prior authorization is required for such dissemination and has marked or indicated such requirement on the medium containing the classified information in accordance with implementing directives issued pursuant to this order.

(2) Classified information originating in one agency may be disseminated by any other agency to which it has been made available to a foreign government in accordance with statute, this order, directives implementing this order, direction of the President, or with the consent of the originating agency. For the purposes of this section, "foreign government" includes any element of a foreign government, or an international organization of governments, or any element thereof.

(3) Documents created prior to the effective date of this order shall not be disseminated outside any other agency to which they have been made available without the consent of the originating agency. An agency head or senior agency official may waive this requirement for specific information that originated within that agency.

(4) For purposes of this section, the Department of Defense shall be considered one agency, except that any dissemination of information regarding intelligence sources, methods, or activities shall be consistent with directives issued pursuant tosection 6.2(b) of this order.

(5) Prior consent of the originating agency is not required when referring records for declassification review that contain information originating in more than one agency.

Sec. 4.2 *Distribution Controls.*

(a) The head of each agency shall establish procedures in accordance with applicable law and consistent with directives issued pursuant to this order to ensure that classified information is accessible to the maximum extent possible by individuals who meet the criteria set forth in section 4.1(a) of this order.

(b) In an emergency, when necessary to respond to an imminent threat to life or in defense of the homeland, the agency head or any designee

APPENDIX

may authorize the disclosure of classified information (including information marked pursuant to section 4.1(i)(1) of this order) to an individual or individuals who are otherwise not eligible for access. Such actions shall be taken only in accordance with directives implementing this order and any procedure issued by agencies governing the classified information, which shall be designed to minimize the classified information that is disclosed under these circumstances and the number of individuals who receive it. Information disclosed under this provision or implementing directives and procedures shall not be deemed declassified as a result of such disclosure or subsequent use by a recipient. Such disclosures shall be reported promptly to the originator of the classified information. For purposes of this section, the Director of National Intelligence may issue an implementing directive governing the emergency disclosure of classified intelligence information.

(c) Each agency shall update, at least annually, the automatic, routine, or recurring distribution mechanism for classified information that it distributes. Recipients shall cooperate fully with distributors who are updating distribution lists and shall notify distributors whenever a relevant change in status occurs.

Sec. 4.3. *Special Access Programs.* (a) Establishment of special access programs. Unless otherwise authorized by the President, only the Secretaries of State, Defense, Energy, and Homeland Security, the Attorney General, and the Director of National Intelligence, or the principal deputy of each, may create a special access program. For special access programs pertaining to intelligence sources, methods, and activities (but not including military operational, strategic, and tactical programs), this function shall be exercised by the Director of National Intelligence. These officials shall keep the number of these programs at an absolute minimum, and shall establish them only when the program is required by statute or upon a specific finding that:

(1) the vulnerability of, or threat to, specific information is exceptional; and

(2) the normal criteria for determining eligibility for access applicable to information classified at the same level are not deemed sufficient to protect the information from unauthorized disclosure.

(b) Requirements and limitations.

(1) Special access programs shall be limited to programs in which the number of persons who ordinarily will have access will be reasonably small and commensurate with the objective of providing enhanced protection for the information involved.

(2) Each agency head shall establish and maintain a system of accounting for special access programs consistent with directives issued pursuant to this order.

(3) Special access programs shall be subject to the oversight program established under section 5.4(d) of this order. In addition, the Director of the Information Security Oversight Office shall be afforded access to these programs, in accordance with the security requirements of each program, in order to perform the functions assigned to the Information Security Oversight Office under this order. An agency head may limit access to a special access program to the Director of the Information Security Oversight Office and no more than one other employee of the Information Security Oversight Office or, for special access programs that are extraordinarily sensitive and vulnerable, to the Director only.

(4) The agency head or principal deputy shall review annually each special access program to determine whether it continues to meet the requirements of this order.

(5) Upon request, an agency head shall brief the National Security Advisor, or a designee, on any or all of the agency's special access programs.

(6) For the purposes of this section, the term "agency head" refers only to the Secretaries of State, Defense, Energy, and Homeland Security, the

Attorney General, and the Director of National Intelligence, or the principal deputy of each.

(c) Nothing in this order shall supersede any requirement made by or under 10 U.S.C. 119.

Sec. 4.4. *Access by Historical Researchers and Certain Former Government Personnel.*

(a) The requirement in section 4.1(a)(3) of this order that access to classified information may be granted only to individuals who have a need-to-know the information may be waived for persons who:

(1) are engaged in historical research projects;

(2) previously have occupied senior policy-making positions to which they were appointed or designated by the President or the Vice President; or

(3) served as President or Vice President.

(b) Waivers under this section may be granted only if the agency head or senior agency official of the originating agency:

(1) determines in writing that access is consistent with the interest of the national security;

(2) takes appropriate steps to protect classified information from unauthorized disclosure or compromise, and ensures that the information is safeguarded in a manner consistent with this order; and

(3) limits the access granted to former Presidential appointees or designees and Vice Presidential appointees or designees to items that the person originated, reviewed, signed, or received while serving as a Presidential or Vice Presidential appointee or designee.

PART 5—IMPLEMENTATION AND REVIEW

Sec. 5.1. *Program Direction.* (a) The Director of the Information Security Oversight Office, under the direction of the Archivist and in consultation with the National Security Advisor, shall issue such directives as are necessary to implement this order. These directives shall be binding on the agencies. Directives issued by the Director of the Information Security Oversight Office shall establish standards for:

(1) classification, declassification, and marking principles;

(2) safeguarding classified information, which shall pertain to the handling, storage, distribution, transmittal, and destruction of and accounting for classified information;

(3) agency security education and training programs;

(4) agency self-inspection programs; and

(5) classification and declassification guides.

(b) The Archivist shall delegate the implementation and monitoring functions of this program to the Director of the Information Security Oversight Office.

(c) The Director of National Intelligence, after consultation with the heads of affected agencies and the Director of the Information Security Oversight Office, may issue directives to implement this order with respect to the protection of intelligence sources, methods, and activities. Such directives shall be consistent with this order and directives issued under paragraph (a) of this section.

Sec. 5.2. *Information Security Oversight Office.* (a) There is established within the National Archives an Information Security Oversight Office. The Archivist shall appoint the Director of the Information Security Oversight Office, subject to the approval of the President.

(b) Under the direction of the Archivist, acting in consultation with the National Security Advisor, the Director of the Information Security Oversight Office shall:

(1) develop directives for the implementation of this order;

APPENDIX

(2) oversee agency actions to ensure compliance with this order and its implementing directives;

(3) review and approve agency implementing regulations prior to their issuance to ensure their consistency with this order and directives issued under section 5.1(a) of this order;

(4) have the authority to conduct on-site reviews of each agency's program established under this order, and to require of each agency those reports and information and other cooperation that may be necessary to fulfill its responsibilities. If granting access to specific categories of classified information would pose an exceptional national security risk, the affected agency head or the senior agency official shall submit a written justification recommending the denial of access to the President through the National Security Advisor within 60 days of the request for access. Access shall be denied pending the response;

(5) review requests for original classification authority from agencies or officials not granted original classification authority and, if deemed appropriate, recommend Presidential approval through the National Security Advisor;

(6) consider and take action on complaints and suggestions from persons within or outside the Government with respect to the administration of the program established under this order;

(7) have the authority to prescribe, after consultation with affected agencies, standardization of forms or procedures that will promote the implementation of the program established under this order;

(8) report at least annually to the President on the implementation of this order; and

(9) convene and chair interagency meetings to discuss matters pertaining to the program established by this order.

Sec. 5.3. *Interagency Security Classification Appeals Panel.*

(a) Establishment and administration.

(1) There is established an Interagency Security Classification Appeals Panel. The Departments of State, Defense, and Justice, the National Archives, the Office of the Director of National Intelligence, and the National Security Advisor shall each be represented by a senior-level representative who is a full-time or permanent part-time Federal officer or employee designated to serve as a member of the Panel by the respective agency head. The President shall designate a Chair from among the members of the Panel.

(2) Additionally, the Director of the Central Intelligence Agency may appoint a temporary representative who meets the criteria in paragraph (a)(1) of this section to participate as a voting member in all Panel deliberations and associated support activities concerning classified information originated by the Central Intelligence Agency.

(3) A vacancy on the Panel shall be filled as quickly as possible as provided in paragraph (a)(1) of this section.

(4) The Director of the Information Security Oversight Office shall serve as the Executive Secretary of the Panel. The staff of the Information Security Oversight Office shall provide program and administrative support for the Panel.

(5) The members and staff of the Panel shall be required to meet eligibility for access standards in order to fulfill the Panel's functions.

(6) The Panel shall meet at the call of the Chair. The Chair shall schedule meetings as may be necessary for the Panel to fulfill its functions in a timely manner.

(7) The Information Security Oversight Office shall include in its reports to the President a summary of the Panel's activities.

Appendix

(b) *Functions.* The Panel shall:

(1) decide on appeals by persons who have filed classification challenges under section 1.8 of this order;

(2) approve, deny, or amend agency exemptions from automatic declassification as provided in section 3.3 of this order;

(3) decide on appeals by persons or entities who have filed requests for mandatory declassification review under section 3.5 of this order; and

(4) appropriately inform senior agency officials and the public of final Panel decisions on appeals under sections 1.8 and 3.5 of this order.

(c) *Rules and procedures.* The Panel shall issue bylaws, which shall be published in the *Federal Register*. The bylaws shall establish the rules and procedures that the Panel will follow in accepting, considering, and issuing decisions on appeals. The rules and procedures of the Panel shall provide that the Panel will consider appeals only on actions in which:

(1) the appellant has exhausted his or her administrative remedies within the responsible agency;

(2) there is no current action pending on the issue within the Federal courts; and

(3) the information has not been the subject of review by the Federal courts or the Panel within the past 2 years.

(d) Agency heads shall cooperate fully with the Panel so that it can fulfill its functions in a timely and fully informed manner. The Panel shall report to the President through the National Security Advisor any instance in which it believes that an agency head is not cooperating fully with the Panel.

(e) The Panel is established for the sole purpose of advising and assisting the President in the discharge of his constitutional and discretionary authority to protect the national security of the United States. Panel decisions are committed to the discretion of the Panel, unless changed by the President.

(f) An agency head may appeal a decision of the Panel to the President through the National Security Advisor. The information shall remain classified pending a decision on the appeal.

Sec. 5.4. *General Responsibilities.* Heads of agencies that originate or handle classified information shall:

(a) demonstrate personal commitment and commit senior management to the successful implementation of the program established under this order;

(b) commit necessary resources to the effective implementation of the program established under this order;

(c) ensure that agency records systems are designed and maintained to optimize the appropriate sharing and safeguarding of classified information, and to facilitate its declassification under the terms of this order when it no longer meets the standards for continued classification; and

(d) designate a senior agency official to direct and administer the program, whose responsibilities shall include:

(1) overseeing the agency's program established under this order, provided an agency head may designate a separate official to oversee special access programs authorized under this order. This official shall provide a full accounting of the agency's special access programs at least annually;

(2) promulgating implementing regulations, which shall be published in the *Federal Register* to the extent that they affect members of the public;

(3) establishing and maintaining security education and training programs;

(4) establishing and maintaining an ongoing self-inspection program, which shall include the regular reviews of representative samples of the agency's

original and derivative classification actions, and shall authorize appropriate agency officials to correct misclassification actions not covered by sections 1.7(c) and 1.7(d) of this order; and reporting annually to the Director of the Information Security Oversight Office on the agency's self-inspection program;

(5) establishing procedures consistent with directives issued pursuant to this order to prevent unnecessary access to classified information, including procedures that:

(A) require that a need for access to classified information be established before initiating administrative clearance procedures; and

(B) ensure that the number of persons granted access to classified information meets the mission needs of the agency while also satisfying operational and security requirements and needs;

(6) developing special contingency plans for the safeguarding of classified information used in or near hostile or potentially hostile areas;

(7) ensuring that the performance contract or other system used to rate civilian or military personnel performance includes the designation and management of classified information as a critical element or item to be evaluated in the rating of:

(A) original classification authorities;

(B) security managers or security specialists; and

(C) all other personnel whose duties significantly involve the creation or handling of classified information, including personnel who regularly apply derivative classification markings;

(8) accounting for the costs associated with the implementation of this order, which shall be reported to the Director of the Information Security Oversight Office for publication;

(9) assigning in a prompt manner agency personnel to respond to any request, appeal, challenge, complaint, or suggestion arising out of this order that pertains to classified information that originated in a component of the agency that no longer exists and for which there is no clear successor in function; and

(10) establishing a secure capability to receive information, allegations, or complaints regarding over-classification or incorrect classification within the agency and to provide guidance to personnel on proper classification as needed.

Sec. 5.5. *Sanctions.* (a) If the Director of the Information Security Oversight Office finds that a violation of this order or its implementing directives has occurred, the Director shall make a report to the head of the agency or to the senior agency official so that corrective steps, if appropriate, may be taken.

(b) Officers and employees of the United States Government, and its contractors, licensees, certificate holders, and grantees shall be subject to appropriate sanctions if they knowingly, willfully, or negligently:

(1) disclose to unauthorized persons information properly classified under this order or predecessor orders;

(2) classify or continue the classification of information in violation of this order or any implementing directive;

(3) create or continue a special access program contrary to the requirements of this order; or

(4) contravene any other provision of this order or its implementing directives.

(c) Sanctions may include reprimand, suspension without pay, removal, termination of classification authority, loss or denial of access to classified information, or other sanctions in accordance with applicable law and agency regulation.

Appendix

(d) The agency head, senior agency official, or other supervisory official shall, at a minimum, promptly remove the classification authority of any individual who demonstrates reckless disregard or a pattern of error in applying the classification standards of this order.

(e) The agency head or senior agency official shall:

(1) take appropriate and prompt corrective action when a violation or infraction under paragraph (b) of this section occurs; and

(2) notify the Director of the Information Security Oversight Office when a violation under paragraph (b)(1), (2), or (3) of this section occurs.

PART 6—GENERAL PROVISIONS

Sec. 6.1. *Definitions.* For purposes of this order:

(a) "Access" means the ability or opportunity to gain knowledge of classified information.

(b) "Agency" means any "Executive agency," as defined in 5 U.S.C. 105; any "Military department" as defined in 5 U.S.C. 102; and any other entity within the executive branch that comes into the possession of classified information.

(c) "Authorized holder" of classified information means anyone who satisfies the conditions for access stated in section 4.1(a) of this order.

(d) "Automated information system" means an assembly of computer hardware, software, or firmware configured to collect, create, communicate, compute, disseminate, process, store, or control data or information.

(e) "Automatic declassification" means the declassification of information based solely upon:

(1) the occurrence of a specific date or event as determined by the original classification authority; or

(2) the expiration of a maximum time frame for duration of classification established under this order.

(f) "Classification" means the act or process by which information is determined to be classified information.

(g) "Classification guidance" means any instruction or source that prescribes the classification of specific information.

(h) "Classification guide" means a documentary form of classification guidance issued by an original classification authority that identifies the elements of information regarding a specific subject that must be classified and establishes the level and duration of classification for each such element.

(i) "Classified national security information" or "classified information" means information that has been determined pursuant to this order or any predecessor order to require protection against unauthorized disclosure and is marked to indicate its classified status when in documentary form.

(j) "Compilation" means an aggregation of preexisting unclassified items of information.

(k) "Confidential source" means any individual or organization that has provided, or that may reasonably be expected to provide, information to the United States on matters pertaining to the national security with the expectation that the information or relationship, or both, are to be held in confidence.

(l) "Damage to the national security" means harm to the national defense or foreign relations of the United States from the unauthorized disclosure of information, taking into consideration such aspects of the information as the sensitivity, value, utility, and provenance of that information.

(m) "Declassification" means the authorized change in the status of information from classified information to unclassified information.

(n) "Declassification guide" means written instructions issued by a declassification authority that describes the elements of information regarding

APPENDIX

a specific subject that may be declassified and the elements that must remain classified.

(o) "Derivative classification" means the incorporating, paraphrasing, restating, or generating in new form information that is already classified, and marking the newly developed material consistent with the classification markings that apply to the source information. Derivative classification includes the classification of information based on classification guidance. The duplication or reproduction of existing classified information is not derivative classification.

(p) "Document" means any recorded information, regardless of the nature of the medium or the method or circumstances of recording.

(q) "Downgrading" means a determination by a declassification authority that information classified and safeguarded at a specified level shall be classified and safeguarded at a lower level.

(r) "File series" means file units or documents arranged according to a filing system or kept together because they relate to a particular subject or function, result from the same activity, document a specific kind of transaction, take a particular physical form, or have some other relationship arising out of their creation, receipt, or use, such as restrictions on access or use.

(s) "Foreign government information" means:

(1) information provided to the United States Government by a foreign government or governments, an international organization of governments, or any element thereof, with the expectation that the information, the source of the information, or both, are to be held in confidence;

(2) information produced by the United States Government pursuant to or as a result of a joint arrangement with a foreign government or governments, or an international organization of governments, or any element thereof, requiring that the information, the arrangement, or both, are to be held in confidence; or

(3) information received and treated as "foreign government information" under the terms of a predecessor order.

(t) "Information" means any knowledge that can be communicated or documentary material, regardless of its physical form or characteristics, that is owned by, is produced by or for, or is under the control of the United States Government.

(u) "Infraction" means any knowing, willful, or negligent action contrary to the requirements of this order or its implementing directives that does not constitute a "violation," as defined below.

(v) "Integral file block" means a distinct component of a file series, as defined in this section, that should be maintained as a separate unit in order to ensure the integrity of the records. An integral file block may consist of a set of records covering either a specific topic or a range of time, such as a Presidential administration or a 5-year retirement schedule within a specific file series that is retired from active use as a group. For purposes of automatic declassification, integral file blocks shall contain only records dated within 10 years of the oldest record in the file block.

(w) "Integrity" means the state that exists when information is unchanged from its source and has not been accidentally or intentionally modified, altered, or destroyed.

(x) "Intelligence" includes foreign intelligence and counterintelligence as defined by Executive Order 12333 of December 4, 1981, as amended, or by a successor order.

(y) "Intelligence activities" means all activities that elements of the Intelligence Community are authorized to conduct pursuant to law or Executive Order 12333, as amended, or a successor order.

Appendix

(z) "Intelligence Community" means an element or agency of the U.S. Government identified in or designated pursuant to section 3(4) of the National Security Act of 1947, as amended, or section 3.5(h) of Executive Order 12333, as amended.

(aa) "Mandatory declassification review" means the review for declassification of classified information in response to a request for declassification that meets the requirements under section 3.5 of this order.

(bb) "Multiple sources" means two or more source documents, classification guides, or a combination of both.

(cc) "National security" means the national defense or foreign relations of the United States.

(dd) "Need-to-know" means a determination within the executive branch in accordance with directives issued pursuant to this order that a prospective recipient requires access to specific classified information in order to perform or assist in a lawful and authorized governmental function.

(ee) "Network" means a system of two or more computers that can exchange data or information.

(ff) "Original classification" means an initial determination that information requires, in the interest of the national security, protection against unauthorized disclosure.

(gg) "Original classification authority" means an individual authorized in writing, either by the President, the Vice President, or by agency heads or other officials designated by the President, to classify information in the first instance.

(hh) "Records" means the records of an agency and Presidential papers or Presidential records, as those terms are defined in title 44, United States Code, including those created or maintained by a government contractor, licensee, certificate holder, or grantee that are subject to the sponsoring agency's control under the terms of the contract, license, certificate, or grant.

(ii) "Records having permanent historical value" means Presidential papers or Presidential records and the records of an agency that the Archivist has determined should be maintained permanently in accordance with title 44, United States Code.

(jj) "Records management" means the planning, controlling, directing, organizing, training, promoting, and other managerial activities involved with respect to records creation, records maintenance and use, and records disposition in order to achieve adequate and proper documentation of the policies and transactions of the Federal Government and effective and economical management of agency operations.

(kk) "Safeguarding" means measures and controls that are prescribed to protect classified information.

(ll) "Self-inspection" means the internal review and evaluation of individual agency activities and the agency as a whole with respect to the implementation of the program established under this order and its implementing directives.

(mm) "Senior agency official" means the official designated by the agency head under section 5.4(d) of this order to direct and administer the agency's program under which information is classified, safeguarded, and declassified.

(nn) "Source document" means an existing document that contains classified information that is incorporated, paraphrased, restated, or generated in new form into a new document.

(oo) "Special access program" means a program established for a specific class of classified information that imposes safeguarding and access requirements that exceed those normally required for information at the same classification level.

APPENDIX

(pp) "Systematic declassification review" means the review for declassification of classified information contained in records that have been determined by the Archivist to have permanent historical value in accordance with title 44, United States Code.

(qq) "Telecommunications" means the preparation, transmission, or communication of information by electronic means.

(rr) "Unauthorized disclosure" means a communication or physical transfer of classified information to an unauthorized recipient.

(ss) "U.S. entity" includes:

(1) State, local, or tribal governments;

(2) State, local, and tribal law enforcement and firefighting entities;

(3) public health and medical entities;

(4) regional, state, local, and tribal emergency management entities, including State Adjutants General and other appropriate public safety entities; or

(5) private sector entities serving as part of the nation's Critical Infrastructure/Key Resources.

(tt) "Violation" means:

(1) any knowing, willful, or negligent action that could reasonably be expected to result in an unauthorized disclosure of classified information;

(2) any knowing, willful, or negligent action to classify or continue the classification of information contrary to the requirements of this order or its implementing directives; or

(3) any knowing, willful, or negligent action to create or continue a special access program contrary to the requirements of this order.

(uu) "Weapons of mass destruction" means any weapon of mass destruction as defined in 50 U.S.C. 1801(p).

Sec. 6.2. *General Provisions.* (a) Nothing in this order shall supersede any requirement made by or under the Atomic Energy Act of 1954, as amended, or the National Security Act of 1947, as amended. "Restricted Data" and "Formerly Restricted Data" shall be handled, protected, classified, downgraded, and declassified in conformity with the provisions of the Atomic Energy Act of 1954, as amended, and regulations issued under that Act.

(b) The Director of National Intelligence may, with respect to the Intelligence Community and after consultation with the heads of affected departments and agencies, issue such policy directives and guidelines as the Director of National Intelligence deems necessary to implement this order with respect to the classification and declassification of all intelligence and intelligence-related information, and for access to and dissemination of all intelligence and intelligence-related information, both in its final form and in the form when initially gathered. Procedures or other guidance issued by Intelligence Community element heads shall be in accordance with such policy directives or guidelines issued by the Director of National Intelligence. Any such policy directives or guidelines issued by the Director of National Intelligence shall be in accordance with directives issued by the Director of the Information Security Oversight Office under section 5.1(a) of this order.

(c) The Attorney General, upon request by the head of an agency or the Director of the Information Security Oversight Office, shall render an interpretation of this order with respect to any question arising in the course of its administration.

(d) Nothing in this order limits the protection afforded any information by other provisions of law, including the Constitution, Freedom of Information Act exemptions, the Privacy Act of 1974, and the National Security Act of 1947, as amended. This order is not intended to and does not create any right or benefit, substantive or procedural, enforceable at law

Appendix

by a party against the United States, its departments, agencies, or entities, its officers, employees, or agents, or any other person. The foregoing is in addition to the specific provisos set forth in sections 1.1(b), 3.1(c) and 5.3(e) of this order.

(e) Nothing in this order shall be construed to obligate action or otherwise affect functions by the Director of the Office of Management and Budget relating to budgetary, administrative, or legislative proposals.

(f) This order shall be implemented subject to the availability of appropriations.

(g) Executive Order 12958 of April 17, 1995, and amendments thereto, including Executive Order 13292 of March 25, 2003, are hereby revoked as of the effective date of this order.

Sec. 6.3. *Effective Date.* This order is effective 180 days from the date of this order, except for sections 1.7, 3.3, and 3.7, which are effective immediately.

Sec. 6.4. *Publication.* The Archivist of the United States shall publish this Executive Order in the *Federal Register*.

THE WHITE HOUSE,
December 29, 2010.

[FR Doc. E9–31418
Filed 1–4–10; 11:15 am]
Billing code 7515–01–P

The Role of International Law in Domestic Courts

4

By Deborah Pearlstein

When and how does international law influence national security decision-making by U.S. government officials? As some of the other chapters in this volume make clear, the short answer is often and in many different ways. This chapter focuses on just one of the paths by which international law may be enforced under domestic U.S. law: through the federal courts. It focuses on the courts not because they are the only government actors that influence U.S. compliance with international law; the president and the Senate, for instance, play essential roles in treaty negotiation and ratification, and the military, by statutory design, professional norms, training, and acculturation, is centrally responsible for day-to-day adherence to the international law of war. But the courts have a unique role in interpreting the effect of law—all law—under our constitutional scheme. Recent debates have thus often centered on how international law guides the courts' actions.

In the past decade alone, prisoners held in U.S. military custody have frequently asked federal courts to weigh in on the legality under international law of their detention, interrogation, and treatment; their right to fair trial procedures and monetary recompense for alleged official misconduct; and restrictions on their transfer to third countries. These questions have generated hundreds of lawsuits since September 11, 2001, and more than a half dozen decisions by the Supreme Court. But as the examples below suggest, international law comes before the courts in any number of cases and influences judicial decision-making in a variety of ways. The basic background provided in this chapter is intended to provide a basic understanding of how U.S. courts respond to lawsuits invoking international law.

WHAT IS INTERNATIONAL LAW?

International law has existed in one form or another for millennia, with scholars typically dating the modern era to the systematic catalog of law and practice compiled by the sixteenth-century Dutch scholar Grotius. While the form and substance of international law has developed substantially since then—beginning with the 1648 European Treaty of Westphalia, establishing the still-prevailing understanding of states as sovereign authorities within their borders—Grotius's influential treatise has been cited by courts from his day to ours to guide legal thinking on topics including just and unjust war, principles of peace and neutrality, the law of the sea, and the rights and freedoms of individuals. These subjects, along with an increasingly elaborate network of international rules governing activities as varied as commercial trade and industry, arms control and terrorism, and human rights and the environment, remain central to the subject of international law today.

The United States, like every other country in the world, is governed by rules of both domestic and international law. In this country, domestic law is contained in the Constitution, in federal statutes and regulations, in a dazzling variety of state and local constitutions, statutes, and lesser rules, and in the written opinions of various authoritative judicial decision-makers. In the same way, modern international law can be found in two kinds of primary sources.

> **International law comes from two primary sources:**
>
> 1. Treaties (written agreements between states); and
> 2. Customary International Law (the general, consistent, and widespread practice of states).

TREATIES

First, international law is contained in treaties, generally defined as written agreements between states, based on state consent, and intended to create a legal obligation among the treaty parties. The United Nations, with which all treaties must be registered, has recorded more than 150,000 bilateral and multilateral treaties formed since 1946. Treaties do not necessarily include "Treaty" in their name—the Geneva Conventions, the U.N. Charter, and the Rome Statute of the International Criminal Court are all in fact treaties. Many treaties set their own rules for what happens if one nation wishes to terminate participation or if one nation violates its terms; many treaties also establish their own institutions for treaty enforcement or compliance.

When a country consents to join a treaty, it takes on an obligation to comply with the treaty as a matter of international law. In contrast, the effect of treaties within that country's *domestic law* varies depending on the country. Some countries make treaties automatically enforceable in their domestic courts as soon as they are ratified. Other countries, like the United States, may have more complex systems. (The enforceability of treaties in U.S. courts is addressed below.) But whatever the effect of a treaty violation under a state's *domestic* law, a state that is party to a treaty that has been breached by another party to the treaty can always complain that the second state has violated *international* law. And the first state will be entitled to whatever remedies for violation may exist under international law.

CUSTOMARY INTERNATIONAL LAW

A second major source of international law is called customary international law, or CIL, a source that accounted for most of international law before the twentieth century. As a popular U.S. treatise on foreign relations law puts it, a CIL rule exists when there is a "general and consistent practice of states followed by them from a sense of legal obligation."[1]

Put differently, CIL depends on

- what most states do (a widespread and actual practice), and
- why they do it (because they think they are legally required to do so).

If a practice is not especially widespread among nations or if nations do it purely out of habit, it is not CIL. Further, if a state has regularly objected to a particular practice while it has been developed—for example, a state has regularly made diplomatic statements objecting to an emerging CIL rule prohibiting the use of land mines—that state is not bound even if the norm eventually becomes so widely adopted that it rises to the level of CIL. Other than that exception, once a norm is recognized as a CIL rule, all countries are bound by it as a matter of law. Among the most readily accepted examples of CIL rules are prohibitions on slavery, genocide, and torture.

While the Supreme Court regularly applied CIL to resolve cases in the eighteenth and nineteenth centuries, the nature of CIL has become a central topic of controversy in the United States today (far less so elsewhere). Scholars and courts disagree on what counts as evidence establishing state practice: How many states have to follow the same practice before it is considered "widespread"? Can you

---

1. RESTATEMENT OF FOREIGN RELATIONS LAW OF THE UNITED STATES § 102(2) (1987).

only count *actions* a state takes, or can you include what a state *says* by signing a nonbinding resolution as evidence as well? Some American scholars also raise concerns about the basic legitimacy of CIL: Why should a nation be considered legally bound by a rule to which it did not consent just because a "widespread" number of other states did consent to it? For example, if the United States decides not to join an international treaty protecting children's rights—which includes a prohibition on the execution of individuals who commit crimes before the age of 18—why should the United States be considered bound by a CIL rule (observed by the vast majority of countries in the world) prohibiting juvenile executions? These and other concerns about the nature of CIL have in part informed how contemporary U.S. courts have addressed cases raising CIL issues, as discussed below.

Two last definitional notes. First, when courts and scholars talk about "international law," they usually do not mean to refer simply to the domestic law of another single country—for example, the property law of France. Foreign law of that nature is often used by American courts and scholars for comparative purposes—that is, to help inform or illuminate the meaning of the domestic law of the United States. Some of the Supreme Court decisions that have generated the most attention and controversy in this realm—for example, the Court's 2005 decision in *Roper v. Simmons* holding that the execution of juveniles violates the Constitution—involve in part this kind of use of foreign or comparative sources.[2] Although judges have varied views on the utility of such methods of interpretation, none claim that it is in any way legally binding on their decision-making, and none suggest that using foreign law to help interpret domestic rules is the same exercise as applying international law in U.S. courts.

Finally, it is worth emphasizing that the term "international law" is not synonymous with the term "international courts." International courts like the International Criminal Court (ICC), the International Court of Justice (ICJ), and the European Court of Human Rights (ECHR) regularly decide cases requiring them to interpret international law. The same may be said for the federal courts of the United States, the state courts of the United States, or for that matter the domestic Constitutional Court of South Africa. Any court with jurisdiction over a particular dispute may be faced with deciding questions of international law. In many of the post-9/11 cases involving detainees, for example, the Supreme Court of the United States had to interpret the effect of various provisions of international law. (Some of these cases are discussed below.) Of course, that does not make the Supreme Court an international court. Conversely, there are many international courts, such as the ICC and ECHR, whose jurisdiction does not extend to disputes involving the United States. The United States is not a party to the treaties creating these courts and is not subject to their jurisdiction. The reality that international law is regularly interpreted by many different courts can sometimes make researching international law difficult for law students. It also makes international law ubiquitous around the world.

---

2. 543 U.S. 551 (2005).

WHEN QUESTIONS OF INTERNATIONAL LAW ARISE BEFORE U.S. COURTS

When do questions of international law arise in U.S. courts, and how do the courts deal with them when they do? Let's consider a few examples taken from recent controversies that illustrate some of the ways that international law—in the form of both treaties and customary international law—arises.

First, a federal statute may be passed to implement an international law obligation the United States has undertaken. The federal criminal law prohibiting torture, for example, was amended in 1994 in order to ensure that the United States was in compliance with the international Convention Against Torture, which it ratified that year.[3] Federal immigration regulations were later enacted to ensure that the United States complied with the Convention's prohibition on the removal of any person to a country where he or she will likely be tortured.[4] When faced with questions arising under such statutes and regulations, courts may refer to the nature of the obligation assumed under international law in order to help them understand how broadly the federal statute means to reach.

Second, a federal statute may incorporate international law by reference—that is, it may make the rule it is prescribing a function of what is required by international law. As the Supreme Court emphasized in holding the Bush administration military commissions invalid in 2006, the federal statutes called the Uniform Code of Military Justice "condition the president's use of military commissions on compliance . . . with the 'rules and precepts of the law of nations.'"[5] Because "compliance with the law of war is the condition upon which the authority" given by the federal statute was granted, and because the military commissions did not comply, they could not proceed.[6]

Congress may take the same approach in incorporating CIL into federal law. The most prominent example in recent years of this kind of law is the Alien Tort Statute, providing the federal courts with jurisdiction over lawsuits by aliens for "a tort only, committed in violation of the law of nations or a treaty of the United States."[7] The Supreme Court has held that the only kind of lawsuits that can be brought under this statute are those that allege violations of particular CIL offenses, such as piracy, or offenses that are similarly as "specific, universal, and obligatory" in nature.[8] How does the Court know what counts as a "tort" that might support a lawsuit under the statute? Only by looking to customary international law.

---

3. 18 U.S.C. § 2340A.
4. *See* Convention Against Torture, Dec. 10, 1984, S. Treaty Doc. No. 100-20, 1465 U.N.T.S. 85, implemented by Foreign Affairs Reform and Restructuring Act of 1998, Pub. L. No. 105-277, Div. G., Tit. XXII, § 2242, 112 Stat. 2681-822; *see also* 8 C.F.R. § 208.18.
5. Hamdan v. Rumsfeld, 548 U.S. 557, 613 (2006).
6. *Id.* at 628.
7. 28 U.S.C. § 1350.
8. Sosa v. Alvarez-Machain, 542 U.S. 692 (2004).

Third, the courts may use international law to help inform their interpretation of statutes, even if the statute does not mention international law by its terms. This was what the Supreme Court did in the case of Yaser Hamdi, the American citizen who was seized in Afghanistan in 2001 by local authorities, turned over to the United States, and later held in military custody in the United States.[9] There, the Supreme Court was asked to decide whether the 2001 Authorization for the Use of Military Force passed by Congress gave the president the power to detain "an individual who . . . was 'part of or supporting forces hostile to the United States or coalition partners'" in Afghanistan and who "engaged in an armed conflict against the United States' there."[10] The statute itself said only that the president had the authority to use all "necessary and appropriate force" against those nations and organizations he deemed responsible for the attacks of September 11.[11] How was the Supreme Court to determine whether detention was part of the "necessary and appropriate" force the statute meant to authorize? It looked to international law—in Hamdi's case, the international law of war, including the Geneva Conventions—to support its holding that the 2001 law should be read to authorize Hamdi's detention. As the Supreme Court put it: "[W]e understand Congress' grant of authority for the use of 'necessary and appropriate force' to include the authority to detain for the duration of the relevant conflict, and our understanding is based on longstanding law-of-war principles."[12]

Separately, there also arise circumstances where there is no federal statute involved. For example, a litigant wants to bring a case alleging that his appearance on a list of people who the United States wishes to target by drone strike in Yemen violates his rights under the International Covenant on Civil and Political Rights, or ICCPR—a treaty to which the United States is party. In the absence of an implementing statute, can an individual still bring a claim under the treaty in federal court? The answer to the broad question is: sometimes. Let's take two different scenarios.

In one scenario, Congress has expressly stated (usually in a Senate statement called a "reservation") at the time it ratified the treaty that it does not intend the treaty to be enforceable—without separate implementing legislation—in U.S. courts. In those cases, the question may be relatively easy. The ICCPR, for example, was accompanied by just such a Senate reservation. As a result, individuals alleging claims under the ICCPR and nothing more have no cause of action in the federal courts.

But for most treaties, the Senate has not said explicitly one way or another whether the treaties should be enforceable in federal courts. In this situation, the answer to whether an individual still can bring a claim under the treaty depends on the court-made doctrine of "self-execution," the subject of the landmark 2008 Supreme Court decision in *Medellin v. Texas*.[13] In that case, Jose Medellin, a

---

9. Hamdi v. Rumsfeld, 542 U.S. 507 (2004).
10. *Id.* at 516.
11. *Id.* at 518 (quoting 115 Stat. 224).
12. *Id.* at 521.
13. 552 U.S. 491, 505 (2008).

> **Recent Cases**
>
> *Hamdan v. Rumsfeld*—Relied on international law as incorporated into domestic law to invalidate the military commissions proposed by President Bush.
>
> *Sosa v. Alvarez-Machain*—Relied on customary international law to define the types of torts (like piracy) that are subject to lawsuit in federal courts.
>
> *Hamdi v. Rumsfeld*—Relied on international law (the laws of war) to help interpret the 2001 Authorization for Use of Military Force to permit detention of U.S. citizens captured in Afghanistan.
>
> *Medellin v. Texas*—Developed a rule for when treaties are "self-executing" and automatically enforceable in U.S. courts and when they require implementing legislation.

Mexican national, was convicted in Texas and sentenced to death for rape and murder. Medellin challenged his conviction, arguing that Texas had violated his rights under the Vienna Convention on Consular Relations, a treaty to which the United States is a party. Specifically, Medellin claimed that his rights under Article 36 of the Vienna Convention had been violated because he had not been advised of his right to contact the Mexican consulate upon his detention (and, for example, seek its assistance in obtaining a lawyer). Medellin's argument relied in part on an International Court of Justice ruling that stated that the United States had violated Article 36 of the Vienna Convention by failing to inform Medellin and 50 other Mexican nationals of their Vienna Convention rights and in part on a memorandum from President George W. Bush that instructed state courts to comply with the ICJ's ruling.

The Supreme Court held that the relevant aspects of the Vienna Convention treaty regime were not self-executing and, therefore, could not take precedence over state procedural rules otherwise applicable in state court, unless enacted into federal law by Congress. It went on to explain the doctrine of self-execution in the following way:

> [A] treaty is equivalent to an act of the legislature, and hence self-executing, when it operates of itself without the aid of any legislative provision. When, in contrast, treaty stipulations are not self-executing[,] they can only be enforced pursuant to legislation to carry them into effect. . . . Our cases simply require courts to decide whether a treaty's terms reflect a determination by the President who negotiated it and the Senate that confirmed it that the treaty has domestic effect.[14]

Even after *Medellin*, the doctrine remains the subject of great ongoing debate.[15]

---

14. *Id.* at 505.
15. Medellin v. Texas (*Medellin II*), 554 U.S. 759 (2008).

To understand self-execution, it is necessary briefly to review what the Constitution has to say about the role of international law in the United States. The Constitution gives all three branches of the federal government some role in the creation, interpretation, or enforcement of international law. Article I of the Constitution gives the Senate the power to advise and consent to undertaking a treaty obligation. And it gives Congress the power to define and punish offenses against the law of nations (a phrase generally thought to include both treaties and CIL). Article II gives the president the power to "make treaties," subject to Senate advice and consent. Article III gives the courts the power to hear cases and controversies "arising under this Constitution, the laws of the United States, and treaties made, or which shall be made, under their authority."[16]

Arguably most important, Article VI of the Constitution provides that "all treaties made, or which shall be made, under the authority of the United States, shall be the supreme law of the land."[17] This provision, called the Supremacy Clause, creates a hierarchy of law in the United States, with the Constitution at the pinnacle of the pyramid, treaties and federal statutes on a par beneath it, and state laws at the base. So, for example, with treaties and statutes at the same level, a later-in-time statute can be passed if Congress wishes to change the effects of an earlier treaty. Note, though, that this effect is only true as a matter of domestic U.S. law; it does not affect the United States' ongoing duty to comply with the treaty as a matter of international law.

So if treaties are the "supreme law of the land," why aren't treaties simply enforceable in federal court even if Congress has not passed separate implementing legislation? For most of U.S. history, the answer was that they *were* automatically enforceable in this way. The courts regularly enforced treaty obligations in the absence of additional implementing legislation, and it was the rare exception that a court found a treaty required further action to make it enforceable. (An early example of a treaty held to require further legislation was one requiring the appropriation of federal funds, an action the Constitution requires be approved by both houses of Congress.)

In *Medellin*, the Supreme Court appeared to back away from that presumption of enforceability. Today, the question of whether a treaty is self-executing—that is, whether it becomes automatically enforceable in federal court upon ratification—depends on a case-by-case assessment of the terms of the particular treaty, the relevant provision within the treaty, and any information that might be gleaned about the intended impact of the treaty from the history of the treaty's negotiation and ratification. It is important to note, however, that it remains unclear what effect, if any, a judgment that a treaty is non-self-executing has on a court's ability to rely on the treaty in any of the other ways noted above. For example, in the case of Salim Hamdan, who admitted to being Osama bin Laden's driver and

---

16. U.S. CONST. art. III, § 2.
17. U.S. CONST. art. VI.

was detained at Guantanamo, the Supreme Court avoided delving into the complex question of the self-execution of the Geneva Conventions and still held that the military commissions were invalid because they failed to comply with that treaty regime. As the Court explained, *whether or not* the Geneva Conventions gave Hamdan an independently enforceable right, the government was required to comply with them because "compliance with the law of war is the condition upon which" the Uniform Code of Military Justice's statutory authority was based.[18]

CONCLUSION

Questions of international law have come before the U.S. courts throughout the country's history, and in the past decade have come with increasing frequency in cases particularly implicating issues of national security. There is little sign this phenomenon will slow down anytime soon. Indeed, America's vigorous ongoing international counterterrorism operations have made it more important than ever for writers and commentators in the national security field to have a basic understanding of the constitutional structure and the many different ways international law might influence judicial decision-making in the United States.

EXPERTS

Philip Alston, New York University School of Law; (212) 998-6173; philip.alston@nyu.edu

Curtis Bradley, Duke University School of Law; (919) 613-7179; cbradley@law.duke.edu

Sarah Cleveland, Columbia Law School; (212) 854-2651; scleve@law.columbia.edu

Donald Donovan, Debevoise & Plimpton, New York, NY; (212) 909-6233; dfdonovan@debevoise.com

Martin Flaherty, Fordham University School of Law; (212) 636-6857; mflaherty17@yahoo.com

Jack Goldsmith, Harvard Law School; (617) 496-2026; qashat@law.harvard.edu (assistant)

Ryan Goodman, New York University School of Law; (212) 992-8180; ryan.goodman@nyu.edu

---

18. Hamdan v. Rumsfeld, 548 U.S. 557, 627–28 (2006).

David Luban, Georgetown University Law Center; (202) 662-9806; luband@law.georgetown.edu

Jenny Martinez, Stanford Law School; (650) 725-2749; jmartinez@law.stanford.edu

Deborah Pearlstein, Benjamin N. Cardozo School of Law; (212) 790-0200; dpearlst@yu.edu

Beth Van Schaack, Santa Clara University School of Law; (408) 554-2349; bvanschaack@scu.edu

David Sloss, Santa Clara University School of Law; (408) 554-2170; DLSloss@scu.edu

Peter Spiro, James E. Beasley School of Law; (215) 204-0911; peter.spiro@temple.edu

Carlos Vazquez, Georgetown University Law Center; (202) 662-9447; vazquez@law.georgetown.edu

Ingrid Wuerth, Vanderbilt University Law School; (615) 322-2304; ingrid.wuerth@vanderbilt.edu

RESOURCES

INTERNATIONAL LAW IN THE U.S. SUPREME COURT: CONTINUITY AND CHANGE (David Sloss et al. eds., Cambridge U. Press 2011).

DAVID J. BEDERMAN, INTERNATIONAL LAW FRAMEWORKS (Foundation, 3d ed. 2010).

SEAN D. MURPHY, PRINCIPLES OF INTERNATIONAL LAW (Thomson/West 2006).

GARY D. SOLIS, THE LAW OF ARMED CONFLICT: INTERNATIONAL HUMANITARIAN LAW IN WAR (Cambridge U. Press 2010).

PHILIP ALSTON ET AL., INTERNATIONAL HUMAN RIGHTS LAW IN CONTEXT (Oxford U. Press 2007).

Anthony Colangelo, *The ATS and Extraterritoriality, Part II*, OPINIO JURIS, Mar. 27, 2012, http://opiniojuris.org/2012/03/27/universal-civil-jurisdiction-and-choice-of-law/, and related posts in the series of commentaries on the Alien Tort Statute.

Deborah N. Pearlstein, *Ratcheting Back: International Law as a Constraint on Executive Power*, 26 CONST. COMMENT. 523 (2010).

Eric Holder, U.S. Att'y Gen., Address at Northwestern University School of Law (Mar. 5, 2012), http://www.justice.gov/iso/opa/ag/speeches/2012/ag-speech-1203051.html.

Harold Hongju Koh, Legal Adviser, U.S. Dep't of State, Address at the Annual Meeting of the American Society of International Law: The Obama Administration and International Law, U.S. DEP'T ST. (Mar. 25, 2010), http://www.state.gov/s/l/releases/remarks/139119.htm.

John B. Bellinger III, Op-Ed., *Why the Supreme Court Should Curb the Alien Tort Statute*, WASH. POST, Feb. 24, 2012, http://www.washingtonpost.com/opinions/why-the-supreme-court-should-curb-the-alien-tort-statute/2012/02/21/gIQA1leZWR_story.html.

John Brennan, Assistant to the President for Homeland Security and Counterterrorism, Address at Harvard Law School Program on Law and Security: Strengthening our Security by Adhering to Our Values and Laws (Sept. 16, 2011), http://www.whitehouse.gov/the-press-office/2011/09/16/remarks-john-o-brennan-strengthening-our-security-adhering-our-values-an.

Kenneth Anderson, *The ATS, Incentives, and Tradeoffs*, OPINIO JURIS (Jan. 29, 2009, 10:04 AM), http://opiniojuris.org/2012/03/06/the-ats-incentives-and-tradeoffs/.

Noah Feldman, *When Judges Make Foreign Policy*, N.Y. TIMES, Sept. 28, 2008, http://www.nytimes.com/2008/09/28/magazine/28law-t.html.

Oona A. Hathaway et al., *International Law at Home: Enforcing Treaties in U.S. Courts*, 37 YALE J. INT'L L. 51 (2012).

Richard M. Buxbaum & David D. Caron, *The Alien Tort Statute: An Overview of the Current Issues*, 28 BERKELEY J. INT'L L. 513 (2010).

SECTION OF INT'L LAW, AM. BAR ASS'N, & AM. SOC'Y OF INT'L LAW, JOINT TASK FORCE ON TREATIES IN U.S. LAW REPORT (tent. draft 2009), *available at* http://www.asil.org/files/TreatiesTaskForceReport.pdf.

Defining Terrorism under International Law

5

By David Scharia[*]

INTRODUCTION

Whenever the debate over the definition of terrorism arises, the discussion inevitably turns to the fact that the international community, despite the horrific consequences of terrorism, is not able to come up with a universal definition of terrorism.

The search for an agreed definition usually stumbles on two issues. The first is the question of whether a definition of terrorism should include states' use of armed forces against civilians, also referred to as "state terrorism." The second question is whether peoples under foreign occupation have a right to resistance, which includes the killing of noncombatants, and whether a definition of terrorism should or should not override this right.

---

[*] The author is Senior Legal Officer and the Legal Coordinator of the United Nations Security Council Counter-Terrorism Executive Directorate. He thanks the Center for Global Affairs at New York University and in particular Dean Vera Jelinek and Professor Mark Galeotti for the hospitality and support provided to conclude this piece during his sabbatical; his research assistant, Aima Raza, for her excellent work and dedication; and Ben Saul and David Unger for their thoughtful comments. The views expressed in this chapter are the author's own and do not represent the views of the United Nations, any of its bodies, or any other institution.

This sums up the core of the difficulty in legally defining terrorism. Because terrorism is a "pejorative term with intrinsically negative connotations,"[1] defining terrorism would simultaneously legitimize or delegitimize both legally and morally acts associated with it.[2] Therefore, it is highly unlikely that any legal creativity or "constructive ambiguity" will allow the international community to overpass these moral and political differences. That being said, terrorism, as a legal concept and as an international crime, has not fallen into absolute relativism. In recent years, there has been much progress in universalizing the concept of terrorism and in criminalizing acts of terrorism.

DEFINING TERRORISM AT THE UNITED NATIONS

The desire to reach an agreed definition of terrorism by the international community started years before the United Nations was established. As early as 1937, the League of Nations prepared a draft defining terrorism as "criminal acts directed against a State and intended or calculated to create a state of terror in the minds of particular persons or a group of persons or the general public."[3] This definition was inherently flawed as it ignored acts targeting civilians except where such acts were directed against a state. However, it did serve as a point of reference for later discussions on terrorism when the United Nations and regional intergovernmental organizations dealt with the issue from a legal and political perspective.

Over the years, the level of awareness of the phenomenon of terrorism at the United Nations has depended on the experience of the international community as a whole at any given time. Following the attack on Lod Airport (now Ben Gurion International Airport) in Tel Aviv and the kidnapping and killing of 11 Israeli athletes during the Olympic Games at Munich, both in 1972, the issue of terrorism became the epicenter of attention and contention in the General Assembly. The controversy between Western and non-Western states became clearly evident. The Arab states and some African and Asian states held the position that people who struggle to liberate themselves may use all methods at their disposal, including the use of force. These member states justified their position by two arguments:

1. Bona fide liberation movements are described as terrorism by a regime against which these freedom struggles are waged.
2. It is not the violence itself that is germane but the root causes—such as despair, frustration, and misery—that cause or produce these violent acts.

---

1. Bruce Hoffman, Inside Terrorism 23 (Colum. Univ. Press 2006).
2. *Id.*
3. 19 League of Nations O.J. 23 (1938) (never entered into force).

From 1972 to 1989, consideration of terrorism at the United Nations reflected this disagreement within the membership as to whether terrorism should be prevented through cooperation in suppressing its manifestations or removal of its root causes.

A second period covers the years 1993 to 2001. During this period, the basic considerations were human rights, terrorism, and measures to eliminate international terrorism, reflecting broader agreement that the existence of root causes does not justify terrorist acts. Since then, the General Assembly, despite inherent disagreements among U.N. member states, has issued numerous resolutions condemning specific acts of terrorism.

The attack on the World Trade Center and the Pentagon with hijacked airliners in 2001 did much to change the orientation of the General Assembly's counterterrorism policy.

In the third (and current) period, the concept and terminology are evolving toward discussions that include genuine measures to eliminate terrorism. The disappearance of the former bipolar confrontation has had a favorable impact on the United Nations and its ability to act. It allowed the United Nations to adopt a Global Counter-Terrorism Strategy in 2006. This comprehensive strategy contains four pillars:

1. Measures to address the conditions conducive to the spread of terrorism;
2. Measures to prevent and combat terrorism;
3. Measures to build states' capacity to prevent and combat terrorism; and
4. Measures to ensure respect for human rights in the fight against terrorism.

The term "root causes" was replaced with "conditions conducive to the spread of terrorism,"[4] which does not imply any sympathy to terrorism but merely reflects the conditions that could be used and abused by terrorists. This was the first time that all member states agreed to a "common strategic approach to fight terrorism." They also sent a clear, unequivocal message that "terrorism is unacceptable in all its forms and manifestation" and committed themselves to taking practical steps "individually and collectively" to prevent and combat terrorism.[5]

Despite lack of a comprehensive agreement on a definition, the United Nations was able to incrementally develop 14 major international conventions against terrorism. Most of these instruments cover specific crimes, such as unlawful seizures of aircrafts, taking of hostages, or crimes against diplomats, which could also fall under a comprehensive definition of terrorism, if reached. This incremental, pragmatic, and very often reactive approach to specific major terrorist attacks started as early as 1963 and allowed the United Nations to conclude

---

4. United Nations, United Nations General Assembly Adopts Global Counter-Terrorism Strategy (2006), http://www.un.org/terrorism/strategy-counter-terrorism.shtml.

5. *Id.*

conventions that require the criminalization of most of the acts that would normally be considered as terrorism. These conventions focus on specific terrorist acts without alluding to the underlying political or other motivation behind the offense. They also established the principle of "extradite or prosecute," which set the basis for extraterritorial jurisdiction of terrorist acts. Of particular interest to our discussion is the Convention for the Suppression of Terrorist Financing (1999), which criminalized for the first time under the United Nations umbrella the financing of terrorism and defined the act, as follows:

(a) An act which constitutes an offense within the scope of and as defined in one of the treaties listed in the annex; or

(b) Any other act intended to cause death or serious bodily injury to a civilian, or to any other person not taking an active part in the hostilities in a situation of armed conflict, when the purpose of such act, by its nature or context, is to intimidate a population, or to compel a government or an international organization to do or to abstain from doing any act.[6]

Many would agree that for all practical purposes, this section provides a comprehensive definition of terrorism. It includes, in its annex, a list of offenses defined as terrorist acts by previous international conventions developed by the United Nations. It also provides a generic definition of terrorism that describes the kind of acts that would normally be considered as terrorism.

International Counterterrorism Instruments

Convention on Offences and Certain Other Acts Committed on Board Aircraft, 1963

Convention for the Suppression of Unlawful Seizure of Aircraft, 1970

Convention for the Suppression of Unlawful Acts against the Safety of Civil Aviation, 1971

    Protocol for the Suppression of Unlawful Acts of Violence at Airports Serving International Civil Aviation, 1988

Convention on the Prevention and Punishment of Crimes against Internationally Protected Persons, including Diplomatic Agents, 1973

International Convention against the Taking of Hostages, 1979

Convention on the Physical Protection of Nuclear Material, 1980

    Amendment to the Convention on the Physical Protection of Nuclear Material, 2005

Convention for the Suppression of Unlawful Acts against the Safety of Maritime Navigation, 1988

---

6. The Convention for the Suppression of Terrorist Financing (1999), art. 2(1), http://www.un.org/law/cod/finterr.htm.

> Protocol to the Convention for the Suppression of Unlawful Acts against the Safety of Maritime Navigation, 2005
>
> Protocol for the Suppression of Unlawful Acts against the Safety of Fixed Platforms Located on the Continental Shelf, 1988
>
> Protocol to the Protocol for the Suppression of Unlawful Acts against the Safety of Fixed Platforms Located on the Continental Shelf, 2005
>
> Convention on the Marking of Plastic Explosives for the Purpose of Detection, 1991
>
> International Convention for the Suppression of Terrorist Bombings, 1997
>
> International Convention for the Suppression of the Financing of Terrorism, 1999
>
> International Convention for the Suppression of Acts of Nuclear Terrorism, 2005
>
> Convention on the Suppression of Unlawful Acts Relating to International Civil Aviation, 2010
>
> > Protocol Supplementary to the Convention for the Suppression of Unlawful Seizure of Aircraft, 2010

Another major development in the consolidation of the United Nations' approach to terrorism is found in the 2004 Report of the Secretary-General's High-Level Panel on Threats, Challenges and Changes. One of the issues the panel discussed in the report was the need to define terrorism universally. The report called upon the United Nations and its member states to adopt a comprehensive definition in line with the one that exists in the Convention for the Suppression of Terrorist Financing.

But the panel did not stop there. The panel tackled in its report the points of contention among the U.N. member states. With regard to the term "state terrorism," the report concluded that since 1945, a set of norms and laws—including the Charter of the United Nations, the Geneva Conventions, and the Rome Statute for the International Criminal Court—has regulated and constrained states' decisions to use force during their conduct in war. Violations of these obligations could and should be prosecuted as war crimes or crimes against humanity. There is no need, therefore, the panel concluded, to include those crimes in the definition of terrorism. Second, with regard to the right to resistance, the panel concluded "that there is nothing in the fact of occupation that justifies the targeting and killing of civilians." Of particular interest is the panel's conclusion that "virtually all forms of terrorism are prohibited by one of 12 [the number now stands at 14] international counter-terrorism conventions, international customary law, the Geneva Conventions or the Rome Statutes."

In 2005, then U.N. Secretary-General Kofi Annan echoed the panel's views in his famous Madrid Address:

> We do not need to argue whether States can be guilty of terrorism because deliberate use of armed force by States against civilians is already clearly prohibited under international law. As for the right to

resist occupation, it must be understood in its true meaning. It cannot include the right to deliberately kill or maim civilians.

The Panel calls for a definition of terrorism, which would make it clear that any action constitutes terrorism if it is intended to cause death or serious bodily harm to civilians and non-combatants, with the purpose of intimidating a population or compelling a government or an international organization to do or abstain from any act. I believe this proposal has clear moral force, and I strongly urge world leaders to unite behind it.[7]

Recent Debates at the United Nations to Define Terrorism

Despite these calls by the high-level panel and the U.N. secretary-general, the General Assembly has been unable to agree on this proposed definition—or, more precisely, on the exclusions to this definition. Since 1996, the U.N. Sixth (Legal) Committee and the Ad Hoc Committee established to conclude a comprehensive convention against terrorism[8] have considered the Draft Comprehensive Convention on International Terrorism.[9] Despite the fact that all member states generally agree on the importance of eradicating international terrorism, the important disagreements continue to exist. They still focus on the legal definition of terrorism and, in particular, on the two above-mentioned disagreements.[10] Several proposals and compromises have been put on the table by the committee's coordinator in order to try to bridge the gap, but as of early 2012 none had been accepted by the member states.[11]

The U.N. Security Council and the Definition of Terrorism

The main role of the U.N. Security Council (UNSC) under the U.N. Charter is to maintain "international peace and security."[12] Over the years, and in particular

---

7. Press Release, United Nations, Secretary-General Offers Global Strategy for Fighting Terrorism in Address to Madrid Summit (Oct. 3, 2005), http://www.un.org/News/Press/docs/2005/sgsm9757.doc.htm.

8. United Nations General Assembly Resolution A/RES/51/210, 88th Plenary Meeting (Dec. 17, 1996), http://www.un.org/documents/ga/res/51/a51r210.htm.

9. Ctr. for Nonproliferation Stud., Inventory of Int'l Nonproliferation Organizations & Regimes, Draft Convention on International Terrorism (May 10, 2010), http://cns.miis.edu/inventory/pdfs/intlterr.pdf.

10. *Id.*

11. The draft Convention that is currently negotiated defines terrorism as follows:

   a person's unlawfully and intentionally causing or threatening to cause violence by means of firearms, weapons, explosives, any lethal devices or dangerous substances, which results, or is likely to result, in death or serious bodily injury to a person, a group of persons or serious damage to property—whether for public use, a State of Government facility, a public transportation system, or an infrastructure facility.

Id.

12. U.N. Charter, Security Council, ch. V, art. 24(1), http://www.un.org/en/documents/charter/chapter5.shtml.

since the 1990s, the Security Council has borne the bulk of the responsibility for treating the threat that terrorism poses to international peace and security. Although the Security Council had done so without defining terrorism, its resolutions have made a huge impact on closing this gap and in preventing any moral ambiguity to terrorist acts. The Council has done so using several tools at its disposal under Chapter VII of the Charter—the chapter dealing with UNSC powers to deal with threats to peace.

The foremost tool available to the UNSC is the use of sanctions against terrorists. On several occasions, the UNSC imposed sanctions against terrorists or states that supported acts of terrorism. For example, in December 1988, Pan Am flight 103 crashed in the Scottish village of Lockerbie when a bomb placed on board the aircraft exploded. The 259 passengers on board and 11 persons on the ground were killed. Less than a year later, in September 1989, a French plane crashed in Niger after a device on board the aircraft exploded, resulting in a loss of 171 lives. Libya was alleged to have been involved in both attacks. In January 1992, the UNSC warned Libya of the consequences if it failed to hand over the suspects. In March of that year, Security Council Resolution 748 (1992) characterized the Libyan actions as a "threat to international peace and security" and imposed a broad range of sanctions. As a result of the sanctions imposed by the Security Council, France obtained from Libya partial satisfaction of its demands in 1996, and six Libyan nationals were tried and convicted of participation in the attacks on the French plane. The two Libyan citizens suspected of having organized the attacks on the Pan Am flight were handed over to the Netherlands on January 5, 1999, to be tried by Scottish judges under Scottish law. One defendant was convicted of murder in 2001 and sentenced to life imprisonment.

On September 12, 2003, after Libya formally stated that it accepted responsibility for the actions of its officials and agreed to pay billions of dollars to the victims' families, the Security Council lifted the sanctions.

In June 1995, a group of terrorists made an unsuccessful attempt on the life of Egyptian President Hosni Mubarak, who was attending a meeting of the Organization of African Unity in Addis Ababa. Three of the suspects sought refuge in Sudan, whose government declined to grant Egypt's request for their extradition. Following Sudan's refusal to grant extradition, the UNSC imposed economic sanctions and a ban on commercial flights. The sanctions, which had an effect on the conduct of the Sudanese authorities, were lifted on September 28, 2001, after Sudan decided to expel various individuals suspected of terrorism, including Osama bin Laden.

Following attacks on American embassies in Kenya and Tanzania, Security Council Resolutions 1189 (1998) and 1267 (1999) were adopted. A number of economic sanctions were imposed on Afghanistan, and a demand for bin Laden was made. Resolution 1267 is of much importance to our discussion regarding the definition because it contains, for the first time in U.N. history, a list of designated individual terrorists associated with al-Qaida or the Taliban who are subject to these sanctions.

Thus, without actually defining terrorism, the UNSC incrementally developed a global framework against terrorism by sanctioning states supporting terrorist acts and by designating individuals and entities as terrorists or terrorist supporters.[13]

RESOLUTIONS REQUIRING MEMBER STATES TO TAKE MEASURES AGAINST TERRORISM

A more comprehensive approach to terrorism was endorsed by the UNSC in response to the terrorist attacks of September 11, 2001. Immediately after the attacks, the Security Council unanimously adopted a resolution[14] embodying the right of individual and collective self-defense against the perpetrators of the attacks. Two weeks later, the Security Council adopted, under Chapter VII, Resolution 1373 (2001), which, without defining terrorism, provided a wide range of legal, financial, police, and cooperation measures against terrorism binding upon all member states.[15] It also called on all member states to ratify and implement the

---

13. In 2009, the Security Council unanimously adopted U.N. Security Council resolution 1904 (2009) setting out bold new reforms of the sanctions regime concerning al-Qaida and the Taliban that include the separation of the sanctions regime against the Taliban and the sanctions regime against al-Qaida. *See* S.C. Res. 1904 (2009), http://www.un.org/Docs/sc/unsc_resolutions09.htm. Over the years the Security Council also improved the due process safeguards provided to designated individuals due largely to a criticism regarding the sanctions regime and its compliance with international human rights law. *See* S.C. Res. 1730 (2006), 1735 (2006), 1904 (2009), and 1989 (2011).
14. S.C. Res. 1368 (2001), http://www.un.org/Docs/scres/2001/sc2001.htm.
15. S.C. Res. 1373 arts 1 & 2 (2001), http://www.un.org/Docs/scres/2001/sc2001.htm:

   1. *Decides* that all States shall:
   (a) Prevent and suppress the financing of terrorist acts;

   (b) Criminalize the willful provision or collection, by any means, directly or indirectly, of funds by their nationals or in their territories with the intention that the funds should be used, or in the knowledge that they are to be used, in order to carry out terrorist acts;

   (c) Freeze without delay funds and other financial assets or economic resources of persons who commit, or attempt to commit, terrorist acts or participate in or facilitate the commission of terrorist acts; of entities owned or controlled directly or indirectly by such persons; and of persons and entities acting on behalf of, or at the direction of such persons and entities, including funds derived or generated from property owned or controlled directly or indirectly by such persons and associated persons and entities;

   (d) Prohibit their nationals or any persons and entities within their territories from making any funds, financial assets or economic resources or financial or other related services available, directly or indirectly, for the benefit of persons who commit or attempt to commit or facilitate or participate in the commission of terrorist acts, of entities owned or controlled, directly or indirectly, by such persons. and of persons and entities acting on behalf of or at the direction of such persons;

international counterterrorism instruments. Resolution 1373 also established the Counter-Terrorism Committee (CTC), a subsidiary organ of the Security Council, comprising all 15 council members. The Security Council charged the CTC with monitoring and implementing the resolution. In late 2003, the UNSC established the Counter-Terrorism Committee Executive Directorate (CTED), a body of professionals to support the work of the CTC. Since then, the CTED has maintained an intensive dialogue with member states concerning the implementation of Resolution 1373 and facilitates necessary assistance to individual countries to help them build capacity to combat terrorism.

Two later resolutions need to be mentioned here.

The first is Security Council Resolution 1540 (2004), which imposes a detailed set of obligations on member states in order to ensure that terrorists, also characterized as "nonstate agents," do not come into possession of unconventional weapons. The second one is Security Council Resolution 1624 (2005), adopted unanimously after the attacks of July 7 and 21 in 2005 on London's public transport system that killed 56 people and injured some 700. This resolution calls upon member states to adopt measures to prohibit incitement to commit an act of terrorism. One of the important elements of this resolution is that it establishes links between incitements to terrorism, attempts to justify or glorify terrorist acts, and the furthering of such terrorist acts.[16]

---

2. *Decides also* that all States shall:

(a) Refrain from providing any form of support, active or passive, to entities or persons involved in terrorist acts, including by suppressing recruitment of members of terrorist groups and eliminating the supply of weapons to terrorists;

(b) Take the necessary steps to prevent the commission of terrorist acts, including by provision of early warning to other States by exchange of information;

(c) Deny safe haven to those who finance, plan, support, or commit terrorist acts, or provide safe havens;

(d) Prevent those who finance, plan, facilitate or commit terrorist acts from using their respective territories for those purposes against other States or their citizens;

(e) Ensure that any person who participates in the financing, planning, preparation or perpetration of terrorist acts or in supporting terrorist acts is brought to justice and ensure that, in addition to any other measures against them, such terrorist acts are established as serious criminal offences in domestic laws and regulations and that the punishment duly reflects the seriousness of such terrorist acts;

(f) Afford one another the greatest measure of assistance in connection with criminal investigations or criminal proceedings relating to the financing or support of terrorist acts, including assistance in obtaining evidence in their possession necessary for the proceedings;

(g) Prevent the movement of terrorists or terrorist groups by effective border controls and controls on issuance of identity papers and travel documents, and through measures for preventing counterfeiting, forgery or fraudulent use of identity papers and travel documents;

16. For an analysis of this resolution, see Daphne Barak-Erez & David Scharia, *Freedom of Speech, Support for Terrorism, and the Challenge of Global Constitutional Law*, 2 HARV. NAT'L SEC. J. 21 (2011), *available at* SSRN: http://ssrn.com/abstract=1735007.

Of particular interest is Resolution 1566 (2004), adopted following the September 2004 terrorist attacks in Beslan, a town in the autonomous region of North Ossetia in the Russian Federation, which claimed the lives of some 350 persons, including 172 children. In this resolution, the Security Council provided the following definition of terrorism:

> Criminal acts, including against civilians, committed with the intent to cause death or serious bodily injury, or taking of hostages, with the purpose to provoke a state of terror in the general public or in a group of persons or particular persons, intimidate a population or compel a government or an international organization to do or to abstain from doing any act, which constitute offences within the scope of and as defined in the international conventions and protocols relating to terrorism, are under no circumstances justifiable by considerations of a political, philosophical, ideological, racial, ethnic, religious or other similar nature.[17]

This resolution brought the United Nations even closer to the adoption of a definition of terrorism.

TERRORISM AS AN INTERNATIONAL CRIME

The International Criminal Court (ICC) was established in 2002. The ICC has jurisdiction over some of the most serious crimes under international law, including war crimes, crimes against humanity, and genocide.[18] One of the questions that was discussed in the negotiations creating the ICC was whether the court would have jurisdiction over the crime of terrorism. The International Law Commission proposed the inclusion of terrorism in this list of crimes.[19] However, the failure to reach a consensus on the definition of the treaty crimes prevented terrorism from falling under the ICC's jurisdiction.[20] Some states were concerned that many terrorism acts are perpetrated in isolation and may carry the "gravity" to become international crime. The concept of gravity reflects the view that the international court will deal only with the most serious crimes. Several recalcitrant states, including the United States, feared that granting the ICC jurisdiction over international terrorism would result in the ICC's politicization.[21]

---

17. S.C. Res. 1566 (2004), art. 3, http://www.un.org/Docs/sc/unsc_resolutions04.html.
18. Richard J. Goldstone & Janine Simpson, *Evaluating the Role of the International Criminal Court as a Legal Response to Terrorism*, 16 Harv. Hum. Rts. J. 13 (Spring 2003); Rome Statute of the International Criminal Court, July 19, 1998, U.N. Doc., art 5(1).
19. *Id.*
20. *Id.*
21. *Id* at 24.

Although acts of terrorism do not fall under the ICC's current mandate, many have argued that some terrorist acts can fall within one of the crimes already under the ICC's jurisdiction. Major terrorist acts, specifically those that have been done as "part of a widespread or systematic attack directed against a civilian population,"[22] could be seen as crimes against humanity and be subject to the jurisdiction of the ICC.[23] Several leading jurists, including Richard Goldstone and Mary Robinson, the former U.N. high commissioner for human rights, have argued that the acts of 9/11 fall under that category and, therefore, their perpetrators could be brought to justice before the ICC.[24] Following the same line of thought, Antonio Cassese,[25] president of the International Criminal Tribunal for the former Yugoslavia, has said that the events of 9/11 call upon the "international community to revisit the Rome Statute with regards to 'crimes against humanity.'"[26] With this approach, and again without defining terrorism, the road to universal criminalization of terrorism edged forward.

---

22. Goldstone & Simpson, *supra* note 18; Rome Statute of the International Criminal Court, July 19, 1998, U.N. Doc., art. 7.
23. Goldstone & Simpson, *supra* note 18.
24. *Id.*
25. Vincent-Joel Proulx, *Rethinking the Jurisdiction of the International Criminal Court in the Post-September 11th Era: Should Acts of Terrorism Qualify as Crimes against Humanity?*, 19 AM. U. INT'L L. REV. 1009, 1025; Antonio Cassese, *Terrorism Is Also Disrupting Some Crucial Legal Categories of International Law*, 12 EUR. J. INT'L L. 993, 994 (2001), http://ejil.oxfordjournals.org/content/12/5/993.full.pdf.
26. Definition of Crimes Against Humanity under Article 7(1) of the Rome Statute:

   Crimes against humanity means any of the following acts when committed as part of a widespread or systematic attack directed against a civilian population, with knowledge of the attack:

   a) Murder;
   b) Extermination;
   c) Enslavement;
   d) Deportation or forcible transfer of population;
   e) Imprisonment or other severe deprivation of physical liberty in violation of fundamental rules of international law;
   f) Torture;
   g) Rape, sexual slavery, enforced prostitution, forced pregnancy, enforced sterilization, or any other form of sexual violence of comparable gravity;
   h) Persecution against identifiable group or collectivity on political, racial, national, ethnic, cultural, religious, gender as defined in paragraph 3, or other grounds that are universally recognized as impermissible under international law, in connection with any act referred to in this paragraph or any crime within the jurisdiction of the Court;
   i) Enforced disappearance of persons;
   j) The crime of apartheid;
   k) Other inhumane acts of a similar character intentionally causing great suffering, or serious injury to body or to mental or physical health.

TERRORISM AS A CRIME UNDER INTERNATIONAL CUSTOMARY LAW

Another important development occurred in the context of the Special Tribunal for Lebanon (STL), which was established in 2007 by the UNSC.[27] The STL is different from other international tribunals because it was the first international court with subject matter jurisdiction over the crime of terrorism.[28] It was established to prosecute those responsible for the assassination of Lebanese Prime Minister Rafiq Hariri in 2005.[29] On February 16, 2011, the STL issued a landmark and much-debated ruling that terrorism is a crime under international customary law.[30] The STL Appeals Chamber found that despite widespread disagreement among scholars and legal experts and their "marked differences of views" on the definition of terrorism, upon closer scrutiny, a definition of terrorism has "gradually emerged."[31] The Appeals Chamber found that the customary international law definition consists of three elements:

1. Perpetration of a criminal act (such as murder, kidnapping, or hostage-taking);
2. Intent to spread fear among the population or directly or indirectly coerce a national or international authority to take some action, or to refrain from taking it; and
3. Inclusion of a transnational element.[32]

The STL further stated that because terrorism is a crime under international customary law, there is a duty on states to prosecute individuals responsible for committing acts of terrorism.[33] This unanimous ruling of the STL Appeals Chamber was signed by Presiding Judge Antonio Cassese,[34] mentioned above, who in

---

27. S.C. Res. 1757 (2007), http://www.un.org/Docs/sc/unsc_resolutions07.htm; *see* Kai Ambos, *Judicial Creativity at the Special Tribunal for Lebanon: Is There a Crime of International Terrorism under International Law?*, 24 LEIDEN J. INT'L L. 655–75 (2011).
28. Michael P. Scharf, *Special Tribunal for Lebanon Issues Landmark Ruling on Definition of Terrorism and Modes of Participation*, 15(6) AM. SOC'Y INT'L L., Mar. 4, 2011, http://www.asil.org/insights110304.cfm.
29. Times Topics, *Saad Hariri*, N.Y. TIMES, Jan. 25, 2011, http://topics.nytimes.com/topics/reference/timestopics/people/h/saad_hariri/index.html.
30. Ambos, *supra* note 27; Scharf, *supra* note 28.
31. Interlocutory Decision on the Applicable Law: Terrorism, Conspiracy, Homicide, Perpetration, Cumulative Charging, Case No. STL-11-01/I (Feb. 16, 2011), accessed at http://www.stl-tsl.org/en/the-cases/stl-11-01/rule-176bis/filings/orders-and-decisions/appeals-chamber/f0010.
32. *Id.* at 85.
33. *Id.*
34. Antonio Cassese, *The Multifaceted Criminal Notion of Terrorism in International Law*, 2006 J. INT'L CRIM. JUST. 933–58. Cassese believes that the definition of terrorism has evolved over the years in the international community under "strong pressure of public opinion." Cassese finds that the main disagreement that exists between states is on the inclusion of an exception to a definition in times of armed conflict of acts committed by freedom fighters engaged in national liberation

his earlier works has supported the notion of the crime of terrorism under international law. However, this ruling has been highly controversial, inviting strong criticism from scholars the likes of international law professor Ben Saul[35] of the University of Sydney and Kai Ambos, an international law professor at the University of Gottingen, who assert that the STL has resorted to "judicial creativity"[36] and overstepped its judicial powers.[37]

CONCLUSION

The international community has yet to reach an agreement on key elements that would constitute a definition of terrorism. However, despite the lack of consensus, there is a shift toward consolidating views on acts that qualify as terrorist offenses under international law, specifically in situations outside the scope of the moral and political controversies that are attached to this much debated issue of terrorism. Despite lack of comprehensive agreement, the international community has accepted a practical understanding of what constitutes terrorism that allowed it to take action and develop a counterterrorism strategy. This has been achieved by a multitude of General Assembly and Security Council resolutions, including 14 universal legal instruments that define specific crimes as terrorist acts, and by the recent establishment and jurisprudence of international tribunals.

---

movements. These should not affect the emergence of such customary law in times of peace. According to Cassese, the spread of fear "is never an end in itself." Terrorist acts must be based on certain political, ideological, or religious motives. Motive in terrorist crimes is important because it serves to differentiate terrorist acts from criminal acts—the motive behind the act is generally immaterial.

35. Ben Saul, *Legislating from a Radical Hague: The United Nations Special Tribunal for Lebanon Invents an International Crime of Transnational Terrorism,* 24 Leiden J. Int'l Law 677–700 (2011).

36. Ambos, *supra* note 27, at 655–75.

37. It should be noted that the decision by the STL was strongly criticized by scholars. Ben Saul and Kai Ambos have strongly contested Antonio Cassese and the STL's assertions on the definition of international crime of terrorism under international customary law. Saul argued that all the sources of custom identified by the STL—national legislation, judicial decisions, regional and international treaties—were "misinterpreted, exaggerated, or erroneously applied" by the Court. Ambos finds that extreme forms of terrorism may be classified as crimes of war or crimes against humanity punishable under international law. However, the elements identified by the STL Appeals Chamber are imprecise, which speaks to the lack of consensus of the international community on the key elements of a definition of international terrorism. Ambos, *supra* note 27, at 655–75; Saul, *supra* note 35, at 677–700.

EXPERTS

Anton Du Plesses, Head, Transnational Threats and International Crimes Division, Institute for Security Studies, South Africa; +27-12-346 9500

Aima Raza, International Affairs Consultant, M.S. Global Affairs, NYU; (917) 892-6032; raza.aima@gmail.com

David Scharia, Senior Legal Officer and Legal Coordinator, CTED United Nations Security Council; (212) 457-1092 or (646) 258-2241; Scharia@un.org or david.scharia@gmail.com

Bibi T. van Ginkel, Senior Research Fellow, Clingendael Netherlands Institute of International Relations; Research Fellow, Clingendael Security and Conflict Program; International Centre for Counter-Terrorism, The Hague; +31 (0)70-3746638, 316-28109185

Howard Wachtel, Political Adviser, United States Mission to the United Nations; (908) 705-5555; Howard.wachtel@gmail.com

RESOURCES

BRUCE HOFFMAN, INSIDE TERRORISM (Colum. U. Press 2006).

United Nations General Assembly Global Counter-Terrorism Strategy, 2006, http://www.un.org/terrorism/strategy-counter-terrorism.shtml.

Ctr. for Nonproliferation Stud., Inventory of Int'l Nonproliferation Organizations & Regimes, Draft Convention on International Terrorism (May 10, 2010), http://cns.miis.edu/inventory/pdfs/intlterr.pdf.

Richard J. Goldstone & Janine Simpson, *Evaluating the Role of the International Criminal Court as a Legal Response to Terrorism*, 16 HARV. HUM. RTS. J. 13 (Spring 2003).

Vincent-Joel Proulx, *Rethinking the Jurisdiction of the International Criminal Court in the Post-September 11th Era: Should Acts of Terrorism Qualify as Crimes against Humanity?*, 19 AM. U. INT'L L. REV. 1009, 1010–36.

Rome Statute of the International Criminal Court, July 19, 1998, U.N. Documents.

Antonio Cassese, *Terrorism Is Also Disrupting Some Crucial Legal Categories of International Law*, 12 EUR. J. INT'L L. 993, 994 (2001), http://ejil.oxfordjournals.org/content/12/5/993.full.pdf.

Kai Ambos, *Judicial Creativity at the Special Tribunal for Lebanon: Is There a Crime of International Terrorism under International Law?*, 24 LEIDEN J. INT'L L. 655–75 (2011).

Michael P. Scharf, *Special Tribunal for Lebanon Issues Landmark Ruling on Definition of Terrorism and Modes of Participation*, 15(6) AM. SOC'Y INT'L L., Mar. 4, 2011, http://www.asil.org/insights110304.cfm.

Antonio Cassese, *The Multifaceted Criminal Notion of Terrorism in International Law*, 2006 J. INT'L CRIM. JUST. 933.

BEN SAUL, DEFINING TERRORISM IN INTERNATIONAL LAW (Oxford U. Press 2006).

Ben Saul, *Legislating from a Radical Hague: The United Nations Special Tribunal for Lebanon Invents an International Crime of Transnational Terrorism*, 24 LEIDEN J. INT'L LAW 677 (2011).

Ben Saul, *Defining "Terrorism" to Protect Human Rights* (U. of Sydney, Sydney Law Sch., Legal Stud. Res. Paper, No. 08/125, October 2008).

C.L. Lim, *The Question of a Generic Definition of Terrorism under General International Law*, ch. 3 *in* GLOBAL ANTI-TERRORISM LAW AND POLICY (Victor V. Ramraj, Michael Hor & Kent Roach eds., Cambridge U. Press 2011).

Michael Lawless, *Terrorism—An International Crime*, INT'L J., Winter 2007/08, at 139–59.

Daphne Barak-Erez & David Scharia, *Freedom of Speech, Support for Terrorism, and the Challenge of Global Constitutional Law*, 2 HARV. NAT'L SECURITY J. 21 (2011).

U.N. OFF. OF DRUGS & CRIME, FREQUENTLY ASKED QUESTIONS ON INTERNATIONAL LAW ASPECTS OF COUNTERING TERRORISM (2009), http://www.unodc.org/documents/terrorism/Publications/FAQ/English.pdf.

Report of the Secretary-General's High-Level Panel on Threats, Challenges and Change to the United Nations, A More Secure World: Our Shared Responsibility (2004), http://www.un.org/secureworld/report2.pdf.

Part II

The Laws of War and Military Operations

The Laws of War: Regulating the Use of Force

6

By Geoffrey S. Corn and Laurie R. Blank

War, or armed conflict, has been subject to regulation since it became an organized societal endeavor. Contrary to the hopes of international society, war has not been eliminated as a tool of national and international power. No nation can predict with certainty if or when it may be compelled to resort to armed force to protect a vital strategic interest or when military action may be necessary to protect its interests against organized armed nonstate groups. Indeed, these "noninternational" armed conflicts have become the predominant source of hostilities in the post-World War II era.

Never before, however, has the law that regulates warfare been more comprehensive or central to the perception of strategic legitimacy. When nation-states—and increasingly even nonstate armed groups—unleash armed violence to achieve their strategic ends, they normally seek to leverage the international legitimacy that flows from compliance with international law. This is unquestionably true for the United States, and especially its armed forces. In the eloquent words of Brig. Gen. Mark J. Martins, an Army lawyer of such exceptional talent that Gen. David Petraeus called him a "once in a generation" officer:

> The question [rule of law in Iraq and Afghanistan] urges inquiry into how law has constrained, enabled and informed our own military operations since September 11th, 2001, even as it also causes us to mull whether and how an abstract concept we all approach with a multitude of assumptions arising from our own experiences

can possibly help oppose ruthless and diverse insurgent groups halfway across the globe. The case I will briefly sketch here today is this: your armed forces heed and will continue to heed the law, take it seriously *and in fact respect it for the legitimacy it bestows* upon their often violent and lethal—necessarily violent and lethal—actions in the field.[1]

In short, law has become the touchstone of military operational legitimacy, and legitimacy the touchstone of strategic credibility. Because of this, no understanding of U.S. national security policy can be complete without understanding how international law influences the conduct of U.S. military operations.

International law includes two legal regimes applicable to war and the use of military force. First, the *jus ad bellum* establishes when a nation may lawfully resort to military force. Second, the *jus in bello* regulates the actual conduct of hostilities and provides the legal foundation for imposing international criminal responsibility for individuals who violate these rules.

It is important to note at the outset, however, the essential separation between these two bodies of law. Although they both apply to the use of force, they have different purposes and different goals. Applying each body of law independent of the other is critical to the fulfillment of these goals and the maximum adherence to their respective key principles. Thus, *jus in bello* rests on the equal application of the law to all parties to an armed conflict. It is a bedrock principle of international law that no party to an armed conflict may disavow respect for the *jus in bello* based on an assertion that the opponent violated the *jus ad bellum* (i.e., launched an illegal war). In other words, just because Saddam Hussein's invasion of Kuwait violated international law, Coalition forces were in no way released from their obligation to follow the rules of war during the conflict. Even in the face of one of the most far-reaching campaigns of aggression in history, the Nuremberg Tribunal firmly rejected the argument that German forces were not entitled to the protections of the law of armed conflict, or LOAC, because they had waged an illegal war of aggression. Thus, in a very real sense this division creates a "no fault" humanitarian protection concept for the simple reason that the people who are required to fight wars and the people who bear the brunt of war's suffering are rarely responsible for the decision to wage wars.

THE *JUS AD BELLUM*: THE INTERNATIONAL LEGAL BASIS FOR THE USE OF FORCE

Jus ad bellum is the law governing the resort to force—that is, when a state may use force within the constraints of the United Nations Charter framework and

---

1. Brig. Gen. Mark J. Martins, Harvard Law School Dean's Distinguished Lecture (July 5, 2011) (emphasis added), http://www.youtube.com/watch?v=g6zBLMpU6Ew.

established legal principles. Article 2(4) of the U.N. Charter prohibits the use of force by one state against another: "All members shall refrain in their international relations from the threat or use of force against the territorial integrity or political independence of any state, or in any other manner inconsistent with the Purposes of the United Nations."[2]

International law provides three justifications that effectively rebut this presumption against the use of force. Any use of force not falling within one of these three justifications is therefore in violation of Article 2(4) and the fundamental prohibition on the use of force by one state against another. These exceptions to the prohibition on the use of force balance two key international law principles: respect for state sovereignty and the collective interests of the international community, including the right to use force in self-defense. Thus, a state's right to protect its sovereignty and territorial integrity is a fundamental aspect of international law and the international system. At the same time, however, states have an inherent right to protect their legally recognized individual and collective interests and their nationals from attack.

Justification One: Consent

First, a state may use force in the territory of another state with the consent of that state. A state engaged in an internal conflict with a rebel group may seek assistance from other states in defeating the rebels and restoring order and security. NATO operations in Afghanistan through the International Security Assistance Force fall within this category of consent, as do individual interventions like the U.S. role in support of the Republic of Vietnam. Alternatively, a state may consent to another state using force in counterterrorism operations, such as Yemen's consent to U.S. drone strikes against al-Qaida and al-Qaida in the Arabian Peninsula operatives in that country. In such cases, however, the territorial state can only consent to such assistance and uses of force in which it could legally engage—no state can consent to actions by another state that would violate international law if undertaken on its own. This means the intervening state may not use the request as a subterfuge for an act of aggression against a neighboring state.

Justification Two: U.N. Authorizations

The second justification is set forth in the U.N. Charter: the collective (multinational) use of force authorized by the Security Council under Chapter VII (Article 42). A recent example of a Security Council–authorized use of force is the multinational military operation to protect civilians in Libya in the spring and summer of 2011. The Security Council first declared that the situation in Libya constituted a threat to international peace and security in Resolution 1970 and

---

2. U.N. Charter art. 2, para. 4.

> Chapter VII of the U.N. Charter covers "action with respect to threats to the peace, breaches of the peace, and acts of aggression." First, Article 39 empowers the U.N. Security Council to determine that a particular situation constitutes a threat to international peace and security and to decide what measures shall be taken under Articles 41 and 42 to maintain or restore peace and security. If nonforceful measures recommended under Article 41 have failed or are not adequate to deter or end the crisis, Article 42 authorizes the Security Council to "take such action by air, sea or land forces as may be necessary to maintain or restore international peace and security . . . [including] operations by air, sea, or land forces of Members of the United Nations."

instituted nonforceful measures, including sanctions, based on Article 41 of the Charter. Some three weeks later, in mid-March 2011, the Security Council passed Resolution 1973, which gave member states the authority to "take all necessary measures . . . to protect civilians and civilian populated areas under threat of attack."[3] The phrase "all necessary measures" is the terminology the Security Council uses when authorizing states to use military force under Chapter VII of the U.N. Charter.

Justification Three: Self-Defense

A state may use force as an act of individual or collective self-defense in response to an armed attack in accordance with Article 51 of the U.N. Charter, which states:

> Nothing in the present Charter shall impair the inherent right of individual or collective self-defence if an armed attack occurs against a Member of the United Nations, until the Security Council has taken measures necessary to maintain international peace and security."[4]

This provision recognizes the preexisting right for states to use force—and to use force in response to another state's request for assistance—in self-defense against an attack. Self-defense is the most commonly relied-upon justification for the use of force. Lawful use of force in self-defense depends on several factors: the existence of an armed attack and the fulfillment of three conditions—necessity, proportionality, and immediacy. Above all, the law focuses on whether the defensive act is appropriate in relation to the ends sought.

The classic formulation of the parameters of the right to self-defense stems from the *Caroline* Incident. In 1837, British troops crossed the Niagara River to the American side and attacked the steamer *Caroline*, which had been running arms and materiel to insurgents on the Canadian side. The British justified the

---

3. S.C. Res. 1973, ¶ 4, U.N. Doc. S/RES/1973 (Mar. 17, 2011).
4. U.N. Charter art. 51.

attack, which killed one American and set fire to the *Caroline*, on the grounds that their troops had acted in self-defense. In a letter to his British counterpart, Lord Ashburton, U.S. Secretary of State Daniel Webster declared that the use of force in self-defense should be limited to "cases in which the necessity of that self-defense is instant, overwhelming and leaving no choice of means, and no moment for deliberation."[5] Furthermore, the force used must not be "unreasonable or excessive; since the act, justified by the necessity of self-defense, must be limited by that necessity, and kept clearly within it."[6] Over the past 60 years, the International Court of Justice has embraced this same formulation.[7]

What Constitutes an Armed Attack?

The prerequisite for any use of force in self-defense is the existence of an armed attack. The International Court of Justice has considered the scale and effects of any particular hostile action directed at a state to see if it rises to the level of an armed attack.[8] For example, deployment of a state's regular armed forces across a border will generally constitute an armed attack (such as Iraq's invasion of Kuwait in 1990), as will a state sending irregular militias or other armed groups to accomplish the same purposes (such as when Rwanda and Uganda sent militias to fight on their behalf in the conflict in the Congo). In contrast, providing assistance—such as weapons or other support—to rebels or other armed groups across state borders will not reach the threshold of an armed attack, such as the United States supplying the mujahedeen in Afghanistan in the 1980s or the Soviets and Cuba supplying the Farabundo Martí National Liberation Front (FMLN) in El Salvador.

A second question pertains to whether only states can launch an armed attack. The International Court of Justice has consistently held that only attacks by states can trigger the right of self-defense.[9] However, nothing in Article 51 of the U.N. Charter specifies that the right of self-defense is only available in response to a threat or use of force by another state. State practice in the aftermath of 9/11 provides firm and increasing support for the existence of a right of self-defense against nonstate actors, even if unrelated to any state.

---

5. Letter from Daniel Webster, U.S. Sec'y of State, to Lord Ashburton, Special British Minister (Aug. 6, 1842), *reprinted in* 2 J. Moore, Digest of Int'l Law § 217, at 409 (1906).

6. *Id.*

7. *See, e.g.*, Military and Paramilitary Activities in and Against Nicaragua (Nicar. v. U.S.), 1986 I.C.J. 14 (June 27); Oil Platforms (Iran v. U.S.), 2003 I.C.J. 161 (Nov. 6); Armed Activities on the Territory of the Congo (Dem. Rep. Congo v. Uganda), 2005 I.C.J. 116 (Dec. 19).

8. Military and Paramilitary Activities in and Against Nicaragua (Nicar. v. U.S.), 1986 I.C.J. 14 (June 27).

9. *See, e.g.*, Military and Paramilitary Activities in and Against Nicaragua (Nicar. v. U.S.), 1986 I.C.J. 14 (June 27); Oil Platforms (Iran v. U.S.), 2003 I.C.J. 161 (Nov. 6); Armed Activities on the Territory of the Congo (Dem. Rep. Congo v. Uganda), 2005 I.C.J. 116, ¶ 147 (Dec. 19); Legal Consequences of the Construction of a Wall in the Occupied Palestinian Territory, Advisory Opinion, 2004 I.C.J. 136, 215 (July 9).

U.N. Security Council Resolution 1368, for example, recognized the United States' inherent right of self-defense against al-Qaida in response to the September 11 attacks and "[u]nequivocally condemn[ed] in the strongest terms the horrifying terrorist attacks . . . as a threat to international peace and security."[10] Similarly, the North Atlantic Council issued a statement activating the collective self-defense provision in Article 5 of the North Atlantic Treaty, as did the Organization of American States regarding its constituent treaty.[11]

Israel's right to act in self-defense against Hezbollah in the summer of 2006 was also generally accepted as a response to Hezbollah's attack on an Israeli army unit and capture of two Israeli soldiers. Similarly, neither Colombia's raid into Ecuador to attack guerrillas of the Revolutionary Armed Forces of Colombia nor Turkey's repeated cross-border raids against Kurdistan Workers' Party forces in Iraq drew condemnation by either the Security Council or the General Assembly. Thus, although debate remains regarding the right of self-defense against nonstate entities, it is now widely accepted that attacks by nonstate actors can amount to armed attacks triggering the right of self-defense.

Responding to an Armed Attack

Like individuals defending themselves against attack, a state must comport with the requirements of necessity, proportionality, and immediacy when acting in response to an armed attack.

Necessity

The requirement of necessity addresses whether there are adequate nonforceful options to deter or defeat the attack, such as diplomatic avenues to halt any further attacks or reparations for injuries caused. In the case of attacks by nonstate actors, states seeking to act in self-defense must first explore whether the territorial state can take action to stop the nonstate actors from launching further attacks and, potentially, to detain those responsible. Necessity includes not only action taken to halt and defeat an initial attack, but can include broader action to eliminate a continuing threat.

---

10. S.C. Res. 1368, 1, U.N. Doc. S/RES/1368 (Sept. 12, 2001).
11. North Atlantic Treaty, art. 5, Apr. 4, 1959, 63 Stat. 2241, 2244, 34 U.N.T.S. 243, 246; Press Release, NATO, Statement by the North Atlantic Council (Sept. 12, 2001); Inter-American Treaty of Reciprocal Assistance, art. 3.1, Sept. 2, 1947, 62 Stat. 1681, 1700, 21 U.N.T.S. 77, 93; Terrorist Threat to the Americas, Res. 1, Twenty-fourth Meeting of Consultation of Ministers of Foreign Affairs, Terrorist Threat to the Americas, OAS Doc. RC.24/RES.1/01 (Sept. 21, 2001). Similarly, Australia activated the collective self-defense provision of the ANZUS Pact. Security Treaty, U.S.-Aust.-N.Z., art. IV, Sept. 1, 1951, 3 U.S.T. 3420, 3423, 131 U.N.T.S. 83, 86; Brendan Pearson, *PM Commits to Mutual Defence*, AUSTRALIAN FIN. REV., Sept. 15, 2001, at 9.

Proportionality

The requirement of proportionality measures the extent of the use of force against the overall military goals, such as fending off an attack or subordinating the enemy. Rather than addressing whether force may be used at all—which is the main focus of the necessity requirement above—proportionality looks at how much force may be used. In doing so, proportionality focuses not on some measure of symmetry between the original attack and the use of force in response, but on whether the measure of counterforce used is proportionate to the needs and goals of repelling or deterring the original attack.[12]

The force used may indeed be significantly greater than that used in the attack that triggered the right to self-defense—what matters is the result sought, not the equivalence between attack and response. For example, in almost all cases, all-out war and occupation would not be a proportionate response to an isolated and limited armed attack. In contrast, the United Kingdom's response to the Argentine invasion of the Falkland Islands in 1982 is an example of a more limited response—a robust campaign to recapture the islands, but no action against the Argentine mainland. Were North Korea to launch an all-out attack on South Korea, however, full-scale invasion of the north and occupation might be the only viable means to terminate the aggression.

Proportionality is one of the most commonly misused terms in international law, and it is therefore important to recognize the differences between the relevant legal regimes. Unlike proportionality in the *jus in bello*, addressed in greater detail below, proportionality here is not concerned with the existence or extent of civilian casualties. The fact that an attack on a particular military objective resulted in excessive civilian casualties (thus constituting a disproportionate attack on civilians under the *jus in bello*) does not mean that the entire military operation to defeat an armed attack is disproportionate as a use of force in self-defense. Similarly, if a state uses force in self-defense beyond the parameters of necessity and proportionality under the *jus ad bellum*, it does not follow that all attacks on individual targets are unlawful as a result (such determinations could only be made by applying the law of armed conflict, as detailed below).

Immediacy

The final requirement for the lawful use of force in self-defense is immediacy. In the case of a response to an ongoing attack, immediacy is not relevant—necessity and proportionality will dominate the analysis of whether the use of force is appropriate. Immediacy considerations arise when a state uses force in self-defense in advance of an attack or long after an attack is over. In the latter case, a forceful response long after an attack will no longer serve defensive purposes, but will be retaliatory, and therefore unlawful. The first scenario is often termed

---

12. YORAM DINSTEIN, WAR, AGGRESSION, AND SELF-DEFENCE 225 (2005).

anticipatory self-defense—the use of force to prevent an imminent attack and the death and damage it will cause. A state need not wait until it is the victim of aggression to act in self-defense. Like domestic law, international law recognizes the right of preemptive self-defense. A classic example of lawful anticipatory self-defense is the Israeli attack on the Egyptian and Jordanian forces massing on its borders at the start of the 1967 Six-Day War. In contrast, the Israeli attack on the Osiraq nuclear reactor in Iraq in 1981 was not generally viewed as a legitimate use of force in anticipatory self-defense because the threat was not seen as sufficiently imminent.

The Bush administration's 2002 National Security Strategy offers another useful lens through which to consider immediacy and imminence. Preemptive self-defense, if construed strictly and narrowly, can in some circumstances comport with existing notions of anticipatory self-defense. When read broadly, however, such concepts of defensive action become preventive self-defense, which extends well beyond the parameters international law has set for the use of force in self-defense. Although the precise contours of the delineation between an imminent threat triggering the lawful use of force in self-defense and actions not so justified are not entirely clear, the *Caroline* requirement that an imminent attack be "instant, overwhelming [and] leaving no moment for deliberation" continues to provide the basic framework.

> ## *Targeted Killing*
>
> The debate over the use of targeted killing as a counterterrorism measure highlights many current considerations inherent in analyzing the lawfulness of the use of force in self-defense. Can a state use force in self-defense in response to an attack or imminent attack by a nonstate actor? How do necessity, proportionality, and immediacy apply to targeted strikes against individual terrorist operatives? As discussed in the text, there is general acceptance that the right to self-defense includes self-defense against attacks by nonstate actors. The nature of the threat posed by the particular individual or terrorist group being targeted will then determine whether the three requirements—necessity, proportionality, and immediacy—are met in each individual case; one cannot make an across-the-board determination regarding all targeted strikes without more individualized analysis of threat, necessity, and other factors.
>
> That said, there is room within the current international law framework for the use of lethal force against nonstate actors when such force is the only means to deter or defeat the threat such persons pose and when the force used is proportionate to the threat. It is important here to distinguish such situations from targeted strikes on terrorist operatives within the framework of an armed conflict against terrorist groups. The lawfulness of any such strikes must be analyzed within the framework of the law of armed conflict, which governs the conduct of hostilities and the protection of persons during armed conflict.

THE *JUS IN BELLO*: REGULATING THE CONDUCT OF HOSTILITIES

The *jus in bello* regulates the conduct of hostilities. Originally known as the laws and customs of war, or laws of war, today it is known as "international humanitarian law" or the "law of armed conflict" (LOAC). The latter characterization is used by the Department of Defense and will be used throughout this chapter.[13]

The law of armed conflict's ultimate objective is to mitigate the suffering of war by balancing the necessity to employ combat power with the interests of humanity. This comprehensive body of treaty and customary international law is based on a rich history of battlefield regulation. Military commanders have always understood that compliance with these rules serves a variety of tactical and strategic interests, ranging from facilitating the submission of enemy forces who expect to be treated humanely upon capture, to minimizing the alienation of the civilian population in order to maximize the opportunity to return to a state of peaceful coexistence, to maintaining the discipline of friendly forces by ensuring that they comply with rules and regulations even in the heat of battle.

Triggering the Law of Armed Conflict

As the term "law of armed conflict" suggests, this body of international law is triggered by situations of armed conflict. Adoption of the term "armed conflict" was a deliberate response to the common practice of the Axis powers in World War II of attempting to avoid humanitarian restraints by claiming that the formal legal requirements of war had not been satisfied. Therefore, the contemporary LOAC applies based on the de facto existence of armed hostilities, maximizing the applicability of humanitarian protections for war victims.

The LOAC includes two types of armed conflicts: international and noninternational. As set forth in Common Article 2 of the Geneva Conventions, international armed conflict is any conflict between two states.[14] The threshold of armed conflict here is intentionally low. For disputes between sovereign states, any hostilities between armed forces, no matter how brief in duration or limited in intensity, trigger the LOAC. Thus, for example, when Syrian forces shot down and captured U.S. Navy Lt. Bobby Goodman while he was flying a mission over the Bekka Valley in Lebanon in 1983 in support of the U.S. peacekeeping forces in Beirut, the United States properly demanded that Syria treat him as a prisoner of war. Although brief, the engagement between Syria and the United States

---

13. Although most of the scholarly community and most experts outside the United States prefer the term "international humanitarian law," "law of armed conflict" is the term used in official Department of Defense Doctrine. *See* U.S. Dep't of Def., Dir. 2311.01 E, DoD Law of War Program (May 9, 2006); *see also* Chairman, Joint Chiefs of Staff, Instr. 5810.01B, Implementation of the DoD Laws of War Program (Mar. 25, 2002).

14. The term "Common Article 2" refers to the provision common to all four Geneva Conventions in Article 2. Note that since all states are parties to the Geneva Conventions, the requirement that the conflict be between two High Contracting Parties essentially means between two states.

qualified as an international armed conflict. In addition, even when states engaged in hostilities insist they are not in a state of war (which is quite common), the objective existence of armed conflict is sufficient to trigger the LOAC. In such situations of state-versus-state conflict, the full corpus of international legal regulation comes into force.

States do not, however, hold a monopoly on organized armed violence. Indeed, violence between states and nonstate organized belligerent groups has been the most common type of armed hostilities since World War II. Prior to 1949, international law did not regulate these conflicts. However, when the drafters of the 1949 Geneva Conventions adopted the armed conflict law trigger, they extended LOAC application to armed conflicts "not of an international character," commonly referred to as noninternational armed conflicts. Common Article 3 of the Geneva Conventions provides a baseline of humanitarian regulation for these conflicts, such as the recent civil war in Libya, or more protracted armed conflicts between state forces and insurgent forces, such as the decades-long civil war in Colombia. As conflicts normally occurring within the sovereign territory of a state, they did not trigger the extent of regulation analogous to international armed conflicts. Originally, the only rule applicable to these conflicts was the obligation to treat humanely any person not actively participating in hostilities, including captured opposition personnel. Since 1949, however, there has been a significant expansion of the rules applicable to noninternational armed conflicts, and the practical distinctions between the two categories of conflict have narrowed. Today, the most significant distinction between international and noninternational armed conflicts is the inapplicability of prisoner of war status to nonstate belligerents—a distinction that has been central to the characterization and treatment of al-Qaida and Taliban operatives captured by the United States, as discussed below.

Identifying the parameters of noninternational armed conflict is more complex than for international armed conflict. The line between government response to internal disturbances and unrest, such as crime and riots, and government response to an armed dissident threat resulting in a situation of armed conflict is often quite blurry. Generally, a noninternational armed conflict involves sustained armed hostilities between government military forces and organized insurgent groups or dissident armed forces, or between two or more organized armed groups such as the warring factions in a failed state like Somalia. The U.S. government characterizes the current struggle against transnational terrorist groups as a noninternational armed conflict.[15] The idea that a state can be engaged in an armed conflict with a transnational terrorist group operating from multiple locations outside

---

15. All three branches of the U.S. government have demonstrated that they view the situation as an armed conflict. *See* Authorization to Use Military Force (AUMF), Pub. L. No. 107-40, 115 Stat. 224(a) (2001); *Hamdan v. Rumsfeld*, 548 U.S. 557 (2006); Detention, Treatment, and Trial of Certain Non-Citizens in the War Against Terrorism, 66 Fed. Reg. 57,833 (Nov. 16, 2001) (stating that the 9/11 attacks "created a state of armed conflict that requires the use of the United States Armed Forces").

its borders thus adds even more complication to the analysis of noninternational armed conflict. Understanding that the rights and duties associated with war may only be invoked during periods of armed conflict—rights that include the right to attack and kill enemy operatives, to preventively detain them without charge or trial, and to prosecute them before military tribunals for violations of the LOAC— shows why this characterization is so critically important to current U.S. national security policy.

Core LOAC Principles: The Foundation of Conflict Regulation

As reflected in the preamble to the 1899 Hague Convention IV,[16] one of the first multilateral international agreements regulating armed conflict, the LOAC in many ways rests on the "desire to diminish the evils of war":

> [I]n cases not covered by the attached regulations, the belligerents remain under the protection and the rule of the principles of the laws of nations as derived from the usages established among civilized people, the laws of humanity and the dictates of the public conscience.[17]

Known as the Martens clause, this statement provides additional support for the proposition that no conflict can be permitted to fall outside the regulation of the foundational principles of the laws of war.[18] These principles provide the foundation for and add meaning to more specific treaty rules. After more than a century of codifying customary rules in the form of treaties, today there is an extensive body of treaty law regulating armed conflict. These treaties fall into two broad categories: the Hague tradition and the Geneva tradition.

The Hague tradition focuses on the regulation of the means (weapons and ammunition) and methods (tactics) of warfare: for example, prohibiting certain types of weapons (like chemical or biological weapons) and defining who and what qualifies as a legitimate target in warfare. The Geneva tradition focuses on the protection of war victims—individuals who are not actively participating in hostilities but are negatively impacted by armed conflict. Thus, each of the four Geneva Conventions of 1949 is devoted to the protection of a distinct category of war victim (the wounded and sick in the field; the wounded, sick, and shipwrecked at sea; prisoners of war; and civilians under the control of an enemy power).

Understanding the core principles upon which the entire LOAC regulatory regime is built will illuminate the framework of conflict regulation. For U.S. armed forces (and the armed forces of many other nations), these principles extend even beyond the context of armed conflict to guide the planning and execution of other

---

16. Convention (II) with Respect to the Laws and Customs of War on Land, Sept. 4, 1899, 32 Stat. 1803, T.S. 403.
17. *Id.* at pmbl.
18. *See* LESLIE C. GREEN, THE CONTEMPORARY LAW OF ARMED CONFLICT 176 (Juris, 2d ed. 2000).

types of military operations, such as peacekeeping missions. While Gen. William T. Sherman's notorious statement that "war is hell"[19] no longer reflects the moral underpinnings of the LOAC, it has and will always reflect the reality of the battlefield. The LOAC's principles thus provide the proverbial azimuth points that guide warriors through the moral abyss of mortal combat. Effective training is the foundation for success in combat; training that must prepare combatants not only for the difficult task of inflicting violence on demand, but also for the equally difficult task of doing so within the limits of the law developed to regulate hostilities and mitigate the suffering associated with war.

Military Necessity: The First Principle of Authority

Military necessity "justifies those measures not forbidden by international law which are indispensable for securing the complete submission of the enemy as soon as possible."[20] Accordingly, military necessity supplies the authority to employ those measures necessary to bring an enemy to submission, including the application of deadly combat power, and to capture and detain enemy personnel until the end of hostilities or until they no longer present a threat. However, the principle also provides an essential constraint on the authority of armed forces. Military necessity therefore reflects a balance between the authority to inflict harm and the obligation to limit suffering that lies at the very core of combat regulation. This balance is reflected in Napoleon's great maxim, "In politics and war alike, every injury done to the enemy, even though permitted by the rules, is excusable only so far as it is absolutely necessary; everything beyond that is criminal."[21]

Crucially, military necessity does not justify departures from the LOAC. Up through World War II, some nations viewed military necessity as a trump card for all other humanitarian constraints. A German doctrine called *Kriegsraison* asserted that war could justify any measures—even in violation of the laws of war—when the necessities of any particular situation purportedly justified it. However, "[w]ar crimes trials after World War II clearly rejected this view. Military necessity cannot justify actions absolutely prohibited by law, as the means to achieve military victory are not unlimited. Armed conflict must be carried on within the limits set by International Law."[22]

---

19. William T. Sherman, Gen., Union Army, Address to the Graduating Class of the Mich. Military Acad. (Jun. 19, 1879).
20. U.S. DEP'T OF ARMY, FIELD MANUAL 27-10: THE LAW OF LAND WARFARE 3–4 (1956) [hereinafter FM 27-10].
21. GEOFFREY BEST, WAR AND LAW SINCE 1945, at 242 (1994) (citing 7 MAX HUBER, ZEITSCHRIFT FUR VOLKERRECHE 353 (1913)).
22. OFFICE OF THE JUDGE ADVOCATE GEN., CANADIAN DEF. FORCES, JOINT DOCTRINE MANUAL OF ARMED CONFLICT: AT THE OPERATIONAL AND TACTICAL LEVELS, B-GJ-005-104/FP-021, 2-1-2-2 (2001), *available at* http://www.forces.gc.ca/jag/publications/oplaw-loiop/loac-ddca-2004-eng.pdf.

Humanity: The First Principle of Constraint

The principle of humanity provides an essential counterbalance to the authority associated with defeating an enemy in armed conflict. In practice, the principle of humanity provides the foundation for two critical limits on the authority to inflict suffering in the context of armed conflict: first, the prohibition against subjecting an opponent to superfluous injury or unnecessary suffering (injury or suffering beyond that which is necessary to bring about the opponent's prompt submission); and second, the obligation to ensure the humane treatment of any person (even a captured enemy) who is no longer or never was actively participating in armed hostilities. The LOAC fully synchronizes the principles of humanity and military necessity by excluding from the measures justified by military necessity anything that violates the principle of humanity.

This principle of humanity is the central focus of the four Geneva Conventions of 1949 and is implemented through numerous LOAC treaty provisions. These include the prohibition against the use of any type of coercion against a prisoner of war or civilian internee; the obligation to search for and collect the wounded and sick and ensure that priority of medical care is based solely on medical considerations; the obligation to search for and collect the shipwrecked at sea; the obligation to provide notice of capture of enemy personnel to the enemy state through a neutral intermediary; the obligation to facilitate the efforts of neutral relief agencies; the extensive immunities from attack afforded to places engaged in medical functions; and even the obligation to maintain and record the location of interment of the enemy dead.[23]

Common Article 3 extended the principle of humanity to noninternational armed conflicts in 1949,[24] leading to a general symmetry in the application of the principle of humanity to both interstate and intrastate armed conflicts. This symmetry is consistent with the universally accepted view that humane treatment is a fundamental principle found at the very core of the Geneva tradition of protecting victims of war in all situations of hostilities.

The principle of humanity also protects participants in hostilities, but to a much more limited extent, prohibiting the use of weapons or tactics that cause unnecessary suffering. However, it is essential to note that inherent within this protection is the assumption that war involves the infliction of substantial necessary suffering. What then is the scope of this protection? It really comes down to

---

23. *See generally* Geneva Convention for the Amelioration of the Condition of the Wounded and Sick in Armed Forces in the Field, Aug. 12, 1949, T.I.A.S. 3362 [hereinafter GWS]; Geneva Convention for the Amelioration of the Condition of Wounded, Sick, and Shipwrecked Members at Sea, Aug. 12, 1949, T.I.A.S. 3363 [hereinafter GWS Sea]; Geneva Convention Relative to the Treatment of Prisoners of War, Aug, 12, 1949, T.I.A.S. 3364 [hereinafter GPW]; Geneva Convention Relative to the Treatment of Civilian Persons in Time of War, Aug. 12, 1949, T.I.A.S. 3365 [hereinafter GC].

24. *See* GWS, *supra* note 23, art. 3; GWS Sea, *supra* note 23, art. 3; GPW, *supra* note 23, art. 3; GC, *supra* note 23, art. 3.

one word: superfluous. War—military necessity, to be more precise—justifies the infliction of suffering on an opponent, but only that amount of suffering necessary to subdue an enemy force. Today, this concept prohibits parties engaged in hostilities from inflicting superfluous injury or unnecessary suffering on their battlefield opponents—injuries that exceed those necessary for bringing about prompt submission. In this regard, it is essential to understand that "prompt submission" applies to the enemy force in the corporate sense, not individual enemy soldiers. Accordingly, it is permissible to employ massive combat power at the decisive place and time of battle to overwhelm enemy forces in order to influence the overall capacity of the enemy writ large. For example, it might appear to many that a massive air and artillery bombardment of retreating enemy forces (for example, the so-called "highway of death" in the first Gulf War) is excessive because the enemy is already in retreat. However, such an attack is justified not only because it ensures the enemy forces will not return to the fight, but also because of the shock effect it has on other enemy forces and enemy leadership that may result in a more timely capitulation. This principle does, however, prohibit armed forces from employing "weapons, projectiles and material, and methods of warfare of a nature to cause superfluous injury or unnecessary suffering."[25]

Over time, it has become apparent that reaching consensus on what weapons and tactics violate this prohibition is extremely difficult. As a result, the modern trend has been to identify particular weapon systems—such as chemical and biological weapons and antipersonnel landmines—and develop treaties for the exclusive purpose of prohibiting their production, stockpile, or use (the United States did not join the antipersonnel landmine ban, however, based on the determination that the technology of our self-neutralizing landmines sufficiently mitigated the risk of collateral casualties and because of the perceived operational importance of being able to utilize this weapon in future conflicts).

Distinction

The principle of distinction requires that combatants always differentiate between lawful objects of attack and all other persons, places, and things in the battle space.[26] Pursuant to this principle, combat power may be deliberately directed

---

25. Protocol Additional to the Geneva Conventions of 12 August 1949, and Relating to the Protection of Victims of International Armed Conflicts (Protocol I), art. 35(2), June 8, 1977, 1125 U.N.T.S. 3 [hereinafter API].

26. *See id* art. 48, which states:

> In order to ensure respect for and protection of the civilian population and civilian objects, the Parties to the conflict shall at all times distinguish between the civilian population and combatants and between civilian objects and military objectives and accordingly shall direct their operations only against military objectives.

See also CUSTOMARY INTERNATIONAL HUMANITARIAN LAW, VOLUME I: RULES, at Rule 1 (J.M. Henckaerts & L. Doswald-Beck eds., 2005) (discussing the customary international law status of the principle of distinction).

only against lawful objects of attack. This principle therefore operates to protect innocent individuals and their property (i.e., individuals and property not actively contributing to enemy military operations) from being made the deliberate object of attack, and ensures that the application of combat power is restricted to targets that contribute to the submission of an opponent's military capability.

In operational terms, the principle of distinction enables commanders to determine what is and is not a lawful target. A target is a person, place, or thing made the object of attack by a military force. The target selection and engagement process begins with the military mission. Operational planners then determine how to best leverage the capabilities of their military units to achieve the effects deemed necessary to accomplish the mission, including destruction, neutralization, denial, harassment, and disruption. Distinction thus mandates that only targets that are lawful military objectives may be attacked.

The principle of distinction thus rests on two presumptions: military personnel, equipment, and facilities are lawful objects of attack; all other persons, places, or things are immune from attack. However, neither of these presumptions is conclusive. A member of the enemy armed forces who surrenders is no longer the lawful object of attack for the obvious reason that disabling him by attack is no longer justified by military necessity. A civilian who takes up arms and engages in hostilities against military forces is no longer immune from attack for the equally obvious reason that disabling that civilian is necessary in order to protect allied forces. These presumptions demonstrate that distinction is unquestionably derived from the concept of military necessity. Because the law presumes that deliberately inflicting death or destruction on civilians or civilian property does not contribute to this objective, distinction prohibits combatants from making civilians or civilian property the deliberate objects of attack. This prohibition is not, however, absolute. If civilians engage in conduct that is considered amounting to a "direct part in hostilities"—in other words, conduct that presents a threat to armed forces analogous to that posed by an enemy soldier—the protection is suspended for the duration of the participation and the civilian may be attacked. Analogous limitations apply to the protections established for places and things; for instance, a hospital being used by enemy forces to launch attacks no longer is presumed to be a protected civilian property.

Compliance with the principle of distinction obviously requires a definition of what constitutes a lawful military objective. The rule of military objective provides this definition by establishing targets that may be made the lawful objects of attack:

> Attacks shall be limited strictly to military objectives. In so far as objects are concerned, military objectives are limited to those objects which by their nature, location, purpose or use make an effective contribution to military action and whose total or partial destruction, capture or neutralization, in the circumstances ruling at the time, offers a definite military advantage.[27]

---

27. *See* API, *supra* note 25, art. 52(2).

Determining whether places or things are, or are not, lawful objects of attack requires a case-by-case analysis of these key factors—nature, location, use, and purpose—based on the mission, enemy, troops available, terrain, time, and presence of civilians.

A second and equally important aspect of distinction is that persons who are fighting (whether soldiers, organized armed groups, or others) must distinguish themselves from innocent civilians. Like the prohibition on deliberately targeting civilians, this obligation is central to the LOAC's fundamental goal of protecting civilians in the course of armed conflict. To this end, the LOAC prohibits perfidy, which occurs when an individual launches an attack while leading the enemy to believe he or she (the attacker) is protected from attack. In other words, an individual cannot pretend to be inoffensive and then attack—such as a suicide bombing by an individual dressed as a local civilian.

Similarly, the LOAC requires that parties to a conflict refrain from locating military objectives in densely populated or civilian areas. As part of this analysis, Article 51 of Additional Protocol I provides that "[t]he presence or movements of the civilian population or individual civilians shall not be used to render certain points or areas immune from military operations, in particular in attempts to shield military objectives from attacks or to shield, favour or impede military operations."[28] Pursuant to this rule, the presence of civilians in or around what qualifies as a military objective does not "immunize" the thing or area from attack. Instead, the operational decision-maker is obligated to analyze the legality of the attack pursuant to the complementary prohibition against engaging in indiscriminate attacks, and assess whether the expected harm to civilians, or civilian property, will be excessive in relation to the concrete and direct military advantage anticipated (commonly referred to as the proportionality analysis and discussed in greater detail below).

Proportionality

The almost inevitable presence of civilians and civilian property in areas of armed hostilities has produced an ever-increasing risk that the effects of combat operations will extend beyond lawful military objectives and harm these civilians and their property. Because of this reality, it is universally recognized that the principle of military objective is insufficient to provide adequate protection for civilians from the harmful effects of hostilities. During the twentieth century, hundreds of thousands of civilians became victims of war, not as the result of a decision to deliberately target them, but as the result of the collateral effects of attacks on lawful military objectives.

The principle of proportionality responds to this reality. Legality of attack is not automatic even after determining that a person, place, or thing satisfies the

---

28. *Id.* art. 51(5)(b).

military objective test. The principle of proportionality imposes an obligation on combatants to refrain from attacks on targets that qualify as lawful military objectives when the expected loss of life and damage to property will be excessive in relation to the *concrete and direct* military advantage anticipated to be gained.[29]

Proportionality is not a separate legal standard as such, but provides a means by which military commanders can balance military necessity against the protection of noncombatants in circumstances when they believe an attack is likely to cause incidental damage to civilian personnel or property. However, it is important to note that an attack does not become indiscriminate when the collateral damage or incidental injury is slightly greater than the military advantage anticipated (as is suggested by the term "disproportionate"), but only when those effects are excessive.

The principle of proportionality requires commanders to balance the anticipated effects of an attack. The two critical components of this balance are the anticipated military advantage to be gained by attacking a lawful target and the expected collateral damage and incidental injury to civilians and civilian property. There are no established numerical equations or ratios for applying this rule, which by its very nature requires case-by-case analysis of the key factors of mission, enemy, troops, terrain, time, and civilians. Any critique regarding application of this rule must be based on this reality and must therefore be made through the subjective perspective of the commander at the time the targeting decision was made. All facts and circumstances available to the commander, including the pressures of time and the proverbial "fog of war," must be considered when rendering an objective assessment of the validity of a targeting decision.

Lawful Combatant Status and Privileges

The LOAC categorizes persons in international armed conflict as combatants or civilians. Combatants (also called privileged belligerents) have the right to participate in hostilities and—as a result—are lawful targets of attack at all times, except when wounded or detained. Upon capture, combatants enjoy prisoner of war status. There are several important requirements that must be met to qualify for POW status and the accordant privileges, like combatant immunity. First, combatant (or POW) status applies only in international armed conflict because the Third Geneva Convention Relative to the Treatment of Prisoners of War applies only in such conflicts. Second, only individuals fighting under state authority may qualify for POW status. Thus, members of the regular armed forces of a state are combatants. Members of regular militia belonging to a state party to the conflict may qualify for POW status if they satisfy four criteria. These four criteria, incorporated into the Geneva POW Convention and derived from treaties dating back to 1899, are

---

29. *See id.* art. 51. *See also* FM 27-10, *supra* note 20, at para. 41.

1. Being commanded by a person responsible for his subordinates;
2. Having a fixed distinctive sign recognizable at a distance;
3. Carrying arms openly;
4. Conducting their operations in accordance with the laws and customs of war.

Members of insurgent groups or other nonstate groups are never entitled to combatant status because they do not operate pursuant to state authority.

Combatant Immunity

Combatant immunity is perhaps the most fundamental privilege that attaches to combatant status. The principle of combatant immunity is based on the premise that because soldiers fight as agents of their respective states, it is unjust to subject them to criminal liability for executing their duty so long as they do so in compliance with the LOAC. Accordingly, if captured by an enemy, the enemy state may not criminally prosecute such prisoners for their lawful precapture conduct, even when that conduct was harmful to the capturing state. As Gen. Telford Taylor stated at the Nuremberg Trials:

> War consists largely of acts that would be criminal if performed in time of peace—killing, wounding, kidnapping, destroying or carrying off other people's property. Such conduct is not regarded as criminal if it takes place in the course of war because the state of war lays a blanket of immunity over the warriors.[30]

For soldiers, this is perhaps the most important benefit associated with the status of prisoner of war. However, only individuals who qualify as "privileged belligerents"—individuals legally entitled to participate in armed conflict pursuant to the laws and customs of war—are combatants and may claim combatant immunity, which sometimes is referred to as the combatant's privilege. Captured enemy belligerent personnel who fail to meet these requirements are not POWs. They accordingly do not qualify for combatant immunity and may be prosecuted for their precapture wartime conduct. It is also important to note that combatant immunity is not absolute and extends only to wartime conduct that complies with the LOAC. Wartime conduct in violation of the LOAC subjects the individual to war crimes liability, even when the individual qualifies as a POW. In other words, wartime conduct in violation of the LOAC falls outside the scope of combatant immunity and subjects the actor and accomplices to international criminal responsibility for such violations.

---

30. Telford Taylor, Nuremberg and Vietnam: An American Tragedy 19 (1970).

Detention

Detention of enemy belligerent personnel is justified as a measure of military necessity in order to prevent their return to hostilities. Because it is preventive in nature (as opposed to punitive), there is no requirement for trial and conviction to justify these detentions. During international armed conflicts, detainees who qualify as POWs may be detained until the end of hostilities. As POWs, these detainees are protected by the Third Geneva Convention, which provides a comprehensive regime of rights and obligations derived from the experiences of conflicts past. The Fourth Geneva Convention also provides for detention of enemy civilians in areas under occupation for imperative reasons of security, although these detentions must be based on individualized threat determinations and must end as soon as the detaining power is satisfied the civilian no longer poses a threat. In Iraq, therefore, Iraqi armed forces captured during the initial phase of the war were designated as POWs. During and after that time, the United States also captured and detained thousands of Iraqi insurgents, who were detained pursuant to the Fourth Geneva Convention based on imperative security concerns (many of these civilians were transferred to Iraq for trial in Iraqi criminal courts).

Captured enemy belligerents who fail to meet POW qualification requirements are detained preventively until the end of hostilities like their privileged belligerent counterparts, but are not POWs. While some experts challenge the validity of this "unprivileged belligerent" detention theory, it received the Supreme Court's endorsement in two important decisions: *Quirin*[31] during World War II and *Hamdi*[32] in 2004. Although these detainees may not invoke the treaty protections provided for POWs, the LOAC nonetheless mandates that they be treated humanely at all times.

Detention related to the conflicts in Afghanistan and against al-Qaida has proven to be significantly more complex and controversial. The U.S. determination that individuals captured in the context of these operations were associated with a belligerent group resulted in their preventive detention for the duration of hostilities. However, the detainees' failure to meet the qualifications for POW status, either because the enemy was not representative of a state (the al-Qaida detainees) or because the enemy armed forces did not satisfy POW qualification requirements (the initial Taliban detainees), resulted in their being denied POW status. This equation has been applied to detentions in Afghanistan and at Guantanamo.

Three central questions lie at the center of the ongoing debate over the Guantanamo Bay detention facility and detention in the course of operations against al-Qaida more broadly: who can be detained, for how long, and where they can be held. In essence, which persons captured in the course of counterterror operations

---

31. *Ex parte* Quirin, 317 U.S. 1 (1942).
32. Hamdi v. Rumsfeld, 542 U.S. 507 (2004).

around the world are properly considered enemy belligerent operatives and may therefore be subject to preventive wartime detention? How long may such persons be detained (for example, when is the end of hostilities with a terrorist group)? And can such persons be held in Guantanamo, only in Afghanistan, or either?

Distinguishing between Law and Policy: Understanding Rules of Engagement

No understanding of the LOAC and how it affects the planning and execution of military operations would be complete without an examination of the relationship between this law and rules of engagement, commonly referred to as ROE. Although the LOAC and ROE are inextricably connected, they are not synonymous, but are instead two distinct sources of operational regulation.

As defined in U.S. military doctrine, ROE are "directives issued by competent military authority that delineate the circumstances and limitations under which United States forces will initiate and/or continue combat engagement with other forces encountered."[33] In other words, ROE are intended to give operational and tactical military leaders greater control over the execution of combat operations by subordinate forces. The history of warfare is replete with examples of what have essentially been ROE. The Battle of Bunker Hill provides an excellent example of such use. Capt. William Prescott imposed a limitation on the use of combat power by his forces in the form of the directive, "Don't shoot until you see the whites of their eyes."[34] Given his limited resources against a much larger and better-equipped foe, he used this tactical control measure to maximize the effect of his firepower. This example of what was, in effect, a ROE is remembered to this day for one primary reason—it enabled the colonial militia to maximize enemy casualties.

Contemporary military operations increasingly manifest the operational necessity for similar constraints on the otherwise lawful scope of the use of force authority. As a result, ROE have become a key aspect of modern warfare[35] and a key component of mission planning for U.S. and many other armed forces.[36] In preparation for military operations, the president and/or secretary of defense personally review and approve the ROE, ensuring they meet the military and political

---

33. CHAIRMAN OF THE JOINT CHIEFS OF STAFF, JP 1-02, DEPARTMENT OF DEFENSE DICTIONARY OF MILITARY AND ASSOCIATED TERMS (Apr. 12, 2001, as amended through Sept. 30, 2010), *available at* http://www.dtic.mil/doctrine/new_pubs/jp1_02.pdf.

34. *See* JOHN BARTLETT, FAMILIAR QUOTATIONS 446 & n.1 (Emily M. Beck ed., Little Brown & Co., 14th ed. 1968), *quoted in* Major Mark S. Martins, *Rules of Engagement for Land Forces: A Matter of Training, not Lawyering*, 143 MIL. L. REV. 1, 34 (1994).

35. *See State Department Conducts Daily Press Briefing*, U.S. FED NEWS, Oct. 3, 2007.

36. *See* INT'L & OPERATIONAL LAW DEP'T, JUDGE ADVOCATE GEN.'S LEGAL CTR. & SCHOOL, OPERATIONAL LAW HANDBOOK 84 (2007); CTR. FOR LAW AND MILITARY OPERATIONS, RULES OF ENGAGEMENT HANDBOOK 1-1-1-32 (May 1, 2000).

The Jus in Bello: Regulating the Conduct of Hostilities

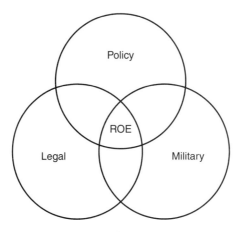

(Originally published in Mark S. Martins, *Rules of Engagement for Land Forces: A Matter of Training, Not Lawyering*, 143 MIL. L. REV. 1 (Winter 1994))

objectives.[37] Ideally, ROE represent the confluence of three important factors: operational requirements, national policy, and the LOAC.[38]

It is particularly important to note that while ROE are not coterminous with the LOAC, they must be completely consistent with it. In other words, while some aspects of the LOAC do not affect a mission's ROE, all ROE must comply with this law. As the diagram reflects, it is common for the authority provided by the ROE to be more limited than the LOAC's parameters. For example, in order to provide greater protection against collateral injury to civilians, the ROE may provide that the engagement of a clearly defined military objective in a populated area is authorized only when the target is under direct observation. This is a fundamental principle and key to the proper formation and application of ROE. In fact, the preeminent U.S. ROE order explicitly directs U.S. forces that they "will comply with the Law of Armed Conflict during military operations involving armed conflict, no matter how the conflict may be characterized under international law, and will comply with the principles and spirit of the Law of Armed Conflict during all other operations."[39] Note that this directive applies to any "armed conflict," not only to international armed conflicts.

To illustrate the interaction between ROE and the LOAC, consider a ROE provision that allows a soldier to kill an enemy. Although this provision is completely

---

37. Dale Stephens, *Rules of Engagement and the Concept of Unit Self Defense*, 45 NAVAL L. REV. 126, 126 (1998).
38. Richard J. Grunawalt, *The JCS Standing Rules of Engagement: A Judge Advocate's Primer*, 42 A.F. L. REV. 245, 247 (1997).
39. Chairman, Joint Chiefs of Staff Instruction 3121.01B, Standing Rules of Engagement/Standing Rules for the Use of Force for US Forces, encl. A, para. 1d (Jun. 13, 2005).

appropriate, it does not implicitly include the authority to kill an enemy who is surrendering, because such conduct would violate the LOAC.[40] Similarly, if a ROE allows for a pilot to destroy a bridge with a bomb, it does not relieve the pilot of his responsibility to terminate the attack if he believes it will violate the principle of proportionality, as explained above.[41] ROE will also often contain provisions that remind soldiers that they can only engage the enemy, or other individuals, who engage in defined conduct endangering soldiers or others. In this way, ROE ensures compliance with the laws of war.

Appreciating this interrelationship is therefore vital to understanding why the violation of a constraint imposed by a specific ROE, or even customarily imposed by ROE, does not ipso facto establish violation of the LOAC. To assess that apparent discrepancy, it is necessary to determine whether the ROE constraint was coterminous with the LOAC, or more restrictive than the scope of permissible authority established by the LOAC. In contemporary military operations, it is common for ROE to be more restrictive than the LOAC in order to satisfy policy considerations related to the application of combat power.

CONCLUSION

Jus ad bellum highlights a balance between the international community's laudable goal of ending war and the respect for state sovereignty with the recognition that states must be able to rely on force when appropriate—and lawful—to protect their individual and collective interests, including the protection and security of their citizens. *Jus in bello*, or the LOAC, balances military necessity with the essential humanitarian considerations of mitigating the inevitable suffering associated with armed hostilities. The separation between these two bodies of law is equally important to the fulfillment of these goals, guarding against claims of just war as justification for violations of the LOAC.

It would, of course, be naïve to suggest that this law is always respected; the reality is quite different. The contemporary record of *jus belli* compliance is indeed a mixed bag. But this in no way diminishes the significance of the law or the importance of continued efforts to improve, understand, and comply with its mandates. Why? The horrors of war throughout the past decades are answer enough, for sure.

Adherence to these central international law norms protects civilians during conflict, minimizes the destructive effects of war, and—equally important—fundamentally bolsters the strategic legitimacy and tactical success of military

---

40. Susan L. Turley, *Keeping the Peace: Do the Laws of War Apply?*, 73 TEX. L. REV. 139, 165 (1994) ("In both cases, Marine snipers said they were firing at men with machine guns, actions allowed under the Americans' 'rules of engagement' (ROE).").
41. *See* API, *supra* note 25, art. 57.2b.

> Another, and to my mind, even more important basis of the laws of war is that they are necessary to diminish the corrosive effect of mortal combat on the participants. War does not confer a license to kill for personal reasons—to gratify perverse impulses, or to put out of the way anyone who appears obnoxious, or to whose welfare the soldier is indifferent. War is not a license at all, but an obligation to kill for reasons of state; it does not countenance the infliction of suffering for its own sake or for revenge.
>
> Unless troops are trained and required to draw the distinction between military and nonmilitary killings, and to retain such respect for the value of life that unnecessary death and destruction will continue to repel them, they may lose the sense for that distinction for the rest of their lives. The consequence would be that many returning soldiers would be potential murderers.
>
> —Gen. Telford Taylor, U.S. chief prosecutor at Nuremberg
> (Telford Taylor, *War Crimes, in* WAR, MORALITY,
> AND THE MILITARY PROFESSION 415, 429
> (Malham M. Wakin ed., Westview 1979)

operations. The *jus ad bellum* and *jus in bello* are equally essential in ensuring that the use of military force remains consistent with rule of law and does not amount to rule by force. Each body of law balances authority and obligation, rights and protections.

EXPERTS

Kenneth Anderson, Professor, Washington College of Law, American University; kanders@wcl.american.edu

Laurie Blank, Director, International Humanitarian Law Clinic, Emory University School of Law; lblank@emory.edu

Robert Chesney, Professor, University of Texas Law School; rchesney@law.utexas.edu

Geoffrey Corn, Professor, South Texas College of Law, and Lieutenant Colonel (Ret.), U.S. Army; gcorn@stcl.edu

Ashley Deeks, Professor, University of Virginia School of Law, and former Legal Officer, U.S. Department of State; adeeks@virginia.edu

Charles Garraway, Colonel (Ret.), UK Armed Forces; charlesgarraway@hotmail.com

Amos Guiora, Professor, S.J. Quinney College of Law, University of Utah, and Lieutenant Colonel (Ret.), Israel Defense Forces; amos.guiora@law.utah.edu

Walter Huffman, Dean Emeritus, Texas Tech University School of Law, and Major General (Ret.), U.S. Army; walter.huffman@ttu.edu

Kate Jastram, Lecturer, Boalt Hall School of Law, University of California, Berkeley; kjastram@law.berkeley.edu

Christopher Jenks, Professor, Southern Methodist University School of Law, and Lieutenant Colonel (Ret.), U.S. Army; cjenks@smu.edu

Eric Jensen, Professor, Brigham Young University Law School, and Lieutenant Colonel (Ret.), U.S. Army; jensene@lawgate.byu.edu

Gregory McNeal, Professor, Pepperdine University Law School; gmcneal @pepperdine.edu

Gregory Noone, Professor, Fairmont State University, and Captain, U.S. Navy Reserve; gnoone@fairmontstate.edu

Gabor Rona, International Legal Director, Human Rights First; RonaG @humanrightsfirst.org

Michael Schmitt, Chair, International Law Department, U.S. Navy War College, and Lieutenant Colonel (Ret.), U.S. Air Force; schmitt.nwc@gmail.com

Gary Solis, Adjunct Professor, Georgetown Law School, and Colonel (Ret.), U.S. Marine Corps; gdsolis@comcast.net

Sean Watts, Professor, Creighton University, and Major, U.S. Army Reserve; seanwatts@creighton.edu

RESOURCES

YORAM DINSTEIN, WAR, AGGRESSION, AND SELF-DEFENCE (5th ed. 2012).

———, THE CONDUCT OF HOSTILITIES UNDER THE LAW OF INTERNATIONAL ARMED CONFLICT (2d ed. 2010).

GEOFFREY S. CORN ET AL., THE LAWS OF ARMED CONFLICT: AN OPERATIONAL PERSPECTIVE (2012).

———, THE WAR ON TERROR AND THE LAWS OF WAR: A MILITARY PERSPECTIVE (2009).

CRIMES OF WAR 2.0 (Roy Gutman, David Rieff & Anthony Dworkin eds., 2007).

GARY SOLIS, THE LAW OF ARMED CONFLICT: INTERNATIONAL HUMANITARIAN LAW IN WAR (2010).

Laurie R. Blank & Gregory P. Noone, International Law and Armed Conflict: Fundamental Principles and Contemporary Challenges in the Law of War (Aspen, forthcoming 2013).

Int'l Comm. Red Cross, International Humanitarian Law: Answers to Your Questions (2002), http://www.icrc.org/eng/resources/documents/publication/p0703.htm.

Secret Operations: Covert Action and Military Activities

7

By Benjamin Powell[1]

Central Intelligence Agency (CIA) and Department of Defense (DoD) secret operations abroad involve some of the most sensitive and opaque areas of U.S. government activities. Following the events of September 11, 2001, both the CIA and the DoD have increased the scope and intensity of these operations, primarily against terrorists affiliated with al-Qaida and in support of combat operations in Iraq and Afghanistan.

This chapter discusses legal authorities governing DoD and CIA secret operations abroad and the two parts of the U.S. Code most pertinent to operations of this type, Title 10 and Title 50. In this context, "Title 10" is usually a shorthand reference to statutes governing the organization of the U.S. military found in Title 10 of the U.S. Code. Similarly, "Title 50" is often shorthand for the provision in Title 50 of the U.S. Code that governs covert action.

Numerous officials and commentators have discussed the difficulties in attempting to define a line between some covert activities led by the CIA ("Title 50") and traditional military activities led by the DoD ("Title 10").[2] Although "covert action" is thought

---

1. Prepared with assistance of Larkin Reynolds and Jason Chipman.
2. *See, e.g.*, Questions for the Record for Adm. Dennis C. Blair upon Nomination to be Director of National Intelligence, Senate Select Comm. on Intelligence, Jan. 22, 2009, http://intelligence.senate.gov/090122/blairresponses2.pdf (explaining that there "is often not a bright line between" traditional secret intelligence missions carried out by the military and covert action); Eric Schmitt, *Clash Foreseen Between C.I.A. and Pentagon*, N.Y. TIMES, May 10, 2006 (quoting Michael Hayden as having stated that it has become

> ### *"Title 10" and "Title 50"*
>
> Title 10 of the U.S. Code, Armed Forces, generally provides the statutory framework governing the military services, including matters related to personnel, organization, and acquisition, but does not generally provide authority for specific offensive military operations against another country or organization.
>
> Title 50, War and National Defense, authorizes the creation and functioning of the CIA and provides the statutory framework for presidential approval of and reporting on covert actions. Specific authorizations for these operations are usually based on congressional enactments or in the president's exercise of executive powers granted in Article II of the U.S. Constitution.
>
> As shorthand terms, "Title 10" and "Title 50" refer to whether an operation is undertaken under the leadership and authority of the military (a "Title 10" operation) or the CIA (a "Title 50" covert action).

of today as a CIA activity, and "traditional military activities" are thought of as DoD activities, the military had a history of carrying out secret activities at the president's direction before the CIA was created—making the precise limits of the term "traditional military activity" difficult to discern. Congress has defined "covert action" as "an activity . . . of the United States Government to influence political, economic, or military conditions abroad, where it is intended that the role of the United States Government will not be apparent or acknowledged publicly."[3] However, reflecting the military's history of performing activities that may in some cases otherwise fit within this definition of covert action, Congress exempted from this definition "traditional . . . military activities or routine support to such activities."[4]

The May 2011 raid on Osama bin Laden's Abbottabad compound in Pakistan is an example of an activity that potentially could be either a covert action or a traditional military activity. The U.S. government has acknowledged that the raid was carried out under the direction of the director of the CIA exercising authority under Title 50, not under the direction of the secretary of defense under Title

---

more difficult to distinguish between traditional secret military and CIA intelligence missions); Advance Questions for Lieutenant General James Clapper USAF (Ret.), Nominee for the Position of Under Secretary of Defense for Intelligence, Senate Armed Servs. Comm., Mar. 27, 2007, *available at* http://armed-services.senate.gov/statemnt/2007/March/Clapper%2003-27-07.pdf (discussing covert actions generally); Advance Questions for the Honorable Michael G. Vickers to Be Under Secretary of Defense for Intelligence, Senate Armed Servs. Comm., Feb. 15, 2011, http://armed-services.senate.gov/statemnt/2011/02%20February/Vickers%2002-15-11.pdf (discussing "operational integration" between the armed services' special operations forces and the intelligence community). For additional discussion, see RICHARD A. BEST JR., CONG. RESEARCH SERV., RL33715, COVERT ACTION: LEGISLATIVE BACKGROUND AND POSSIBLE POLICY QUESTIONS, Dec. 27, 2011.

3. 50 U.S.C. § 413b(e).
4. 50 U.S.C. § 413b(e)(2).

10. But even though the raid likely could have been carried out as a traditional military activity against an enemy force pursuant to Title 10, and despite the fact that the U.S. role in the successful raid was widely acknowledged, the president ordered that the raid be carried out under CIA direction. His policy reasons for this decision might have included foreign relations considerations, such as the sensitivity of Pakistan to the presence of U.S. troops in a formal combat mission on its territory, or the desire to keep some measure of deniability in the event that the mission encountered difficulties.

Although the bin Laden raid demonstrates the flexibility the executive branch has to pursue certain operations under either Title 10 or Title 50, there are significant differences in how the operations are approved and overseen within the executive branch and in Congress. Whether an operation is pursued as a covert action or as a traditional military activity can affect a number of areas, including how operations are funded, how Congress is informed about operations, whether the president personally directs that an operation occur, and how the U.S. public or the international community may react to a failed operation. However, as the bin Laden raid demonstrates, placing an activity under one authority does not exclude another organization, such as the military, from providing personnel or equipment in support of the activity.

MILITARY ACTIVITIES UNDER TITLE 10 OF THE U.S. CODE

Title 10 does not provide the underlying authority to conduct specific operations, such as combat in Afghanistan or targeting operations against al-Qaida. The authority to conduct a military operation flows from different sources, such as the Constitution or congressional enactments. In general, one of two sources authorizes direct military engagements abroad:

- *Article II authorization.* Certain military engagements can be authorized pursuant to the president's authority in Article II of the Constitution,[5] with authority for operations flowing from the president through the secretary of defense to the soldiers on the ground.
- *Congressional authorization.* Congress can authorize the carrying out of military activities. Formal declarations of war marked the United States' entries into World Wars I and II. For the past 60 years, however, Congress has enacted "use of force" resolutions to authorize certain military engagements, such as those passed prior to both Iraq wars and the Authorization for Use of Military Force enacted on September 18, 2001.[6]

---

5. U.S. CONST. art. II, § 2.
6. Authorization for Use of Military Force, Pub. L. No. 107-40, 115 Stat. 224 (2001).

Title 10 provides the statutory basis for the organization, training, and equipping of DoD components. It also provides a framework for executive branch policy directives relevant to secret DoD operations. Such operations may be authorized by the secretary of defense in written execute orders, often referred to as EXORDs, that detail the nature of a military mission and particular limitations on a military commander's authority in executing the assigned mission, including when higher-level approvals may be needed before engaging in certain activities. Those operations do not require—as a matter of statutory law—formal, written presidential-level decisions or congressional notifications of the kind required in Title 50 for covert action.

The Senate and House armed services committees have oversight jurisdiction over those DoD operations and matters of the "common defense."[7] Although the Senate and House intelligence committees have oversight jurisdiction for intelligence matters,[8] appropriations authority for both the DoD and the intelligence community, including operations under both Title 10 and Title 50, is exercised by defense subcommittees of the Senate and House appropriations committees.

COVERT ACTION UNDER TITLE 50 OF THE U.S. CODE

Title 50 of the U.S. Code contains provisions applicable to national security and the intelligence community. In particular, Title 50 contains the statutory provisions defining "covert action" and the procedures setting forth how covert actions are authorized and how Congress is informed of covert actions. The statutory requirements for a covert action include the following: (1) the president must authorize covert actions in a written "finding"; (2) certain members of Congress must be informed of the finding; and (3) Congress must be kept informed of significant changes to activities authorized by a finding and of any significant activity undertaken pursuant to a previously issued finding.[9]

Historically, some activities we consider today to be "covert actions" began in the military departments as a subset of the normal activities the military engaged in to accomplish its missions, including secret activities, and there were no statutes defining the precise contours of operations and procedures for these types of

---

7. RULES OF THE HOUSE OF REPRESENTATIVES FOR THE 112TH CONGRESS, Rule X, http://clerk.house.gov/legislative/house-rules.pdf (Jan. 5, 2011) [hereinafter HOUSE RULES]; *see also* S. Doc. 107-1, Senate Manual, Rule XXV, Rule. 25.1c 110th Cong., *available at* http://www.gpoaccess.gov/smanual/index.html.

8. HOUSE RULES, *supra* note 7, Rule X(3)(m) (giving jurisdiction for House Permanent Select Committee on Intelligence to "review and study on a continuing basis laws, programs, and activities of the intelligence community and [to] review and study on an exclusive basis the sources and methods of entities described in [Rule X], clause 11(b)(1)(A)"; S. Res. 400 (94th Cong.) (creating the Senate Select Committee on Intelligence) and charging it with oversight responsibility for "the intelligence activities and programs of the United States Government."

9. 50 U.S.C. § 413b.

actions. Sensitive government operations took place under the president's authorization, and Congress largely deferred to presidential assessments of the necessity of the activity. During World War II, the military's Office of Strategic Services commanded these activities (many of which involved espionage behind enemy lines), and they were carried out by military personnel.[10]

The National Security Act of 1947 created the CIA and defined its duties. Though the CIA's core mission was to coordinate and evaluate intelligence relating "to the national security," Congress authorized a category of CIA activity that would encompass the type of activities previously performed by the OSS.[11] The authorization, which came to be known as the "fifth function" because it was enacted as subpart five of section 102(d) of the Act, permitted the CIA to perform "such other functions and duties related to intelligence affecting the national security as the National Security Council may from time to time direct."[12] This language codified the mandate for the CIA to conduct activities that were neither intelligence collection nor analysis when directed by the National Security Council.[13]

Congress first enacted specific legislation asserting some authority over covert actions in 1974 in response to CIA activities that were reported to have been excessive or otherwise improper, such as certain actions connected to the Vietnam War, domestic surveillance of U.S. citizens, and perceived excesses in Chile and in the Angolan Civil War.[14] Since 1974, Congress has created additional statutory restrictions on covert action and generally required congressional visibility into the activities themselves. "Covert action" is defined today in Title 50 of the U.S. Code as

> an activity or activities of the United States Government to influence political, economic, or military conditions abroad, where it is intended that the role of the United States Government will not be apparent or acknowledged publicly.[15]

But in defining "covert action," Congress had to be careful to exclude the broad array of U.S. government activities that may influence international conditions in a nonpublic manner but that had long been performed by other government departments—such as military activities or diplomatic activities. Congress dealt with this issue by specifying four activities that were excluded from the definition of covert action, specifically:

---

10. Peter Raven-Hansen & William C. Banks, *Targeted Killing and Assassination: The U.S. Legal Framework*, 37 U. RICH L. REV. 667, 691–94 (2003), and sources cited therein.
11. *Id.* at 697–98.
12. *Id.* Currently this provision is codified at 50 U.S.C. § 403-4a(d)(4), and tasks the CIA to perform such intelligence-related national security functions and duties as the "President or the Director of National Intelligence may direct."
13. *See, e.g.*, Raven-Hansen & Banks, *supra* note 10.
14. A. John Radsan, *An Overt Turn on Covert Action*, 53 ST. LOUIS U. L.J. 485, 529–36 (2009).
15. 50 U.S.C. § 413b(e).

(1) Activities the primary purpose of which is to acquire intelligence, traditional counterintelligence activities, traditional activities to improve or maintain the operational security of United States Government programs, or administrative activities;

(2) Traditional diplomatic or military activities or routine support to such activities;

(3) Traditional law enforcement activities conducted by United States Government law enforcement agencies or routine support to such activities; or

(4) Activities to provide routine support to the overt activities (other than activities described in paragraph (1), (2), or (3)) of other United States Government agencies abroad.[16]

The congressional conference committee report accompanying the statute explained the conferees' understanding of traditional military activities:

> It is the intent of the conferees that "traditional military activities" include activities by military personnel under the direction and control of a United States military commander (whether or not the U.S. sponsorship of such activities is apparent or later to be acknowledged) preceding and related to hostilities which are either anticipated (meaning approval has been given by the National Command Authorities for the activities and for operational planning for hostilities) to involve U.S. military forces, or where such hostilities involving United States military forces are ongoing, and, where the fact of the U.S. role in the overall operation is apparent or to be acknowledged publicly. In this regard, the conferees intend to draw a line between activities that are and are not under the direction and control of the military commander. Activities that are not under the direction and control of a military commander should not be considered as "traditional military activities."[17]

According to this interpretation of the statutory language, the "traditional military activities" exception contemplates a number of factors, such as whether the personnel executing and commanding the operation are military, when the operation occurs in relation to the "hostilities," whether those hostilities are ongoing or anticipated, and official intent to publicly acknowledge the activity.

Congress has spoken more clearly in defining the nature of and specific requirements for covert actions. Under section 413b of Title 50, covert action can be pursued only if the president has signed a written "finding." A finding must

---

16. *Id.* (emphasis added).
17. Joint Explanatory Statement of the Committee of Conference, H.R. Rep. No. 102-166, at 23 (1991) (Conf. Rep.), reprinted in 1991 U.S.C.C.A.N. 243, 251.

Traditional Military Activities and Covert Action

contain the president's determination that "such an action is necessary to support identifiable foreign policy objectives of the United States and is important to the national security of the United States."[18] The finding must also identify all government agencies involved and state whether any third party will be involved.[19]

Section 413b also requires the president to notify the congressional intelligence committees in advance of any covert action authorized by the finding.[20] In certain circumstances, the president can limit the members of Congress notified to the so-called "Gang of Eight," whose members include the chairmen and ranking minority members of the congressional intelligence committees, the speaker and minority leader of the House of Representatives, and the majority and minority leaders of the Senate.[21] However, the requirement to notify Congress is expressly not a precondition to carrying out a covert action,[22] and the president may delay notification to members of Congress until after the operation has commenced or occurred. In such instances, the statute still requires the president to "fully inform the congressional intelligence committees in a timely fashion and . . . provide a statement of the reasons for not giving prior notice."[23]

Although few findings and covert action programs have been officially acknowledged, the 9/11 Commission Report discusses a 1986 presidential finding that authorized the CIA to conduct covert action worldwide to combat terrorism as well as steps taken in 1998 to prepare a draft "Memorandum of Notification"—a formal notice of significant undertakings pursuant to previously issued findings—of a plan to capture bin Laden in Afghanistan.[24] The CIA's paramilitary operation to drive the Soviet army out of Afghanistan in the mid-1980s is another example of a covert action now publicly discussed.

TRADITIONAL MILITARY ACTIVITIES AND COVERT ACTION

As many commentators have noted since 9/11, the military and CIA at times appear to engage in very similar activities under distinct authorities.[25] In the face of opposition from the executive branch to legislation attempting to restrict the president's ability to exercise his powers in the area of national defense and foreign affairs, Congress has provided little guidance on understanding the boundary

---

18. 50 U.S.C. § 413b.
19. 50 U.S.C. § 413b(a)(3)–(4).
20. 50 U.S.C. § 413b(c)(1).
21. 50 U.S.C. §§ 413b(c)(2), 416b(c)(5).
22. 50 U.S.C. § 413(a)(2).
23. 50 U.S.C. § 413b(c)(3).
24. Final Report of the National Commission on Terrorist Attacks Upon the United States 113 (2004).
25. *See, e.g.*, Robert Chesney, *Military-Intelligence Convergence and the Law of the Title 10/Title 50 Debate*, 5 J. Nat'l Sec. L. & Pol'y 539–629 (2012).

SECRET OPERATIONS: COVERT ACTION AND MILITARY ACTIVITIES

between those activities that are covert actions and those activities that are traditional military activities.[26] In the bin Laden operation, for example, given its successful outcome, the deep personal involvement of the president and White House staff, and the publicly acknowledged role of the CIA and the military, the decision to place the operation under Title 50 appears to have not been particularly significant as a matter of statutory law beyond who was nominally "in command." But if the operation had failed or had encountered significant problems, the Departments of Defense and State may have been able to preserve diplomatic flexibility and avoid harm to the United States by denying that the United States had carried out a military operation in Pakistan because the operation was a CIA-led activity.

Thus, because a number of intricate policy questions may accompany the planning and execution of any given mission, a president may choose to place an operation with tactical military characteristics under CIA leadership to create additional flexibility if the operation fails or if certain contingencies arise in the course of executing it (if, for example, in the case of the bin Laden raid, the operators had encountered armed resistance from Pakistani forces).[27] CIA direction may also permit the DoD to deny that U.S. armed forces had engaged in combat activities and thus avoid claims that the United States had engaged in activity amounting to an act of war or a violation of state sovereignty. Further, proceeding under Title 50 may be appealing if an operation involves influencing economic or political conditions abroad and takes place outside of active conflict or conflict planning areas—such as the CIA's covert financial support to Radio Free Europe and Radio Liberty during the Cold War.[28]

The statutory framework for Title 50 operations also sets forth a clear and documented process for authorization and oversight of covert action. Planning a mission to be carried out under Title 50 requires a finding signed by the president, specific notification to Congress, and continuing oversight functions by the administration and Congress. Title 10 operations as a matter of administration policy may also be documented in writing and notified to Congress (although perhaps not the intelligence committees), but in contrast to Title 50, operations do not follow a specific statutory framework.

---

26. The DoD's internal definition of "clandestine" activity does not fully resolve the distinction between covert action and traditional military activities, either. The military defines a clandestine operation as "an operation sponsored or conducted by governmental departments or agencies in such a way as to assure secrecy or concealment." Joint Publication 3-05.1, Joint Special Operations Task Force Operations, Apr. 26, 2007. A clandestine operation "differs from a covert operation in that emphasis is placed on concealment of the operation rather than on concealment of identity of the sponsor. In special operations, an activity may be both covert and clandestine and may focus equally on operational considerations and intelligence-related activities." *Id.*

27. *See, e.g.*, Nicholas Schmidle, *Getting Bin Laden*, NEW YORKER, Aug. 8, 2011 (explaining officials' concerns that Pakistan's military forces might have engaged the Black Hawk helicopters that carried the Navy SEALs to the bin Laden compound to conduct the raid).

28. Jonathan Fredman, *Covert Action Policy and Procedure*, 31 A.B.A NAT'L SEC. L. REP., July–Oct. 2009, at 6, 7.

These differences have led to some controversy in recent years over the proper amount of congressional oversight over Title 50 activities. For example, in 2009, the House Permanent Select Committee on Intelligence (HPSCI) stated in its report on the fiscal year 2010 Intelligence Authorization Act that the military had been "frequently label[ing] [its secret activities] as 'Operational Preparation of the Environment' (OPE) to distinguish particular operations as traditional military activities and not as intelligence functions."[29] In HPSCI's view, this practice was being used to shield intelligence operations from being categorized as such, and thus from being reported to HPSCI and the Senate Select Committee on Intelligence. HPSCI warned that "if DoD does not meet its obligations to inform the Committee of intelligence activities, the Committee will consider legislative action clarifying the Department's obligation to do so."[30]

Operating in the cyber realm may also challenge the divisions between Title 10 and Title 50 given the difficulty of determining what "traditional military activities" are in the context of cyber operations. For example, the Internet allows enemies of the United States located in one part of the world to conduct operations using communications systems located in entirely different countries. It is not entirely clear how the United States should respond to such a threat. Steven Bradbury, who led the Office of Legal Counsel at the Department of Justice from 2005 to 2009, has publicly stated his view that websites found in neutral countries could be legitimate military targets in some circumstances (and thus subject to military-led operations):

> [A] server might be a valid military target because it's being used for the communications or command and control of the enemy fighters in the area of hostilities (after all, al Qaeda regularly uses the Internet in planning and ordering operations). The server might have no connection to the host country's military, government, or critical infrastructure, and it might be readily targeted for a computer attack without inflicting widespread damage on unrelated systems used for civilian purposes.[31]

If an administration decides to act in the cyber realm in secret, that activity may likely also fit within the definition of covert action. According to some congressional reports, a nonpublic, military-led cyber operation does also qualify as a "traditional military activity" exception, especially if it is an operation "under the direction and control of a United States military commander . . . preceding and related to hostilities."[32] In enacting the fiscal year 2012 National Defense

---

29. Intelligence Authorization Act for Fiscal Year 2010, H.R. REP. NO. 111-186 (2009) (accompanying H.R. 2701).
30. *Id.*
31. Steven G. Bradbury, The Developing Legal Framework for Defensive and Offensive Cyber Operations, Keynote Address at Harvard Law School Symposium, Law, Security, and Liberty after 9/11: Looking to the Future (Sept. 16, 2011), *available at* http://harvardnsj.org/wp-content/uploads/2011/04/Vol.-2_Bradbury_Final.pdf.
32. Joint Explanatory Statement of the Committee of Conference, *supra* note 17.

Authorization Act, Congress recognized that there was "a lack of historical precedent for what constitutes traditional military activities in cyberspace," and included language that affirmed the military's authority to conduct cyber operations consistent with DoD policies for "kinetic capabilities" and the War Powers Resolution.[33] This language indicates support for the view that some offensive cyber activities can fall within the traditional military activities exception to the definition of covert action.

The overlap between covert action and traditional military activities is particularly large when DoD is engaged in combat operations against an organization or country. In the absence of such hostilities, administrations may be more likely to look to the CIA to perform secret operations because of the authority, flexibility, and secrecy provided by use of the CIA. However, the existence of expanded numbers and capabilities of elite military forces that are able to engage in activities that are not directly related to an ongoing combat role could result in the military seeking to assume a greater role in activities traditionally categorized as covert action. As the United States continues to confront widely dispersed hostile state and non-state actors, we can expect the debate to continue over whether specific activities to respond to threats should be undertaken pursuant to Title 10 or Title 50.

EXPERTS

Steven G. Bradbury, Partner, Dechert LLP; former Acting Assistant Attorney General, Office of Legal Counsel; (202) 261-3483; steven.bradbury@dechert.com

Robert M. Chesney, Charles I. Francis Professor in Law, University of Texas School of Law; Distinguished Scholar of the Robert S. Strauss Center for International Security and Law; Non-Resident Senior Fellow of the Brookings Institution; (512) 232-1298; rchesney@law.utexas.edu

Jamie Gorelick, Partner, WilmerHale; former DoD General Counsel; former Deputy Attorney General; former 9/11 Commissioner; (202) 663-6500; jamie.gorelick@wilmerhale.com

Gen. (Ret.) Michael Hayden, Principal, The Chertoff Group; former Director of the Central Intelligence Agency; former Principal Deputy Director of National Intelligence; former Director of the National Security Agency; (202) 649-4260; info@chertoffgroup.com

---

33. National Defense Authorization Act for FY2012, Pub. L. No. 112-81, § 954; Conference Comm. Report 112-329, § 962, at 216–18.

Jeffrey H. Smith, Partner, Arnold & Porter LLP; former General Counsel of the Central Intelligence Agency; member of the Director of CIA's External Advisory Board; (202) 942-5115; Jeffrey.Smith@aporter.com.

RESOURCES

Robert Chesney, *Military-Intelligence Convergence and the Law of the Title 10/Title 50 Debate*, 5 J. NAT'L SEC. L. & POL'Y 539–629 (2012).

A. John Radsan, *An Overt Turn on Covert Action*, 53 ST. LOUIS U. L.J. 485 (2009).

Peter Raven-Hansen & William C. Banks, *Targeted Killing and Assassination: The U.S. Legal Framework*, 37 U. RICH. L. REV. 667 (2003).

Andru E. Wall, *Demystifying the Title 10-Title 50 Debate: Distinguishing Military Operations, Intelligence Activities & Covert Action*, 3 HARV. NAT'L SECURITY J. 85–142 (2011).

Jonathan Fredman, *Covert Action Policy and Procedure*, 31 A.B.A. NAT'L SECURITY L. REP., July–Oct. 2009, at 6, 7.

Exec. Order No. 12,333, 46 Fed. Reg. 59,941, 59,952 (Dec. 4, 1981), *as amended by* Exec. Order Nos. 13,284 (2003), 13,355 (2004), and 13,470 (2008).

RICHARD A. BEST JR., CONG. RESEARCH SERV., RL33715, COVERT ACTION: LEGISLATIVE BACKGROUND AND POSSIBLE POLICY QUESTIONS (Dec. 27, 2011).

Piracy

By Eugene Kontorovich

The explosion of Somali piracy in the Gulf of Aden in 2008 captured international attention with high-profile seizures of ships like the *Faina*, bearing battle tanks for Kenya; other ships carrying crude oil from the Persian Gulf or relief supplies to Africa; or simply European pleasure boats. It also opened up a dusty treasure chest of legal questions. A U.S. Navy frigate spots a boat full of men with Kalashnikovs speeding toward a Greek cargo vessel in the Indian Ocean. Can the frigate attack or stop the boat? What can the cargo ship do to defend itself? If the Navy does apprehend the boat's crew, can the crew members be tried for piracy, and if so, where and under what rules?

BACKGROUND

Piracy has a unique and storied legal status: it is perhaps the first international law crime. Normally, nations can prosecute only those crimes that occurred within their jurisdiction, which includes ships under their flag. Pirates, however, can be tried by any nation that catches them. The idea behind this "universal jurisdiction" is that pirates threaten the commerce of all nations. The law calls them *hostis humani generis*, enemies of all mankind. The U.S. Constitution even addresses piracy: article I, section 8, clause 10 authorizes Congress to "define and punish" piracy on the high seas—one of the very few federally punishable offenses specifically mentioned in the founding document.

The First Congress criminalized piracy, and the law has been on the books almost unchanged since then.

"Piracy" is often used as a general term for maritime violence, but its meaning in international law is narrower. The act of piracy is violence or robbery committed on the high seas by private parties. Thus, warships cannot commit piracy regardless of what they do (though they can commit war crimes), and attacks within a nation's 12-mile territorial waters do not amount to piracy in international law.

Classically, the prohibition on piracy was part of customary, or unwritten, international law, but the comprehensive United Nations Convention on Law of the Sea (UNCLOS) has codified piracy and defines it in Article 101(a)(1) as "any illegal acts of violence or detention, or any act of depredation, committed for private ends by the crew or the passengers of a private ship or a private aircraft, and directed, on the high seas, against another ship or aircraft, or against persons or property on board such ship or aircraft."[1]

The requirement of "another ship" means that the hijacking of a vessel by its own passengers or crew does not amount to piracy. After the 1985 incident in which the *Achille Lauro* was seized by Palestinian terrorists who had sailed on the ship, the United Nations drafted another treaty to deal with such situations, the Convention for the Suppression of Unlawful Acts against the Safety of Maritime Navigation. While this instrument applies to most acts of piracy and gives states

---

Piracy in History

During the Age of Sail, when ships were an important means of transportation, piracy usually spiked between major international wars, when sailors in national naval fleets and privateering vessels found themselves unemployed. Privateers in time of war furnished pirates in times of peace, a popular saying went.

Major piracy outbreaks occurred in the late 1600s, when Henry Morgan ravaged the Spanish in the Caribbean until he died of natural causes. The "Golden Age" of Atlantic piracy peaked in 1715–1725, after the War of Spanish Succession. The most famous pirate of this period was Edward Teach, or Blackbeard, a terrifying and brutal man known for carrying lit fuses in his beard. A final wave of piracy roiled the Caribbean and Atlantic in the 1820s, during the lawlessness of the Latin American revolutionary wars.

The "Barbary Pirates" of North Africa, with which the United States clashed in the early 1800s, were actually not pirates but rather the ill-behaved navies of sovereign Mahgreb sultanates. They were called pirates as a term of abuse, but no one thought to prosecute them.

---

1. While the United States has famously not joined the third round of the Law of the Sea treaty, it did sign the first one in the 1950s, which contained the same provisions on piracy.

more flexibility in prosecuting, it does not enjoy the broad national membership of UNCLOS and has rarely been invoked.

In recent years the U.N. Security Council has passed numerous resolutions, and more than 30 nations have deployed vessels to protect shipping and catch the Somali pirates. Yet Somali piracy quadrupled from 2007 to 2010, though it has declined since then. Pirate ransoms grew from a few hundred thousand dollars to more than $11 million in some notable 2012 deals. The gangs have become increasingly sophisticated, using motherships and more sophisticated navigation equipment to roam far outside the Gulf of Aden and deep into the Indian Ocean.

Modern-day piracy did not start with nor is it limited to the current Somali gangs, though they have been among its most successful practitioners. Piracy has been an ongoing problem for decades in places such as the Straits of Malacca, where vessels must transit through a narrow passage and where local naval authorities are ineffective, and in the oil-rich Gulf of Guinea area in West Africa, which saw a major rise in attacks in 2012 and may be poised to replace the Aden as the world's piracy hotspot. Somali pirates have, however, set records in the scale of their activities. Their innovative business model is to ransom the ship and crew back to its owners. Though far away from the United States, Somali pirates "threaten international security, the global economy and American citizens and commercial interests," according to the State Department.[2] This chapter focuses primarily on the problems presented by Somali piracy, which currently accounts for most of the world's hijackings at sea.

CAUSES OF SOMALI PIRACY

There has been considerable speculation about the motives and root causes of Somali piracy. Two competing narratives have emerged. In one, the pirates are the naval affiliates of al-Shabaab, the radical Islamist movement with al-Qaida ties fighting for control of the country's Mogadishu-based government. In the second, the pirates are a kind of volunteer coast guard that took to banditry to chase off the foreign fishing vessels and liners that took advantage of Somalia's lack of governmental authority to deplete its resources and dump waste.

There is almost no evidence for the jihadist navy theory; Somali pirates and al-Shabaab operate in entirely different parts of the country, and the pirates are not particularly devout. They have probably done some business with al-Shabaab, but do not appear to have any alliance.

Nor is there anything to support the environmental crusader story. While it is true that European fishing boats have made free with Somali resources, this began nearly 20 years ago. Most of the pirates were not even born then and can

---

2. U.S. State Department, Threats from Piracy off Coast of Somalia, *available at* http://www.state.gov/t/pm/ppa/piracy/c32661.htm.

hardly claim to be out-of-work fishermen. Moreover, the pirates themselves never mention this issue; in negotiations for the release of captured vessels, their only demand is money.

One does not need a theory to explain pirates' motives. The average per capita income in Somalia is $600, making it one of the five poorest countries in the world.[3] The pirates see billions of dollars sail by every day, unguarded. The lowest-ranking pirates will get a five-figure payday for taking a single ship—more than they would otherwise make in their entire lives.

On a larger level, the piracy problem is said to be a result of state failure in Somalia. This suggests that the problem cannot significantly improve until Somalia itself is fixed—a daunting task. However, Somalia's government collapsed 15 years before the piracy boom. Moreover, all pirates are based out of the northern semi-independent provinces, where government has not failed and is relatively stable, though weak. Indeed, looking globally at where maritime banditry happens, political scientists have found that state weakness, rather than failure, contributes to piracy: in a failed state, life and property are too precarious for even piracy to be worthwhile.

PRIVATE MILITARY CONTRACTORS AND RULES OF ENGAGEMENT

The hijacking of the *Maersk Alabama* dominated headlines in 2009 and focused American attention on the Somali piracy problem. The captain of the U.S.-flagged vessel, which was carrying relief supplies for the United Nations, was held hostage by pirates in a lifeboat for four days before Navy SEALS rescued him in a dramatic raid. It was the first piratical seizure of a U.S. vessel in more than 100 years. Much had changed. Historically, merchant vessels with valuable cargo carried at least some armament to deter predators. The *Alabama*'s crew had been trained in small arms and antiterror tactics by their trade union. Yet, like almost all civilian vessels at the time, they had no weapons on board. If the ship had not been in the U.S. government service—guaranteeing a strong naval response—the story could have ended in tragedy.

While the attack on the *Alabama* remains the most famous pirate attack in recent American history, the media devoted far less attention to the second and third attacks on the same vessel in March and May of 2011. This time the story played out quite differently. Now the ship had armed security guards who fired on the pirates as they attempted to board and chased them off. The sequels to the 2009 *Alabama* hijacking illustrate a fact known widely in the shipping industry: no ship

---

3. *See* CIA World Factbook, *available at* https://www.cia.gov/library/publications/the-world-factbook/rankorder/2004rank.html.

with armed security guards on board has ever been taken by pirates. Yet armed vessels are still the exception. This is in large part because the law and policy of most countries has, at least until very recently, seriously discouraged armed security.

The question of arming vessels has been the subject of heated debate among shippers, insurers, and governments since the eruption of Somali piracy. Some of the debate has been simply whether it is a wise policy or whether it would provoke escalation by pirates. But many shippers have avoided armed security because of legal concerns.

Most countries restrict private firearm possession significantly more than the United States does. A ship might have to comply with a multitude of such national regulations: the laws of the flag state plus those of every port at which it calls. In many countries, firearms possession is either illegal or requires navigating a maze of approvals and permits. African and Persian Gulf coastal states in particular have a confusing patchwork of regulation. Indeed, in 2011, South Africa detained several vessels in port when they declared they had arms on board for security purposes. In addition, Western countries' arms-trafficking laws have hampered the arming of vessels. Even though it is not the guns that are being shipped—rather, they are used to protect the goods being shipped—one could say the guns are being exported, in the sense that they are taken overseas.

The sentiment of many maritime nations began to turn in late 2011. The United Kingdom, which had taken one of the toughest stances against armed security details, made a dramatic reversal, with Prime Minister David Cameron himself calling for armed guards on British ships. Many countries began announcing similar policies, and ship security has become a growth industry.

Still, thorny legal questions remain about the level of force guards may use and the liability for mistakes. Generally, the rules of the flag state, as well as those of where the ship and the contractors are based, govern private military companies. There are no special international principles allowing pirates to be shot on sight, and indeed it is unclear what pirates look like on sight. Thus, the assumption is that the security teams merely get to use the standard domestic criminal law self-defense doctrine of the relevant country. In most countries, lethal force cannot be used merely to defend property, and the pirates say they were not seeking to injure anyone. Thus, the new enthusiasm for armed security by many nations has nonetheless not eliminated the uncertainty about the circumstances in which lethal force can be used. Pirates and suspected pirates could presumably sue security guards for improper or excessive force.

Related questions attend the use of force by naval ships against pirates. Pirates are treated by international law as civilians, albeit criminals. Thus, the navies in the area use rules of engagement borrowed from law enforcement rather than hostilities. Even so, India, Italy, and Russia, among others, have been much quicker on the trigger—in a few cases mistakenly firing on an innocent fishing vessel. (This shows that concerns about improper use of force, typically raised in the relation to private security, apply at least as much to public armed force.) The use of force rules dictated by international law, if any, remain unclear. Just as most nations do not believe they can just blast pirates out of the water, it is even clearer that they cannot hang them from the yardarm when caught. The days when pirates could be summarily tried and punished on board a naval ship have long passed. (Even in the Age of Sail, such practices were rare.)

DIFFICULTIES IN PROSECUTION

The forces patrolling the Gulf of Aden and the Indian Ocean have caught thousands of suspected pirates. Yet approximately 90 percent of the captured pirates have been promptly released, and sometimes even given a comfortable ride back to Somalia. While piracy is a crime that any nation can prosecute under international law, in practice few nations are eager to do so.

Trying pirates is a complex, costly business that could lead to long-term obligations for the forum nation. To be clear, many nations have brought pirates back to face trial for attacks on vessels flying their own flag. The United States has sentenced scores of pirates caught attacking American ships, as have France, Holland, South Korea, and other states. What countries are loath to do is to apply international law to try pirates for attacking vessels of other countries.

There are two sets of difficulties with trying suspected pirates.

The first focuses on the logistics of trial. Proving piratical intent can be tricky. Pirates invariably claim they are simply innocent fishermen, and indeed Somali fishermen are typically armed. Having guns on a boat in the high seas is not in itself an international crime. To be sure, boarding ladders, rocket-propelled grenades, fast engines, and other equipment seem quite incriminating, but may not rise to the level of attempt in many countries' laws;[4] such equipment can also be easily tossed overboard. When pirates manage to seize a ship, it becomes a hostage situation and ransom negotiations generally ensue, often including an amnesty. Thus, the sweet spot for catching pirates in the act is when they are speeding toward a target, but this chase is usually quite short. Other evidentiary problems include the difficulties of having military forces collect and preserve evidence, rounding up witnesses from the victim vessels long after they have dispersed around the world, getting Somali translators for the trial, and actually getting the defendants from the ship to the court, which takes a ship's only helicopter out of service.

A more serious problem is the likelihood that pirates will remain in the forum country indefinitely when they are acquitted or serve their sentences. The international law doctrine of nonrefoulement may bar sending pirates back to Somali, where they may face treatment that falls short of international human rights standards. This is part of the reason most nations do not simply send captured suspects to Somalia for trial. Moreover, pirates could potentially seek

---

4. However, in 2012, the Seychelles Supreme Court ruled in several groundbreaking cases that possession of such equipment is evidence of intent to commit piracy.

asylum in the prosecuting country. In most European countries, in keeping with their broader penal norms, pirate sentences have run from five to 10 years when there are no injuries. In the United States, by contrast, where criminal law is generally tougher, piracy carries a mandatory life sentence, though defendants can sometimes plea bargain to lesser charges. Either way, bringing pirates into one's country is a long-term commitment.

The current pirate trials are the first in most nations in hundreds of years. Because of the lack of precedent, even the most routine questions can stump courts. For example, in the first pirate trials in the United States, two federal district courts divided on the very definition of piracy, with one throwing out the international law charges against the defendants, who were caught after confusing a U.S. warship with a civilian vessel. The question turned on whether piracy, which is generally thought of as robbing a vessel, includes *attempts* at piracy. One district court said no, another said yes. In May 2012, the U.S. Court of Appeals for the Fourth Circuit weighed in—the first appellate court to do so—and upheld the attempt charges. An even more unusual piracy prosecution in D.C., involving a Somali official who helped negotiate the ransom and release of a vessel taken by pirates, raises the novel and somewhat surprising question of whether, as the Justice Department maintains, the international crime of piracy can take place on dry land, in a nation's sovereign territory. The trial court at least has rejected this theory.[5]

TRANSFERS FOR TRIAL

Because of the unwillingness of the capturing nations to prosecute pirates for attacks on other countries' ships, much of legal thinking and international diplomacy has focused on finding other nations willing to take pirates. Years of discussion about possible international courts or extraterritorial Somali courts have gone nowhere, and the practical efforts have refocused on working with other countries in the region. Kenya, which neighbors Somalia, stepped forward first. Pirates captured by the United States and Europe were transferred to Mombasa, a port city in south Kenya, for trial. After less than a year, Kenya canceled the arrangement, saying it did not want to be the world's pirate dumping ground. Now Seychelles and Tanzania have agreed to try some pirates. But both nations have very limited judicial and prison capacities and can accommodate only a small fraction of the captured pirates.

These transfer agreements raise several legal issues. First, UNCLOS Article 105, which codifies the universal jurisdiction status of piracy, provides:

> [E]very State may seize a pirate ship or aircraft . . . and arrest the persons and seize the property on board. The *courts of the State which carried out the seizure* may decide upon the penalties to be imposed. [Emphasis added.]

---

5. U.S. v. Ali, 2012 WL 2870263 (D.D.C. 2012).

The treaty language seems to permit universal jurisdiction prosecution only by the capturing states, not by entirely unrelated ones, which raises difficulties for the systematic transfer policy agreements. There seems to be little or no precedent for universal jurisdiction-by-rendition. On the other hand, many scholars argue that the provision permits prosecution by the captor but does not prohibit transfers, and the general principle of universal jurisdiction for piracy, as well as the actual current practice of states in this regard, supports the permissive interpretation of Article 105.

International law and domestic sentiment restrict the ability of nations to transfer suspects to places with deeply flawed judicial systems or poor human rights practices. Yet the transfers generally go downhill from Western countries with elaborate judicial safeguards and high-quality penal conditions. The transfer agreements require the receiving country to make a variety of guarantees about the trial and treatment of the defendants. The United Nations and various governments assist these countries with improving their judicial and prison systems. Yet ensuring the rights of transferees requires long-term monitoring of conditions in a foreign country, and the transferring states have not developed procedures for this. Indeed, Seychelles has adopted a policy of transferring pirates it has received from Western navies and convicted back to Somalia to serve their sentences. There is some possibility that capturing nations could be held liable for such transfers and retransfers. Indeed, in late 2011, a German administrative court ruled that Germany had violated the prohibition of torture and inhumane and degrading treatment in various human rights treaties when it handed pirates over to Kenya pursuant to an EU transfer agreement.

EXPERTS

Law

Douglas Guilfoyle, Professor, University College, London; +44 (0)20 7679 1546; d.guilfoyle@ucl.ac.uk

Eugene Kontorovich, Professor of Law, Northwestern University; (312) 503-0429; e-kontorovich@law.northwestern.edu

Cdr. James Kraska, Naval War College; (401) 841-6983; james.kraska@usnwc.edu

Political Science

Peter Lehr, Lecturer, School of International Relations, University of St. Andrews; pl17@st-andrews.ac.uk

Security

Nigel Booker, Asia Director, Neptune Maritime Security; +61 (0)412 871782; nigel.booker@neptune-ms.com

Graeme Gibbon Brook, Dryad Maritime Intelligence; graeme@dryadmaritime.com

RESOURCES

Lauren Ploch et al., Cong. Research Serv., Piracy off the Horn of Africa (April 2011), http://assets.opencrs.com/rpts/R40528_20110427.pdf.

House of Commons, Foreign Affairs Committee, Piracy off the Coast of Somalia (Jan. 2012), http://www.publications.parliament.uk/pa/cm201012/cmselect/cmfaff/1318/1318.pdf.

U.S. Gov't Accountability Office, GAO-10-856, Maritime Security: Actions Needed to Assess and Update Plan and Enhance Collaboration among Partners Involved in Countering Piracy off the Horn of Africa (Sept. 2010).

U.N. Secretary-General, *Report of the Special Adviser to the Secretary-General on Legal Issues Related to Piracy off the Coast of Somalia*, U.N. Doc. S/2011/30 (Jan. 24, 2011), http://cil.nus.edu.sg/wp/wp-content/uploads/2010/10/Lang_report_S-2011-301.pdf.

Douglas Guilfoyle, *Counter-Piracy Law Enforcement and Human Rights*, 59 Int'l & Comp. L.Q. 141–69 (2010).

Eugene Kontorovich, *The Pirate Prosecution Paradox*, 13.2 Geo. J. Int'l Aff. (2012).

Eugene Kontorovich, *"A Guantanamo on the Sea": The Difficulty of Dealing with Pirates and Terrorists*, 98 Cal. L. Rev. 234 (2010).

Robin Geiss & Anna Petrig, Piracy and Armed Robbery at Sea: The Legal Framework for Counter-Piracy Operations in Somalia and the Gulf of Aden (Oxford 2011).

James Kraska & Brian Wilson, Contemporary Maritime Piracy: International Law, Strategy, and Diplomacy at Sea (ABC CLIO 2011).

The United Nations Convention on the Law of the Sea

9

By Glenn M. Sulmasy and Chris Tribolet

INTRODUCTION

The principles embodied in the United Nations Convention on the Law of the Sea, whether ratified as a treaty or viewed simply as customary international law, are an essential element of national security in oceans governance. The oceans cover 70 percent of Earth and provide our most important highways for commerce. One need look no further than the recent concerns over the passage rights of vessels in the Strait of Hormuz to comprehend the significance of these provisions in the twenty-first century.

The U.S. government has long supported efforts to codify the law of the sea in an international agreement. The country entered into four treaties on the law of the sea in 1958, but those quickly proved inadequate to deal with contemporary ocean uses and political developments. By 1970, President Richard Nixon supported a new U.N. initiative for a more robust convention on the law of the sea. The United States had two overriding objectives for the new convention: First, find a legal method to secure fundamental navigation rights in the face of rapidly expanding coastal state claims purporting to enclose large swaths of the littoral ocean. Second, provide ordered access and management to natural resources of the ocean beyond the current jurisdiction of coastal states—and do it in a way that would not undermine the U.S. desire for enhanced protections for the freedom of navigation.

As explained below, the United Nations Convention on the Law of the Sea, or UNCLOS, achieved both objectives. The treaty significantly expanded, by several orders of magnitude, the right of nations to claim both sovereignty and sovereign rights further to sea. The treaty also codified a right to "transit passage" through strategic straits that was not well defined in customary international law. With very minor exceptions, UNCLOS committed to treaty all the rights the United States had previously claimed as a matter of customary international law. In addition, UNCLOS permitted the United States to claim sovereign rights over the natural resources in more than 3.4 million square miles of the oceans. No other country gained such a massive area of the earth for exclusive economic development. Yet UNCLOS also came with some provisions that made the treaty less palatable. Part XI of the treaty, in particular, had language that echoed socialist values as the Reagan administration fought a pitched battle between free-market ideals and communism during the Cold War. Provisions of Part XI that required transfer of technology and the redistribution of wealth—presumably from Western powers to third world and possibly communist countries—were unacceptable to a number of influential political leaders. President Ronald Reagan declined to sign the treaty, but he did not completely abandon it. On balance, the treaty did much to enhance the sovereign rights and the national security imperatives of the United States. Therefore, Reagan proclaimed that, with the exception of Part XI of the treaty, the United States viewed UNCLOS as reflective of customary international law and thus binding on the community of nations. The United States promised to honor the rights of other nations off their coasts in accordance with the treaty and also to enforce its own rights to freedom of navigation in accordance with the convention.

In 1994, the United Nations facilitated an amendment to Part XI of the treaty that answered many of the objections of the United States. Provisions requiring the transfer of technology involved in deep sea mining were stricken, and the United States was offered a permanent right to veto distributions of royalties. President Bill Clinton signed the treaty, but the Senate has yet to ratify it, although Senate hearings were held as recently as May 2012.

EARLY DEVELOPMENT OF THE LAW OF THE SEA

In the days of Christopher Columbus, as state powers rose, there were efforts by maritime nations to claim exclusive rights over entire oceans. But starting in the 1600s, Western maritime powers increasingly looked at the oceans as global highways open to all users. By the 1700s, most states subscribed to the idea of *mare liberum*—the freedom of the seas. Proponents of *mare liberum* argued the sea's resources were vast and all nations had an equal right to navigation, commerce, and fishing on the high seas. The physical nature of the ocean was unlike the land. It was impossible to occupy the ocean, guard it, or secure it from others. *Mare liberum* promoted communication, transportation, and trade across the ocean. Freedom of navigation also permitted global powers to move their navies and armies to coastal areas of military or economic importance.

Even strong advocates of *mare liberum* recognized a limited exception whereby countries could claim "territorial seas." The "territorial sea" was (and is) a narrow band of water along the coast of a nation that is treated much like the land territory of a country. The stated purposes and rights within territorial seas varied between nations, but the idea that the territorial sea should not exceed three miles was broadly accepted by the community of nations.[1] Within this band of water, the coastal state could assert its laws and exclude foreigners who threatened the peace or security of the state.[2] Resigning such a small sliver of the littoral zone to the coastal states left the vast majority of the world's oceans open to all users.

JURISDICTION CREEP BEGINS

The close of World War II opened a new chapter in the law of the sea. States began to assert more jurisdiction and claim greater sovereign rights farther offshore. In 1945, the United States recognized the opportunity to harvest offshore oil and gas resources in the Gulf of Mexico. President Harry Truman proclaimed American jurisdiction over the "subsoil and sea bed of the continental shelf" contiguous to the United States. Truman also proclaimed the right of coastal states to establish fisheries conservation zones in the high seas contiguous to the United States. (The high seas existed in the waters just beyond the territorial seas.) Truman's proclamations were careful to reserve freedom of navigation for all other ocean users. Even in those areas where the United States claimed exclusive rights to conserve, manage, or exploit natural resources in or beneath the water column, other nations would still enjoy unimpeded navigation and all other traditional high seas freedoms.

Shortly following the Truman proclamations, South American countries broadened their territorial seas. In 1947, Chile claimed a 200-mile territorial sea. Ecuador and Peru did the same in 1951. Under the Santiago Declaration, these countries claimed not just limited jurisdiction over resources in and under the sea, but exclusive sovereignty and jurisdiction out to 200 miles. The Santiago Declaration claimed much stronger powers for the South American countries than the Truman proclamations had for the United States. The United States protested the Santiago Declaration.

---

1. The breadth of the territorial sea was said by Thomas Jefferson to be determined by the "cannon shot" rule—a coastal state could claim a territorial sea only over those waters its armies could defend from ashore.

2. In 1900, 30 of 31 states claiming a territorial sea claimed a breadth of just three nautical miles. Until the late 1950s, even excessive territorial seas claims were fairly modest. For example, Scandinavian countries claimed a four-mile territorial sea, some Mediterranean countries claimed a six-mile territorial sea, and Russia claimed 12 miles.

THE 1958 CONVENTIONS ON THE LAW OF THE SEA

In the view of maritime countries like the United States, stronger international rules on the territorial seas, protection of the high seas freedoms, and conservation of fishing stocks were needed. A partial answer was the first United Nations Conference on the Law of the Sea—later known as UNCLOS I.

In 1958, UNCLOS I produced four short conventions on the law of the sea. The treaties defined rights in (1) the high seas, (2) fisheries, (3) the continental shelf, and (4) the territorial sea and contiguous zone. The first three treaties codified or supported the American view of customary international law on the high seas and the positions enunciated in the Truman proclamations on the continental shelf and certain high seas fisheries.

The fourth treaty, the convention on the territorial sea, clarified that states have "sovereignty" over both their territorial sea and the airspace above it, but preserved the right of foreign vessels to traverse another state's territorial sea when engaged in "innocent passage." Innocent passage is navigation that is not "prejudicial to the peace, good order or security of the coastal State." Fishing in a foreign territorial sea is not innocent passage. For a submarine to be in innocent passage it must be surfaced and show its flag. Most other forms of navigation are innocent, even when exercised by warships. The United States signed, ratified, and remains party to all four of the 1958 conventions.

A major shortcoming of the 1958 conventions was their failure to define the maximum breadth of the territorial sea. In order to reach agreement on the convention, the drafters left this contentious issue—how big the territorial sea may be—unresolved. This was an important matter for the United States and other maritime and air powers. Excessive territorial seas may impede navigation essential for projection of power. Although ships may enjoy "innocent passage" through a territorial sea, aircraft do not. Further, even the right of ships to innocent passage is subject to "suspension" by the coastal state when "essential for the protection of its security."

In 1960, a second conference on the law of the sea was convened to resolve the maximum breadth of the territorial sea and other issues. The problems proved too divisive, and the second conference—UNCLOS II—produced no treaty.

THE PUSH FOR A COMPREHENSIVE LAW OF THE SEA TREATY

Overfishing, maritime pollution, and an increasing thirst for offshore resources in the 1960s created demand for new agreements on the law of the sea. Coastal states wanted to protect their offshore resources. Developing states desired to share in wealth they believed would be garnered from exploitation of the deep seabed. Many commentators and policy makers were concerned that without new agreements, the seabed would be "militarized" through the emplacement of weapons and quickly appropriated to national use by the world's large military and commercial powers. Some—including Presidents Lyndon Johnson and Richard Nixon—called for the deep seas to be managed for the "legacy of all human beings" and the "common heritage of mankind." But the United States was most concerned by the increasing number of nations with excessive territorial sea claims. Freedom of navigation through international straits overlapped by territorial seas could be impaired absent adequate international rules. Without freedom of navigation, U.S. naval and air forces may not be able to protect the country's national interests.

Beginning in 1967, and spanning more than 14 years of negotiations, the Third United Nations Conference on the Law of the Sea produced one of the most comprehensive international treaties in history. More than 150 countries participated in the treaty development. This conference produced a treaty with 320 articles and nine annexes.

THE UNITED NATIONS CONVENTION ON THE LAW OF THE SEA (UNCLOS III)

The Law of the Sea Convention is divided into 17 parts, summarized below.

Part I of the treaty, spanning less than a page, simply provides definitions.

Part II of the convention concerns the territorial sea and the contiguous zone adjacent to it. The treaty establishes that the territorial sea may not exceed 12 miles from the "baseline." Achieving a concrete rule on the maximum breadth of the territorial sea was a primary policy objective and major victory for the U.S. delegation.

But where is the 12-mile territorial sea measured from? Part II of the convention also establishes rules for the baseline. Under the general rule, the baseline is drawn along the low water mark of the coast. An exception to the normal rule allows countries to draw "straight baselines" across deeply indented coasts or coasts with fringing islands. In a relatively benign application of this exception, Norway closes its fjords with straight baselines.

Vietnam's use of straight baselines has been more controversial. Vietnam uses straight baselines through a series of islands that sit, on average, more than 30 miles offshore and in several cases are more than 100 miles apart. Using straight baselines, Vietnam thus extends what should be a 12-mile territorial sea to more than 60 miles in many locations.[3] The United States has similarly complained about China's use of straight baselines where its coast is neither indented nor fringed by islands.

---

3. Technically, the territorial sea would still be just 12 miles wide. The waters landward of the baseline would be considered internal waters. But the effect, in this instance, is the same.

THE UNITED NATIONS CONVENTION ON THE LAW OF THE SEA

Regardless of the breadth of the territorial sea, Part II protects the rights of vessels to engage in innocent passage through the territorial sea. Some nations claim military vessels must receive clearance prior to entering their territorial sea in innocent passage. Such a restriction is not supported by UNCLOS.

JURISDICTIONAL AREAS

[Diagram showing jurisdictional areas from baseline outward: Territorial Sea (1), (2), Contiguous Zone (3), (4), Exclusive Economic Zone (5), High Seas (6), Foreign Territorial Sea (7), with features like MD, Interstate Lake, Internal Waters, VA, Exclusive State Waters, Inland Waters, NC, and a Foreign Country (Not claiming EEZ).]

This diagram is adapted from Title 33, Code of Federal Regulations, Part 2 (2011). The footnotes have been simplified to eliminate the need to refer to the text of the regulations in Part 2.

1. This illustrates the breadth of territorial sea currently claimed by the United States for international law purposes.
2. This illustrates the breadth of our territorial sea prior to UNCLOS III and President Reagan's proclamation (1983).
3. This illustrates the breadth of our contiguous zone (CZ) today for international law purposes.
4. Prior to 1983, the CZ reached only to 12 miles. The CZ is still only from 3 to 12 miles for some domestic laws, like the Federal Water Pollution Control Act.
5. The exclusive economic zone (EEZ) reaches as far as 200 miles from the "baseline." The EEZ begins at the seaward edge of the territorial sea and overlaps the CZ. Importantly, "islands" may have their own EEZ.
6. The high seas are those waters seaward of any EEZ. Many high seas freedoms also exist on the EEZ.
7. The United States recognizes foreign territorial seas up to 12 miles in breadth.

Part II also codifies the purpose and scope of the contiguous zone (CZ). The CZ is a band of water beyond the territorial sea that extends not more than 24 miles from the baseline. In the CZ, the coastal state has fewer rights than it has within its territorial sea. In this zone, the coastal state may prevent or punish infringement of its fiscal, immigration, customs, and sanitation laws. Pollution and drug trafficking laws are among the many domestic laws that may be enforced under these provisions.

Part III of the convention created the right of "transit passage" for both ships and aircraft through international straits such as the Strait of Gibraltar (access to the Mediterranean) and the Strait of Hormuz (access to the Persian Gulf). The new right of transit passage in international straits was much stronger and broader than the right of innocent passage through the territorial sea. Transit passage applies not just to ships but also to aircraft. Additionally, ships may operate in their

---

UNCLOS and the Arctic

UNCLOS has received special attention as it applies to the Arctic. As the Arctic becomes less icy, the Northwest Passage may become a viable traffic lane across the top of Alaska and Canada. On the other side of the Arctic Ocean, the Northern Sea Route (on top of Russia) may reduce transits from Asia to Europe by as much as 4,000 miles compared to transit through the Suez Canal.

UNCLOS allows Arctic nations to impose special rules on vessels travelling through "ice covered areas" to prevent irreversible ecological damage. Perhaps more importantly, UNCLOS rules on baselines, bays, territorial seas, and international straits may determine where ships may navigate pursuant to the rights of innocent passage and transit passage. If an area of the Arctic is internal water (inland of a state's territorial sea), there may or may not be a right of innocent passage through that water.

Proponents of UNCLOS argue that one of the most important reasons to join the convention is to lay claim to the resources on and in the continental shelf extending beyond the exclusive economic zone in the Arctic. UNCLOS defines the criteria for establishing an extended continental shelf and requires that member states submit their claims to the Commission on the Limits of the Continental Shelf (CLCS). Because the United States is not yet party to the convention, it may not submit claims to CLCS. While the United States is able to comment on foreign claims, the fear is that the CLCS will make decisions on claims by nations party to UNCLOS that are contrary to U.S. interests. Supporters of UNCLOS suggest that the United States must accede to the treaty to protect our interests. Others argue, however, that the melting Arctic was not foreseen when UNCLOS was drafted and a separate regime should govern activities and claims in that unique sea.

"normal mode," meaning submarines need not surface. There are fewer restrictions on vessels engaged in transit passage through a strait—they may launch and recover boats and aircraft so long as they do not threaten the coastal state. The right of transit passage through straits may not be suspended.

Part IV of UNCLOS establishes special rules for archipelagic states—countries consisting wholly of islands. Under UNCLOS III, the archipelagic states may draw baselines around their outermost islands. From this baseline extends the archipelagic nation's territorial sea and other zones. Within the baseline are archipelagic waters that, like the territorial sea, are subject to innocent passage by foreign vessels. To ensure freedom of navigation through archipelagic waters, UNCLOS also created a right to "archipelagic sea lanes passage," which is similar to the regime of transit passage for international straits. The purpose of the archipelagic sea lanes passage provision, particularly important to the United States, was to preserve traditional passage routes used for international navigation or overflight.

Part V establishes the coastal state's right to an exclusive economic zone (EEZ) that may extend up to 200 miles from the baseline. Within the EEZ, the coastal state has sovereign rights over the exploration and exploitation of all natural resources in, on, and under the water column. These resources include fish, gas, oil, and wind. To further these rights, the coastal state can regulate marine research, pollution, and artificial installations within its EEZ.

A country may establish an EEZ extending from its mainland coasts and from its islands. Because the United States has such long coastlines and numerous islands, it netted the largest EEZ of any nation—more than 3.4 million square miles.[4]

Under the rules of Part V, the coastal state may not regulate activities unrelated to resources in its EEZ. Thus, the coastal state may not exclude foreign vessels from sailing in its EEZ. Whether states may prevent other countries from conducting military activities within their EEZ is more controversial. The United States, along with the majority of other nations, considers it a right of all nations to conduct military activities within the EEZ.

Part VI of the treaty permits coastal states to claim exclusive sovereign rights over the exploration and exploitation of the continental shelf. While Part V of the treaty also grants coastal states the rights to natural resources on the sea floor within the EEZ, Part VI potentially extends those rights farther offshore. The treaty uses complex terms to determine the maximum extent of the continental shelf, but in the most favorable case the continental shelf may extend up to 350 miles from the baseline.

Determining the exact extent of the continental shelf has become a priority for many states vying for oil and gas far offshore. The United States is actively mapping its continental shelf in the Arctic in anticipation of capturing oil and gas there and defending its claims against other nations. Proponents of U.S. accession to UNCLOS argue claims to the continental shelf must be submitted to the Commission on the Limits of the Continental Shelf, a body established pursuant to the

---

4. U.S. law generally prohibits any foreign vessels from fishing within its EEZ.

treaty. Those opposed to the treaty claim the Commission interferes with U.S. sovereign rights. Further, opponents argue, Part VI requires payment of production royalties to an international body established for the purpose of redistributing wealth.

While recognizing coastal state rights on the continental shelf, UNCLOS preserves the status of the waters above the shelf as high seas and protects the traditional uses of the high seas. UNCLOS specifically prohibits interference with navigation or other high seas freedoms.

Part VII[5] of UNCLOS is concerned with the "high seas" beyond the territorial sea, the CZ, and the EEZ. In the years prior to the Third United Nations Conference on the Law of the Sea, the substantial concern of major maritime nations was protecting traditional freedoms of the sea from expanding claims of sovereignty. Part VII codifies important high seas freedoms, many of which also apply in the EEZ.

The exercise of U.S. law enforcement jurisdiction against foreign vessels in international waters must be based on one of the exceptions to this general rule. Each exception is carefully defined and limited. Exceptions to the general rule of exclusive flag-state jurisdiction represent encroachments by coastal states upon the traditional concept of freedom of the seas.

Creation of zones such as the CZ and the EEZ have expanded coastal state jurisdiction. However, the general rule of jurisdiction on the high seas remains the same. Foreign vessels are subject to the exclusive jurisdiction of the flag state.

There are, however, a number of exceptions to Article 92's proposition of exclusive flag-state jurisdiction over vessels on the high seas. Those exceptions include

- right of visit and right of approach
- consent of the vessel's master
- consent of the flag state
- consent by a foreign coastal state
- hot pursuit
- constructive presence
- "universal" crimes

Right of Visit and Right of Approach

Under customary international law, warships were permitted to stop and board foreign flag vessels in international waters in certain circumstances. This doctrine is called the right of visit or right of approach. The principal difference between this doctrine and those that confer full jurisdiction is that right of visit authorizes only a boarding. Unless additional information supporting jurisdiction is found, the warship may not seize the vessel or arrest any of the people onboard.

---

5. Portions of this discussion were adapted from Cases and Materials on Maritime Law Enforcement, published by the Law Section, U.S. Coast Guard Academy, and from Naval Warfare Publication 1–14, The Commander's Handbook on the Law of Naval Operations.

The customary international law of right of visit was first codified in 1958 in Article 22 of the Convention on the High Seas. Before exercising this right, law enforcement officers must have "reasonable grounds for suspecting" the ship is engaged in piracy, slavery, or unauthorized broadcasting (the "universal" crimes); or have "reasonable grounds" to believe the vessel is either stateless or of the same nationality as the warship.

The U.S. Coast Guard often uses the doctrine of right of visit to board and determine the nationality of vessels that, although claiming a foreign flag, are suspected of being U.S. vessels.

The right of visit is extremely limited in scope. It justifies a boarding only for the purpose of determining the vessel's nationality. Once the nationality has been determined, the justification for the boarding under the right of visit ceases. Boarding personnel have no further law enforcement jurisdiction based on the right of visit doctrine and must turn to other rules of international law to justify further enforcement action.

Consent of the Vessel's Master

The second Article 92 exception that confers certain rights to an enforcing state, but does not confer full international jurisdiction, is consent of the vessel's master. It is important to distinguish between master consent, which grants law enforcement officials of a foreign nation certain rights aboard the vessel but can never convey the authority to assert jurisdiction over the vessel or those aboard it, and consent by the flag state, which can grant full law enforcement jurisdiction over the vessel and those aboard it. For example, the master of a vessel may consent to law enforcement authorities from a nonflag state boarding his vessel, searching it in whole or in part, and remaining aboard while flag-state consent to assert law enforcement jurisdiction aboard the vessel is sought. However, the master does not have the authority to consent to any further assertion of law enforcement jurisdiction, either to arrest the crew or seize the vessel. That jurisdiction must come from a representative of the flag state's government.

Consent of the Flag State

The flag state, as part of its right to assert jurisdiction over its vessels in international waters, may consent to another nation's request to assert jurisdiction over the vessel.

Special arrangements may be either formal documents intended to cover a whole class of cases or less formal agreements dealing with a particular case.

Another method of obtaining flag-state consent is on a case-by-case basis. The nationality of the vessel is determined (through a right-of-visit boarding, if necessary), and then its flag state is contacted to see if it will agree to the exercise of another nation's jurisdiction over its vessel.

Consent by a Foreign Coastal State

A third-party nation may acquire jurisdiction over a foreign vessel that is located in a maritime jurisdictional zone of another coastal state if that coastal state consents to the third party's exercise of jurisdiction. For example, suppose a U.S. Coast Guard cutter detects a Dominican Republic vessel in Haiti's EEZ and desires to arrest the crew for attempting to smuggle drugs to the United States. The vessel does not comply with an order to stop and flees into Haiti's territorial sea. At this point, Haiti, by virtue of the boat's presence in its sovereign waters, would gain coastal state international jurisdiction as to place over the Dominican vessel. If it so desired, Haiti could consent to the United States standing in its shoes, so to speak, and asserting jurisdiction on its behalf.

Hot Pursuit

Article 111 of UNCLOS codifies another Article 92 exception, the customary rule of international law known as "hot pursuit."[6] Hot pursuit allows a coastal state to preserve its jurisdiction to take law enforcement action against a foreign vessel that flees beyond normal jurisdictional limits after it has committed a violation of the coastal state's law. A foreign vessel committing a violation in a zone over which the coastal state has jurisdiction (internal waters, territorial sea, or EEZ) must first be signaled to stop. If the vessel fails to heed the signal, the coastal state may pursue the vessel anywhere on the high seas as long as pursuit is continuous and the vessel does not enter the territorial sea of another country.

Constructive Presence

Constructive presence, another doctrine of customary international law, is closely related to the doctrine of hot pursuit. The constructive presence doctrine is also codified in Article 111 of UNCLOS. The doctrine was recognized as early as 1888, when Russian officials seized the Canadian vessel *Araunah*. The *Araunah* was 16 miles off a Russian island in the Bering Sea, but the vessel's boats were seal hunting within a half mile of the island in violation of Russian law. The Russians argued that although the vessel was outside their waters, it was, by means of its boats, carrying on fishing without the prescribed license and, therefore, subject to seizure. The British government agreed and did not protest the seizure.

The rationale for this exercise of jurisdiction is the legal fiction that the target vessel is constructively present in such a zone by virtue of its criminal partnership

---

6. 18 U.S.C. § 2237(a)(1), enacted in 2006, makes it a federal felony offense for the master, operator, or person in charge of a vessel of the United States, or a vessel subject to the jurisdiction of the United States, to knowingly fail to obey an order by an authorized federal law enforcement officer to heave to that vessel. See full statute in statutory supplement.

with the contact vessel. Conversely, if any of three elements fail at any time to exist, the right to assert jurisdiction under the constructive presence doctrine is lost.

"Universal" Crimes

The oldest exception to the exclusivity of flag-state jurisdiction over a vessel on the high seas is the exception for certain crimes at sea that were determined to be such a threat that all nations were called on to suppress these acts: piracy, unauthorized broadcasting, and slavery.

Piracy: The principal and only "true" universal crime for the purpose of this maritime-focused chapter is piracy. The customary law against piracy is codified in Articles 100–107 of UNCLOS. Piracy is treated uniquely—any nation may seize a pirate vessel without the flag state's consent and try those onboard in the seizing state's own courts. In 2010 alone, 489 acts or attempted acts of piracy were reported to the International Maritime Organization's Maritime Safety Committee.[7]

Unauthorized broadcasting: A second type of piracy, pirate radio, or, more broadly, unauthorized (unlicensed) broadcasting, is also a universal crime at sea. Fearing the political instability often created or spurred by unregulated radio transmissions, the international community has long agreed that unauthorized, unregulated broadcasts may be investigated and prosecuted by an entire class of potentially affected parties. While not as "universal" in nature as piracy—in that not just any nation may enforce its laws against foreign flagged vessels engaged in such acts; the actor nation must fall within a prescribed class of affected parties, such as those actually receiving the unauthorized signal—unauthorized broadcasts provide a legitimate jurisdictional hook for action where it might not otherwise exist.

Slavery: Slave trading is not a true universal crime like piracy in that a third-party state must obtain flag-state consent to seize a slave vessel or to make arrests thereon. Thus, although slave trading has been universally condemned for almost two centuries and remains a legitimate ground for conducting a right-of-visit boarding, it does not provide true universal enforcement jurisdiction. While not automatically able to seize or arrest those involved in a slave-trading operation (absent flag-state authorization), third-party nations are permitted, under international law, to liberate any slaves encountered. Note, though, the crime of human trafficking is generally not considered to constitute slavery for these purposes.

Part VIII of the treaty, a mere three sentences long, defines the regime of islands. An island is "a naturally formed area of land, surrounded by water, which is above water at high tide" and can support "human habitation or economic life." As mentioned above, islands may have their own EEZs, while rocks (not capable of supporting life) are entitled only to a territorial sea.

---

7. MSC.4/Circ.169 (Apr. 1, 2011).

There are frequent news reports about countries contesting each other's claims to small islands—especially the Spratly Islands in the South China Sea. These disputes are often not so much over the island but the potential resources of the EEZ it would support. There is periodically international discord as to whether a particular feature is a rock or an island.[8]

Part IX of the treaty requires cooperation of coastal states that share access to enclosed or semi-enclosed areas.

Part X grants landlocked states access to the sea.

Part XI of the treaty created an international regime for the management of all resources on and in the seabed beyond national jurisdiction. Part XI was the most repugnant feature to the Reagan administration when the UNCLOS treaty opened for signature. Reagan objected to the methods of administration of the authority responsible for allocating leases in the deep seabed, sharing technology, and disbursing the royalties received from mining operations in the area. In 1994, a new agreement was reached. The 1994 agreement modified Part XI to meet U.S. demands. In addition to eliminating technology transfer requirements, the modified provisions guarantee the United States a permanent seat in the administration. The provisions of Part XI, which once looked antithetical to business interests in the deep seabed, now are viewed by drilling and mining corporations as essential. These companies desire a body that can grant them a lease or title to tracts and resources on the deep seabed. The companies would still be required to pay a royalty, but generally view the royalties as a reasonable business cost.

Part XII of UNCLOS addresses marine pollution and established a framework for many other international pollution prevention and response treaties that have followed.

Part XIII regulates marine scientific research in the EEZ and territorial sea. The treaty reserves coastal states the right to control research in these zones, but establishes methods to encourage research in the EEZ absent objection from the coastal state.

Part XIV requires states to work together to develop and share technology. However, the U.S. government's view is that Part XIV would result in little obligation to the United States or changes in practice. The United States did not find the provisions of Part XIV objectionable.

Part XV creates options for states for dispute resolutions. States may choose any peaceful means for settlement of disputes. Further, Part XV accommodates states by exempting sensitive issues, like fisheries management questions, from binding procedures under the treaty.

Part XVI has just a handful of general provisions. Among them, Article 301 requires states to refrain from threats of force "against the territorial integrity or political independence of any state." Opponents of the treaty look at this provision as impeding U.S. sovereignty and its right to self-defense. Those favoring the treaty reply that Article 301 mirrors nearly identical language in Article 2(4)

---

8. An Internet search for "Rockall" or "Okinotorishima" will quickly illustrate the issue.

of the U.N. Charter. Further, military activities conducted in accordance with international law would not be prohibited by this treaty, and the inherent right of self-defense, reflected in Article 51, is always retained.

Part XVII, the final part of the U.N. Convention on the Law of the Sea, explains how the treaty will come into force.

THE STATUS OF UNCLOS III IN U.S. LAW

The United States was one of four nations that did not sign the treaty. President Reagan declared, however, that the United States would view most provisions of the UNCLOS III as customary international law and thus binding on the United States. Reagan did, however, object to the deep-seabed-mining provisions. Moreover, the United States did not accept the premise of the deep-seabed-mining provisions as being customary, and thus, was not legally bound by them.

The collapse of the Soviet Union and the presidency of George H.W. Bush provided an opportunity to address the concerns raised by Reagan in the 1980s. The international community subsequently drafted an annex to the treaty that answered virtually all of the concerns regarding deep-seabed-mining provisions. After Bush, the Clinton administration finalized and signed UNCLOS III. However, it still awaited ratification by the Senate.

In 2004, with the support of President George W. Bush, the Senate Foreign Relations Committee unanimously voted in favor of ratification. However, the treaty, for myriad reasons, never reached the floor of the Senate for a vote.

In 2007, Bush decided to work with the Senate to have the treaty ratified before the end of his term. In the spring of 2012, the Senate had still not voted to accede to the treaty. By June of 2012, Senators Kerry and Lugar led another push to accede to the treaty. They were joined by the Secretaries of Defense and State and an impressive list of military, corporate, and civil leaders. But even with this advocacy, the treaty was never brought to a vote.

Within the United States, there remains strong opposition to the passage of this international instrument. Most opponents view ratification as an unnecessary ceding of sovereignty to nations or international bodies, such as the Law of the Sea Tribunal. Common allegations are that such entities or nations will politicize the issues and ensure that the United States does not obtain as much as it would by not participating. Essentially, such arguments rest on the premise of the United States being a superpower that should not limit itself or give others equal status. Groups supporting such positions include the Heritage Foundation, the Center for Security Policy, and some members of the armed forces.

But the treaty currently receives strong support from most of the military and business community. It has received support from both Republican and Democratic presidents and senators. Many on the Senate Foreign Relations Committee have been Republicans with internationalist philosophies arguing that accession would help our military conduct transit and operations, benefit business, and send a positive message to international partners. Republican Sen. Richard Lugar of Indiana, who in 2012 lost a primary reelection battle, and others believe the United States needs to have a "seat at the table" when issues of the oceans are discussed. In particular, they worry about not being able to participate in negotiations on resource and territorial issues dealing with the Arctic.

Regardless of whether the United States eventually does or does not accede to UNCLOS, since 1983 UNCLOS has been a part of the U.S. understanding and implementation of the international law of the sea.

EXPERTS

Professor Craig Allen, University of Washington School of Law; (206) 616-8302; challen@uw.edu

Baker Spring, Heritage Foundation; media information line (202) 675-1761

CDR James Kraska, USN, U.S. Naval War College; (401) 841-6983; James.Kraska@usnwc.edu

David Caron, U.C. Berkeley School of Law; (510) 642-7249; ddcaron @law.berkeley.edu

Martin J. Durbin, American Petroleum Institute, Washington, D.C.; (202) 682-8000

Frank Gaffney, Center for Security Policy, Washington, D.C., 20006; (202) 835-9077

Steven Groves, Heritage Foundation, Washington, D.C.; (202) 546-4400

R. Bruce Joster, U.S. Chamber of Commerce, Washington, D.C.; (202) 463-5300; http://www.uschamber.com

Professor Norton Moore, University of Virginia School of Law; (434) 924-7441; jnm9s@virginia.edu

Capt. Raul (Pete) Pedrozo, USN (ret.), U.S. Naval War College, Newport, RI; (401) 841-7457; Raul.Pedrozo@USNWC.edu

Edwin Williamson, Partner at Sullivan & Cromwell, former legal advisor to the State Department (1989–1993); (202) 956-7505; williamsone@sullcrom.com

RESOURCES

U.S. Dep't of State, Law of the Sea Convention, http://www.state.gov/e/oes/lawofthesea/.

The Commander's Handbook on the Law of the Naval Operations (NWP 1-14), available through the Stockton Portal at the U.S. Naval War College, http://usnwc.libguides.com/LOAC-IHL.

Proceedings on Leadership for the Arctic, www.uscga.edu/arctic.

Targeted Killings and the Law   10

By Amos N. Guiora*

The U.S. government's drone policy, as initiated by President George W. Bush and significantly enhanced by President Barack Obama, has been the subject of innumerable articles, commentaries, and public discussions.[1] Commentary has focused on the policy's legality, morality, and effectiveness. Particular attention was drawn to the policy in the aftermath of the drone attack on Anwar al-Awlaki, a leading figure of al-Qaida in the Arabian Peninsula. Critics of the policy expressed concern that the U.S. government would kill an American citizen devoid of due process and external review of executive decision-making.

Additional critical voices have commented both on collateral damage that has resulted in the aftermath of many drone attacks and on the broad definition of a legitimate target and its subsequent application in determining who poses a threat to U.S. national security. Conversely, proponents note that the policy minimizes potential harm to U.S. military personnel, whose "on the ground" presence is reduced when the killing of identified targets is conducted from unmanned aerial vehicles. It is widely assumed that drone warfare will play an increasing, if not dominant, role in operational counterterrorism in the years to come.

---

*The author expresses thanks for research assistance to Felicity Murphy and Alison Satterlee, graduates of S.J. Quinney College of Law, University of Utah.

1. Paul Harris, *Drone Wars and State Secrecy: How Barack Obama Became a Hardliner*, GUARDIAN, June 2, 2012, http://www.guardian.co.uk/world/2012/jun/02/drone-wars-secrecy-barack-obama.

The Obama administration articulated a broad rationale for the al-Awlaki killing, reflecting aggressive self-defense.² More broadly, the administration has acknowledged the general drone program, again defending it as lawful:

> In practice, the U.S. approach to targeting in the conflict with al-Qaida is far more aligned with our allies' approach than many assume. This administration's counterterrorism efforts outside of Afghanistan and Iraq are focused on those individuals who are a threat to the United States, whose removal would cause a significant—even if only temporary—disruption of the plans and capabilities of al-Qaida and its associated forces. Practically speaking, then, the question turns principally on how you define "imminence."
>
> We are finding increasing recognition in the international community *that a more flexible understanding of "imminence" may be appropriate* when dealing with terrorist groups, in part because threats posed by nonstate actors do not present themselves in the ways that evidenced imminence in more traditional conflicts. After all, al-Qaida does not follow a traditional command structure, have uniforms, carry its arms openly or mass its troops at the borders of the nations it attacks. Nonetheless, it possesses the demonstrated capability to strike with little notice and cause significant civilian or military casualties. Over time, an increasing number of our international counterterrorism partners have begun to recognize that the traditional conception of *what constitutes an "imminent" attack should be broadened in light of the modern-day capabilities, techniques, and technological innovations of terrorist organizations.*³

The renewed debate in the United States regarding the legality, morality, and utility of killing terrorists has focused on a number of issues, including

- the decision-making process of targeted killing
- the definition of a "legitimate target"
- the definition of "collateral damage"
- the definition of "imminent threat"
- effectively assessing intelligence information

The bottom line is that U.S. officials and scholars are just beginning to grasp the full legal and moral ramifications of modern targeted killing. Technology and

---

2. Eric Holder, U.S. Att'y Gen., Speech at Northwestern Univ. (Mar. 5, 2012), http://www.justice.gov/iso/opa/ag/speeches/2012/ag-speech-1203051.html.

3. John O. Brennan, Assistant to the President for Homeland Security and Counterterrorism, Address at Harvard Law School: Strengthening our Security by Adhering to our Values and Laws (Sept. 16, 2011) (emphasis added), http://www.whitehouse.gov/the-press-office/2011/09/16/remarks-john-o-brennan-strengthening-our-security-adhering-our-values-an.

fundamental changes in how we understand war and the actors within it have pushed targeted killing to the forefront of scholarly legal thought. But officials, scholars, and journalists are flying blind, as there truly is no "law" on targeted killing, encapsulating and nicely defining how, what, when, why, and who. Indeed, the main argument advanced by the Obama administration in support of its actions and in opposition to judicial review is that its internal procedures have provided ample protections that render the actions lawful—but that is a new and unique understanding of the legal process.

That said, addressing the issues listed above is essential to understanding targeted killing policy. This chapter seeks to shed light on these issues. In doing so, I draw on my experiences while serving in the Judge Advocate General's Corps of the Israel Defense Forces, particularly legal advice I provided military commanders regarding targeted killing decisions. In addition, this chapter draws on my scholarship and public engagement on targeted killing both in the United States and internationally.

Targeted killings are indeed legal under certain conditions. However, like all other counterterrorism measures, the decision to order a targeted killing must be rooted in four overarching principles (see figure).

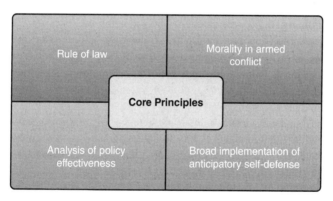

HISTORICAL BACKGROUND OF SELF-DEFENSE

One possible legal ground for defending targeted killings is that they are a legitimate act of self-defense by a nation-state; in that spirit, the United States asserts a right to self-defense under Article 51 of the U.N. Charter.[4] Within the context of self-defense, however, international law does not provide clear criteria or criteria extending beyond the four "holy grails" of international law: the principles

---

4. U.N. Charter art. 51, http://www.un.org/en/documents/charter/chapter7.shtml.

of military necessity, collateral damage, proportionality, and alternatives.[5] These principles date back to St. Augustine in the fifth century,[6] and they are still the guiding principles used today. Historically, self-defense has required a sense of imminence—a context that is lacking in targeted killings.

In 1837, Secretary of State Daniel Webster articulated a definition of self-defense that would eventually evolve into customary international law. Webster's definition was the result of what has become known as the *Caroline* Incident. The *Caroline* was a U.S. steamboat attempting to transport supplies to Canadian insurgents. A British force interrupted the *Caroline*'s voyage, shot at it, set it on fire, and allowed it to wash over Niagara Falls. Webster claimed that Britain's act did not qualify as self-defense because self-defense is justified only "if the necessity of that self-defense is instant, overwhelming, and leaving no choice of means, and no moment for deliberation."[7] Webster believed that in this instance, Britain could have dealt with the *Caroline* using diplomacy rather than force. Webster's definition, which has become known as the Caroline Doctrine, limited the right to act in self-defense to the following situations:

- an imminent threat has been identified;
- the response to the threat is essential and proportional; and
- all peaceful means of resolving the conflict have been exhausted.

In contrast to the Caroline Doctrine, the U.N. Charter (Article 51) limits self-defense to those instances when an armed attack "occurs."[8] The definition of self-defense has changed from a customary international law principle allowing preemption to a treaty-based definition dependent upon the occurrence of an armed attack.

A word of caution: Nations are making critical decisions in an age of uncertainty. There is no specific law, either domestic or international, that solely governs targeted killings. Rather, there is a complex interplay between domestic law, international law, and morality.

---

5. These principles are often articulated as the principles of military necessity, distinction, proportionality, and humanity. *See, e.g.*, U.S. DEP'T OF THE ARMY, JUDGE ADVOCATE GEN.'S SCH., INT'L & OPERATIONAL LAW DEP'T, LAW OF WAR HANDBOOK 164 (2005), *available at* http://www.loc.gov/rr/frd/Military_Law/pdf/law-war-handbook-2005.pdf (listing the "four key principles of the law of war"); U.S. DEP'T OF ARMY, FIELD MANUAL 27-100, at 164.

6. *See* Colin B. Donovan, *What Is Just War?*, GLOBAL CATHOLIC NETWORK, http://www.ewtn.com/expert/answers/just_war.htm (explaining that the Just War Doctrine, first enunciated by Saint Augustine, teaches what constitutes the just defense of a nation against an aggressor). For an excellent survey of the moral issues surrounding military history, see generally MICHAEL WALZER, JUST AND UNJUST WARS: A MORAL ARGUMENT WITH HISTORICAL ILLUSTRATIONS (Basic Books, 4th ed. 2006).

7. Emanuel Gross, *Thwarting Terrorist Acts by Attacking the Perpetrators or Their Commanders as an Act of Self-Defense: Human Rights Versus the State's Duty to Protect Its Citizens*, 15 TEMP. INT'L & COMP. L.J. 195, 211 (2001).

8. U.N. Charter, art. 51, http://www.un.org/en/documents/charter/chapter7.shtml.

Historical Background of Self-Defense

In this context, however, there is one additional wrinkle to address: Historically, laws of war have governed actions between nation-states. International law, in its current articulation, is inadequate regarding the state/nonstate conflict; after all, the laws of armed conflict were codified in an era when warfare was conducted between nation-states with rules clearly articulated and understood, though tragically not always respected.[9] Thus, today nations often must engage an enemy who looks just like any other civilian: He wears no identifying insignia, obeys no laws of warfare, and does so on purpose. In the present state/nonstate actor paradigm, the rules are known and largely respected by the nation-state and largely ignored by the nonstate actor, who ignores the laws of war by arguing that the rules do not apply to him.[10] To accept the lawfulness of targeted killing under international law we must accept an arguable premise—that the existing laws of armed conflict are fully applicable.

It also must be asked, of course, if domestic U.S. law permits targeted killings. Here, the answer is clearer. Domestically, Congress acted under its own authority[11] in the wake of 9/11 to give an expansion of powers to the president to use "all necessary and appropriate force" against nations—as well as organizations—involved in the 9/11 attacks and to prevent future attacks from occurring.[12]

Acting under this framework becomes even more complex when American citizens are involved. Every U.S. citizen is guaranteed the rights and freedoms found in the Constitution, including the Fifth and Fourteenth Amendments' due process clauses. Briefly, the United States cannot deprive a citizen of "life, liberty, or property without the due process of law."[13] Due process generally refers to procedural safeguards in the context of a fair system of law. A citizen is therefore

---

9. *See generally* Convention (II) with Respect to the Laws and Customs of War on Land, July 29, 1899, 32 Stat. 1803, 1 Bevans 247; Convention (IV) Respecting the Laws and Customs of War on Land, Oct. 18, 1907, 36 Stat. 2277, 1 Bevans 631; Convention for the Amelioration of the Condition of the Wounded and Sick in Armed Forces in the Field, Aug. 12, 1949, 6 U.S.T. 3114, 75 U.N.T.S. 31; Convention for the Amelioration of the Condition of Wounded, Sick and Shipwrecked Members of Armed Forces at Sea, Aug. 12, 1949, 6 U.S.T. 3217, 75 U.N.T.S. 85; Convention Relative to the Treatment of Prisoners of War, Aug. 12, 1949, 6 U.S.T. 3316, 75 U.N.T.S. 135; Convention Relative to the Protection of Civilian Persons in Time of War, Aug. 12, 1949, 6 U.S.T. 3516, 75 U.N.T.S. 287; Protocol Additional to the Geneva Conventions of 12 August 1949, and Relating to the Protection of Victims of International Armed Conflicts (Protocol I), June 8, 1977, 1125 U.N.T.S. 3; Protocol Additional to the Geneva Conventions of 12 August 1949, and Relating to the Protection of Victims of Non-International Conflicts (Protocol II), June 8, 1977, 1125 U.N.T.S. 609.

10. Walter Laqueur, *The Terrorism to Come*, 126 POL'Y REV. Aug. 1, 2004, http://www.hoover.org/publications/policy-review/article/7371 ("Terrorism does not accept laws and rules, whereas governments are bound by them. . . .").

11. 50 U.S.C. § 1541.

12. Authorization for Use of Military Force, Pub. L. No. 107-40, 115 Stat. 224 (2001), *available at* http://www.gpo.gov/fdsys/pkg/PLAW-107publ40/html/PLAW-107publ40.htm.

13. U.S. CONST. amends. V & XIV.

guaranteed—or "due"—the process of law. However, the level of threat to a nation-state's security that an individual poses may overcome such protections. For example, police are authorized to shoot to kill if a citizen poses an immediate threat to the nation or others. Again, the essence of targeted killing revolves around determining legitimate targets. Put another way, the Obama administration's argument is that if administrative procedures are used appropriately to correctly judge that an individual is a national security threat, that process itself satisfies domestic requirements.

DIFFERENTIATING EXTRAJUDICIAL KILLING FROM TARGETED KILLING

One counterargument is that targeted killings run afoul of the domestic prohibition on assassination. However, targeted killing is not assassination, which is defined by international law as the killing of a political leader or a statesman involving treachery or perfidy.[14] In contrast, terrorists are not considered political leaders or statesmen.[15] Extrajudicial killing, according to Amnesty International, is an unlawful and deliberate killing carried out by order of a government or with its acquiescence reflecting a policy to eliminate individuals even though arrest is an option.[16] Unlike extrajudicial killing, targeted killing occurs only when arrest *is not* an option. It is critical to distinguish between the two practices. Extrajudicial killings are not part of counterterrorism; instead, they are domestic in orientation and violate civil rights. These killings often occur in an effort to incapacitate political opponents rather than protect a state against terrorists. Targeted killing, on the other hand, is a form of preemption and is not punitive in its purpose.

THE DECISION-MAKING PROCESS

In the end, then, the lawfulness of targeted killing depends in large part on the efficacy of the internal administrative measures adopted to identify targets. The more credence one gives those procedures, the more likely one is to find the actions resulting from those procedures lawful. It is therefore of great use to understand more clearly precisely what those targeting procedures are.

---

14. BLACK'S LAW DICTIONARY 109 (7th ed. 1999).
15. Patricia Zengel, *Assassination and the Law of Armed Conflict*, 43 MERCER L. REV. 615, 629–31 (1991–92).
16. J. Nicholas Kendall, *Israeli Counter-Terrorism: "Targeted Killings" Under International Law*, 80 N.C. L. REV. 1069, 1073 (2001–02).

The Decision-Making Process

Effective counterterrorism requires the nation-state to apply self-imposed restraint; otherwise violations of both international law and morality in armed conflict are all but inevitable. It is how counterterrorism is carried out that will determine its legality under governing international instruments. Therefore, in any targeted killing decision, the following important questions must be addressed:

1. Can the target be identified accurately and reliably? (Is the target legitimate?)
2. Does the target pose a threat such that an attack on the target *at that moment* is justified, or are there alternatives available? (Is the intelligence actionable?)
3. What is the anticipated extent of collateral damage? (Is the response proportional?)

To answer these questions legally, morally, and effectively, decision-makers must use a criteria-based process. Criteria-based decision-making increases the probability of correctly identifying and attacking a legitimate target while minimizing collateral damage, thereby enhancing the policy's effectiveness. The criteria-based process is dependent upon the gathering of intelligence information from three separate sources: human intelligence, or HUMINT; signal intelligence, or SIGINT; and open-source information. Intelligence analysts determine whether the information is actionable.

Who Are Legitimate Targets?

In order to implement legal, moral, and effective operational counterterrorism, decision-makers must initially evaluate the threat. This evaluation must include the following:

- analysis of the threat's nature
- identification of the threat's source
- identification of the timeline when the threat is anticipated to materialize
- assessment of the threat's imminence

The foundation for determining the legality of targeted killing is assessing whether the threat's imminence justifies the action in order to protect an innocent civilian population. The suicide bomber infrastructure is instructive in highlighting the complexities of determining whether an individual is a legitimate target; it is important to recall that four distinct actors are necessary for a successful suicide bombing:

1. *Planner*—Legitimate target at all times.
2. *Bomber*—Legitimate target solely when operationally engaged.
3. *Logistician*—Legitimate target when involved in all aspects of

implementing suicide bombing but, unlike the planner, not a legitimate target when not involved in a specific, future attack.

4. *Financier*—A largely unexplored subject in the context of targeted killings, the financier is a legitimate target when involved in wiring or laundering money, both of which are essential for terrorist attacks. There is significant room for debate regarding when the financier is not in the act of financing. To that extent, the question is whether the financier is more akin to the bomber or the logistician. Arguably, due to the central role the financier plays in the structure, the correct placement is between the logistician and the planner.

Imminence must be understood from two distinct perspectives: the imminent threat posed by the bomber and the future threat posed by a planner or financier who are considered legitimate targets, even when not directly engaged in planning or implementing a suicide bombing. In order for a state's actions under either scenario to be considered legal, limits of self-defense must be defined. The policy of targeted killing should be used only in response to imminent threats rather than to those that are distant, unviable, or merely foreseeable. Such a response is grounded in revenge and emotion rather than in objective, criteria-based decision-making.

A legitimate target is an individual who, according to intelligence information, poses a direct and immediate threat to national security.

Is the Intelligence Actionable?

Threat analysis refers to the nature of the target and his or her planned activities and attacks. Assessing the source of the information about the target and the planned attack is an equally vital aspect of the decision-making process. Therefore, source analysis becomes a fundamental component of the criteria-based approach.

Information provided by a human source should be analyzed closely for possible biases, grudges, or personal agendas that might taint its reliability. Signal intelligence includes information gathered from sources such as intercepted phone and e-mail conversations. Open sources, such as the Internet and newspapers, are generally available and can often help paint a landscape against which a perceived threat can be evaluated. The combination of these three sources allows the intelligence community to develop an operational picture from which to work.

Ultimately, the question central to this operational puzzle is whether the acquired information is actionable. The main goal of decision-makers is to enhance the objectivity in their decision-making process. The test prong table, developed to evaluate detention decisions, is an example of articulated guidelines for determining whether the intelligence is sufficiently actionable.

TEST PRONG	DEFINITION/USE
Reliable	• Past interactions show the source to be a dependable provider of correct information. • The information is determined to be useful and accurate. • The case officer has analyzed the source's personal agendas or grudges with respect to the identified target.
Viable	• It is both possible and feasible that an attack could occur in accordance with the source's information.
Relevant	• The information has bearing on upcoming events. • The information is both timely and time sensitive—immediate counterterrorism measures are needed.
Corroborated	• Another source confirms the information in part or whole. • This second source also meets the above reliability test.

Is the Response Proportional?

Even if a legitimate target is identified and the intelligence about that target is actionable, the use of lethal force, in this example the ordering of a targeted killing, can be considered lawful only if it meets the four-part proportionality test as identified by international law:

1. An attack must be proportionate to the threat posed by the individual;
2. Collateral damage must be minimal;
3. Alternatives have been considered and eliminated as operationally impossible; and
4. Military necessity justifies the action.

Of the principles being discussed, proportionality receives the greatest attention and is the most scrutinized. It is also the most problematic, most misconstrued, and least attainable. Clearly, it is poorly defined. In simplest terms, how can there be proportionality in the context of state/nonstate conflict? It is a conflict that is inherently disproportionate. History is replete with examples of disproportionate warfare between nation-states, much more between states and nonstates.

While the principle of proportionality was intended to protect the civilian population, the reality of war, unless conducted by foes of equal power, is characterized by disproportionate force. War is often won in large part by the use of significant force in order to defeat the other military.

In the person-specific operational counterterrorism model, proportionality means that state action, proactive and reactive alike, must be proportional to the threat posed, whether actual or perceived. Operationalized, the term means the commander must be very selective both with respect to force used and individuals targeted.

CONCLUSION

The nation-state's right to engage in aggressive, preemptive self-defense must be subject to powerful restraints and conditions. A measured, cautious approach to targeted killing is the understanding that the nation-state has the absolute—but not unlimited—right, and obligation, to protect its civilian population. International law is ill-equipped to deal with the terrorist issues of today. If Article 51 does not apply to a situation where a state wishes to defend itself against nonstate actors, what is left to guide that state in its response? The answer lies with the fundamental principles of the laws of war regarding military necessity, proportionality, collateral damage, and alternatives. It is these principles that underlie the development of criteria-based decision-making policies and will act as a compass for states in their efforts to steer international law in a new direction, a direction that will allow states to effectively defend themselves against nonstate actors.

Targeted killing is a legal, legitimate, and effective form of active self-defense provided that it is conducted in accordance with clear international law principles and a narrow definition of what is a legitimate target; otherwise it reflects state action bound neither by the rule of law nor by constraints of morality. Although recognized by international law, the principle of self-defense is not limitless. Additionally, relying on intuition in the heat of the moment leads to seeing everyone and everything as an imminent threat, thereby risking a disproportionate response.

By engaging in operational counterterrorism conducted within the rule of law, a nation-state must apply self-imposed limits when implementing aggressive self-defense. By developing a mechanism to weigh and measure the reliability of intelligence, the decision-makers will be able to identify a legitimate target and determine whether engaging that target is justified by the circumstances. Such mechanisms facilitate lawful and effective targeted killing.

EXPERTS

Kenneth Anderson, Professor, Washington College of Law, American University; (202) 274-4212; kanders@wcl.american.edu

Robert Chesney, Professor, University of Texas Law School; (512) 232-1298; rchesney@law.utexas.edu

Monica Hakimi, Professor, University of Michigan Law School; (734) 763-0404; mhakimi@umich.edu

Gregory McNeal, Professor, Pepperdine University School of Law; (310) 506-7292; gregory.mcneal@pepperdine.edu

Mary Ellen O'Connell, Professor, Notre Dame Law School; (574) 631-7953; MaryEllenOConnell@nd.edu

Jordan Paust, Professor, University of Houston Law Center; (713) 743-2177; JPaust@central.uh.edu

Afsheen John Radsan, Professor, William Mitchell School of Law; (651) 290-6402; john.radsan@wmitchell.edu

RESOURCES

Kenneth Anderson, *Targeted Killing in U.S. Counterterrorism Strategy and Law* (May 11, 2009), http://ssrn.com/abstract=1415070.

Richard Brust, *Uneasy Targets: How Justifying the Killing of Terrorists Has Become a Major Policy Debate*, 98 A.B.A. J. 50 (2012).

Claire Finkelstein, Jens David Ohlin & Andrew Altman, Targeted Killings: Law and Morality in an Asymmetrical World (Oxford Univ. Press 2012).

W. Jason Fisher, *Targeted Killing, Norms, and International Law*, 45 Colum. J. Transnat'l L. 711 (2012).

Emanuel Gross, *Thwarting Terrorist Acts by Attacking the Perpetrators or Their Commanders as an Act of Self-defense: Human Rights Versus the State's Duty to Protect Its Citizens*, 15 Temp. Int'l & Comp. L.J. 195, 211 (2001).

Amos Guiora, *Drone Strikes: What the U.S. Could Learn from Israel*, L.A. Times, Sept. 29, 2011, http://opinion.latimes.com/opinionla/2011/09/drone-strikes-us-learn-israel-blowback.html.

———, Targeted Killing and the Law (Oxford Univ. Press forthcoming 2013).

———, *Targeted Killing: A Proposal for Criteria Based Decision Making*, in Targeted Killings: Law and Morality in an Asymmetrical World (C. Finkelstein ed., Oxford Univ. Press 2012).

———, *Targeted Killing as Active Self-Defense*, 36 Case W. Res. J. Int'l L. 319, 322–30 (2004).

Cheri Kramer, *The Legality of Targeted Drone Attacks as U.S. Policy*, 9 Santa Clara J. Int'l L. 375 (2011).

Jane Mayer, *The Predator War*, NEW YORKER, Oct. 2009.

Jordan J. Paust, *Self-Defense Targetings of Non-State Actors and Permissibility of U.S. Use of Drones in Pakistan*, 19 J. TRANSNAT'L L. & POL'Y 237 (2009).

Vincent-Joel Proulx, *If the Hat Fits, Wear It, if the Turban Fits, Run for Your Life: Reflections on the Indefinite Detention and Targeted Killing of Suspected Terrorists* (2005).

Afsheen John Radsan & Richard Murphy, *Measure Twice, Shoot Once: Higher Care for CIA-Targeted Killing*, 2011 U. ILL. L. REV. 1201 (2011).

Daniel Statman, *Targeted Killing*, 5 THEORETICAL INQ. L. 179 (2004).

U.N. Charter art. 51, http://www.un.org/en/documents/charter/chapter7.shtml.

Mark Vlasic, *Assassination and Targeted Killing: A Historical and Post-Bin Laden Legal Analysis*, 43 GEO. J. INT'L L. 259 (2012).

John Yoo, *Assassination or Targeted Killings After 9/11*, 56 N.Y. L. SCH. L. REV. 5 (2011–12).

Patricia Zengel, *Assassination and the Law of Armed Conflict*, 43 MERCER L. REV. 615, 629–31 (1991–92).

Military Commissions | 11

By David W. Glazier

President George W. Bush surprised the legal world in November 2001 by issuing a military order calling for the use of military commissions to try suspected terrorists.[1] The order relied upon the congressional Authorization for Use of Military Force,[2] enacted a week after the attacks of September 11, 2001, as the basis for treating the fight against al-Qaida as an actual armed conflict rather than a matter for law enforcement and traditional criminal prosecution in regular federal courts.

The order resurrected the military commission from relative historical obscurity to the forefront of the American legal vernacular while provoking an often fierce public debate over the commissions' legitimacy. Historically, the military commission has been a "common law" court, conducted using the same general rules and procedure as the better-known court-martial, but relying on legal authority derived from the customary international law governing armed conflict rather than the formal statutes that regulate court-martial jurisdiction and practice. The military commission has thus served as a flexible jurisdictional gap-filler while the court-martial has been strictly limited to trying only those persons and crimes Congress has specifically made subject to its jurisdiction.

---

1. George W. Bush, Military Order of Nov. 13, 2001: Detention, Treatment, and Trial of Certain Non-Citizens in the War Against Terrorism, 3 C.F.R., 2001 Comp., at 918 (2002).
2. Authorization for Use of Military Force, Pub. L. No. 107-40, 115 Stat. 224 (2001).

Trials envisioned under Bush's original order offered only very rudimentary due process,[3] but the Guantanamo military commissions have significantly evolved in the intervening years. Trials conducted under the Military Commissions Act of 2009 now conform more closely to court-martial procedure, facially limit the use of evidence obtained through coercion, and establish the right of the defendants to be present and hear all the evidence against them. The effective bipartisan support for their use that emerged during the Obama administration has largely quieted public criticism. Nevertheless, there are still significant legal issues with both the procedural standards and the substantive law being applied, and their limitation to the trial of foreign nationals is unprecedented.

MILITARY COMMISSION HISTORY

Contemporary proponents of military commission use almost invariably claim precedents dating back to the American Revolution. But the military commission has a discrete origin in the Mexican War of 1846–48, where it was created by the army's commanding general, Winfield Scott, to address gaps in statutory court-martial jurisdiction and permit the trial of American servicemen for offenses falling outside the scope of the written military law of the day, the Articles of War, which were the forerunner of the modern Uniform Code of Military Justice.

The Articles of War in effect in 1846 were a slightly amended version of those enacted by the Continental Congress in 1776 at the urging of John Adams and Thomas Jefferson. They provided for punishing a wide range of military-unique offenses such as desertion, disobedience of orders, and misbehavior in the face of the enemy, but did not extend to common crimes such as assault, murder, or rape. Reflecting the Framers' implicit view that the U.S. Army would be used defensively, the Articles mandated that any soldier accused of committing offenses against civilians be turned over to the local civil magistrate for trial. The 1846 invasion of Mexico placed the army outside the jurisdiction of U.S. civilian courts, however, and after an American soldier murdered a Mexican national, the secretary of war determined that the only available sanction was to discharge the killer and send him home.

Scott recognized that this situation was untenable. He planned to conduct an audacious campaign, marching an army of approximately 10,000 troops inland from Vera Cruz to capture the Mexican capital from an enemy force several times larger than his own while buying provisions locally to obviate the need to garrison an extended supply line back to the coast. Anticipating modern counterinsurgency doctrine's concern with "hearts and minds," Scott recognized the need to

---

3. For a comparison between the initial Bush military commission rules and contemporary court-martial procedures, see David Glazier, *Kangaroo Court or Competent Tribunal?: Judging the 21st Century Military Commission*, 89 VA. L. REV. 2005, 2015–20 (2003).

sufficiently win what he termed the "minds and feelings" of the civilian Mexican population that they would at least acquiesce to the American presence, if not welcome it.

Scott resolved to invoke authority from the law of war to declare martial law in the areas controlled by his troops and issued general orders defining a set of common law crimes that would be prosecuted by courts he called "military commissions" if committed by, or upon, his forces. He left jurisdiction over Mexican-on-Mexican offenses with the existing local courts.

Military commission procedures were based closely upon the court-martial; they essentially differed only in terms of jurisdiction. Roughly three-quarters of the more than 400 persons tried by these tribunals during the war were Americans. Scott created a less formal tribunal he called the "council of war" to try actual law-of-war violations, but only a handful of these were ever convened, and most documented trials were for what was then considered to be an offense of encouraging desertion. Even the councils of war treated persons of all nationalities equally, trying at least one American and a Belgian in addition to a score or so of Mexican nationals.

Military commissions saw extensive use again during the Civil War when they served in three roles: as martial law courts in northern states where habeas corpus was suspended; as military government courts in areas of the South under Union occupation during the war and the Reconstruction period; and as law-of-war courts replacing the short-lived Mexican War council of war. Collectively the three types of commissions tried close to 6,000 individuals.

These multiple roles highlight the fact that historical military commission jurisprudence must be considered in light of the jurisdictional basis for the trial. Commissions sitting as martial law or military government courts actually apply "domestic" criminal law. They can enforce the local national criminal law already in existence, or military authorities can promulgate new rules, which can be enforced from that date forward. Scott had adopted this latter approach in Mexico, issuing general orders published in English to his troops and in Spanish to the local populace. Because these commissions are enforcing domestic rather than international law, their precedents are not directly applicable to trials based on the law of war.

Several Civil War military commissions proved highly controversial, including the trial of eight Lincoln assassination conspirators, which resulted in the execution of Mary Surratt, the first woman put to death by the federal government.[4] The next year the Supreme Court overturned the conviction and death sentence of Indiana Democrat Lambdin P. Milligan, holding that commissions could not exercise jurisdiction over civilians lacking direct ties to hostilities where federal courts were open.[5]

---

4. For an objective assessment of the case against Surratt, see Laurie Verge, *Mary Elizabeth Surratt*, in THE TRIAL (Edward Steers Jr. ed., Univ. of Ky. Press 2003).

5. *Ex parte* Milligan, 71 U.S. (4 Wall.) 2 (1866).

MILITARY COMMISSIONS

Congress also addressed military commissions for the first time during the war, requiring the newly created post of judge advocate general of the army to review both court-martial and military commission convictions.[6] These reviews enforced commission compliance with court-martial procedures, overturning convictions for failing to do so.

The close conformance of court-martial and military commission practice was reinforced by army experience during the Philippine Insurrection of 1899–1902, which saw more than 800 commission trials. Most of those tried were Filipinos, but this number also included several American defendants. Army leaders insisted upon rigorous application of court-martial rules, including the same rules of evidence used in U.S. federal courts, and barred admission of confessions not proven to be voluntary or the admission of ex parte statements.

Perhaps the most well-known military commission trial is that of eight German would-be saboteurs landed by U-boats on East Coast beaches in June 1942. Their arrest prompted a massive public outcry for swift justice, but they had not committed any serious violations of ordinary criminal law before their capture. Attorney General Francis Biddle recommended that Roosevelt authorize their military trial and persuaded him to sign a military order establishing a commission, which could take unprecedented shortcuts from standard court-martial practice, such as dispensing with traditional U.S. rules of evidence and admitting anything "of probative value to a reasonable man." The order also purported to foreclose judicial review. Nevertheless, lead defense attorney (and later the first secretary of the army) Kenneth C. Royall persuaded the Supreme Court to convene in a special July term to consider a challenge to the trial.

Although the court ultimately upheld the proceedings in *Ex parte Quirin*,[7] just by meeting it repudiated the president's claim of authority to foreclose judicial review, and the opinion required military commission charges to state a valid violation of the law of war for military jurisdiction to be permissible. The court did not consider the commission's unprecedented departure from court-martial practice, focusing its holding on the question of jurisdiction. The court did also hold that the claim to American citizenship on the part of at least one defendant was irrelevant; their association with an adversary force made them liable to military detention and trial. These results were confirmed by the Supreme Court in reviewing several postwar military trials in which it upheld military jurisdiction from the declaration of war through the conclusion of a final peace agreement.[8]

---

6. Act of July 17, 1862, ch. 201, § 5, 12 Stat. 597, 598 (1862).

7. *Ex parte* Quirin, 317 U.S. 1 (1942).

8. *See In re* Yamashita, 327 U.S. 1 (1946) (requiring valid military commission charges to state a violation of the law of war); Madsen v. Kinsella, 343 U.S. 341 (1952) (upholding jurisdiction of a U.S. military occupation court over a U.S. civilian military spouse).

BUSH ADMINISTRATION MILITARY COMMISSIONS

Bush's military commission order, which was based almost verbatim on that used for the Nazi saboteurs' trial a half-century earlier, generated immediate controversy as legal scholars and commentators debated its constitutionality and more controversial provisions, including its extremely relaxed rules of evidence.[9] It was almost three years, however, before any individuals were actually identified for military trial. Early proceedings were confused, with rapidly evolving and frequently changing rules essentially being developed as hearings proceeded, and two defendants were actually excluded from their own proceedings while "classified" information was being discussed.

In November 2004, U.S. district judge James Robertson halted the military commissions, ruling that they unnecessarily departed from court-martial procedure in contravention of language in Article 36 of the Uniform Code of Military Justice and violated Geneva Conventions language limiting trials to "regularly constituted" courts.[10] The D.C. Circuit Court of Appeals reversed this ruling the next year in an opinion joined by John Roberts prior to his elevation to chief justice of the United States,[11] before the Supreme Court reversed again, halting the trials on essentially the same logic employed by Robertson.[12]

The Supreme Court's decision was grounded on a statutory and treaty, rather than constitutional, basis, leaving the door open for Congress to redress these issues via legislation. Under pressure from the administration, the Republican congressional majority passed the Military Commissions Act (MCA) of 2006[13] as one of its final enactments before the November 2006 elections. The MCA codified military commission procedures and jurisdiction. Procedural enhancements included providing for actual military judges, limiting use of evidence obtained through coercion, and establishing a formalized appellate process. The statute also defined a fairly extensive set of crimes that could be prosecuted. Although the commissions were justified solely on the basis of being "law of war" courts, the offenses defined in the MCA included "providing material support to terrorism" and "conspiracy" even though most law-of-war scholars believe that these are not valid war crimes.

The Bush administration nevertheless pressed ahead with prosecutions based almost exclusively on these two charges. In March 2007, Australian David Hicks pleaded guilty to providing material support under a secret plea agreement facilitated by his government's intervention, which required him to serve just nine months of postconviction confinement in an Australian prison. Despite having

---

9. For a discussion of this early debate, see Jack L. Goldsmith & Cass Sunstein, *Military Tribunals and Legal Culture: What a Difference Sixty Years Makes*, 19 CONST. COMMENT. 261 (2002).
10. Hamdan v. Rumsfeld, 344 F. Supp. 2d 152 (D.D.C. 2004).
11. Hamdan v. Rumsfeld, 415 F.3d 33 (D.C. Cir. 2005).
12. Hamdan v. Rumsfeld, 548 U.S. 557 (2006).
13. 10 U.S.C. §§ 948a–950w.

prevailed in the Supreme Court, Salim Hamdan was put on trial in July 2008 and convicted of providing material support but acquitted of conspiracy charges. Hamdan's military trial panel clearly rejected the government's assertions about his dangerousness, sentencing him to less than six months of additional confinement once credit for time served was computed.

The final commission judgment of the Bush administration saw the conviction of Ali Hamza al Bahlul, an admitted al-Qaida propagandist, essentially for making a video that can be legally purchased via Amazon.com. Al Bahlul had previously made it clear that he wanted to be represented by a Yemeni attorney he could trust, but as a fallback demanded to represent himself. Although self-representation was explicitly authorized by the MCA, the judge denied his request and al Bahlul then directed that his assigned military attorney remain silent throughout his trial, which he did. Al Bahlul was convicted and given a life sentence, which he is serving at Guantanamo.

GUANTANAMO TRIALS UNDER THE MILITARY COMMISSIONS ACT OF 2009[14]

President Barack Obama criticized military commission use as a senator, voted against the MCA, and pledged to close Guantanamo immediately after taking office. Nevertheless, he surprised many observers by announcing on May 21, 2009, that his administration would continue to prosecute some cases before commissions even while pledging to try others in federal courts. In support of this endeavor, Congress passed an updated Military Commissions Act of 2009 on October 28 of that year, making further modest improvements to the procedural mandates specified in the MCA 2006 such as establishing a "voluntariness" standard for admission of any statements by a defendant.[15] The MCA 2009 also adopts commission rules for dealing with classified evidence that are closely based on the Classified Information Procedures Act employed in regular federal courts.[16] (Curiously, this calls into question one common argument for commission use: the idea that they are superior to regular federal courts in their ability to handle classified information.)

---

14. A detailed history of military commissions during the first three years of the Obama administration can be found in David Glazier, *Still a Bad Idea: Military Commissions Under the Obama Administration*, Loyola-LA Legal Studies Paper No. 2010-32, http://papers.ssrn.com/sol3/papers.cfm?abstract_id=1658590.

15. 10 U.S.C. § 948r(c)–(d). For a detailed comparison of the MCA 2009 with the MCA 2006, see JENNIFER K. ELSEA, CONG. RESEARCH SERV., THE MILITARY COMMISSIONS ACT OF 2009: OVERVIEW AND LEGAL ISSUES 1 (Apr. 6, 2010), http://www.fas.org/sgp/crs/natsec/R41163.pdf.

16. *Compare* 10 U.S.C. §§ 949p-1 to 949p-7 (MCA 2009 classified information procedures) *with* 18 U.S.C. App. (CIPA).

The Obama commissions then proceeded to obtain guilty pleas from four individuals: Sudanese detainees Ibrahim Ahmed Mahmoud al Qosi and Noor Uthman Muhammed; the better-known young Canadian, Omar Khadr; and Pakistani national Majid Khan. The first three cases each saw a trial panel vote a long notional sentence, letting the government proclaim these outcomes as "victories," even though they were accompanied by plea deals requiring comparatively short terms and ultimate repatriation to their home countries. (Khan will not be sentenced until after he testifies against other "high value" detainees in U.S. custody.) This creates the perverse irony that, with the exception of al Bahlul, those convicted of "war crimes" at Guantanamo have gotten comparatively quick tickets home while many of those never charged linger in prolonged—potentially lifetime—detention.

GUANTANAMO MILITARY COMMISSION ISSUES

Obama's decision in favor of military commission use resulted in a general bipartisan endorsement of the MCA 2009 and has substantially reduced the overall criticism of these tribunals. Nevertheless, there are still potentially serious issues remaining with the substantive law being applied, procedural rules, and potential lack of prosecutorial good faith.

All convictions to date have involved charges of providing material support to terrorism, and several have added conspiracy, even though these are arguably not war crimes. This is an important issue because the Supreme Court held in several World War II–era cases that military commission jurisdiction is limited to recognized war crimes. Even if Congress might be able to enlarge commission jurisdiction prospectively,[17] both the Constitution and law-of-war treaties such as the Third and Fourth Geneva Conventions of 1949 explicitly bar ex post facto crime creation. Guantanamo detainees, who were generally captured in 2001 or 2002, can only lawfully be prosecuted under a statute first enacted in 2006 if the conduct was already a recognized crime at the time committed, a fact recognized by Congress in the MCA text itself.[18]

Another potential substantive issue is the timing of conduct charged. Abd al-Rahim al-Nashiri, for example, is being prosecuted for his role in the October 2000 suicide bombing of the USS *Cole*. Given that the conflict with al-Qaida was not formally recognized by the United States as an armed conflict until 9/11, however, it is problematic whether this attack, or earlier events such as the 1998 embassy bombings in Africa, can lawfully be prosecuted before the commissions even though there would be no issue with trials in regular federal courts.

---

17. *See* Stephen I. Vladeck, *The Laws of War as Constitutional Limit on Military Jurisdiction*, 4 J. Nat'l Sec. L. & Pol. 295 (2010) (arguing that the Constitution places strict limits on congressional authority to prescribe military commission jurisdiction).
18. 10 U.S.C. § 950p(d).

The use of a civilian convening authority who performs multiple roles including making final prosecution decisions, selecting the chief judge (who then assigns individual trial judges), appointing trial panel pools, approving plea bargains, reviewing trial results, and exercising general oversight over the Department of Defense Office of Military Commissions is problematic. Although court-martial convening authorities perform similar roles, this is arguably justified on the grounds that these are actual military commanders legally accountable for the maintenance of good order and discipline within their chain of command, and based on the need for military justice to be able to function in the field while deployed, considerations absent from the Guantanamo commission process. But even in the uniformed military context, it is worth noting that virtually all other leading democracies have now rejected these multiple roles as unduly compromising the administration of justice.

One of the most significant procedural issues calling into question commission fairness is the inability of defendants to choose counsel other than U.S. citizens. Past law-of-war tribunals have routinely allowed defendants to be represented by attorneys of their own nationality, and the right to counsel of choice is well established by current law-of-war and human rights treaties. Oddly, an individual facing a U.S. court-martial, applying actual U.S. military law, can elect foreign counsel, but a non-U.S. citizen facing charges based on the international law of armed conflict rather than U.S. law cannot.

A related issue is the inequity between commission treatment of prosecution and defense. Modern international tribunals rigorously enforce an "equality of arms" between prosecution and defense with respect to all matters within the court's control. The Uniform Code of Military Justice statutorily mandates that court-martial defendants have "equal" access to evidence. But the MCA mandates only a "reasonable opportunity to obtain witnesses and evidence."

In actual commission practice, defense teams are at a serious disadvantage compared with the government in terms of such matters as access to expert witnesses, with the Military Commission Convening Authority regularly denying defense requests even while spending hundreds of thousands of dollars on prosecution witnesses. Guantanamo defense attorneys have also experienced significant difficulty getting prosecutors to comply with their discovery obligations. This is particularly critical given commission rules permitting the admission of hearsay, placing the burden on the defense to demonstrate the unreliability of evidence the government intends to admit without information from the government about the circumstances under which the statement was obtained. Despite the categorical MCA bar on evidence obtained via coercion, it is readily possible for the prosecution to get such evidence admitted if the prosecution controls all information about how such statements were obtained.

Another unique challenge faced by the defense is the government's effort to conceal information about Central Intelligence Agency (CIA) interrogation practices. The government insists that anything that a defendant who has previously been in CIA custody says, even in privileged conversations with his attorney, is "presumptively classified information," making it a federal crime for the attorney to disclose it to any third party. And because the detainees lack security clearances, lawyers are also barred from discussing any information contained in government interrogation records with the detainee who was being questioned at the time. These rules, coupled with a requirement that the defense must notify the judge and prosecution 30 days in advance of any possible use of classified information in court, seriously impair the ability of defense counsel to represent detainees. While these restrictions are enforced out of public view and have largely escaped public or media scrutiny, the fact that the media and public spectators are placed behind a soundproof glass barrier (or allowed to view at remote sites) and can only hear audio delayed 40 seconds after review and potential censorship by CIA security officers further undermines the tribunals' credibility as "fair and open" proceedings.

In light of these problematic aspects of military commission law and procedure, the MCA limitation that the commissions can try only "alien" enemy unprivileged belligerents creates the impression that the government recognizes that they provide justice to which it would be inappropriate, or even unconstitutional, to subject U.S. nationals. This limitation is entirely unprecedented; all previous U.S. military tribunals could, and did, try Americans. This overt denial of equal protection may well violate the Constitution if any fundamental protections are held to apply there, which seems likely given the Supreme Court's holding in *Boumediene v. Bush* that Guantanamo detainees had a constitutional right to habeas review.[19] And this inequality based on nationality is subject to particular criticism given that special considerations have been given at Guantanamo to nationals of countries closely allied with the United States, including Great Britain, Australia, and Canada.

CONCLUSION

Historically, the military commission is a legitimate tribunal for the trial of criminal violations of the law of war or for the administration of domestic criminal law in areas under military occupation. Reputable prior military commissions have been closely modeled on court-martial practice, essentially differing only in terms of jurisdiction. Although the Guantanamo military commissions conducted under the MCA 2009 are an improvement over those initially envisioned by the Bush administration, they remain potentially problematic in several ways. First, their procedural protections fall short of those provided by modern courts-martial or legitimate international war crimes courts. Second, there are real questions about

---

19. Boumediene v. Bush, 553 U.S. 723 (2008).

the substantive law being applied in most cases, which would not be an issue with corresponding federal trials. Finally, their limitation to the trial of foreign nationals raises serious equal protection issues, suggesting they are deliberately employed to provide substandard justice to noncitizens.

EXPERTS

Geoffrey Corn, Associate Professor of Law, South Texas College of Law; (713) 646-2973; gcorn@stcl.edu

David Frakt, Associate Professor of Law, Barry University Dwayne O. Andreas School of Law; (321) 206-5600 ext. 5693; dfrakt@mail.barry.edu

David Glazier, Professor of Law, Loyola Law School Los Angeles; (213) 736-2242; david.glazier@lls.edu

Andrea Prasow, Human Rights Watch; (212) 216-1832; prasowa@hrw.org

Stephen Vladeck, Professor of Law, American University Washington College of Law; (202) 274-4241; svladeck@wcl.american.edu

RESOURCES

David Glazier, *Precedents Lost: The Neglected History of the Military Commission*, 46 VA. J. INT'L L. 5 (2005).

———, *A Self-Inflicted Wound: A Half-Dozen Years of Turmoil Over the Guantánamo Military Commissions*, 12 LEWIS & CLARK L. REV. 131 (2008).

———, *Still a Bad Idea: Military Commissions Under the Obama Administration*, Loyola-LA Legal Studies Paper No. 2010-32, http://papers.ssrn.com/sol3/papers.cfm?abstract_id=1658590.

Office of Military Commissions website, http://www.mc.mil.

Military Commission Act of 2009, http://www.mc.mil/Portals/0/MCA20Pub20Law200920.pdf.

THE MANUAL FOR MILITARY COMMISSIONS (2010), http://www.mc.mil/Portals/0/2010_Manual_for_Military_Commissions.pdf.

Courts-Martial and Other Military Legal Proceedings

12

By Jim McPherson

The foundations of military justice are found in the Uniform Code of Military Justice (UCMJ) and the Manual for Courts-Martial (MCM). The Uniform Code is the code of military criminal laws applicable to all active duty U.S. military members worldwide.

The Manual is essentially the procedural rules for courts-martial and consists of the Rules for Courts-Martial (RCM) and the Military Rules of Evidence (MRE). Both mirror procedures in the federal court system. Military courts often are referred to as Article I courts. This distinguishes them from federal courts or Article III courts; the names refer to articles of the Constitution under whose authority each type of court is created.

In addition, each of the armed services supplements the UCMJ and the MRE with its own regulations. (The Air Force calls its regulations "instructions.") In many cases, violations of these service regulations may be dealt with administratively and also may be punishable under criminal codes at a court-martial.

ADMINISTRATIVE PERSONNEL PROCEEDINGS

An adjunct to the military justice system, and in many cases an alternative forum for taking court-martial or criminal action against a service member, is the administrative personnel proceeding. These proceedings are analogous to traffic courts, where traffic citations result in administrative sanctions rather than criminal convictions. Administrative personnel proceedings are likewise considered noncriminal actions, although the sanctions or punishments can be relatively severe.

The most common administrative personnel proceeding is provided in the UCMJ under Article 15.[1] In the Army and Air Force, the proceedings are known as Article 15; in the Coast Guard and Navy as Mast; and in the Marine Corps as Office Hours.[2] Punishment can include forfeiture of pay; restriction to certain geographic limits such as a base, fort, or ship; loss of rank, referred to as "reduction in grade"; and other adverse personnel actions. However, punishment at an administrative proceeding is not considered a criminal conviction, whereas conviction at a court-martial is a federal criminal conviction.

Common Proceedings

The most common event that causes senior military officers to face administrative personnel proceedings under Article 15 of the UCMJ is an accident occurring in their command. For naval officers, it is a ship under their command colliding with another ship or running aground; for Army, Air Force, or Marine officers, it is a training accident involving personnel in the unit they command. In each of these instances, commanding officers are responsible for the safe operation of their units, whether the unit be a ship, aircraft, tank, or even the individual soldier, sailor, Marine, or airman firing a weapon. The principle of ultimate responsibility in the commanding officer is enforced through the legal standard of negligence. If a commanding officer is negligent through failure to provide adequate or proper equipment for his or her command or unit, fails to adequately train the members of the command or unit, approves an operation that is unnecessarily hazardous or dangerous, fails to adequately supervise the command or unit, or through a host of other circumstances fails to perform his or her duties and the result is an accident or mishap, the commanding officer may be guilty of dereliction of duty—one of the uniquely military offenses under the UCMJ.[3] Depending upon the severity of the accident or mishap, as well as many other factors, the most common disciplinary action that will be taken against the commanding officer is an administrative hearing under UCMJ Article 15.

A More Serious Charge and Proceeding

Following any incident involving injury or loss of life of a service member or damage to military equipment or property, the officer next in line in the chain

---

1. 10 U.S.C. § 815.
2. In the Navy, "Mast" for purposes of addressing service members' misconduct should not be confused with the term "Request Mast." "Request Mast" is a sailor's request to speak with his or her commanding officer about a complaint.
3. 10 U.S.C. § 892.

of command to the commanding officer of the unit involved will convene an investigation. This officer is called the convening officer. The investigating officer is typically an officer senior to the commanding officer of the unit and usually on the convening officer's staff (as, for example, when an admiral commanding a fleet assigns one of his or her staff to investigate an incident on a particular ship).[4] In the Army, this investigation is referred to as an AR 15-6; in the Air Force, an Administrative Investigation; in the Navy and Marine Corps, a JAGMAN Investigation. The investigation is an administrative, not criminal, investigation. In rare cases involving significant events, or where intentional criminal conduct is suspected, a criminal investigation may be opened by one of the services' criminal investigation organizations.[5]

The investigating officer's report will include a summary of the evidence, factual conclusions, and recommendations. This report will be given to the convening officer, who will decide how to handle the personal responsibility of the commanding officer involved. This could include holding an administrative hearing during which the personal responsibility of the commanding officer would be decided. If such a hearing is held, the commanding officer must be present; must have the opportunity to read all material considered, including a copy of the investigative report; may present material for consideration; may have a personal representative present who can be an attorney; and may request the hearing be open to the public or closed.

Administrative Punishment

If the officer conducting the hearing finds by a preponderance of the evidence (i.e., more than 50 percent) that the commanding officer was culpably negligent, or derelict, then a wide range of administrative punishment can be imposed.

The most common is a punitive letter of reprimand or censure. The letter is from the officer imposing the punishment to the officer involved and, most importantly, a copy is placed in the officer's personnel records. This action all but precludes any future promotions or career-enhancing assignments for the officer and can result in subsequent proceedings leading to discharge. The officer receiving a punitive letter can appeal that decision to the next higher officer in the chain of command.

One important note: Except in rare circumstances involving the Navy and Marine Corps, a service member may decline to have the matter decided under UCMJ Article 15. In that case, any charges may be referred to a court-martial.

---

4. The term "investigating officer" in this context should not be confused with the Article 32 Investigating Officer discussed in the next section.

5. In the Army that would be the Criminal Investigation Division (CID); in the Air Force it would be the Office of Special Investigations (OSI); in the Navy and Marine Corps it would be the Naval Criminal Investigative Service (NCIS); and in the Coast Guard the Coast Guard Investigative Service (CGIS).

These proceedings can also take place in cases where an officer or enlisted service member commits minor misconduct that does not warrant a court-martial. The range of possible punishments for junior enlisted service members includes reduction in rank, forfeitures of pay, restrictions, and extra duties. All punishments awarded at administrative personnel proceedings are placed in the service member's personnel record and can result in subsequent action to discharge them from the service.

COURT-MARTIAL PROCEEDINGS

Court-martial proceedings are the military's equivalent of civilian criminal court proceedings and are governed by the UCMJ and MCM as well as service-specific procedural regulations. The UCMJ provides for three types of court-martial: summary court-martial, special court-martial, and general court-martial. Depending upon the severity of the alleged crimes, the accused's[6] commanding officer or the court-martial convening authority has great discretion in which type of court-martial to convene and send the charges to.[7] The three types of courts-martial correspond to the three types of criminal charges in civilian jurisdictions—summary courts-martial handle minor misdemeanor offenses, special courts-martial handle routine misdemeanor offenses, and general courts-martial handle felony offenses.

One Scenario

The following hypothetical case illustrates how a typical court-martial transpires:

Petty Officer Smith, 25, had been in the Navy for six years. He recently returned from an overseas deployment and was assigned to a naval base in the United States. His job was to stand a rotational duty at the entrance to the headquarters building at the naval base. He was single, had a lot of debt, and lived in an off-base apartment in the city. He decided that the best way out of debt was to rob a local market just outside the base, using a stolen car so that if someone got a look at the license plate, the car could not be traced to him. While on duty one evening, he changed out of his uniform into civilian clothes, left the headquarters building, hot-wired a car in the parking lot adjacent to the building, and drove to the market. He entered the market wearing a mask and pulled out a gun he had brought from his home. The two clerks at the store emptied the cash into a shopping bag and gave it to Smith. He then drove back to the base, left the car in the parking lot, changed back into his uniform, and resumed his duties at the entrance to the headquarters building. A clerk told local police the car had a naval

---

6. Under the UCMJ, the defendant is called "the accused."
7. The act of sending the charges to a court-martial is termed "referral," as in "The Commanding General referred the charges to a general court-martial."

base decal in the window. Police asked the Naval Criminal Investigative Service (NCIS) for assistance.

The next morning, the owner of the car Smith had used noticed it had been tampered with and reported that to naval base police, who realized the car met the description put out by NCIS. Fingerprints were lifted from the car and run through the FBI's fingerprint system. Smith's fingerprints were identified along with several others, but he was the only person not known by the owner of the car. NCIS, accompanied by local police, went to Smith's apartment to interview him. Although Smith was not in custody, NCIS agents advised him of his rights under the UCMJ.[8] Smith waived his rights and denied any involvement in or knowledge of the robbery. Nevertheless, the local police arrested Smith and charged him with robbery. The police obtained a search warrant for Smith's apartment; there, officers accompanied by NCIS found the bag of money, the gun, and the mask Smith had worn.

The next day, the district attorney asked the base staff judge advocate whether the Navy would pursue the charges, given that Smith had allegedly robbed the market while he was on duty at the naval base headquarters and the get-away car was stolen from the base.[9] The answer was yes. Smith was transferred from the local jail to the brig at the naval base.[10]

Investigation and Prosecution

Within seven days of a service member's being placed in pretrial confinement, an officer acting as a neutral authority is formally appointed as a reviewing officer and required to determine whether there is probable cause to believe that the service member, in this case Smith, committed the offenses he is charged with and confinement is warranted.[11]

---

8. 10 U.S.C. § 31 requires that any service member, whether in custody or not, be given the *Miranda* warning before being questioned by military authorities.

9. Under the Supreme Court decision in *Solorio v. United States,* 483 U.S. 435 (1987), service members are subject to court-martial jurisdiction for violation of the UCMJ regardless of where the offense took place. All that is required is that the service member be "subject to the UCMJ" at the time of the offense—in other words, on active duty in the military.

10. Many military installations have informal agreements with local prosecutors regarding who will take jurisdiction of service members who commit a crime off base in the local community. Most provide that if the victim of the crime is another service member or a service member's family member, the military will take jurisdiction. Likewise, if the crime committed off base was part of a sequence of events that included crimes committed on base, the military will normally take jurisdiction.

11. The Reviewing Officer's hearing is very similar to a civilian Magistrate's Hearing. Unless he waives the right to an attorney, Petty Officer Smith will be appointed a military defense counsel to represent him at this hearing. He may also hire a civilian attorney to represent him at this hearing. The hearing is very informal and is usually conducted at the confinement facility. It is not normally open to the public. The military justice system does not have any provisions for release on bond or bail. Either the service member remains in pretrial confinement or he is released on his own recognizance.

Simultaneous to Smith being transferred to Navy custody, his commanding officer is required to conduct an informal inquiry of the incidents, which consists of nothing more than reviewing the police and NCIS investigations and deciding the appropriate disposition of the matter. The commanding officer has the options of taking no action, initiating an administrative personnel proceeding, referring charges to a summary or special court-martial, or convening a formal pretrial or UCMJ Article 32 Investigation.

One of the most significant differences between the military justice system and the civilian criminal justice system is who decides to bring charges against an accused person. In the civilian criminal justice system, the decision is made by a district, state, or U.S. attorney.[12] Under the UCMJ, the service member's immediate commanding officer makes that decision. In the case of Smith, since the charges were serious, his commanding officer decided to convene a formal investigative hearing, the required precursor to a general court-martial.[13]

In nearly all civilian state court and federal jurisdictions, before felony charges can be filed against a defendant, there must be either a grand jury hearing and indictment issued or a preliminary hearing. In the military justice system, this step is known as an Article 32 Investigation (a reference to 10 U.S.C. § 832). Smith's commanding officer convened the investigation by appointing a commissioned officer to conduct the investigation. Although not required, most often a judge advocate general is appointed as the Article 32 investigating officer. Unlike grand jury proceedings, at the Article 32 Investigation, the defendant will be present, will have a military defense counsel appointed to represent him, will be able to see the evidence and hear the testimony, and will be able, through his counsel, to cross-examine witnesses and present any evidence he desires.

A few weeks after Smith's commanding officer ordered the Article 32 Investigation, the investigating officer held the hearing at the base legal office. Smith was there along with the military defense counsel appointed to represent

---

12. This basic difference in who exercises prosecutorial discretion is one of the most hotly debated issues in military justice. In the civilian community, an attorney—a district attorney, state's attorney, or attorney general in the state and a U.S. attorney in the federal system—always exercises prosecutorial discretion. In the military justice system, prosecutorial discretion is exercised by a nonattorney; that is, the service member's commanding officer or a flag or general officer. In the civilian criminal justice system, the underpinnings are protecting society both physically and economically. In the military justice system, the underpinnings are maintaining good order and discipline of the armed force. Every few years, there are proposals before Congress to limit military justice jurisdiction to purely military offenses. Such proposals have never been successful.

13. For both a summary and special court-martial, the commanding officer can simply refer the charges to either of those levels of courts. However, if the commanding officer believes that the charges warrant prosecution before a general court-martial, he or she must first convene a formal investigative hearing under Article 32, UCMJ, which will determine whether there is probable cause to believe that a crime has been committed and that the service member committed it.

him.[14] The government was represented by the trial counsel assigned to prosecute the matter.

Before the hearing began, the trial counsel would have prepared the "charges and specifications" against Smith and placed those on the formal charging document, called a charge sheet. Smith was charged with several offenses: absence without leave (UCMJ Article 86—leaving the headquarters building without permission during his work shift); violation of an order (UCMJ Article 92—having a gun on base without permission); theft of a car (UCMJ Article 121); and armed robbery (UCMJ Article 122). The trial counsel called the witnesses and presented various documents and pieces of evidence, including the headquarters duty list, laboratory reports, the shopping bag, the money, and the handgun found in Smith's apartment.

The military rules of evidence regarding testimony and physical evidence do not apply at an Article 32 Investigation hearing. So, for example, the police may testify as to what they were told by witnesses, and lab reports can be presented without any witnesses from the lab. Like a grand jury proceeding or preliminary hearing in the civilian criminal justice system, at an Article 32 Investigation hearing, the trial counsel must present sufficient evidence to establish probable cause that Smith committed the offenses.

Following the hearing, the investigating officer prepared her report to Smith's commanding officer, recommending that the charge of having the gun on the naval base be dismissed for lack of evidence and that the remaining charges be referred to a general court-martial for trial. Smith's commanding officer forwarded the report to the base commander, a two-star admiral, concurring with the investigating officer's recommendations.[15]

Upon receipt of the report, the admiral is required to have his staff judge advocate review the report and prepare a recommendation for disposition of the charges. The staff judge advocate recommended that the charges of absence without leave, theft of the car, and robbery of the market be referred to a general court-martial. The admiral agreed and signed two documents. The first, a convening order, was the formal document that convenes the court-martial and lists the court-martial "members." The "members" of a court-martial are the jury panel, which is selected by the convening authority. Typically, the panel members are officers assigned to local commands for whom court-martial duty is a collateral duty. Smith had the right to have one-third of the members be enlisted service members if he desired.

---

14. A member of the military who is the defense counsel is called the "detailed defense counsel." Smith also may hire a civilian attorney and he may request a specific military defense counsel if that counsel is available.

15. While Smith's commanding officer has the authority to convene a summary and special court-martial, only certain designated flag or general officers may convene a general court-martial. Such officers are called General Court-Martial Convening Authorities (GCMA). In most cases, if a flag or general officer commands the base, camp, or fort, that officer is the GCMA for the installation and surrounding areas.

The second document the admiral signed was the charge sheet. In this two-step process, the convening authority (the base commander) convenes the general court-martial and then refers the charges to that court-martial.

Once the admiral signed the documents, they were sent to the base legal office and the Circuit Trial Judiciary. The senior military judge in the geographical area of the installation assigned one of the military judges in the area to preside over the court-martial.[16] The assigned judge called the attorneys in the case to his office and set a trial date. Smith had to decide if he wanted to be tried by the military judge alone or by the members assigned to the court-martial.[17] If Smith decided to be tried by the court-martial members, both the defense and the prosecution would have the opportunity to question the members and excuse them just as in the civilian criminal justice system. A general court-martial must have at least five members, a special court-martial at least three.[18]

Typically, a few weeks before the scheduled trial date, there would be a session of the court-martial for the military judge to hear and rule on any motions, such as a motion to dismiss any charges or suppress any evidence.

On the day scheduled for trial, the court-martial would begin and look very much like a typical criminal trial in a civilian court. If Smith chose trial by a jury, the members would be there, the military judge would preside, there would be a court reporter making a record, Smith would be seated next to his counsel, and the prosecution would be at the opposite table. If Smith decided to be tried by the military judge alone, the members would not be there. The trial would proceed with the attorneys making opening statements followed by the prosecutor presenting evidence first. The traditional rules of evidence familiar in a civilian trial are applicable to the court-martial as the MRE. After the prosecutor finished, the defense counsel would have the opportunity to present any evidence in defense of Smith.

Smith may testify or not—it is his decision. If he decided to testify, he would be sworn and cross-examined by the prosecutor. After the prosecutor finished presenting evidence, the defense would have the opportunity to offer any rebuttal evidence. Both attorneys would then give closing arguments. If the trial was before the members, there would be a short hearing without the members present during which the military judge would go over the proposed jury instructions. The judge then would instruct the members on the law, and they would deliberate

---

16. Military judges are selected and geographically assigned by their respective service Judge Advocate General and, following successful completion of specialized training on court-martial practice, are certified by the service Judge Advocate General to preside over special and general court-martials. This ensures a completely independent judiciary, because every military judge reports directly to the Service Judge Advocate General and not a local commanding officer.

17. The decision to be tried by the military judge or the court-martial members is the accused's except in a case where the accused could be sentenced to death. In a capital case, the court-martial members must try the accused.

18. If at a general court-martial the possible sentence includes death, there must be at least 12 members.

on the verdict.[19] If the trial was before the military judge alone, there would be a recess during which he would decide the verdict. As in civilian criminal justice, the government must prove the accused guilty beyond a reasonable doubt.

The finding of guilt by members at a court-martial is sufficiently different from the civilian criminal justice process to warrant comment here. In most civilian jurisdictions, the jury verdict must be unanimous to find a defendant guilty. At a court-martial with members, a guilty finding requires a two-thirds majority of the members voting for guilt except under two circumstances: First, if the possible sentence exceeds 10 years' confinement, the majority vote requirement increases to three-quarters. Second, if the possible sentence includes death, a unanimous vote for guilt is required. In addition, the members may only take one vote—if the required majority is not reached, the vote has resulted in a not-guilty verdict. There is no such thing as a hung jury in military justice practice.

Smith was found guilty of the three charges he faced. Unlike most civilian criminal justice systems, the court-martial moves immediately into determining the sentence. There is no sentencing or probation report prepared. The sentencing portion of the court-martial consists of the same players as the findings (or guilt) portion. If the military judge alone tried him, the judge determines the sentence. If the members tried him, they determine the sentence. The prosecutor again goes first, presenting evidence of Smith's service history and any aggravating circumstances surrounding the crimes not already in evidence. The defense attorney then presents any evidence establishing extenuating or mitigating circumstances surrounding the crimes. Smith may testify under oath or make an unsworn statement to the court. If he testifies under oath, he may be cross-examined by the prosecutor. If he makes an unsworn statement, the prosecutor may not cross-examine him. At this point, the military judge gives instructions to the members or calls a recess to determine the sentence if the trial was before the judge alone.

A word about sentencing. The Manual for Courts-Martial contains the maximum sentences a court-martial may impose (in military terms, "award") for each crime. Both summary and special courts-martial are limited by a cap on the sentence that may be awarded.[20] A general court-martial has no such limitation and may award the maximum punishment listed for each offense. The sentencing body (either the members or the military judge) has the discretion to award any punishment up to the maximum. For example, in Smith's case, he was convicted of leaving his place of duty, which carries a maximum sentence of three months' confinement; theft of the car, which carries a maximum sentence of two years' confinement; and robbery with a firearm, which carries a maximum sentence of 15 years' confinement. In this case, those terms are combined for a total possible sentence to confinement of 17 years and three months. In addition, the Manual

---

19. In military justice practice, the verdict is called "findings."
20. At a summary court-martial, the sentence is limited to reduction in rank, fines, or forfeitures, and restriction for up to 60 days. At a special court-martial, the sentence is limited to reduction in rank, fines or forfeiture, confinement for up to 12 months, and a punitive discharge.

provides for reduction in rank or pay grade, forfeiture and fines, and punitive discharges (either a bad conduct discharge or dishonorable discharge for enlisted members or dismissal for officers). Unlike many civilian jurisdictions, a sentence to confinement is not specified in terms of a range (e.g., three to five years) but in a certain term (e.g., five years). Under the military justice system, a service member sentenced to confinement may be paroled.[21]

POSTTRIAL PROCEEDINGS

After the court-martial, the verbatim record of the trial is sent to the base staff judge advocate (SJA) and the convening authority (the officer who convened the court-martial) for review and action. The SJA provides a written, formal review for the convening authority, who has the discretion to approve both the findings of guilty and the sentence, disapprove any findings of guilty, and reduce the sentence. The convening authority cannot change a not-guilty finding to guilty nor increase the sentence. Once the convening authority completes the action, the record is forwarded to service headquarters for appellate review.

All special and general court-martial convictions receive an automatic review at the service Court of Criminal Appeals if the sentence included confinement for one year or more, a punitive discharge, or a sentence to death.[22] If the conviction is affirmed by the service Court of Criminal Appeals, the service member may request review by the Court of Appeals for the Armed Services and the U.S. Supreme Court. Review by these courts is discretionary. The service member will be assigned a military attorney to represent him or her in the appeal process.

---

21. A quick word here about plea agreements or, as they are called in the military justice system, pretrial agreements (PTAs). Pretrial agreements are provided for in the military justice system. The agreement is negotiated between the accused and his or her attorney and the convening authority. The typical PTA consists of the charges the accused will plead guilty to and limitations upon a potential sentence. Unlike many civilian criminal jurisdictions, the military judge or court-martial members (jury) will not know the limitations on the sentence. A hearing will be held before the military judge alone during which the accused will be placed under oath and be required to relate the facts that establish his or her guilt. Service members may plead guilty only if they are in fact guilty of the charged offense(s). There is no nolo contendere or *Alford* plea in the military justice system. After a guilty plea is accepted, a sentencing hearing is held. The accused will be awarded a sentence, and if that sentence exceeds the one agreed to with the convening authority, only that portion that was agreed to will be approved. If the sentence by the court-martial is less than that agreed to, the accused will be given the one awarded by the court-martial.

22. The judges of the service Court of Criminal Appeals are senior judge advocates who have been appointed by the service Judge Advocate General.

EXPERTS

Charles J. Dunlap, Jr., Professor, Duke University School of Law; Maj. Gen. (Ret.), Judge Advocate Corps; former Deputy Judge Advocate General of the Air Force; (919) 613-7233; dunlap@law.duke.edu

Victor M. Hansen, Vice President, National Institute of Military Justice and Professor of Law, New England Law School; (617) 422-7252; vhansen@nesl.edu

David A. Schlueter, Hardy Professor of Law and Director of Advocacy Programs, St. Mary's School of Law; (210) 431-2212; dschlueter@stmarytx.edu

RESOURCES

R. CHUCK MASON, CONG. RESEARCH SERV., MILITARY JUSTICE: COURTS-MARTIAL, AN OVERVIEW (2011), http://www.fas.org/sgp/crs/natsec/R41739.pdf. An excellent reference document for very basic information.

DAVID A. SCHLUETER, MILITARY CRIMINAL JUSTICE: PRACTICE AND PROCEDURE (LexisNexis Matthew Bender 2008). The definitive textbook on military criminal justice from the professor of law and director of advocacy programs at St. Mary's School of Law.

CHARLES A. SHANOR, NATIONAL SECURITY AND MILITARY LAW IN A NUTSHELL (West 2003). An excellent handbook on military justice.

Part III

Domestic Law Enforcement and Counterterrorism

U.S.-Based Intelligence: The Law and Organizational Structure

13

By W. Renn Gade and Harvey Rishikof

Intelligence or information that involves U.S. citizens at home or abroad under current U.S. laws creates challenges of how to categorize and handle information sharing. Likewise, intelligence activities conducted within the United States to collect information on foreign powers and their agents can generate significant debate. To some, domestic intelligence connotes the specter of government overreach—"domestic spying." Condoleezza Rice, when she was the national security adviser, rather famously told the 9/11 Commission that America is allergic to domestic intelligence.[1] Americans' ingrained commitment to the First Amendment and some notable historical incidents may explain why the concept of U.S.-based intelligence generates such debate and controversy.

Because of its relative geographical isolation and the fact that it did not rise to world power status until the late nineteenth century, the United States had little need, historically, for national intelligence. Intelligence was essentially limited to those times when military commanders, for immediate tactical and operational necessity, functioned as their own intelligence officers.[2]

---

1. Henry A. Crumpton, *Intelligence and Homeland Defense*, in TRANSFORMING U.S. INTELLIGENCE 206 (Jennifer E. Sims & Burton Gerber eds., Georgetown Univ. Press 2005).
2. MARK M. LOWENTHAL, INTELLIGENCE: FROM SECRETS TO POLICY (CQ Press 2006).

U.S.-BASED INTELLIGENCE: THE LAW AND ORGANIZATIONAL STRUCTURE

There were, however, sporadic instances when the federal government responded to perceived external and internal threats by constraining dissent, and these reactions consequently left a mark on the American psyche. For example, the 1798 Alien and Sedition Acts were used by the Federalists against their political opponents, and the public outcry against this abuse was widespread. In the Civil War, the Habeas Corpus Act allowed the government to arrest suspected spies, secessionists, and Confederate sympathizers, and this also left an indelible dark spot on our history.[3]

The Federal Bureau of Investigation (FBI), established in 1908 as the Bureau of Investigation, has collected intelligence since its inception. The FBI is recognized as the world's premier crime-fighting force, but it has had times of excess and overreaching that have registered in the national identity as well. During World War I, Congress passed a series of laws commonly known as the Espionage and Sedition laws in response to threats from draft resisters, saboteurs, anarchists, Bolsheviks, and other radicals. In 1919 and 1920, Attorney General Mitchell Palmer created a General Intelligence Division (GID), led by J. Edgar Hoover, within the Department of Justice. In response to a series of bombings, the GID directed raids in numerous American cities that resulted in the arrest of more than 10,000 people. Those detained in the "Palmer Raids" were later exonerated, and the raids were seen as due process violations that were ultimately investigated by the Senate Judiciary Committee.[4] Similarly, during the 1940s and 1950s the public became concerned about the communist threat, and the FBI infiltrated domestic organizations believed to be communist affiliated.[5]

The 1947 National Security Act reorganized the military, created the Central Intelligence Agency (CIA), and generally created a permanent national intelligence framework. The act resulted in a divide between foreign and domestic intelligence.[6] Between 1956 and 1970, the FBI investigated those believed to be engaged in "subversive" activities as part of various counterintelligence programs. As later revealed by the Church and Pike Committees, the government used the FBI to collect intelligence on prominent African Americans, black nationalists, white hate groups, communists, and opponents of the war in Vietnam.[7]

In response to these abuses, new rules were imposed on the intelligence community, or IC, including the FBI, which constrained U.S.-based intelligence. In

---

3. Agnes Gereben Schaefer, *The History of Domestic Intelligence in the United States: Lessons for Assessing the Creation of a New Counterterrorism Intelligence Agency*, in THE CHALLENGE OF DOMESTIC INTELLIGENCE IN A FREE SOCIETY: A MULTIDISCIPLINARY LOOK AT THE CREATION OF A U.S. DOMESTIC COUNTERTERRORISM INTELLIGENCE AGENCY 14–15 (Brian A. Jackson ed., RAND Corp. 2009).
4. *Id.* at 18–21.
5. *Id.* at 27–31.
6. *Id.* at 31; *see also* National Security Act of 1947, U.S.C. 50 § 401, as amended.
7. *Id.* at 30–39, *see also* S. SELECT COMM. TO STUDY GOVERNMENTAL OPERATIONS WITH RESPECT TO INTELLIGENCE ACTIVITIES, SUPPLEMENTARY DETAILED STAFF REPORTS ON INTELLIGENCE ACTIVITIES AND THE RIGHTS OF AMERICANS, BOOK III: FINAL REPORT (CHURCH COMMITTEE REPORTS) 548 (Apr. 26, 1976).

U.S.-Based Intelligence: The Law and Organizational Structure

1976 and 1977, Congress established the Senate Select Committee on Intelligence and the House Permanent Select Committee on Intelligence to provide oversight of the IC.[8] In 1978, Congress passed the Foreign Intelligence Surveillance Act[9] (FISA), establishing rules for conducting electronic surveillance for foreign intelligence purposes, and provided procedures for the surveillance of U.S. citizens and others whom the Foreign Intelligence Surveillance Court determines to be "agent[s] of a foreign power."[10] Similarly, in 1981 President Ronald Reagan signed Executive Order 12333, which among other things provided guidance to other U.S. agencies on the design and direction of the intelligence community and, importantly for this analysis, the rules for intelligence agencies on the collection, retention, and dissemination of "U.S. person" information.[11]

This FISA/12333 framework contributed to the building of the so-called wall between intelligence activities and criminal investigations. The "wall" became shorthand for the authorities that governed law enforcement and foreign intelligence investigations targeted against Americans. These authorities, designed to prevent a recurrence of abuses, always recognized that international terrorism was both a law enforcement and intelligence matter. However, this shorthand understanding was frequently misunderstood by prosecutors, FBI agents, and CIA officers to mean that the law prohibited sharing information between law enforcement and intelligence communities. This misunderstanding became the subject of much discussion in the 9/11 Commission Report, and the USA PATRIOT Reauthorization and Improvement Act was passed in 2001 to, among other things, address this misunderstanding by eliminating the wall and promoting intelligence sharing.[12]

While "domestic intelligence" may be a loaded term, some simply view the term as descriptive of legitimate law enforcement activities. Others view the term as aptly describing an evolutionary turn of government operations in the post-9/11 world. The intent of this chapter is to define "U.S.-based intelligence," describe the architecture of this enterprise after changes in the law post-9/11, and then briefly list the structural and legal challenges that lie ahead in this arena. While the U.S.-based intelligence enterprise includes U.S.-based collection of foreign intelligence, counterintelligence of foreign agents, and the assembling of information on purely domestic concerns collected at fusion centers (e.g., natural disasters and disaster relief), this chapter focuses on that aspect of the U.S.-based intelligence enterprise that centers on counterterrorism, or CT, because that was the prime impetus for change in legal and organizational structures.

---

8. Frederick M. Kaiser, Cong. Research Serv., Congressional Oversight of Intelligence: Current Structure and Alternatives 1 (2010).
9. Foreign Intelligence Surveillance Act, 50 U.S.C. §§ 1801 *et seq.*, as amended (1978).
10. Schaefer, *supra* note 3, at 40.
11. Eric Rosenbach & Aki J. Peritz, Confrontation or Collaboration? Congress and the Intelligence Community 60 (Belfer Ctr. for Sci. & Int'l Affairs, Harvard Kennedy Sch. 2009).
12. Harvey Rishikof, *The Evolving FBI: Becoming a New National Security Enterprise Asset*, in The National Security Enterprise: Navigating the Labyrinth 186–89 (Roger Z. George & Harvey Rishikof eds., Georgetown Univ. Press 2011).

"U.S.-BASED INTELLIGENCE" DEFINED

There is no universally recognized definition of intelligence, or any of the terms rather loosely called domestic intelligence.[13] The lack of an agreed-upon definition for domestic intelligence complicates the often emotional policy debate. We will use "U.S.-based intelligence" as a descriptive and hopefully not emotionally laden term for the purposes of this chapter. As a starting point in this discussion, the National Security Act of 1947 defines foreign intelligence as "information relating to the capabilities, intentions, or activities of foreign governments or elements thereof, foreign organizations, or foreign persons."[14] That type of intelligence is commonly associated with the secret activities of government for the advancement of its own purposes in international affairs. More recently, however, intelligence has taken on a broader meaning and has even been adopted by the business community to describe how information is collected and analyzed for a competitive advantage in the marketplace.[15]

In layman's terms, U.S.-based intelligence can be defined as intelligence activities conducted on U.S. soil to collect information concerning threats to national security. However, a more precise definition of U.S.-based intelligence can be found in a recent RAND study: "efforts by government organizations to gather, assess, and act on information about individuals or organizations in the United States or U.S. persons elsewhere that are not related to the investigation of a known past criminal act or a specific planned criminal activity."[16] This is a useful definition because it hones in on the tactical collection and use of information to identify and disrupt threats to national security or to the homeland as opposed to a more general study of possible societal or criminal threats.

It is generally accepted that the lines between law enforcement and intelligence have been blurred in the past decade. Contrary to the views of those who consider domestic intelligence as law enforcement by another name, the latter is focused on past events and is case-oriented toward a prosecution. In contrast, U.S.-based intelligence is forward-looking and is focused on preventing threats or informing national policy. To the extent that it is focused on crimes, it is oriented toward preventing potential crimes before they occur, rather than prosecuting them after the events occur. In an era of persistent conflict and incidents of terrorism at home, the emphasis on domestic intelligence would appear to be the approach of a state focused on prevention.

---

13. Michael Warner, *Wanted: A Definition of Intelligence*, STUDIES IN INTELLIGENCE, Apr. 4, 2007, https://www.cia.gov/library/center-for-the-study-of-intelligence/csi-publications/csi-studies/studies/vol46no3/article02.html.

14. 50 U.S.C. § 401(a); *see also* Exec. Order 12333, 3.4.

15. *See, e.g.*, KIRK W. M. TYSON, THE COMPLETE GUIDE TO COMPETITIVE INTELLIGENCE (Leading Edge, 4th ed. 2006).

16. Brian A. Jackson, *Introduction, in* THE CHALLENGE OF DOMESTIC INTELLIGENCE IN A FREE SOCIETY: A MULTIDISCIPLINARY LOOK AT THE CREATION OF A U.S. DOMESTIC COUNTERTERRORISM INTELLIGENCE AGENCY 3–4 (Brian A. Jackson ed., RAND Corp. 2009).

POST-9/11 CHANGES AND THE STRUCTURE OF THE U.S.-BASED INTELLIGENCE ENTERPRISE

The prime characteristic of U.S.-based intelligence is the extreme diversity of federal, state, and local governmental actors. This defining attribute has become even more pronounced since 9/11, though terrorism was not a new problem for the United States in 2001. The years immediately preceding that attack saw numerous bombings—by the Unabomber, the 1993 World Trade Center bombing, the 1995 Oklahoma City bombing, the 1996 Atlanta Olympics bombing, the 1996 Khobar Towers bombing, the 1998 U.S. embassy bombings in Africa, and the 2000 attack on the USS *Cole*—yet terrorism was not the number one priority within the U.S. government prior to 2001. State and local officials were invested in the counterterrorism field, and the CT activities fit squarely within the federal law enforcement function of the FBI—albeit with a lower priority than criminal prosecutions.

The September 2001 attacks, followed by the anthrax attacks in the postal system, changed the national perception of the threat. The 9/11 Commission Report lucidly related the events that led to the September attacks: "As 2001 began, counterterrorism officials were receiving frequent but fragmentary reports about threats. . . . Yet no one working on these late leads in the summer of 2001 connected the case in his or her in-box to the threat reports agitating senior officials and being briefed to the President. Thus, these individual cases did not become national priorities . . . no one looked at the bigger picture; no analytic

U.S.-Based "Intelligence" Enterprise*

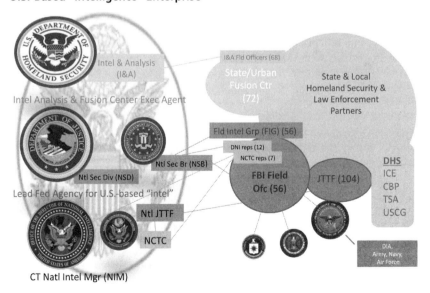

*Not inclusive; a general depiction.

work foresaw the lightning that could connect the thundercloud to the ground."[17] The problems evident on September 11 were, at their core, about the failures and obstacles to share information among the federal partners charged with protecting the country. The consequent changes in the federal, state, and local U.S.-based intelligence enterprise, detailed in the chart, were intended to reprioritize the CT effort and improve the organization and effectiveness of our U.S.-based intelligence.

DEPARTMENT OF HOMELAND SECURITY

In response to the September 11, 2001, terrorist attacks, Congress passed the Homeland Security Act of 2002 on November 25, 2002.[18] It has been amended more than 30 times since then. The act created the Department of Homeland Security (DHS), consolidating nearly two dozen executive branch organizations, including the Border Patrol, Immigrations and Customs Enforcement, the Transportation Security Administration, the Federal Emergency Management Administration, and the coast guard under one cabinet-level department. The DHS lists five core homeland security missions: preventing terrorism, safeguarding cyberspace, securing borders, enforcing immigration laws, and ensuring resilience to disasters.[19]

In an operational context, DHS creates and uses U.S.-based intelligence. The Office of Intelligence and Analysis is the central organizational element for intelligence within DHS. DHS operates the National Operations Center (NOC), which collects and fuses information from more than 35 federal, state, territorial, tribal, and private-sector agencies.[20] Much of the information flowing to the NOC comes from the DHS-funded fusion centers that are found in 50 states and 22 urban centers around the nation.[21] The purpose of the fusion centers is to centralize in one location federal and state representatives in order to synthesize intelligence, law enforcement, and investigative information.[22] The creation of DHS was the largest U.S. government reorganization since the Department of Defense (DoD)

---

17. THE 9/11 COMMISSION REPORT: FINAL REPORT OF THE NATIONAL COMMISSION ON TERRORIST ATTACKS UPON THE UNITED STATES 254, 277 (2004).
18. Homeland Security Act of 2002, Pub. L. No. 107-296 (Nov. 25, 2002).
19. Gary M. Shiffman & Jonathan Hoffman, *The Department of Homeland Security: Chief of Coordination*, in THE NATIONAL SECURITY ENTERPRISE: NAVIGATING THE LABYRINTH 207–10 (Roger Z. George & Harvey Rishikof eds., Georgetown Univ. Press 2011).
20. Brian A. Jackson, Darcy Noricks & Benjamin W. Goldsmith, *Current Domestic Intelligence Efforts in the United States*, in THE CHALLENGE OF DOMESTIC INTELLIGENCE IN A FREE SOCIETY, *supra* note 16, at 59.
21. Danielle Keats Citron & Frank Pasquale, *Network Accountability for the Domestic Intelligence Apparatus*, 62 HASTINGS L.J. 1441, 1448–49 (2011).
22. *Id.* at 1449–55; Matthew Waxman, *Police and National Security: American Local Law Enforcement and Counterterrorism After 9/11*, 3 J. NAT'L SEC. L & POL'Y 389–90 (2009).

was created 50 years earlier. DHS contains a wide variety of agencies that are involved in intelligence activities in the United States and at its borders.

DIRECTOR OF NATIONAL INTELLIGENCE

The perception that the IC failed to "connect the dots" prior to September 11 created a sense of urgency to correct the shortfalls in information sharing and to remove the sharp distinctions between foreign and domestic intelligence. The 9/11 Commission Report served as a prime catalyst to the IC reform efforts.

Passage of the Intelligence Reform and Terrorism Prevention Act (IRTPA) on December 17, 2004, created the Office of the Director of National Intelligence. The Director of National Intelligence (DNI) supplanted the Director of Central Intelligence as the senior intelligence official in government and principal intelligence officer to the president and the National Security Council. The IRTPA also placed the National Counterterrorism Center, commonly known as NCTC and created only months earlier by Executive Order 13,354, under the DNI.[23] Under IRTPA, the DNI was charged with managing the 17-organization IC, improving information sharing, and ensuring integration across the IC. The IRTPA also created the Information Sharing Environment to facilitate sharing of terrorism information among federal agencies, and adoption of federal steps to support the development of state and local information fusion centers.[24] The IRTPA sets out the DNI's primary responsibilities as follows:

- serve as the president's principal intelligence adviser;
- oversee the National Intelligence Program budget ($54.6 billion in FY2011);
- establish IC priorities with clear and measurable goals and objectives;
- set direction through policies and budgets;
- ensure integration of IC personnel, expertise, and capabilities;
- provide leadership on IC cross-cutting issues; and
- monitor IC agency and leadership performance.[25]

The IRTPA also lays out NCTC's responsibility to "[l]ead our nation's efforts to combat terrorism at home and abroad by analyzing the threat, sharing that information with our partners and integrating all instruments of national power to ensure unity of effort."[26] NCTC serves as the primary organization within the U.S. government for "analyzing and integrating all intelligence possessed or acquired by

---

23. Intelligence Reform and Terrorism Prevention Act of 2004 (IRTPA), Pub. L. No. 108-458, 118 Stat. 3638, enacted Dec. 17, 2004. *See also* LOWENTHAL, *supra* note 2, at 30–31.
24. Section 1016 of the IRTPA directs the president to create the ISE. 6 U.S.C. § 48.
25. Office of Dir. of Nat'l Intelligence, ODNI FAQ (Oct. 2011).
26. *Hearing before the H. Permanent Select Comm. on Intelligence*, 112th Cong. 7 (Oct. 6, 2011) (statement of Matthew G. Olsen, Director, Nat'l Counterterrorism Ctr.) [hereinafter Olsen statement].

the government pertaining to terrorism and counterterrorism, except intelligence pertaining exclusively to domestic terrorism and domestic counterterrorism" (the FBI remains the lead federal agency in the domestic area).[27] NCTC also serves as the federal government's "central and shared" knowledge bank on known and suspected terrorists and terrorist groups, and toward this end has developed the Terrorist Identities Datamart Environment, or TIDE. NCTC provides U.S.-based intelligence support by

- integrating information and passing it along to federal, state, and local partners through the NCTC Watch Center (which is colocated with the FBI's Counterterrorist Division Watch Center);
- exporting data to the FBI's Terrorist Screening Center;
- providing information to the DHS on individuals who have overstayed their visas; and
- disseminating on a classified website finished intelligence products to DHS, other executive branch users, fusion centers, and Joint Terrorism Task Forces.[28]

Following the attempted airplane bombing on Christmas Day 2009, the NCTC created the Pursuit Group in January 2010. The purpose of the Pursuit Group is to develop tactical leads and pursue terrorism threats. The Pursuit Group is divided into interagency teams that use the widest range of terrorism information available to develop nonobvious connections to produce relevant, actionable leads that are provided to operational elements such as the FBI, CIA, or DHS.[29]

DEPARTMENT OF JUSTICE AND THE FBI

The Department of Justice (DoJ) oversees a wide variety of federal law enforcement activities that concern not only domestic counterterrorism, but also counterintelligence (CI), counterespionage (CE), organized crime, and narcotics trafficking. The nexus between counterthreat finance, organized crime, and narco-trafficking is becoming increasingly important, and DoJ-led organizations such as the Drug Enforcement Administration, U.S. Marshals Service, and the Bureau of Alcohol, Tobacco, Firearms, and Explosives, commonly known as ATF, are prominent in this area. The mission of those organizations is to collect, analyze, and share data on individuals and their activities in the United States or activities abroad that affect the United States.

The reorganization of the national security enterprise was also felt at the DoJ. The National Security Division (NSD) was created in March 2006 by the Patriot

---

27. *Id.*
28. *Id.* at 7–8; Jackson, Noricks & Goldsmith, *supra* note 20, at 57–58.
29. Olsen statement, *supra* note 26, at 9.

Act.[30] The creation of the NSD consolidated a number of Justice Department national security sections: the CT and Counterespionage Sections, the Office of Justice for Victims of Overseas Terrorism (all previously found in the Criminal Division), an Executive Office, and a new Office of Law and Policy. The mission of the NSD is to "carry out the department's highest priority: to combat terrorism and other threats to national security."[31] The NSD's organizational structure was designed to ensure improved coordination between prosecutors and law enforcement agencies on one hand, and intelligence attorneys and the IC on the other. The NSD is led by an assistant attorney general for national security.[32]

Most prominent among the DoJ organizations involved in U.S.-based intelligence is the FBI. After the 9/11 attacks, the FBI in particular was assessed to have missed opportunities to prevent or disrupt the attacks by focusing on its reactive law enforcement mission at the expense of identifying and preventing terrorist threats. The Senate and House intelligence committees conducted a joint inquiry into the IC in connection with the terrorist attacks. The inquiry criticized the FBI for failing to collect, analyze, and share U.S.-based intelligence internally and with the IC.[33] In response to the criticism, the FBI undertook nothing less than a paradigm shift from a traditional law enforcement organization to a "national security organization that fuses traditional law enforcement and intelligence missions."[34]

It did this by elevating counterterrorism to its highest priority, with CI and cybercrime filling out the top three priorities. It also sought to transform and upgrade its intelligence program by employing the traditional intelligence cycle used by the rest of the IC. The goal was to move the FBI away from its arrest and prosecution focus and make it a threat-driven organization with intelligence collection as the top priority. To meet this post-9/11 demand, the FBI shifted resources from criminal investigations to national security matters. Nearly 2,000 agents were added to national security programs in the year following the 9/11 attacks. Director Robert Mueller, who took over only one week before the attacks, also sought to change the culture of the FBI by centralizing control and management of CT and CI operations at the Washington headquarters. This removed

---

30. USA PATRIOT Improvement and Reauthorization Act of 2005, Pub. L. No. 109-177 (Mar. 9, 2006).

31. U.S. Dep't of Justice, Nat'l Sec. Div., About the Division, http://www.justice.gov/nsd/about-nsd.html (last visited Jan. 23, 2012).

32. *Id.*

33. H. PERMANENT SELECT COMM. ON INTELLIGENCE & S. SELECT COMM. ON INTELLIGENCE, JOINT INQUIRY INTO INTELLIGENCE COMMUNITY ACTIVITIES BEFORE AND AFTER THE TERRORIST ATTACKS OF SEPTEMBER 11, 2001 (JIC INQUIRY), H. REP. NO. 107-792, S. REP. NO. 107-351, at xv, 37–39, 337–38 (2002), http://www.gpoaccess.gov/serialset/creports/911.html; Jackson, *supra* note 16, at 3–4.

34. *Hearing before the S. Permanent Select Comm. on Intelligence*, 112th Cong. 1–2 (Sept. 13, 2011) (statement of Robert S. Mueller III, Director, Fed. Bureau of Investigation), http://www.fbi.gov/news/testimony/ten-years-after-9-11-are-we-safer [hereinafter Mueller statement].

some of the autonomy that special agents in charge may have previously enjoyed, but it avoided the "stovepiping" of terrorist information in the 56 field offices.[35]

The infrastructure changes that took place to prioritize CT and intelligence collection and sharing included the establishment of prominent intelligence organizations within FBI headquarters and the creation of a Field Intelligence Group (FIG) composed of intelligence analysts and special agents at each field office in the country. The mission of the regional FIGs is to identify the threats in their area of operations and "develop 'domain awareness' through collecting, exploiting, analyzing and disseminating intelligence."[36] In June 2005, President George W. Bush directed Attorney General Alberto Gonzales to create a National Security Service within the FBI, as recommended by the Commission on the Intelligence Capabilities of the United States Regarding Weapons of Mass Destruction, commonly known as the WMD Commission.[37] Gonzales implemented the president's directive in September 2005 by creating the FBI's National Security Branch (NSB)—perhaps the biggest structural change within the FBI in decades. The NSB combined the missions and capabilities of the national security components of the FBI—the CT Division, the CI Division, the Directorate of Intelligence, and, in 2006, the Weapons of Mass Destruction Directorate. The newly created executive assistant director for the NSB serves as the bureau's lead representative to the IC.[38] The Directorate of Intelligence (DI) was created first by presidential memorandum in 2003 and later authorized by IRTPA in 2004 as a dedicated national intelligence workforce within the FBI—a service within a service. DI manages intelligence collection within the United States by maintaining a presence in each operational division of the bureau and managing the FIGs. The CT Division runs the National Joint Terrorism Task Force (NJTTF), an interagency task force with representatives from more than 35 agencies that provides administrative, logistical, budgetary, and training support to the JTTFs. The JTTFs existed prior to 9/11, but their number has increased from about three dozen to more than 100.[39] The previously discussed DHS-funded fusion centers operate as information clearinghouses, while the JTTFs help coordinate operations of the participating agencies.[40] The NSB also has administrative responsibility for two interagency groups—the High-Value Detainee Interrogation Group (HIG, created by executive order in 2010) and the Terrorist Screening Center (TSC, created in 2003).[41]

---

35. *Id.* at 1–2.
36. *Id.* at 7–8.
37. ALFRED CUMMING & TODD MASSE, CONG. RESEARCH SERV., RL32336, FBI INTELLIGENCE REFORM SINCE SEPTEMBER 11, 2001: ISSUES AND OPTIONS FOR CONGRESS 7–9 (Apr. 6, 2004), http://www.fas.org/irp/crs/RL32336.html.
38. Mueller statement, *supra* note 34, at 3.
39. Jackson, Noricks & Goldsmith, *supra* note 20, at 61.
40. Waxman, *supra* note 22, at 7.
41. Mueller statement, *supra* note 34, at 3.

Intelligence collection is done by people, and since 2001, the FBI has more than doubled the number of agents and analysts assigned to its national security missions from 3,537 (2,514 agents and 1,023 analysts) to 7,933 (4,815 agents and 3,118 analysts). The FBI has also increased its presence domestically and globally with 56 field offices, 399 resident agencies, and 62 legal attaché offices, known as LEGATs, around the world (an increase of 18 LEGATs since 2001).[42]

DEPARTMENT OF DEFENSE

The common perception is that DoD IC elements conduct intelligence efforts in support of the warfighter entirely abroad. However, as should be expected, the DoD actively engages in CI activities in the United States. The DoD also conducts domestic information collection in support of its force protection and criminal investigation missions. These law enforcement and CT force protection missions are routinely conducted by the armed services at the base level by military police and criminal investigators. Moreover, at least three combatant commands have areas of responsibility, or AORs, that include the United States and missions that interact with the U.S.-based intelligence enterprise.

The U.S. Southern Command's AOR includes Central and South America, and much of its activities involve counterdrug operations. USSOUTHCOM, headquartered in Miami, operates the Joint Interagency Task Force-South, or JIATF-South, in Key West, which brings a variety of interagency law enforcement and military assets together to counter drug trafficking in the Caribbean.[43] U.S. Pacific Command, headquartered in Hawaii, is responsible for the Pacific and East Asia. USPACOM manages the JIATF-West, which targets threats and smuggling in its AOR.[44] Finally, U.S. Northern Command, headquartered in Colorado Springs, Colorado, was created after 2002 to provide command and control of DoD homeland defense efforts and to coordinate defense support of civil authorities. USNORTHCOM's AOR includes air, land, and sea approaches and encompasses the continental United States, Alaska, Canada, Mexico, and the surrounding water out to approximately 500 nautical miles. It also includes the Gulf of Mexico, the Straits of Florida, and portions of the Caribbean region that include the Bahamas, Puerto Rico, and the U.S. Virgin Islands. Joint Task Force North, headquartered at Fort Bliss, Texas, is a subordinate command of USNORTHCOM that is tasked to support federal law enforcement agencies in the interdiction of suspected transnational threats such as international terrorism, narco-trafficking, alien smuggling,

---

42. *Id.* at 5–7.
43. U.S. Southern Command, About Us, http://www.southcom.mil/aboutus/Pages/About-Us.aspx.
44. U.S. Pacific Command, USPACOM Facts, http://www.pacom.mil/about-uspacom/facts.shtml.

and weapons of mass destruction within and along the approaches to the continental United States.[45]

The National Security Agency (NSA) is a DoD intelligence component and the largest intelligence agency in the U.S. government. The NSA conducts electronic and signals intelligence collection for intelligence and CI purposes to support military missions against targets outside the United States, foreign citizens traveling through the United States, and communications between foreign citizens and U.S. citizens. With advancements in communications, the importance and scope of this collection has increased considerably.[46] Lastly, the Defense Intelligence Agency's Joint Intelligence Task Force for Combating Terrorism, JITF-CT, was established in 2007 to provide enhanced analysis and production to support worldwide efforts to counter terrorism. JITF-CT analysts produce daily assessments of possible terrorist threats to DoD personnel, facilities, and interests in the United States and abroad. JITF-CT's products are shared with a variety of agencies within the IC.[47]

FUTURE CHALLENGES WITH U.S.-BASED INTELLIGENCE

As illustrated by this brief history, the United States seems to struggle to find a balance between overreaction to perceived threats and overreaction to the responses after unconstitutional excesses. This political and cultural tension between intelligence collection and law enforcement on one hand, and personal privacy and civil liberties on the other, is part of the American constitutional framework and will be challenged again given the perpetual advances in digital and electronic communications.[48] It is cliché to say that U.S. legal structures have difficulty in keeping up with the dynamic technological domain. It is also reasonable to state that America's views on privacy in the digital age may be changing. Americans now share volumes of personal information with others. Justice Sonia Sotomayor asked in *United States v. Jones* whether the expectation of privacy has changed, and the concurring opinion by Justice Samuel Alito and three others stated that the court should have tried to apply the expectations of privacy analysis to the vexing

---

45. U.S. Northern Command, About USNORTHCOM, http://www.northcom.mil/About/index.html.
46. Nat'l Sec. Agency, Mission, http://www.nsa.gov/about/mission/index.shtml; Jackson, Noricks & Goldsmith, *supra* note 20, at 63–64.
47. *Id.* at 64.
48. *See* Jack Goldsmith, *The Cyberthreat, Government Network Operations, and the Fourth Amendment*, Future of the Constitution Series (Brookings Inst. 2010), http://www.brookings.edu/~/media/Files/rc/papers/2010/1208_4th_amendment_goldsmith/1208_4th_amendment_goldsmith.pdf; *but see* BENJAMIN WITTES, AGAINST A CRUDE BALANCE: PLATFORM SECURITY AND THE HOSTILE SYMBIOSIS BETWEEN LIBERTY AND SECURITY (Harvard Law Sch. & Brookings Inst. 2011), http://www.brookings.edu/~/media/Files/rc/papers/2011/0921_platform_security_wittes/0921_platform_security_wittes.pdf (the author rejects the liberty-security balance and posits a "hostile symbiosis" or a relationship of "profound mutual dependence yet, simultaneously, mutual danger and hostility").

issues presented in our age.[49] How does one define "search" and "seizure" under the Fourth Amendment in the digital age? Third parties control and store vast amounts of information on individuals, and the government is a subpoena away from access to that information. This tension between privacy and intelligence will manifest itself in numerous ways in the upcoming years as the Supreme Court continues to define or divine Americans' "reasonable expectations of privacy."

This tension over the sphere of privacy will be exacerbated by the evolving nature of the national security threats. At this juncture it appears that the core of al-Qaida senior leadership has taken heavy blows, and it would appear today that the centrally organized al-Qaida groups are a lesser threat than the numerous informal wannabe groups that compose the so-called "leaderless jihad."[50] It would also seem that the homegrown violent extremists, or HVEs—people inspired by the al-Qaida global extremist agenda, extreme right-wing militias, and violent environmental activists—are another key evolution and diversification of the threat.[51] These small groups of free-agent terrorists and lone-wolf actors present unique and difficult challenges to the law and the structure of U.S.-based intelligence and also pose unique privacy problems.

Similar to the changes in the IC enterprise, the changes in the legal architecture have been profound. Passage of the Patriot Act in 2001, and the law's reauthorization in 2005 and 2011, generated robust debate.[52] The Patriot Act is a massive and complicated piece of legislation. The act's key changes were in the Foreign Intelligence Surveillance Act—FISA,[53] the Electronic Communications Privacy Act of 1986—ECPA,[54] the Money Laundering Control Act of 1986,[55] the Bank Secrecy Act,[56] and the Immigration and Nationality Act.[57] Technology advancements may allow for greater anonymity, but they may also provide the federal government an even greater capacity to monitor and draw connections between individuals and groups. In the cyberworld the distinction between foreign and domestic is dissolved in a sea of 1s and 0s. The ability to harness information

---

49. United States v. Jones, 132 S. Ct. 945 (2012).
50. *See, e.g.*, MARC SAGEMAN, LEADERLESS JIHAD: TERROR NETWORKS IN THE TWENTY-FIRST CENTURY (Univ. of Pa. Press 2008).
51. Olsen statement, *supra* note 26, at 5.
52. Uniting and Strengthening America by Providing Appropriate Tools Required to Intercept and Obstruct Terrorism Act of 2001 (USA PATRIOT ACT), Pub. L. No. 107-56 (Oct. 12, 2001); USA PATRIOT Improvement and Reauthorization Act of 2005, Pub. L. No. 109-177 (Mar. 9, 2006); PATRIOT Sunsets Extension Act of 2011, Pub. L. No. 112-14 (May 26, 2011), 50 U.S.C. § 1801.
53. Foreign Intelligence Surveillance Act of 1978, 50 U.S.C. ch. 36.
54. Electronic Communications Privacy Act of 1986, U.S.C. 18, §§ 2510–2522, 2701–2711, 3121–3127.
55. Money Laundering Control Act of 1986, 18 U.S.C. § 1956.
56. Bank Secrecy Act of 1970 (also known as the Currency and Foreign Transactions Reporting Act), 31 U.S.C. §§ 5311–5332e. Several anti-money-laundering acts, including provisions in title III of the USA PATRIOT Act, have been enacted to amend the BSA, *see* 31 U.S.C. §§ 5311–5330, 31 C.F.R. ch. X, Financial Crimes Enforcement Network, Dept. of Treasury.
57. Immigration and Nationality Act of 1952 (INA), 8 U.S.C. § 1101, as amended.

technology to fuse intelligence and "big data" such as travel, financial, biometric, and business data is unprecedented. Whether current laws designed to protect personal privacy (e.g., the Privacy Act,[58] ECPA, and the Data Mining Statute[59]) function as needed or present an advantage to a skilled adversary will be the subject of much public debate and media commentary in the future.

EXPERTS

Jamie Baker, Chief Judge, U.S. Court of Appeals for the Armed Forces; (202) 761-1466; sheila.moretz@armfor.uscourts.gov (assistant)

Spike Bowman, former FBI Senior Counsel; former Deputy, Office of the National Counterintelligence Executive; (301) 439-9898; spikebowman@verizon.net

Michael Chertoff, former Secretary of the Department of Homeland Security; (202) 662-5060; mchertoff@cov.com

Susan Ginsburg, Senior Counsel and Team Leader, 9/11 Commission; (212) 535-1391; sginsburg@uscivilsecurity.org

David Kris, former Assistant Attorney General for National Security; (425) 677-2868 (Pam Miller, assistant); davidskris@aol.com

Gordon Lederman, former Majority Staff Counsel on the Senate Homeland Security and Governmental Affairs Committee; (202) 494-8728; gordonlederman1@aol.com

Harvey Rishikof, Professor, National Security Law, National War College, FBI, NCIX, DoD; rishikh@me.com

Suzanne Spaulding, DHS Deputy Undersecretary for the National Protection and Programs Directorate; (202) 282-8000; suzanne.spaulding@hq.dhs.gov

RESOURCES

James E. Baker, In the Common Defense: National Security Law for Perilous Times (Cambridge Univ. Press 2007).

Bank Secrecy Act (also known as the Currency and Foreign Transactions Reporting Act), 31 U.S.C. §§ 5311–5332e (1970).

---

58. Privacy Act of 1974, 5 U.S.C. § 552a.
59. Federal Agency Data Mining Reporting Act of 2007 (Data Mining Act), 42 U.S.C. § 2000ee-3(c).

RICHARD A. BEST JR., CONG. RESEARCH SERV., INTELLIGENCE REFORM AFTER FIVE YEARS: THE ROLE OF THE DIRECTOR OF NATIONAL INTELLIGENCE (DNI) (June 22, 2010), http://www.fas.org/sgp/crs/intel/R41295.pdf.

Danielle Keats Citron & Frank Pasquale, *Network Accountability for the Domestic Intelligence Apparatus*, 62 HASTINGS L.J. 1441, 1448–49 (2011).

Henry A. Crumpton, *Intelligence and Homeland Defense*, in TRANSFORMING U.S. INTELLIGENCE 206 (Jennifer E. Sims & Burton Gerber eds., Georgetown Univ. Press 2005).

ALFRED CUMMING & TODD MASSE, CONG. RESEARCH SERV., RL32336, FBI INTELLIGENCE REFORM SINCE SEPTEMBER 11, 2001: ISSUES AND OPTIONS FOR CONGRESS (Apr. 6, 2004), http://www.fas.org/irp/crs/RL32336.html.

ALFRED CUMMING & TODD MASSE, CONG. RESEARCH SERV., RL33033, INTELLIGENCE REFORM IMPLEMENTATION AT THE FEDERAL BUREAU OF INVESTIGATION: ISSUES AND OPTIONS FOR CONGRESS (Aug. 16, 2005), http://www.fas.org/sgp/crs/intel/RL33033.pdf.

Ken Dilanian, *A Key Sept. 11 Legacy: More Domestic Surveillance*, L.A. TIMES, Aug. 29, 2011, sec. A.

Electronic Communications Privacy Act, 18 U.S.C. §§ 2510–2522, 2701–2711, 3121–3127 (1986).

Exec. Order No. 12333, 46 Fed. Reg. 59,941, 59,952 (Dec. 4, 1981), *as amended by* Exec. Order Nos. 13,284 (2003), 13,355 (2004), and 13,470 (2008).

Federal Agency Data Mining Reporting Act, 42 U.S.C. § 2000ee-3(c) (2007).

Foreign Intelligence Surveillance Act, 50 U.S.C. §§ 1801 *et seq.*, as amended (1978).

Jack Goldsmith, *The Cyberthreat, Government Network Operations, and the Fourth Amendment*, Future of the Constitution Series (Brookings Inst. 2010), http://www.brookings.edu/~/media/Files/rc/papers/2010/1208_4th_amendment_goldsmith/1208_4th_amendment_goldsmith.pdf.

Intelligence Reform and Terrorism Prevention Act, 42 U.S.C. § 2000ee; 50 U.S.C. §§ 403-1 *et seq.*, §§ 403-3 *et seq.*, §§ 404 *et seq.* (2004).

Immigration and Nationality Act, 80 U.S.C. §§ 1101 *et seq.*, as amended (1952).

FREDERICK M. KAISER, CONG. RESEARCH SERV., CONGRESSIONAL OVERSIGHT OF INTELLIGENCE: CURRENT STRUCTURE AND ALTERNATIVES (2010).

MARK M. LOWENTHAL, INTELLIGENCE: FROM SECRETS TO POLICY (CQ Press 2006).

U.S.-BASED INTELLIGENCE: THE LAW AND ORGANIZATIONAL STRUCTURE

KATE MARTIN, DOMESTIC INTELLIGENCE AND CIVIL LIBERTIES (SAIS Review 2004).

Money Laundering Control Act, 18 U.S.C. §§ 1956 *et seq.* (1986).

National Security Act, 50 U.S.C. §§ 401 *et seq.*, as amended (1947).

Office of Dir. of Nat'l Intelligence, ODNI FAQ (Oct. 2011), http://www.dni.gov/content/ODNI%20Fact%20Sheet_2011.pdf.

RICHARD A. POSNER, PREVENTING SURPRISE ATTACKS: INTELLIGENCE REFORM IN THE WAKE OF 9/11 (Hoover Inst. 2005).

Privacy Act, 5 U.S.C. §§ 552a *et seq.*, as amended (1974).

Harvey Rishikof, *The Evolving FBI: Becoming a New National Security Enterprise Asset*, in THE NATIONAL SECURITY ENTERPRISE: NAVIGATING THE LABYRINTH 186 (Roger Z. George & Harvey Rishikof eds., Georgetown Univ. Press 2011).

ERIC ROSENBACH & AKI J. PERITZ, CONFRONTATION OR COLLABORATION? CONGRESS AND THE INTELLIGENCE COMMUNITY (Belfer Ctr. for Sci. & Int'l Affairs, Harvard Kennedy Sch. 2009).

MARC SAGEMAN, LEADERLESS JIHAD: TERROR NETWORKS IN THE TWENTY-FIRST CENTURY (Univ. of Pa. Press 2008).

Agnes Gereben Schaefer, *The History of Domestic Intelligence in the United States: Lessons for Assessing the Creation of a New Counterterrorism Intelligence Agency*, in THE CHALLENGE OF DOMESTIC INTELLIGENCE IN A FREE SOCIETY: A MULTIDISCIPLINARY LOOK AT THE CREATION OF A U.S. DOMESTIC COUNTERTERRORISM INTELLIGENCE AGENCY 14–15 (Brian A. Jackson ed., RAND Corp. 2009).

THE 9/11 COMMISSION REPORT: FINAL REPORT OF THE NATIONAL COMMISSION ON TERRORIST ATTACKS UPON THE UNITED STATES (2004).

GREGORY F. TREVERTON, REORGANIZING UNITED STATES DOMESTIC INTELLIGENCE: ASSESSING THE OPTIONS (RAND Corp. 2008).

KIRK W. M. TYSON, THE COMPLETE GUIDE TO COMPETITIVE INTELLIGENCE (Leading Edge, 4th ed. 2006).

Uniting and Strengthening America by Providing Appropriate Tools Required to Intercept and Obstruct Terrorism Act of 2001 (USA PATRIOT ACT), Pub. L. No. 107-56 (Oct. 12, 2001); USA PATRIOT Improvement and Reauthorization Act of 2005, Pub. L. No. 109-177 (Mar. 9, 2006); PATRIOT Sunsets Extension Act of 2011, Pub. L. No. 112-14 (May 26, 2011), 50 U.S.C. § 1801.

U.S. Congress. *Hearing before the H. Permanent Select Comm. on Intelligence*, 112th Cong. (Oct. 6, 2011) (statement of Matthew G. Olson, Director, Nat'l Counterterrorism Ctr.).

U.S. Congress. *Hearing before the H. Permanent Select Comm. on Intelligence*, 112th Cong. (Oct. 6, 2011) (statement of Robert S. Mueller III, Director, Fed. Bureau of Investigation).

U.S. Congress. H. PERMANENT SELECT COMM. ON INTELLIGENCE & S. SELECT COMM. ON INTELLIGENCE, JOINT INQUIRY INTO INTELLIGENCE COMMUNITY ACTIVITIES BEFORE AND AFTER THE TERRORIST ATTACKS OF SEPTEMBER 11, 2001 (JIC INQUIRY), H. REP. NO. 107-792, S. REP. NO. 107-351 (2002), http://www.gpoaccess.gov/serialset/creports/911.html.

U.S. Congress. S. SELECT COMM. TO STUDY GOVERNMENTAL OPERATIONS WITH RESPECT TO INTELLIGENCE ACTIVITIES, SUPPLEMENTARY DETAILED STAFF REPORTS ON INTELLIGENCE ACTIVITIES AND THE RIGHTS OF AMERICANS, BOOK III: FINAL REPORT (CHURCH COMMITTEE REPORTS), 94th Cong. (Apr. 26, 1976).

U.S. Congress. *Hearing before the S. Permanent Select Comm. on Intelligence*, 112th Cong. (Sept. 13, 2011) (statement of Robert S. Mueller III, Director, Fed. Bureau of Investigation).

U.S. DEP'T OF HOMELAND SEC., IMPLEMENTING 9/11 COMMISSION RECOMMENDATIONS: PROGRESS REPORT 2011 (July 21, 2011), http://www.dhs.gov/xlibrary/assets/implementing-9-11-commission-report-progress-2011.pdf.

Press Release U.S. Dep't of Justice, Oversight Changes, One Year Progress Report: The Department's Comprehensive National Security Oversight Initiative (July 31, 2008), http://www.justice.gov/opa/pr/2008/July/08-nsd-678.html.

U.S. Dep't of Justice, Nat'l Sec. Div., About the Division, http://www.justice.gov/nsd/about-nsd.html.

Michael Warner, *Wanted: A Definition of Intelligence*, STUDIES IN INTELLIGENCE, Apr. 4, 2007, https://www.cia.gov/library/center-for-the-study-of-intelligence/csi-publications/csi-studies/studies/vol46no3/article02.html.

Matthew Waxman, *Police and National Security: American Local Law Enforcement and Counterterrorism After 9/11*, 3 J. NAT'L SEC. L & POL'Y 377 (2009).

BENJAMIN WITTES, AGAINST A CRUDE BALANCE: PLATFORM SECURITY AND THE HOSTILE SYMBIOSIS BETWEEN LIBERTY AND SECURITY (Harvard Law Sch. & Brookings Inst. 2011), http://www.brookings.edu/~/media/Files/rc/papers/2011/0921_platform_security_wittes/0921_platform_security_wittes.pdf.

Pete Yost, *Rise in FBI Use of National Security Letters*, WASH. POST, May 9, 2011, sec. A.

National Security Investigations

14

By Todd Hinnen

National Security Investigations (NSIs) are investigations conducted by the U.S. government, led by the Federal Bureau of Investigation (FBI), to acquire information that the government can use to protect the United States and its citizens from foreign threats to national security. NSIs take place within a legal framework that includes the Constitution, federal laws and regulations, and executive orders. The Attorney General Guidelines for Domestic FBI Operations and the FBI's Domestic Investigations and Operations Guide exist within this legal framework and govern the FBI's national security investigative activities.

NSIs are coordinated among all of the departments and agencies in the national security community and with law enforcement at the state and local levels. They also often depend on the support and assistance of foreign law enforcement and intelligence partners. They complement traditional investigative activities with foreign intelligence collection activities, such as the issuance of National Security Letters (NSLs) and search or surveillance orders under the Foreign Intelligence Surveillance Act[1] (FISA). They draw on all of the authorities and capabilities of the national security community and may result in a wide variety of national security activity, including increased security around the targets of national security threats, exclusion or removal of foreign persons illegally in the United States, arrest and prosecution of perpetrators, imposition of economic sanctions, diplomatic

---

1. 50 U.S.C. §§ 1801 *et seq.*, as amended (1978).

overtures to foreign governments, and actions undertaken by U.S. intelligence services or armed forces overseas.

This chapter provides historical context and a general overview of the institutions and authorities principally involved in NSIs and outlines how several formative historical events—including abuses in the 1950s and '60s, the end of the Cold War, and the increased threat of international terrorism—shaped the legal framework governing, and institutions involved in, modern NSIs. It also explains the legal and policy framework within which the FBI conducts modern NSIs and examines the oversight and other safeguards that aim to ensure that NSIs are conducted consistent with the rule of law and with due regard for privacy and civil liberties.

THE HISTORICAL FOUNDATIONS OF MODERN NATIONAL SECURITY INVESTIGATIONS

The institutions, legal authorities, and capabilities involved in national security investigations have evolved continuously since the modern national security community was created after World War II in the early days of the Cold War. Three particularly formative historical events—the Church Committee's exposure of abuse and recommendations for reform, the collapse of the Soviet Union, and the rise to prominence of international terrorism as a threat to the United States—shape the manner in which modern national security investigations are conducted.

Early Abuses and the Church Committee

In their 2007 treatise *National Security Investigations and Prosecutions*, David Kris and Douglas Wilson note: "Beginning after World War II, the intelligence community conducted investigations, and otherwise gathered information, in ways that systematically broke the law . . . [and] routinely violated . . . privacy rights of Americans."[2] Members of the intelligence community opened Americans' mail, surreptitiously entered their homes, conducted surveillance of their phone calls, and slipped them narcotics, such as LSD, to determine whether they became more amenable to recruitment or malleable in response to interrogation. The FBI also conducted sweeping, unrestrained investigations of groups dedicated to causes as diverse (and lawful) as women's liberation and racial equality.

In 1975, Congress established the Senate Select Committee to Study Governmental Operations with Respect to Intelligence Activities, more commonly called the Church Committee after its chairman, Sen. Frank Church of Idaho. In 1976, the Church Committee issued an extensive report on intelligence activities

---

2. DAVID S. KRIS & J. DOUGLAS WILSON, NATIONAL SECURITY INVESTIGATIONS AND PROSECUTIONS 2–3 (Thomson/West 2007).

that transgressed U.S. laws and Americans' rights. The recommendations for reform would become the foundation for the legislation, executive orders, policies, and guidelines that constitute the modern legal and oversight framework for intelligence activities, including national security investigations. This historic episode resulted in the first imperative of national security investigations: conduct them in a manner that respects privacy, civil liberties, and the rule of law.

The Collapse of the Soviet Union and the End of the Cold War

From its inception following World War II, the modern intelligence community was overwhelmingly focused on the threat posed by the Soviet Union and its satellites and regional proxies. The intelligence community's institutions and capabilities reflected this focus—they were designed to respond to a superpower nation-state adversary that threatened to undermine American interests around the world by incrementally expanding its own sphere of influence. The Soviet Union's collapse in 1991 left the intelligence community adrift and without particular focus. As Tim Weiner notes in *Legacy of Ashes*, his history of the Central Intelligence Agency (CIA), Director Robert Gates identified in his 1992 testimony before Congress "176 threats, from climate change to cybercrime," including nuclear, chemical, and biological weapons, narcotics and terrorism.[3] The CIA's budget fell for each of the next six years.

The Rise of the Threat of International Terrorism

In February 1998, a new threat to American national security announced its presence. Osama bin Laden issued a religious proclamation, stating:

> The ruling to kill the Americans and their allies—civilians and military—is an individual duty for every Muslim who can do it in any country in which it is possible to do it . . . We—with God's help—call on every Muslim who believes in God and wishes to be rewarded to comply with God's order to kill Americans and plunder their money wherever and whenever they find it.

On August 7, 1998, bin Laden's organization, al-Qaida, conducted synchronized suicide bombings of the U.S. embassies in Dar es Salaam, Tanzania, and Nairobi, Kenya, killing more than 220 people and injuring more than 4,000. On September 11, 2001, al-Qaida's coordinated suicide attacks on New York City and Washington, D.C., claimed nearly 3,000 lives. Three years too late, the national security community scrambled to adapt to a new and different threat to U.S. national security.

---

3. Tim Weiner, Legacy of Ashes: The History of the CIA 433–34 (Doubleday 2007).

Al-Qaida practiced some of the same tradecraft as the Soviet Union and other traditional nation-state adversaries of the United States—for instance, it communicated surreptitiously and sought to infiltrate secret operatives into the United States—but there were also crucial differences. Principal among these was objective: Al-Qaida was not interested in incremental gains in geopolitical influence; it was interested in spectacular, mass-casualty attacks against American civilian targets. Al-Qaida's objective, at least in the short term, was to undermine the U.S. economy, destabilize the U.S. political system, and exact revenge for perceived historic injustices by killing U.S. citizens. Unlike the Cold War, this conflict could not be mediated, or kept "cold," by mutual deterrence. Al-Qaida was not a nation-state with an economy, political system, and citizenry to protect. The asymmetry of this threat changed both the nature and the stakes of national security investigations.

More than ever, the intelligence community has to collect all of the threat information it may lawfully collect, share it broadly within the community, sift and analyze it, centralize it, and scrutinize it from multiple perspectives—a process still undergoing refinement, as evidenced by the November 5, 2009, attack by Army Maj. Nidal Hasan at Fort Hood in Texas and the December 25, 2009, failed attempt to blow up a commercial passenger airplane in flight by Umar Farouk Abdulmutallab. The intelligence community has to be infallible. Every plot has to be detected and prevented. Although infallibility cannot be achieved, it can be closely approximated by increasing the sources and volume of intelligence collection, diversifying and strengthening the cadre of analysts scrutinizing the data, and practicing "defense in depth," multiple layered security measures beginning halfway around the globe and ending at local hardware or beauty supply stores.

The September 11 attacks resulted in the second imperative of national security investigations: Detect and prevent every plot. The institutional structure and legal framework governing modern national security investigations seeks to satisfy both imperatives simultaneously—to protect the United States against every plot and to respect privacy, civil liberties, and the rule of law.

THE EMERGENCE OF A LEGAL FRAMEWORK

The Creation of the Modern Legal Framework

The principal components of a legal framework governing national security investigations followed quickly on the heels of the Church Committee report.

Executive Order 12,333

In 1976, President Gerald Ford issued Executive Order 11,905, controlling and directing intelligence organizations, setting forth their duties and responsibilities, and restricting and providing for oversight of their activities.[4] In 1981, President Ronald Reagan issued a successor order, Executive Order 12,333, which, with the incorporation of several subsequent amendments, delineates the current roles and responsibilities of each member institution of the intelligence community, sets forth procedural and substantive restrictions on their activities, and subjects them to oversight.[5] The order establishes the FBI as the lead agency responsible for the collection of foreign intelligence in the United States. Taking its cue from the Church Committee's finding that "the Attorney General is the most appropriate official to be charged with ensuring that the intelligence agencies conduct their activities in accordance with the law,"[6] the order also vests the attorney general with broad power to oversee the activities of the intelligence agencies, particularly those activities inside the United States and those relating to U.S. persons.

The Foreign Intelligence Surveillance Act

In 1978, Congress enacted FISA, a statute generally permitting the government to apply for, and a court to issue, an order authorizing electronic surveillance of agents of foreign powers inside the United States for foreign intelligence purposes, and providing for executive, legislative, and judicial oversight of such surveillance. FISA was subsequently amended to permit the government to apply for orders authorizing physical searches (1994), real-time acquisition of data relating to communications (but not the content of those communications) (1998), compelled production by a U.S. business of its records (1998), and compelled production by a U.S. business of "any tangible thing" (2001). In 2006, FISA was further amended to govern the government's acquisition in the United States of the communications of persons outside the United States, and its acquisition outside the United States of U.S. persons' communications.

For many years, law enforcement and intelligence officers were prevented, originally by internal Justice Department policy but eventually by Foreign Intelligence Surveillance Court (FISC) orders as well, from sharing information or collaborating. This created dangerous disconnects in which the law enforcement community had some information about a plot, the intelligence community had other information, but no one had the whole picture. After September 11, the government challenged a FISC order preventing cooperation between law enforcement and intelligence officers. For the first time in the 33 years since FISA was enacted, a FISC ruling was appealed to the Foreign Intelligence Surveillance Court of Review (FISCR).

In *In re Sealed Case*, the FISCR found that there was no basis in FISA's text or legislative history for preventing law enforcement and intelligence officers from

---

4. Exec. Order No. 11,905, 41 Fed. Reg. 7703 (Feb. 18, 1976).
5. Exec. Order No. 12,333, 46 Fed. Reg. 59,941 (Dec. 4, 1981), *as amended by* Exec. Order Nos. 13,284 (2003), 13,355 (2004), and 13,470 (2008).
6. Final Report of the Select Committee to Study Governmental Operations with Respect to Intelligence Activities, United States Senate, Report No. 755, 94th Cong., 2d Sess. Book II at 332 (1976).

sharing information and collaborating in the investigation of criminal activity that threatens national security.[7] To the contrary, the FISCR noted, "arresting and prosecuting terrorist agents of, or spies for, a foreign power may well be the best technique to prevent them from successfully continuing their terrorist or espionage activity."[8] Federal courts had misinterpreted case law that appeared to suggest the contrary, the FISCR held, and their reliance upon such precedent to impose strict separation between these core, overlapping government functions had been in error.

Ironically, as the FISCR noted, the executive branch had sought to address these erroneous judicial opinions in the USA PATRIOT Act. As a result of the changes codified in the act, FISA was amended to clarify that law enforcement and intelligence personnel could collaborate on investigations, including by using FISA, so long as obtaining foreign intelligence was a "significant purpose" of the surveillance activity. This legislative clarification, the FISCR noted, though *less* restrictive than the misunderstanding of law under which the executive and judicial branches had been laboring (i.e., that foreign intelligence collection had to be the *only* purpose for the surveillance), was *more* restrictive than the original FISA statute (which, the FISCR found, required only that foreign intelligence collection had to be *a* purpose for the surveillance). As a result, as the FISCR noted, today FISA surveillance can be utilized in a national security investigation "[s]o long as the government entertains a realistic option of dealing with the agent other than through criminal prosecution."[9]

Institutional Reform and the Creation of the National Security Division

National security institutions also changed in response to the September 11 attacks. In 2002, the Department of Homeland Security was created to prevent and respond to emergencies, from terrorist attacks to natural disasters. In 2004, the Office of the Director of National Intelligence was established to direct and oversee the intelligence community. And in 2005, the Commission on the Intelligence Capabilities of the United States Regarding Weapons of Mass Destruction, known as the WMD Commission, recommended the creation of a National Security Division (NSD) to consolidate the national security functions within the Department of Justice, to help "synthesize intelligence and law enforcement investigations," and to provide "more thoughtful, innovative, and constructive legal guidance" to the FBI and other national security agencies.[10] In 2006, Congress created the National Security Division in the Justice Department along with the position of assistant attorney general for national security, who would lead NSD and "serve

---

7. *In re* Sealed Case, 310 F.3d 717, 727 (FISA Ct. Rev. 2002).
8. *Id.* at 724.
9. *Id.* at 735.
10. The Commission on the Intelligence Capabilities of the United States Regarding Weapons of Mass Destruction, Report to the President of the United States 473 (March 31, 2005).

as the primary liaison to the Director of National Intelligence for the Department of Justice."[11]

NSD is the Department of Justice component responsible for, among other things, investigating and prosecuting terrorism, espionage, and other activities that threaten national security; representing the United States government in matters before the FISC; overseeing the development and implementation of department policy with regard to intelligence and national security matters; and advising the attorney general and the White House on matters relating to national security.

The Attorney General Guidelines and the FBI Guide

On October 31, 2003, Attorney General John Ashcroft signed the Guidelines for FBI National Security Investigations and Foreign Intelligence Collection (NSI Guidelines). They inaugurated several important concepts regarding national security investigations that endure in the current 2008 Attorney General Guidelines.

First, they are avowedly disposition-neutral. They do not reflect a preference or predisposition for prosecution over any of the other instrumentalities the government may use to address a threat to national security; the objective is to neutralize the threat in the most effective way possible. The NSI Guidelines note that there are

> a variety of measures to deal with threats to national security, . . . includ[ing], for example, recruitment of double agents and other assets; excluding or removing persons involved in terrorism or espionage from the United States; freezing assets of organizations that engage in or support terrorism; securing targets of terrorism or espionage; providing threat information and warnings to other federal agencies and officials, state and local governments, and private entities; diplomatic or military actions; and actions by other intelligence agencies to counter international terrorism or other national security threats.[12]

Second, they establish three stages of investigative activity with increasing authorities and constraints: assessments, preliminary investigations, and full investigations.

Third, they reflect the Church Committee's recommendation that national security authorities should be exercised as part of a legal framework that is mindful of privacy and civil liberties and that provides for effective oversight. The oversight provisions for national security investigations in the NSI Guidelines, in the successor 2008 AG Guidelines, and elsewhere are discussed briefly later in this chapter.

---

11. 28 U.S.C. § 507A.
12. THE ATTORNEY GENERAL'S GUIDELINES FOR FBI NATIONAL SECURITY INVESTIGATIONS AND FOREIGN INTELLIGENCE COLLECTION 2 (Oct. 31, 2003).

NATIONAL SECURITY INVESTIGATIONS

On September 29, 2008, Attorney General Michael Mukasey issued the current Guidelines for Domestic FBI Operations. These guidelines set forth the levels of investigation, the investigative methods an agent may use at each level, the approvals that an agent must obtain, and the documentation that an agent must maintain. The FBI, according to the document, is to be "both an agency that effectively detects, investigates, and prevents crimes, and an agency that effectively protects the national security and collects intelligence."[13] The objective of the guidelines is to provide for "full utilization of all authorities and investigative methods, consistent with the Constitution and laws of the United States, to protect the United States and its people from victimization by all crimes in violation of federal law, and to further the foreign intelligence objectives of the United States."[14] The general principles and directives contained in the 2008 AG Guidelines are translated into practical detail by the FBI's Domestic Investigations and Operations Guide (DIOG), more than 400 pages of rules that FBI agents must follow when exercising investigative and intelligence-gathering authorities.

The 2008 AG Guidelines and the resulting FBI guide begin with certain core principles intended to ensure that investigative and intelligence-gathering activities are lawful and duly respect Americans' privacy and civil liberties. All investigative and intelligence-gathering activities must have one or more valid purpose(s) set forth in the 2008 AG Guidelines and the DIOG. Agents must use the least intrusive means possible to obtain information. Agents must comply with the laws and the U.S. Constitution. Agents must report violations of law or noncompliance with the AG Guidelines or the DIOG committed during the course of investigative or intelligence collection activities. Agents may not collect or maintain information on U.S. persons solely for the purpose of monitoring activities protected by the First Amendment or the lawful exercise of other constitutional or legal rights.

The 2008 AG Guidelines and the DIOG require all FBI investigative and intelligence-gathering activity to occur within a three-tiered taxonomy. Assessments are the most basic level of investigative activity. Assessments can be conducted only for purposes authorized by the 2008 AG Guidelines and the DIOG, but agents need not satisfy any particular factual predication standard in order to open an assessment. Assessments are generally used to check investigative leads, identify potential human sources, or obtain available information about criminal activity or threats to national security. Only nine relatively unintrusive investigative methods are authorized for use in an assessment, including obtaining publicly available information, checking government records, interviewing members of the public, obtaining information from human sources, observing activities in plain view of the public, and issuing grand jury subpoenas to identify subscribers of a telephone or e-mail service. For each assessment, FBI agents are required to document "the authorized purpose and the clearly defined objective(s), as well as the use of any investigative

---

13. THE ATTORNEY GENERAL'S GUIDELINES FOR DOMESTIC FBI OPERATIONS 5 (Sept. 29, 2008).
14. Id.

methods."[15] The FBI receives tens of thousands of national security tips and leads each year and, while the FBI must look into every tip or lead, only a small fraction—typically less than 5 percent—result in preliminary or full investigations.

Suppose, for instance, that a worker doing repairs on the Brooklyn Bridge notices that on two consecutive days just before dusk, a car has parked under the bridge and a man, acting furtive and nervous, has gotten out and taken pictures of the bridge's support structure. The worker calls the FBI field office. The FBI opens an assessment for the purpose of determining whether the man poses a threat to the bridge. An agent can interview the bridge worker and conduct physical surveillance the following day to see if the man returns. If he does, the agent can take down his license plate number, access state motor vehicle records to determine who owns the car, and review the FBI's records for any other information regarding the owner. The agent can also ask the individual why he is taking pictures of the bridge. If the agent is satisfied there is an innocent explanation, he can close the assessment. If the agent has only grown more concerned and wants to use more intrusive investigative techniques, he must satisfy the factual predication standard (that is, document facts that indicate that a federal crime is occurring or a threat to national security exists) and approval and documentation requirements to open a preliminary investigation.

There are two types of "predicated investigations," or investigations for which agents must, among other requirements, satisfy a factual predication standard: preliminary investigations and full investigations. An agent may open a preliminary investigation (PI) only with the approval of a supervisor and only if there is information or an allegation indicating that a federal crime or threat to national security exists or that an individual, group, or property requires protection against attack or victimization. PIs must be concluded within six months, unless the special agent in charge of a field office extends the PI an additional six months. An agent may use any authorized investigative method in a PI *except for* electronic surveillance under the Wiretap Act or Foreign Intelligence Surveillance Act; physical searches authorized by a warrant or court order; and acquisition of foreign intelligence information pursuant to the FISA Amendments Act.

An agent may open a full investigation only with approval of a supervisor and only if there is a reasonable, articulable basis to believe that a federal crime or threat to national security has occurred, is occurring, or may occur; an individual, group, or property requires protection against attack or victimization; or the investigation may result in the acquisition of foreign intelligence. The FBI must notify the Department of Justice National Security Division of every full investigation of a U.S. person relating to a threat to national security or intended to result in the acquisition of foreign intelligence. An agent may use any of the 24 investigative methods authorized by the attorney general in a full investigation so long as he or she meets the factual predication, supervisory approval, and documentation requirements for each method used.

---

15. Domestic Investigations and Operations Guide, Federal Bureau of Investigation 5-1 (Oct. 15, 2011).

> The DIOG authorizes the following investigative methods: (1) consulting public information; (2) consulting FBI or Department of Justice records or information; (3) obtaining records or information from another federal or a state, local, or tribal government agency; (4) obtaining information from online services and resources; (5) using a confidential human source; (6) interviewing or requesting information from a person or entity; (7) receiving information from a person or entity; (8) physical surveillance not requiring a court order; (9) consensual monitoring of communications; (10) intercepting the communications of a computer trespasser; (11) using monitoring devices; (12) issuing administrative subpoenas; (13) issuing grand jury subpoenas; (14) issuing National Security Letters; (15) issuing a FISA order for business records; (16) obtaining stored communications; (17) installing a pen register or trap and trace device; (18) conducting a mail cover (obtaining information available on the outside of an envelope or package); (19) conducting a polygraph examination; (20) searching a subject's trash once it has been left in a public place for retrieval; (21) conducting an undercover operation; (22) executing a warrant or court order authorizing a search; (23) conducting criminal electronic surveillance; and (24) conducting FISA surveillance.

OVERSIGHT OF NATIONAL SECURITY INVESTIGATIONS

All three branches of government are actively involved in the oversight of NSIs. The means and level of oversight may vary with the intrusiveness of the investigative activity.

Executive Oversight

Agents, like all members of the intelligence community, are required to use the least intrusive means possible to achieve a valid investigative objective. An agent contemplating an investigative activity must also comply with the approval, predication, and documentation requirements in the 2008 guidelines and the DIOG. Substantial noncompliance must be reported to the FBI's Office of Integrity and Compliance and Office of the General Counsel (OGC). The most intrusive investigative techniques require the approval of a president-appointed, Senate-confirmed official at the Department of Justice. Investigative activity cannot be based solely on protected First Amendment speech, or on religion, race, ethnicity, or national origin. FBI supervisors are required to conduct regular "file reviews" of the documentation relating to each investigation. In addition, NSD and FBI OGC conduct regular reviews at each FBI field office of all aspects of the FBI's national security and foreign intelligence activities. Finally, the Department of Justice's Office of Inspector General can, and does with some vigor, investigate the use of national security authorities.

Judicial Oversight

Intrusive investigative activities are subject to the review of a federal judge. The most intrusive of these, such as regular or FISA search warrants and surveillance orders and FISA business records orders, require prior approval from a judge. Other intrusive activities, such as the issuance of NSLs and subpoenas, provide a mechanism for their recipients to seek judicial review. An individual subject to these authorities has another opportunity to subject them to judicial review if the government intends to use the information obtained as a result of them in a trial or other proceeding against that individual. And, of course, individuals can sue the government if they suffer harm or injury as a result of an improper exercise of national security authorities.

Legislative Oversight

The national security community is required to keep Congress "fully and currently informed of the Intelligence Activities of the United States."[16] The statutes granting intrusive investigative authorities, such as FISA and the NSL statutes, require regular reporting to Congress on the use of those authorities. In addition, the intelligence and judiciary (and often other) committees of both houses of Congress frequently hold oversight hearings regarding the use of national security investigative authorities (those hearings may be closed and classified in appropriate cases, to ensure that Congress receives a thorough briefing). Finally, some of those authorities sunset—that is, expire if Congress does not renew them—guaranteeing legislative review every two or three years.

CONCLUSION

National security investigations seek to harness and coordinate the authorities and capabilities of all members of the national security community, state and local law enforcement, and foreign law enforcement and intelligence partners. The objective of such investigations is to collect intelligence that can be used to address threats to national security. Such threats may be addressed in a variety of ways, including increased security around the targets of national security threats, exclusion or removal of foreign persons illegally in the United States, arrest and prosecution of perpetrators, imposition of economic sanctions, diplomatic overtures to foreign governments, and actions undertaken by our intelligence services or armed forces overseas. NSIs are conducted at the crossroads of two imperatives, which are the legacies of formative historical experiences: (1) conduct investigations in a manner that respects privacy, civil liberties, and the rule of law, and

---

16. 50 U.S.C. § 413(a)(1).

(2) detect and prevent every plot. Whether the current institutional structure and legal framework best accomplishes these two imperatives is, appropriately, the subject of ongoing debate and discussion.

EXPERTS

Todd Hinnen (author), former Deputy Assistant Attorney General and Acting Assistant Attorney General for National Security; (202) 654-6259; (202) 821-8962 (m); THinnen@perkinscoie.com

David Kris, former Assistant Attorney General for National Security; (425) 283-4738; david@intven.com

Pat Rowan, former Assistant Attorney General for National Security; (202) 857-1758; prowan@mcguirewoods.com

Ken Wainstein, former Assistant Attorney General for National Security; (202) 862-2474; ken.wainstein@cwt.com

RESOURCES

Exec. Order No. 12,333, 46 Fed. Reg. 59,941 (Dec. 4, 1981), *as amended by* Exec. Order Nos. 13,284 (2003), 13,355 (2004), and 13,470 (2008).

THE ATTORNEY GENERAL'S GUIDELINES FOR FBI NATIONAL SECURITY INVESTIGATIONS AND FOREIGN INTELLIGENCE COLLECTION (Oct. 31, 2003).

THE ATTORNEY GENERAL'S GUIDELINES FOR DOMESTIC FBI OPERATIONS (Sept. 29, 2008).

FED. BUREAU OF INVESTIGATION, DOMESTIC INVESTIGATIONS AND OPERATIONS GUIDE (Oct. 15, 2011).

DAVID S. KRIS & J. DOUGLAS WILSON, NATIONAL SECURITY INVESTIGATIONS AND PROSECUTIONS (Thomson/West 2007).

Electronic Surveillance and Cybersecurity

15

By James X. Dempsey

This chapter focuses on the law concerning government surveillance of communications for national security purposes. It describes the rules for real-time interception of communications as well as the rules for government access to stored communications (e-mail, for example) and to transactional data regarding communications. It describes the basic elements of the Foreign Intelligence Surveillance Act[1] (FISA) and the parallel set of laws regulating surveillance in criminal investigations. It also touches upon government access to other records, such as banking and credit card transactions. Finally, the chapter reviews some special issues associated with government monitoring for cybersecurity purposes.

CONSTITUTIONAL ORIGINS

The law of electronic surveillance has its roots in the Fourth Amendment to the Constitution, whose basic standards are interpreted by the courts and supplemented by congressional statute.

Note that the amendment regulates only "searches and seizures." If something is not a search or a seizure, it falls outside the limits of the amendment. The Supreme Court has a two-prong test for what constitutes a "search:"

---

1. Foreign Intelligence Surveillance Act, 50 U.S.C. §§ 1801 *et seq.*, as amended (1978).

1. A physical intrusion on private property for the purpose of obtaining information;
2. An activity that infringes on a reasonable expectation of privacy. (This is known as the "reasonable expectation of privacy test;" it is not very well defined but has been applied in many cases.)[2]

Leaving aside arrests, a "seizure," the Court has said, is any meaningful interference with a person's possessory interest in property—that is, taking control of the property and denying control to others.

The Fourth Amendment to the Constitution

"The right of the people to be secure in their persons, houses, papers, and effects, against unreasonable searches and seizures, shall not be violated, and no Warrants shall issue, but upon probable cause, supported by Oath or affirmation, and particularly describing the place to be searched, and the persons or things to be seized."

Content versus Noncontent

The courts have perennially struggled to apply the Fourth Amendment to new technology, dating back to the Supreme Court's 1928 ruling that wiretapping was not a search or seizure and was, therefore, outside the Fourth Amendment.[3] That decision was reversed in 1967, when the Court articulated the reasonable expectation of privacy test.[4] It is now widely accepted that the interception of the contents of any private electronic communication in transit—voice, e-mail, texts, instant messages, and other private Internet communications—is a search under the Fourth Amendment.

On the other hand, the Supreme Court held in the 1970s that individuals have no reasonable expectation of privacy in the dialed-number information showing who called whom and when.[5] When you voluntarily disclose data to a third party (such as a telephone company or a bank in the case of financial data), the Supreme Court said, you surrender your privacy interest in that data. This means, the Court concluded, that the interception of dialed-number information, unlike the interception of the contents of a communication, is not a search.

Until recently, these 1970s cases were read to mean that there is no constitutional privacy interest in any of the noncontent data that is associated with electronic communications—for example, the dialed-number information or Internet-address information showing who is communicating with whom—even

---
2. Katz v. United States, 389 U.S. 347 (1967).
3. Olmstead v. United States, 277 U.S. 438 (1928).
4. *Katz*, 389 U.S. 347.
5. Smith v. Maryland, 442 U.S. 735 (1979). *See also* United States v. Miller, 425 U.S. 435 (1976).

in very large volumes and even though that data can be highly revealing of a person's associations and patterns of activity. That assumption guided Congress in drafting the statutes governing electronic surveillance, and it also was key to the executive branch's view of its surveillance powers. However, in January 2012, in *United States v. Jones*, the Supreme Court cast doubt on the broader readings of the so-called third-party doctrine.[6] *Jones* involved the government's planting of a GPS device on a drug suspect's car. The government argued that Jones had voluntarily disclosed his location to anyone who happened to observe him on the public streets, but the Court unanimously concluded that the use of the device to track Jones for 28 days was a search. Most importantly, five justices were of the view that the collection of location data over a prolonged period of time was a search even without the physical intrusion involved in attaching the GPS device to the bottom of the suspect's car; in other words, the use of the GPS device violated a reasonable expectation of privacy. It will be years before the courts flesh out the implications of the *Jones* case, but it seems clear that it can no longer be assumed quite so confidently that the collection of broad swaths of transactional data is not a "search."

"Reasonableness" in the National Security Context

Note that the Fourth Amendment does not prohibit all searches and seizures—only "unreasonable" ones. Generally, an unreasonable search or seizure is one conducted without a judicial warrant. The second half of the amendment describes how a warrant should be issued and what its essential elements are. However, the courts have recognized many exceptions to the warrant requirement, finding searches in various circumstances reasonable without a warrant (for example, searches at the border, pursuant to arrest, or in emergencies).

One may hear general comments about a "national security exception to the Fourth Amendment," but in fact it seems pretty clear that the Fourth Amendment applies to all foreign intelligence surveillance activity inside the United States. Instead, the question is whether there is a national security exception to the warrant requirement. Even the drafters of the initial FISA recognized that there were some types of searches or seizures carried out inside the United States for national security purposes that were "reasonable" in the absence of a warrant. For example, FISA includes an emergency exception, permitting surveillance for up to 48 hours without a warrant in defined emergency circumstances.

The Supreme Court has never ruled on the question of whether there is a national security or foreign intelligence exception to the warrant requirement. However, in 2008, the Foreign Intelligence Surveillance Court of Review (FISCR) squarely held that "a foreign intelligence exception to the Fourth Amendment's warrant requirement exists when surveillance is conducted to obtain foreign

---

6. United States v. Jones, 132 S. Ct. 945 (2012), *available at* http://www.supremecourt.gov/opinions/11pdf/10-1259.pdf.

intelligence for national security purposes and is directed against foreign powers or agents of foreign powers reasonably believed to be located outside the United States."[7] The court found that intelligence collection fit within the so-called "special needs" exception recognized by the Supreme Court, under which compliance with the warrant clause could be excused where the purpose behind the government action went beyond routine law enforcement and insisting on a warrant would materially interfere with the accomplishment of that purpose. Such searches remain subject to the Fourth Amendment's reasonableness standard, which should be assessed, the court said, considering the "totality of the circumstances." The court found that the searches at issue (conducted under the now-expired Protect America Act) were reasonable because they were conducted pursuant to "a matrix of safeguards" that included targeting and minimization procedures and a finding of probable cause by the attorney general.[8] The decision of the FISCR is binding only on the judges of the FISC. Since the attacks of September 11, 2001, other trial and appellate courts have upheld FISA as amended by the USA PATRIOT Act and have rejected arguments that the court orders issued under FISA do not satisfy the Fourth Amendment, but no other appellate court since 9/11 has ruled so flatly on whether there is a foreign intelligence exception to the warrant requirement.

"Agent of a Foreign Power"

One more item of historical background may be helpful. In 1972, the Supreme Court decided the so-called *Keith* case involving the warrantless wiretapping of a group opposed to the Vietnam War.[9] The Supreme Court rejected the government's argument that there is a "domestic security" exception to the warrant requirement. However, the Court explicitly declined to address "issues which may be involved with respect to activities of foreign powers or their agents."[10] The *Keith* case set the stage for adoption of FISA. A consensus developed between Congress and the executive branch that it would be best to put foreign intelligence and national security wiretapping on a firm basis with the adoption of a statute. The Court's reference to "foreign powers or their agents" in the *Keith* case became a crucial concept in subsequent court cases and in FISA.

---

7. *In re* Directives [Redacted Text] Pursuant to Section 105B of the Foreign Intelligence Surveillance Act, 551 F.3d 1004 (FISA Ct. Rev. 2008).

8. The PAA authorized senior intelligence officials to issue directives to communications service providers ordering them to assist in acquiring foreign intelligence when the surveillance targeted persons reasonably believed to be located outside the United States.

9. United States v. U.S. District Court, 407 U.S. 297 (1972).

10. *Id.* at 321–22.

STATUTES REGULATING ELECTRONIC SURVEILLANCE AND RELATED ACTIVITIES

As explained in chapter 14, national security investigations can take place under two parallel sets of authority, one for law enforcement investigations and one for foreign intelligence or counterintelligence investigations. ("Foreign intelligence" in this context means information about threats from abroad—about the activities and intentions of foreign powers—whether that information is collected inside or outside the United States.) In straight criminal investigations, electronic surveillance and related collection activities are governed by the federal Wiretap Act[11] (sometimes called Title III because it was first enacted as Title III of the 1968 omnibus anticrime bill), the Stored Communications Act[12] (sometimes referred to as the Electronic Communications Privacy Act, or ECPA, although it is only one part of that 1986 statute), and statutory provisions governing use of pen registers and trap and trace devices, which were adopted as part of ECPA. FISA governs surveillance in intelligence investigations.

With the dismantling of the "wall" in the Patriot Act (discussed below), information collected in criminal investigations can be shared with the intelligence community, and information collected under FISA can be shared with law enforcement officials and used in criminal investigations, but the twin sets of authority remain.

The statutes in question are very complicated—they share some definitions, but each uses some unique terms—and it is impossible to give here anything but an overview. One way to describe how the varying laws work is to examine key techniques used by the government in the following areas:

- real-time interception of the content of communications
- physical searches
- access to stored communications (such as e-mails maintained by a service provider)
- acquisition of noncontent in real time
- access to stored noncontent
- access to other noncontent records and things

Content Interception

As a general rule, the federal Wiretap Act makes it a crime to intercept within the United States the content of an electronic communication without a court order. (As a result of the Electronic Communications Privacy Act, the Wiretap Act applies to all kinds of communications in transit, including both voice and data, and all kinds

---

11. 18 U.S.C. §§ 2510–2522, as amended.
12. 18 U.S.C. §§ 2701–2712 (1986).

of Internet communications over a wire or by wireless means.) Title III has various exceptions—for example, permitting surveillance with the consent of one party to the communication. The next few paragraphs focus on the rules authorizing the government to intercept communications with a court order issued under either Title III or FISA. Later, the chapter addresses the acquisition of information under the special procedures authorized in the FISA Amendments Act of 2008.

Under Title III, a federal prosecutor, with the approval of a senior official, may apply to a court of competent jurisdiction for an order to intercept communications while investigating certain crimes listed in the statute. The list of these "predicate crimes" was once very short, limited only to serious offenses, but the list has been expanded vastly over time. The various terrorism offenses, as well as espionage and sabotage, are all predicate offenses. The statute spells out what must be contained in the government's application, including a detailed sworn statement of supporting facts. (Title III also authorizes state officials, where the state has adopted its own wiretap law with comparable procedures, to apply for wiretap orders from state courts.) An order can be issued only if the court finds probable cause (the words used in the Fourth Amendment) to believe that (1) an individual is committing, has committed, or is about to commit a crime; (2) particular communications concerning the offense will be obtained through such interception; and (3) except in the case of roving taps, the facilities to be tapped are being used in connection with the commission of the offense. The court must also find that normal investigative techniques have been unsuccessful, appear to be unlikely to succeed, or appear to be too dangerous. The order must generally specify the facility (the phone number or Internet account) to be monitored and the identity of the person, if known, whose communications are to be intercepted. Title III authorizes roving taps, which specify the target rather than the facility. Wiretap orders are generally issued for 30 days, subject to renewal. The order authorizing the surveillance generally also includes a direction to a telephone company or other entity to furnish the assistance necessary to accomplish the surveillance. Within a reasonable time after completion of the surveillance, the targets must be notified that their communications were intercepted.

As a general rule, FISA also requires a court order to intercept a communication inside the United States. However, there are some major differences between Title III and FISA:

- While Title III requires probable cause of criminal activity, FISA requires probable cause to believe that the target of the surveillance is a foreign power or an agent of a foreign power.
- While Title III applies the same rules to U.S. citizens and noncitizens, FISA sets somewhat different rules for "U.S. persons" and "non-U.S. persons."
- While Title III regulates "interception," FISA regulates "electronic surveillance," which is defined in a very complicated four-part definition; the definition of "electronic surveillance" is both somewhat narrower and somewhat broader than the Title III definition of "interception."

- While the initial length of Title III wiretaps is 30 days, FISA authorizations vary in length from 90 days to a year, depending on the nature of the target.
- While persons whose communications are intercepted under Title III are entitled to notice after the investigation concludes, FISA taps remain secret forever, unless the government seeks to use evidence from one in a criminal prosecution.

A lot of the substance of FISA is contained in its definitions section, so a summary of key terms is essential to understanding the statute.

First, a term already used in this chapter: A "U.S. person" is basically a U.S. citizen, a permanent resident alien, an unincorporated association of which a substantial number of members are citizens or permanent resident aliens, or a corporation incorporated in the United States and not controlled by a foreign government.

Two other key terms are "foreign power" and "agent of a foreign power." "Foreign power" is defined to include a foreign government, an entity controlled and directed by a foreign government, a foreign-based political organization not substantially composed of U.S. persons, or "a group engaged in international terrorism or activities in preparation therefor." The definition of an "agent of a foreign power" is more complicated. It is any non-U.S. person who (1) acts in the United States as an officer or employee of a foreign power or as a member of an international terrorist organization, (2) acts for or on behalf of a foreign power that engages in clandestine intelligence activities in the United States, or (3) engages in international terrorism or activities in preparation for international terrorism (the "lone wolf"). A U.S. person (and any non-U.S. person as well) is an agent of a foreign power if he or she (1) knowingly engages in clandestine intelligence-gathering activities for or on behalf of a foreign power that involve or may involve a criminal violation; (2) knowingly engages in sabotage, international terrorism, or activities to prepare for sabotage or international terrorism for or on behalf of a foreign power; or (3) knowingly aids, abets, or conspires with any person in the conduct of such activities.

Another crucial term in FISA is "electronic surveillance," which, in the simplest terms, is defined as

- the acquisition of the contents of any wire or radio communication to or from a particular, known U.S. person who is in the United States by intentionally targeting that person;
- the acquisition of any wire communication to or from a person in the United States if the acquisition occurs in the United States;
- the intentional acquisition of the contents of any radio communication under circumstances in which a person has a reasonable expectation of privacy and a warrant would be required for law enforcement purposes, if both the sender and all intended recipients are inside the United States;

- the installation and use of a bug or other device in the United States for monitoring to acquire information, other than from a wire or electronic communication.

With those definitions in mind, the essence of FISA's wiretapping provisions can be stated fairly simply: FISA authorizes the U.S. government to apply for a court order to conduct electronic surveillance inside the United States for the purpose of obtaining foreign intelligence information, and it authorizes judges of a special court to issue orders approving the electronic surveillance if they find probable cause to believe that the target of the surveillance is a "foreign power" or an "agent of a foreign power" and that the facilities or places at which the surveillance is directed are being used by a foreign power or agent of a foreign power. The special court, the Foreign Intelligence Surveillance Court (FISC), is made up of 11 sitting federal judges designated by the chief justice of the United States for additional duty on the FISC. Denials of the government's applications and other decisions of the FISC can be appealed to a three-judge Foreign Intelligence Surveillance Court of Review (FISCR).

Physical Searches

While this chapter deals mainly with electronic surveillance, it should not be forgotten that the Fourth Amendment at its core protects Americans' homes, offices, and physical effects. Generally, to conduct a physical search of a home or office, the government must obtain a warrant from a judge, and generally the government must serve the warrant on the occupant at the time of the search. However, both under the criminal law and on the intelligence side, the government carries out secret searches pursuant to a warrant but without notice, which critics call "black-bag jobs."

In the criminal context, the government refers to these as "delayed-notice searches." Prior to the Patriot Act, several federal courts had approved search warrants in criminal cases allowing the government to enter a person's house when he was away, search the premises and take or copy things, and delay notifying the subject for days or months. In the Patriot Act, Congress codified the practice, authorizing its use in any criminal case not only when notifying the suspect would endanger someone's life or lead the suspect to flee from prosecution, but also whenever notice would "otherwise seriously jeopardize an investigation or unduly delay a trial."[13]

FISA also contains a provision for physical searches, authorizing the FISA court to issue orders permitting surreptitious entry in cases meeting the basic FISA standard—probable cause to believe that the target of the search is a foreign power or an agent of a foreign power. In contrast to the criminal justice use

---

13. 18 U.S.C. § 2105, incorporated by reference in § 213 of the United and Strengthening America by Providing Appropriate Tools Required to Intercept and Obstruct Terrorism Act of 2001 (USA PATRIOT ACT), Pub. L. No. 107-56, 115 Stat. 286 (Oct. 12, 2001).

> ### The "Wall" and FISA's Purpose Requirement
>
> When FISA was first enacted, it required a senior official to certify that "the purpose" of the surveillance was to obtain foreign intelligence information. That provision led to the belief that FISA could not be used to collect information if the purpose was criminal prosecution. Rigid interpretation of the purpose requirement contributed to the "wall" that prevented information collected under the criminal justice powers of Title III from flowing to intelligence agencies and that prevented foreign intelligence collected under FISA from being shared with criminal investigators. The wall became so thick that agents on criminal squads were prohibited from talking with agents on intelligence squads even when they were investigating the same group. The interpretation and application of the wall generated intense but secret debate inside the executive branch and led to sharp disagreement with the FISA court, lasting through the months leading up to 9/11.
>
> Provisions in the USA PATRIOT Act helped tear down the wall, permitting information sharing in both directions. Section 203 revised the Wiretap Act and Federal Rule of Criminal Procedure 6(e) to permit sharing of Title III and grand jury material involving foreign intelligence or counterintelligence with intelligence or national security officials to assist them in performing their duties. In terms of FISA, perhaps the most important change that the Patriot Act made was a "cut and bite" amendment that changed the word "the" to "a significant" so that FISA could be used when "a significant purpose" of the surveillance was to collect foreign intelligence. By implication, the change meant that FISA could be used when the primary purpose was to collect evidence of a crime being carried out by or on behalf of a foreign power.
>
> In 2002, the Foreign Intelligence Surveillance Court of Review held that the use of FISA for investigation of "foreign intelligence crimes" is constitutional. Noting that Congress in the Patriot Act had required that "a significant purpose" of the surveillance must be to obtain foreign intelligence, the court also held that the wall was never required under the initial FISA.

of the technique, physical searches under FISA remain secret forever unless the government seeks to introduce as evidence the information obtained in the course of such a search.

Access to Stored Communications

The Wiretap Act only applies to the real-time interception of electronic communications. A separate statute, the Stored Communications Act (SCA), adopted in 1986 as part of ECPA (and sometimes referred to as ECPA, as noted above), regulates government access to stored communications in criminal investigations. It has its own complications. In limited circumstances, the SCA requires a judicial warrant for the government to compel an e-mail service provider to disclose stored e-mail. However, under the terms of the SCA, the warrant requirement only applies to stored e-mail less than 181 days old. Moreover, the government argues that the warrant requirement only applies to unread e-mail in someone's in-box, not to e-mail in one's out-box, nor to opened e-mail. All of those communications, the government argues, are available with a subpoena, issued by a prosecutor, a Federal Bureau of Investigation (FBI) agent, or another official without approval of a judge. Likewise, the government argues that a subpoena can be used to compel disclosure of documents stored "in the cloud." Many Internet users probably do not understand that by storing their documents remotely, rather than on their local hard drive, they are, in the view of the Justice Department, giving up Fourth Amendment protection and making such documents available to the government without a court order.

The U.S. Court of Appeals for the Sixth Circuit has held the Stored Communications Act unconstitutional to the extent that it allows access to stored e-mail without a warrant.[14] In 2011, the initial author of ECPA, Sen. Patrick Leahy of Vermont, introduced legislation to amend ECPA to require a warrant in most cases for government access to e-mail or other private content stored with a service provider; the legislation had not been approved. Leading service providers take the position that access to their customers' content requires a warrant.

In contrast to ECPA, FISA does not expressly address the standards for government access to stored e-mail. Stored e-mail and voicemail communications are neither "wire communications" nor "radio communications" under FISA, and until recently it was quite unclear how stored communications fit within the FISA scheme. However, recent court decisions regarding e-mail privacy in ordinary criminal cases make it likely that stored e-mail is covered by FISA either under the fourth prong of the definition of electronic surveillance or under FISA's provision for physical searches. Both of those sections regulate situations where the government acquires information "under circumstances in which a person has a reasonable expectation of privacy and a warrant would be required for law enforcement purposes."[15] In December 2010, the U.S. Court of Appeals for the Sixth Circuit, in the case mentioned just above, held that persons have a reasonable expectation of privacy in their stored e-mail and that a warrant is required for law enforcement access. In an earlier case, the U.S. Court of Appeals for the Ninth Circuit held the same with respect to stored text messages.[16] (The Supreme Court reversed and remanded the Ninth Circuit's decision on other grounds, leaving untouched the ruling on reasonable expectation of privacy.) Conversely, no federal appeals court holds the view that there is no reasonable expectation of privacy in

---

14. United States v. Warshak, 631 F.3d 266 (6th Cir. 2010).
15. Foreign Intelligence Surveillance Act, *supra* note 1, 50 U.S.C. §§ 1801(f)(4) and 1821(5) (1978).
16. Quon v. Arch Wireless Operating Co., 529 F.3d 892 (9th Cir. 2008), *rev'd on other grounds sub nom.* City of Ontario v. Quon, 130 S. Ct. 2619 (2010).

stored e-mail. These cases seem to represent the direction of the law and would seem likely to be followed in a case arising under FISA.

Transactional Data

Just as the surveillance laws have different provisions for access to the content of communications in real time and from storage, there are also separate provisions for access to transactional data in real time and from storage.

On the criminal side, access to dialed-number information in real time, which is carried out using a pen register or trap and trace device, requires a court order. For stored transactional data, the Stored Communications Act authorizes the government to use a subpoena to require a provider of electronic communication service or remote computing service (a term that encompasses cloud storage services) to disclose subscriber identifying information and local and long distance telephone connection records (call detail records similar to those that would be collected by a pen register). To obtain records of Internet activity, such as web-browsing logs and to-and-from e-mail information, the government cannot use a subpoena. It must obtain at least a so-called (d) order, issued by a court only if the government offers "specific and articulable" facts showing that there are reasonable grounds to believe that the records are relevant and material to an ongoing criminal investigation.

On the foreign intelligence side, various statutes authorize the government to compel companies to disclose records about their customers using what are called National Security Letters (NSLs). Mostly, the FBI issues these NSLs. Generally, they can be issued whenever the material sought is relevant to a national security investigation. Under ECPA, the FBI may use NSLs to obtain subscriber identifying information, telephone billing records, and, arguably, transactional records regarding electronic communications. Under the Right to Financial Privacy Act, the FBI has the authority to issue NSLs for the financial records of a person or entity from various types of financial institutions, such as banks, credit unions, and credit card companies. Under provisions of the Fair Credit Reporting Act, the FBI has the authority to issue three different, but related, types of NSLs to credit reporting agencies. Finally, under special standards, certain agencies have the authority to issue NSLs pursuant to the National Security Act in the course of investigations of improper disclosure of classified information by government employees; in those cases, the records sought must pertain to a person who is or was an executive branch employee and who provided consent to the government to access his financial records, consumer reports, and travel information as a condition of his access to classified information. All of the National Security Letter statutes contain provisions barring recipients from disclosing the NSLs or even the fact that one has been received (except to an attorney or other person whose assistance is required to comply) based upon a certification by the government that nondisclosure is necessary.

Pen Registers and Trap and Trace Devices

Traditionally, a pen register was a device that recorded the numbers dialed on outgoing phone calls; a trap and trace device captured the number of origination for incoming calls. Today, the functions are essentially computerized, and a pen register is normally operated in conjunction with a trap and trace device, recording not only number of origin and destination for calls but also other transactional data. As explained above, the Supreme Court has held that the Fourth Amendment affords no privacy protection to the dialing information showing who is calling whom. Lower courts and Congress have assumed that the Court's reasoning applies to other forms of signaling and routing information.

By statute, Congress has adopted rules requiring a court order for the interception of metadata in real time. In criminal cases, the Pen Register Act (18 U.S.C. §§ 3121–3127) requires a court order, but it does not require a finding of probable cause. In fact, it requires no finding of suspicion at all by the court. Instead, the statute says that the court "shall" approve the government's application so long as the government certifies that the information sought is relevant to an ongoing investigation. The USA PATRIOT Act included a provision making it clear that the pen/trap authority applies to e-mail and Internet communications. Thus, the e-mail equivalent of a pen/trap device can collect to and from lines of e-mail (but not the subject line, which is considered content).

FISA has its own provisions authorizing applications and orders for pen/trap collection in foreign intelligence investigations. As amended by the Patriot Act, FISC judges and certain specially designated magistrates can authorize installation and use of a pen/trap if the government certifies that the information likely to be obtained is foreign intelligence information not concerning a U.S. person or is relevant to an ongoing investigation to protect against international terrorism or clandestine intelligence activities, provided that such investigation of a U.S. person is not conducted solely on the basis of activities protected by the First Amendment.

Access to Other Noncontent Records and Tangible Things

FISA has a provision for court orders requiring the production of "any tangible things (including books, records, papers, documents and other items) for an investigation to obtain foreign intelligence information not concerning a United States person or to protect against international terrorism or clandestine intelligence activities."[17] (Such investigation cannot be conducted solely on the basis of activities protected by the First Amendment.) Before the Patriot Act, the court orders were limited to certain travel-related records and records regarding the use of storage facilities, and the court order for disclosure could be issued

---

17. Foreign Intelligence Surveillance Act, *supra* note 1, 18 U.S.C. § 1861.

only if there were "specific and articulable" facts giving reason to believe that the person to whom the records being sought pertained was a foreign power or an agent of a foreign power.

Section 215 of the Patriot Act rewrote the provision to apply to any record or tangible thing, and it required only that the government specify in its application that the records concerned were sought for an authorized investigation to obtain foreign intelligence information not concerning a U.S. person or to protect against international terrorism or clandestine intelligence activities. The change drew particular opposition and came to be known as the "library records provision."

In 2006, Congress amended section 215 to require the government to include in its application for a disclosure order a statement of facts showing that there are reasonable grounds to believe that the records or other tangible things sought are relevant to an authorized investigation (other than a mere threat assessment) to obtain foreign intelligence information not concerning a U.S. person or to protect against international terrorism or clandestine intelligence activities. If the records sought are library circulation records, library patron lists, book sale records, book customer lists, firearms sales records, tax return records, or educational or medical records, the application can be submitted only with the approval of the FBI director or one of two other senior FBI officials.

In 2005, the Department of Justice reported to Congress that it had obtained 35 orders under section 215. In contrast, the FBI issued 49,425 National Security Letters in 2006 and 24,287 in 2010 regarding 14,212 people.

The Warrantless Surveillance Program and the FISA Amendments Act

Soon after the 9/11 attacks, the government began a warrantless wiretapping program. The exact nature of the program is not publicly known, but it apparently involved some form of surveillance that required a warrant under FISA. After the program was revealed in December 2005 by *The New York Times*, the Bush administration publicly offered a number of justifications. Most prominently, it argued that the 2001 Authorization for Use of Military Force[18] provided statutory authority to engage in electronic surveillance outside the "exclusive means" prescribed by FISA. Also, the Justice Department suggested that FISA was unconstitutional to the extent that it interfered with a core exercise of the president's powers as commander in chief. The constitutional question was mooted, but not resolved, with the enactment of the FISA Amendments Act of 2008[19] (FAA), in which Congress authorized a new form of activity not requiring the type of judicial orders traditionally associated with FISA surveillance.

---

18. Pub. L. No. 107-40, 115 Stat. 224 (2001).
19. H.R. 6304, 110th Cong. (2008).

The FAA added to FISA a new title that does not rely on the term "electronic surveillance." Instead, its key concept is "acquisition," which the new provisions do not define. The new title states that the attorney general and the director of national intelligence may authorize jointly, for a period of up to one year on a renewable basis, "the targeting of persons reasonably believed to be located outside the United States to acquire foreign intelligence information."[20] There is no need to believe that the targets are foreign powers or their agents. Instead, the main substantive determination concerns the location of the targeted person. "Person" means any individual, group, entity, association, corporation, or foreign power.

The acquisition authority granted by the statute is subject to several requirements and limitations, including:

- An acquisition may be conducted only in accordance with "targeting procedures" that are "reasonably designed" to ensure that any acquisition is limited to targeting persons reasonably believed to be located outside the United States and to "prevent the intentional acquisition" of any communication as to which the sender and all intended recipients are known at the time of the acquisition to be located in the United States.
- An acquisition may be conducted only in accordance with "minimization procedures" adopted by the attorney general.

The targeting procedures and the minimization procedures must be submitted to the FISC. The court must review the targeting procedures to assess whether they are reasonably designed to ensure that an acquisition is limited to targeting persons reasonably believed to be located outside the United States and to prevent the intentional acquisition of domestic-to-domestic communications. The court must review the minimization procedures to assess whether they meet the definition of minimization in FISA. If the court finds that the procedures are consistent with the requirements of the statute and with the Fourth Amendment, the court shall enter an order approving their use for an acquisition. Upon the issuance of such an order, or upon the determination of the attorney general and director of national intelligence in exigent circumstances, the attorney general and the director of national intelligence may direct, in writing, an electronic communication service provider to provide the government with all information, facilities, or assistance necessary to accomplish the acquisition. Providers may challenge such directives in the FISC, and the government may seek FISC orders compelling compliance from a recalcitrant provider.

The FISA Amendments Act of 2008 made two other relatively small but significant changes. First, it made it clear that when the government seeks to conduct surveillance inside the United States targeting a U.S. person who is located outside the United States, the government must obtain a FISA court order based on the basic showing of probable cause to believe that the target is an agent of a

---

20. *Id.*

foreign power. (An example might be a U.S. person living abroad whose e-mail is available from a service provider inside the United States.)

Second, the FAA required the government, when it wants to conduct surveillance outside the United States against a U.S. person reasonably believed to be outside the United States, to obtain a FISA court order. This is the one situation in which the FISC has jurisdiction to issue an order authorizing conduct outside the United States. It appears that the authority covers not only electronic surveillance but other forms of "acquisition" as well.

The American Civil Liberties Union brought suit on behalf of various individuals and organizations to challenge the FAA immediately after it was enacted. The government argued that the plaintiffs did not have "standing" to challenge the law because they could not show that their communications were in fact being monitored.[21] In March 2011, the U.S. Court of Appeals for the Second Circuit ruled that the case could go forward without the plaintiffs first showing with certainty that they had been spied on under the statute. In May 2012, the Supreme Court, at the government's request, took the case to determine whether the plaintiffs had standing.

CYBERSECURITY

The electronic surveillance laws allow telephone companies, Internet service providers, and other service providers to monitor their own systems for cybersecurity purposes and to disclose to the government and to their peers information about cyberattack incidents for the purpose of protecting their own networks. In particular, the Wiretap Act provides that it is lawful for any provider of electronic communication service to intercept, disclose, or use communications passing over its network while engaged in any activity that is a necessary incident to the protection of the rights and property of the provider. This includes the authority to disclose communications to the government or to another private entity when doing so is necessary to protect the service provider's network from cyberattacks. Likewise, under ECPA, a service provider, when necessary to protect its system, can disclose stored communications and customer records to any governmental or private entity. Furthermore, under the Wiretap Act, it is lawful for a service provider to invite the government to intercept the communications of a "computer trespasser."

However, there is widespread concern that these provisions do not give service providers enough latitude to share information for their mutual defense. In 2012, Congress was considering legislation that would amend the surveillance laws to create a wider exception for information sharing for cybersecurity purposes. Already, under existing authorities, the National Security Agency is sharing

---

21. Amnesty Int'l USA v. McConnell, 646 F. Supp. 2d 633 (S.D.N.Y. 2009), *summary judgment granted*, No. 09-4112 (2nd Cir. 2011), *cert. granted sub. nom.* Clapper v. Amnesty Int'l USA, No. 11-1025, 132 S. Ct. 2431 (May 21, 2012).

with the major Internet service providers information it has about cyberattack signatures, which the providers are using to better protect their customers, especially those working on defense contracts.

EXPERTS

Todd Hinnen, Partner, Perkins Coie; former Acting Assistant Attorney General for National Security; (202) 654-6259; (202) 821-8962 (m); THinnen@perkinscoie.com

Jameel Jaffer, ACLU, lead attorney on ACLU's FISA cases; (212) 519-7814; jjaffer@aclu.org

Orin Kerr, Law Professor, The George Washington University; former Department of Justice lawyer; (202) 994-4775; okerr@law.gwu.edu

Martin Lederman, Law Professor, Georgetown University; former Deputy Assistant Attorney General in the Justice Department's Office of Legal Counsel; (202) 662-9421; msl46@law.georgetown.edu

Kate Martin, Director, Center for National Security Studies; (202) 721-5650; cnss@cnss.org

Peter Swire, Law Professor, Ohio State University; former Chief Privacy Officer in the Clinton administration; (614) 292-2547; swire.1@osu.edu

RESOURCES

DAVID S. KRIS & J. DOUGLAS WILSON, NATIONAL SECURITY INVESTIGATIONS AND PROSECUTIONS (Thomson/West 2007).

The Permanent Provisions of the PATRIOT Act: Hearing Before the House Judiciary Subcomm. on Crime, Terrorism & Homeland Sec. (Mar. 30, 2011), http://www.justice.gov/nsd/opa/pr/testimony/2011/nsd-testimony-110330.html (statement of Todd Hinnen, Acting Assistant Att'y Gen. for National Security).

The Electronic Communications Privacy Act: Promoting Security and Protecting Privacy in the Digital Age: Hearing Before the Senate Judiciary Comm. (Sept. 22, 2010), http://www.judiciary.senate.gov/pdf/10-09-22DempseyTestimony.pdf (statement of James X. Dempsey, Vice President for Public Policy, Ctr. for Democracy & Technology).

J. BECKWITH BURR, THE ELECTRONIC COMMUNICATIONS PRIVACY ACT OF 1986: PRINCIPLES FOR REFORM (2010), http://www.digitaldueprocess.org/files/DDP_Burr_Memo.pdf.

Material Support of Terrorism: Tool for Public Safety or Recipe for Overreaching?

16

By Peter Margulies

Laws that prohibit the provision of "material support" to terrorists and terrorist organizations are a powerful tool that prosecutors must use wisely. The material support laws serve compelling and legitimate law enforcement goals, particularly in the challenging environment after the September 11, 2001, attacks. Courts have generally upheld convictions under these provisions, which build on time-honored principles of conspiracy doctrine and foreign relations law. Moreover, the courts have said that the First Amendment does not bar prosecutions under material support laws, as long as the government takes care to leave safe harbors for crucial areas such as independent expression, scholarship, human rights monitoring, legal advocacy, journalism, and international mediation.

To understand the laws' rationale and scope, consider three hypothetical cases:

1. Three young men, Eric, Ibn, and Michael, from the suburbs of Washington, D.C., seek to go to Pakistan to train in a camp that teaches attendees how to use violence against established governments in the Middle East. Alumni of the camp have informed the three men that the camp will teach them how to operate automatic weapons and build improvised explosive

devices (IEDs). After landing in Pakistan, the men are apprehended by Pakistani authorities and sent back to the United States, where they await trial.

2. In a New York City restaurant, an engaging and experienced person (Ali) who appears to be prosperous approaches two younger men, Abu and Sami, and makes conversation, deploring American policy toward Israel as one-sided. The older man asks that the younger men take part in a plan to bomb three Brooklyn synagogues. The two men initially express reluctance. However, over the next few months, the older man persists, building a relationship with the younger men and eventually asserting that his own life will be in danger if the younger men do not help. Alarmed by the older man's worries, the younger men go shopping the next day for pipe to build explosives. The older man turns out to be a Federal Bureau of Investigation (FBI) informant. The younger men are arrested; their trial is pending.

3. Beth, a woman in Los Angeles, is concerned about the humanitarian toll of a recent earthquake in Turkey. She knows that portions of Turkey affected by the earthquake are partly under the control of the Kurdistan Workers' Party (PKK). The PKK has been designated by the Secretary of State as a foreign terrorist organization. The woman contacts another person she knows who has ties with the PKK and offers to help train the PKK to solicit money from international organizations for disaster relief. After hearing about a 2010 Supreme Court decision, *Holder v. Humanitarian Law Project*,[1] the woman fears that her volunteer efforts will lead to her arrest and prosecution.[2]

The federal material support statute would permit prosecution in each of these cases. The law, which prohibits material support of both terrorist activity and terrorist groups such as Hamas, serves vital law enforcement and national security objectives, allowing authorities to stop terrorist threats at an early stage, before they ripen into fatal plots. It also gives prosecutors a powerful weapon that supplements the wide discretion already accorded them by the United States'

---

1. 130 S. Ct. 2705 (2010).
2. The first two hypotheticals are fictional accounts that highlight significant issues raised by the material support laws. They are inspired by actual cases and questions raised by scholars and practitioners. In each scenario, most or all of the subjects are Muslim. The material support provisions in the U.S. criminal code, *see* 18 U.S.C. §§ 2339A, B (2012), draw no distinction between Muslim and non-Muslim individuals or groups. The material support provisions would also prohibit aid to a group such as the Revolutionary Armed Forces of Colombia (FARC). *See* United States v. Vergara, 612 F. Supp. 2d 36 (D.D.C. 2009). However, the substantial majority of material support prosecutions have involved Muslims. This should not be surprising when viewed against the backdrop of the September 11 attacks and other terrorist incidents around the world; *see, e.g.*, United States v. Odeh, 552 F.3d 177 (2d Cir. 2008) (upholding conviction in 1998 bombing of U.S. embassies in Kenya and Tanzania). However, that law enforcement trend reinforces the need for sound prosecutorial judgment.

broad conspiracy laws. Critics of the law challenged its constitutionality, arguing that it stifled political speech that is central to a democracy.[3] The Supreme Court rejected this view, citing the protections for speech that Congress had included in the statute.[4] However, responsible prosecutors will need to ensure that enforcing the law does not alienate communities such as Muslim Americans, whose cooperation is vital to counterterrorism policy.

A (VERY) SHORT HISTORY OF CONSPIRACY

The accusation of conspiracy has long been a favorite tool of American prosecutors because it permits prosecution far earlier in a criminal plot.[5] For example, a prosecutor charging defendants with conspiracy to murder need not show that a murder was committed. Indeed, she need not prove that the defendants even made an attempt. A jury need only find an agreement among two or more people, sometimes joined by a relatively modest act in furtherance of that agreement.

As an example, suppose that three people plan to rob a bank and purchase a gun or car to assist that effort. Evidence of an agreement to rob the bank and buying a gun or car to execute the plan would support a conviction for conspiracy. Indeed, evidence of acts taking place earlier in the plan's preparations, such as casing the bank to discern its security level and the availability of escape routes, would support conviction of the defendants, as long as prosecutors persuaded a jury that the conduct described actually furthered the plot. Moreover, recorded conversations between two of the people about the role of the third would be admissible to prove the third person's guilt, even though testimony of this kind is usually deemed inadmissible hearsay outside the conspiracy context.

Courts have long recognized that prosecutions of this type respond to the special challenges of group criminality. Groups typically conspire in secret, where each member's commitment bolsters the others.[6] Hearsay evidence between conspirators may be more reliable than other kinds of hearsay, precisely because conspirators need to communicate reliably about the progress of their plans. Moreover, the very secrecy of conspirators' conversations would make prosecution difficult

---

3. *See* David Cole, *The First Amendment's Borders: The Place of* Holder v. Humanitarian Law Project *in First Amendment Doctrine*, 6 HARV. L. & POL'Y REV. 147 (2012); Wadie E. Said, *Humanitarian Law Project and the Supreme Court's Construction of Terrorism*, 2011 BYU L. REV. 1455 (2011); Amanda Shanor, *Beyond* Humanitarian Law Project*: Promoting Human Rights in a Post-9/11 World*, 34 SUFFOLK TRANSNAT'L L. REV. 519, 524–36 (2011); Timothy Zick, *The First Amendment in Transborder Perspective: Toward a More Cosmopolitan Perspective*, 52 B.C. L. REV. 941, 966–69 (2011).

4. *See Humanitarian Law Project*, 130 S. Ct. at 2728 (noting that statute excludes independent speech).

5. PETER MARGULIES, LAW'S DETOUR: JUSTICE DISPLACED IN THE BUSH ADMINISTRATION 101–06 (N.Y.U. Press 2010).

6. Neal Kumar Katyal, *Conspiracy Theory*, 112 YALE L.J. 1307 (2003).

without some relaxation of evidentiary rules. The breadth of conspiracy law and the evidentiary innovations that ease prosecution are usually considered legitimate responses to a particularly challenging problem. However, they also require prosecutors to act as gatekeepers to ensure that prosecutions target dangerous individuals.

HISTORY OF THE MATERIAL SUPPORT LAWS

The power of conspiracy law ratchets up several notches when combined with legislation that bars material support of terrorism. The material support law is actually two laws: 18 U.S.C. § 2339A, passed in 1994, bars material support of terrorist activity, generally;[7] section 2339B bars material support of designated terrorist groups, such as Hamas. "Material support" covers a broad range of activity, including tangible items, such as explosives and weapons, and intangible items, including financial services, personnel, and training. Section 2339A, which Congress enacted first, also requires proof that a defendant specifically intended to promote attacks on persons or property. After the Oklahoma City bombing, Congress came to believe that this requirement unduly limited terrorism prosecutions. Accordingly, it passed 2339B, which banned *any* contribution of material support to groups like Hamas that the Secretary of State designated as foreign terrorist organizations, also known as DFTOs.

History teaches that Congress's use of the criminal law to shape conduct of our foreign relations, including relationships with rogue states and nonstate actors, is not new. Since the founding era, Congress has enacted laws that criminalized trade and other activity with certain states regarded as causing problems for the United States on the world stage. To avoid entanglement in the conflict between Britain and France in the 1790s, Congress enacted legislation that imposed penalties on U.S. citizens' trade with France. More recent laws have criminalized unauthorized travel to Cuba or to states that support terrorism, such as Iran. Courts have regularly upheld such bans,[8] although since the McCarthy era in the early 1950s, courts have also been careful on First Amendment grounds to distinguish such laws from laws that directly regulate the expression of ideas.

More-recent history has also affected the evolution and interaction of the two material support laws. The laws triggered investigations in the 1990s but few if any actual prosecutions. After 9/11, however, the government decided that the laws were a useful building block in efforts to stop terrorist attacks before they

---

7. Robert M. Chesney, *The Sleeper Scenario: Terrorism-Support Laws and the Demands of Prevention*, 42 HARV. J. LEGIS. 1, 12–18 (2005).
8. Regan v. Wald, 468 U.S. 222 (1984).

reached a critical stage. Prosecutors brought dozens of cases under each statute.[9] In addition, as part of the Patriot Act, Congress added to the conduct criminalized by the statutes, including the broad term "services," as well as "expert advice or assistance" as prohibited forms of material support.

A lawsuit brought in federal court in California resulted in a decision holding that a number of these provisions were too vague to comply with the Constitution's requirement that the public receive clear guidance about the borders of illegal conduct.[10] Responding to this vagueness, Congress amended the statute in 2004, explaining that the term "personnel" did not include people who were merely expressing an independent opinion that happened to coincide with views expressed by Hamas or another DFTO.[11] In other words, an individual who stands up in the public square and proclaims Hamas's virtues, would not violate the statute as long as Hamas exercises no control over his activities. A sensible reading of the statute also exempts scholarship, journalism, human rights monitoring, legal advocacy, and mediation à la the Carter Center.[12] Moreover, the statute does not cover domestic organizations, such as militia groups.[13] Congress also added other clarifications, which the Supreme Court addressed in a 2010 case, *Holder v. Humanitarian Law Project*, discussed later in this chapter.

PROSECUTIONS FOR AIDING TERRORIST ACTIVITY UNDER SECTION 2339A

Before discussing the *Humanitarian Law Project* case, which deals with our third hypothetical, it is useful to examine further how section 2339A would criminalize the conduct in hypotheticals 1 and 2. The government used section 2339A to prosecute Jose Padilla, a U.S. citizen arrested in Chicago whom it had detained for three and a half years without charges because of the government's concerns that Padilla was seeking to build a "dirty bomb" that would spew radiation along with explosive debris.[14] It turned out that the dirty bomb scenario, which many observers judge to be a plausible allegation in Padilla's case, could not be proven in court because it would have required the use of evidence obtained through coercion.

---

9. Richard B. Zabel & James J. Benjamin, Jr., *In Pursuit of Justice: Prosecuting Terrorism Cases in the Federal Courts—2009 Update and Recent Developments* (2009) (discussing prosecutions and noting that prosecutors have been successful in obtaining convictions).
10. *See* Humanitarian Law Project v. Reno, 205 F.3d 1130, 1137–38 (9th Cir. Cal. 2000).
11. *Humanitarian Law Project*, 130 S. Ct. at 2722.
12. Peter Margulies, *Advising Terrorism: Material Support, Safe Harbors, and Freedom of Speech*, 63 Hastings L.J. 455, 506–12 (2012) (arguing that this reading of the statute is consistent with constitutional precedent).
13. *See Humanitarian Law Project*, 130 S. Ct. at 2730.
14. *See* Margulies, Law's Detour, *supra* note 5, at 112–13.

After 2004, when the courts' pushback against unreviewable detention suggested that Padilla's days in detention were numbered, the government charged Padilla with violations of section 2339A.

The government's charges against Padilla illustrate the value of 2339A as a counterterrorism tool. The charges did not mention the dirty bomb plot, or indeed any post-9/11 conduct. Instead, they focused on allegations that Padilla had traveled abroad with the intention of aiding violent jihad in the Balkans, the Middle East, and South Asia. The government did not prove that Padilla had participated in any specific attack. Rather, under the statute, the government needed only to prove that Padilla and his codefendants had (1) conspired to provide material support to (2) a *broader* conspiracy that violated section 956 of the criminal code, which bans conspiracies to "murder, kidnap, or maim overseas."

The combination of section 2339A's counterterrorism provisions and section 956's broad conspiracy language is particularly powerful. Participation in a terrorist training camp overseas, for example, constitutes a section 956 violation, even without proof that a defendant has planned to participate in any specific terrorist plot. Rather, courts have treated a terrorist training camp as one big terrorist enterprise, on the theory that aspiring participants know they are not attending a Michael Jordan basketball camp. Once courts make this legal link between sections 2339A and 956, conspiracy law permits a conviction based on relatively slender evidence. In Padilla's case, for example, the government introduced a completed application for attendance at a camp with Padilla's fingerprints, a few phone conversations including Padilla, and a substantial number of phone conversations between Padilla's codefendants discussing his activities. The latter would ordinarily be considered hearsay and thus would be inadmissible, but as noted earlier, conspiracy law permits the use of hearsay to prove the existence and scope of a conspiracy. The prosecution of Padilla was successful; he was convicted, and a federal appeals court recently affirmed the conviction.[15]

The cases also offer wide latitude on evidence in other respects. For example, suppose that the aspiring camp attendees in hypothetical case 1 have expressed opinions hostile to the United States and generally favorable to violent jihad. Under the First Amendment, the government cannot ban expression of such opinions unless they rise to the level of incitement to violence. To meet this test, the opinions have to be reasonably likely to spur imminent violence, and the speaker has to intend for them to have this effect.[16] The material support laws do not challenge this bedrock "content-neutrality" of modern free speech doctrine. However, in a material support prosecution, the government may introduce the speaker's opinions as *evidence* of the speaker's intention to agree to provide material support.

---

15. *See* United States v. Jayyousi, 657 F.3d 1085, 1105–06 (11th Cir. 2011).
16. Brandenburg v. Ohio, 395 U.S. 444 (1969).

Suppose, for example, that one of the defendants claims that he merely planned to see relatives or visit tourist destinations while he was in Pakistan. The government may use the defendant's expressed beliefs to show that his actual intent was to participate in a terrorist training camp. A jury, even though it will often receive an instruction from the judge that the defendant's opinions are protected speech and are not in themselves criminal, may nonetheless be tempted to hold the speaker's views against him in a way that the First Amendment forbids. On appeal, as long as the government has shown other evidence of an agreement and some overt act and the jury could have viewed the speaker's words as showing intent, a conviction based in part on this evidence will stand.

The cases also feature government and other witnesses offering opinions on amorphous matters where the basis for an opinion is hotly contested. For example, in the *Padilla* case, an FBI agent who had listened to many of the phone calls between Padilla's coconspirators stated his opinion that the callers used terms like "football" and "wedding" as a code referring to terrorist activity.[17] Because the agent had listened to many of the calls, the court accepted his lay opinion testimony that the use and placement of the terms listed indicated the existence of a code. This opinion was helpful to the jury, which lacked the experience of the agent, an appellate court reasoned in denying Padilla's appeal. Moreover, the court observed, defendants were free to cross-examine the agent to highlight weaknesses in his testimony and free to present evidence that the government had not properly translated terms from another language, such as Arabic. The jury was in turn free to credit the defense theory of the case, or the government's.

In many cases, the government has introduced the testimony of experts on terrorism, who testify about the organizational structure and aims of groups like al-Qaida.[18] Experts confront inherent limits on their expertise, since al-Qaida and other terrorist groups are often secretive organizations that do not cooperate in social science experiments. Defendants often assert that this evidence does not assist the jury and therefore is not appropriate expert testimony. However, courts have decided that the prosecution can provide jurors with a "road map" to aid in understanding terrorist groups, just as prosecutors can introduce testimony about the structure of organized crime families or drug cartels. Here, again, the defense is free to cross-examine the government's expert and/or offer witnesses of its own.

The point here is not to revisit the question of Padilla's factual guilt. Rather, the discussion above serves a descriptive purpose in showing how the material support statutes, specifically 2339A, facilitate prosecution of Padilla and others in the hypothetical 1 training camp scenario.

---

17. *Jayyousi*, 657 F.3d at 1095–98.
18. United States v. El-Mezain, 2011 U.S. App. Lexis 2416, at 97–98 (11th Cir. 2011) (testimony of ex-Treasury Department official Matthew Levitt on Hamas); *cf.* MATTHEW LEVITT, HAMAS: POLITICS, CHARITY, AND TERRORISM IN THE SERVICE OF JIHAD 135 (2006).

USE OF INFORMANTS

Both the first and second hypotheticals also illustrate another element of these cases: the government's use of informants. The government has often used informants in material support cases to gain the trust of individuals the government wishes to investigate. The informant, who as in most criminal cases has reasons of his or her own for working with the government, persuades the targets of the investigation to agree to take part in a plot, such as the synagogue bombing described in hypothetical 2, based on an actual case in New York City.[19] Sometimes persuasion can involve psychological or financial inducements, such as the hypothetical informant's assertion that he will be at risk of harm if the plot does not proceed. Courts have long held, however, that the informant's own agenda makes no legal difference, as long as a jury is persuaded that the defendant believed he was actually involved in a genuine terrorist plot.

Defendants can argue that they were entrapped. However, an entrapment defense presents virtually insurmountable hurdles for the defense. To succeed, a defendant must show that he was not otherwise disposed to commit the crime. However, the defendant's participation in the plot makes that a tough sell. In hypothetical 2, for example, the defendants would have to demonstrate to a jury that they were disposed to be law-abiding citizens, despite their willingness to participate in a plot to bomb a synagogue. Jurors will typically reason that no law-abiding person would remain in the same room with someone proposing such a plan. This inference will doom an entrapment defense.

MATERIAL SUPPORT OF DESIGNATED ORGANIZATIONS

Section 2339B criminalizes not only material support to illegal activity, but *any* aid that is coordinated with, or under the direction and control of, a designated foreign terrorist group. Most of the activity prohibited by this section involves cash contributions or similar aid, which courts have uniformly viewed as imposing merely incidental restrictions on speech.[20] In one decision, however, *Holder v. Humanitarian Law Project* (*HLP*),[21] the Supreme Court in a 6–3 vote held that Congress could limit the *content* of speech.[22] To avoid ceding too much power to Congress, the Court's decision in *HLP* suggested that the constitutional power to

---

19. *See* Kareem Fahim, *4 Convicted of Attempting to Blow Up 2 Synagogues*, N.Y. TIMES, Oct. 19, 2010, A21.
20. *Humanitarian Law Project v. Reno*, 205 F.3d 1130, 1136 (9th Cir. 2000), *cert. denied*, 532 U.S. 904 (2001) (holding that Congress could prohibit financial contributions to foreign terrorist groups).
21. 130 S. Ct. 2705 (2010); cf. Margulies, *Advising Terrorism*, *supra* note 12 (analyzing decision).
22. Chief Justice Roberts wrote the majority opinion in *Humanitarian Law Project*. Justices Alito, Kennedy, Scalia, Stevens, and Thomas joined that opinion. Justice Breyer dissented, joined by Justices Ginsburg and Sotomayor.

regulate such speech was narrow and that individuals and groups had a number of safe harbors available.

The comprehensive framework set out in section 2339B starts with designation of a foreign terrorist organization. Under the designation process, the secretary of state determines there is evidence indicating that particular organizations such as al-Qaida, Hamas, or the LTTE (the Tamil Tigers of Sri Lanka) have a track record of violence, particularly violence against innocents. The government then informs the organization's representatives, who have a chance to review unclassified evidence and rebut the government's claims.[23] If the government designates the group as a foreign terrorist organization, the group can appeal to a federal court. Courts will reject a designation that is arbitrary, not based on substantial support, or inconsistent with procedural safeguards.[24]

While critics of the designation process charge that courts merely rubber-stamp the government's determination,[25] judicial review has proven to be more robust than many critics acknowledge. In one case, *Holy Land Foundation v. Ashcroft*,[26] a court considered the organization's evidence that its aid to families of "martyrs" was not assistance for relatives of suicide bombers, but merely aid to families of anyone killed by the government. Upon closer examination, the court discovered that the organization used a different term to describe families in the latter context, suggesting that its use of the term "martyrs" in fact referred to suicide bombers. After this inquiry, the court sustained the designation.

Some advocates and scholars argue that individuals should be free to provide money to nonviolent activities of a group like Hamas, which runs hospitals and schools as well as engaging in violence. These critics of the section 2339B framework assert that the government should have to prove that an individual providing financial aid to a DFTO *specifically intended* to promote violence. Courts, however, have uniformly upheld Congress's view that DFTOs, like state sponsors of terrorism, "are so tainted by their criminal conduct that any contribution to such an organization facilitates that conduct" (Antiterrorism and Effective Death Penalty Act of 1996 (AEDPA) § 301(a)(7)).

---

23. 8 U.S.C. § 1189(c)(3); *cf.* People's Mojahedin Org. of Iran v. U.S. Dep't of State, 613 F.3d 22 (D.C. Cir. 2010) (discussing process and holding that the government had violated due process by failing to give DFTO an opportunity to view unclassified evidence prior to making a final decision denying petition to revoke designation).

24. *See* United States v. Afshari, 426 F.3d 1150, 1160 (9th Cir. 2005) (upholding process and barring collateral review of designation in subsequent criminal cases).

25. *See* Susan N. Herman, Taking Liberties: The War on Terror and the Erosion of American Democracy 41–43 (Oxford U. Press 2011).

26. 219 F. Supp. 2d 57, 71–73 (D.D.C. 2002), *aff'd*, 333 F.3d 156, 164 (D.C. Cir. 2003).

Once courts uphold a designation, it seems logical to prohibit the provision of any and all financial support to the group.[27] Courts take this view because groups like Hamas disdain traditional accounting principles.[28] Once a donor contributes money to a group such as Hamas, he or she has no way to ascertain where the money is actually going. DFTOs have no compunction about shifting a contribution intended for a nonviolent activity to programs supporting violence. Moreover, as courts have repeatedly found, money is fungible, so cash contributed to one phase of a group's operations necessarily frees up money that can be used for violent activities. Finally, a DFTO uses social services not merely for help for the needy, but for recruitment and maintenance of operatives whose families have become dependent on the DFTO's largesse.[29]

Courts have uniformly held that restrictions on financial or other tangible aid are merely incidental restrictions on speech.[30] Incidental restrictions are content-neutral, involve important governmental interests, and are appropriately tailored to serve those interests. Section 2339B's ban on cash assistance is content-neutral; an individual who wishes to express his or her support for the DFTO is still free to shout that sentiment from the rooftops.[31] The section serves an important governmental interest: limiting DFTOs' access to funds. Finally, it is tailored to achieve that purpose, given the futility of less restrictive measures, such as arrest and prosecution by foreign governments of individuals abroad who provide aid directly connected to violence. Hypothetical 3, although it nominally involves speech, should be viewed in the same light as the prohibition on cash support. Beth, hypothetical number 3's protagonist, has offered to train the PKK, a DFTO that has engaged in violence in Turkey to promote Kurdish autonomy, to seek earthquake aid from humanitarian organizations. The Supreme Court found in *HLP* that the PKK had exploited the sanctuary provided by a United Nations refugee camp to enhance its capacity for violence.[32] The LTTE, or Tamil Tigers, dangled humanitarian assistance before needy Tamil families, extorting them to provide child

---

27. *See* David Cole, *Hanging with the Wrong Crowd: Of Gangs, Terrorism, and the Right of Association*, 1999 SUP. CT. REV. 203.
28. *See* Kilburn v. Socialist People's Libyan Arab Jamahiriya, 376 F.3d 1123, 1130 (D.C. Cir. 2004) (commenting that "terrorist organizations can hardly be counted on to keep careful bookkeeping records").
29. *See HLP*, 130 S. Ct. at 2725; Boim v. Holy Land Found. for Relief & Dev., 549 F.3d 685, 698 (7th Cir. 2008); Margulies, *Advising Terrorism*, *supra* note 12, at 484.
30. *See* Humanitarian Law Project v. Reno, 205 F.3d 1130, 1136 (9th Cir. 2000).
31. Of course, the Supreme Court has also recently equated money with speech in the context of campaign contributions. *See* Citizens United v. FEC, 130 S. Ct. 876 (2010). However, the *Citizens United* Court did not suggest that its decision would affect the many areas, such as commercial finance and foreign relations, in which government has traditionally regulated money.
32. *See HLP*, 130 S. Ct. at 2729–30.

soldiers for LTTE in return for aid.[33] Providing instruction to a DFTO on raising money is just as dangerous as contributing money directly.

A recent case, *United States v. Mehanna*, takes section 2339B beyond the realm of cash help and into the provision of propaganda to al-Qaida. Tarek Mehanna was convicted in December 2011 in federal court in Massachusetts of conspiring to commit violence in this country, go to an al-Qaida training camp abroad, and furnish al-Qaida with propaganda.[34] This last charge has First Amendment implications, since propaganda is speech. In principle, the rule should be no different for DFTOs. For such groups, propaganda is linked to operations; terrorist plots are not random, but are carefully planned to maximize propaganda value. Propaganda spread by the group is not separate from, but indeed is crucial to, the group's operations.

> U.S. courts have regularly permitted prosecutions of individuals, such as World War II's infamous Tokyo Rose, who knowingly provided propaganda to nations engaged in war against the United States.

Mehanna made two claims at trial to counter the government's claims. First, he claimed the material he provided consisted of translations into English of prominent texts justifying violent jihad by religious and political thinkers. Mehanna said that these texts were of scholarly value and had a merely abstract relationship to any particular acts of violence. Second, Mehanna said that he had posted these texts to an online chat room visited by others with a purely intellectual interest in these texts. Members or organizers of the chat room who had requested that Mehanna translate the documents were, according to Mehanna, acting independently of al-Qaida. The expression of abstract support for violence by someone acting independently of a DFTO is protected by the First Amendment, even when those views happen to coincide with those of DFTO leaders. At least in the domestic setting, such views do not meet the test for incitement, which as noted earlier requires the intent to cause imminent harm and the reasonable likelihood that such harm will result.

The government saw the case differently. It argued that Mehanna knew that the chat room, sponsored by an entity called Tibyan Publications, was in fact run by persons who were part of al-Qaida's network. It also introduced evidence, culled from Mehanna's own e-mails, that he had knowingly provided specific

---

33. Peter Popham, *Tamil Tigers Break UN Pledge on Child Soldiers*, INDEPENDENT (LONDON), Feb. 4, 2000, at 18.
34. *See* Abby Goodnough, *U.S. Citizen Is Convicted in Plot to Support Al Qaida*, N.Y. TIMES, Dec. 21, 2011, A26.

individuals with religious authorizations for going abroad to kill U.S. personnel.[35] The government took the position that terrorist networks are not hierarchical, but instead are widely dispersed. Security concerns mean that al-Qaida's former leader, Osama bin Laden, or current leader, Dr. Ayman al-Zawahiri, rarely offer specific operational advice. Instead, most orders and advice come from a broad group of people around the world. Courts have never required the government to prove that conspirators in ordinary cases involving drugs or organized crime had contact with the kingpins of the organization. The government can prevail in such cases by simply showing that defendants were "spokes in a wheel" who had agreed with other conspirators to further the conspiracy's objectives. Proving conspiracy under section 2339B should be no different, the government has contended.

HLP itself addressed an issue that was closer than *Mehanna* or hypothetical number 3 to protected political speech. The *HLP* Court, in an opinion by Chief Justice Roberts, held that Congress could prohibit speech by those who coordinated their activity with a DFTO or acted under the DFTO's direction or control. This activity is more dangerous than independent speech, the Court said, because it allows the DFTO to tailor its interactions to maximize its tactical advantage. Recall that courts have said that DFTOs are poor accountants.[36] In *HLP*, the Court extended this concern from the context of financial contributions to the realm of speech coordinated with a DFTO, such as instructions on international law or nonviolence or negotiating on a DFTO's behalf with a state. This narrow band of speech, the Court asserted, entailed a relationship with a terrorist organization and was therefore more dangerous than speech outside the DFTO's ambit.

---

35. *See* Trial Transcript at 98–101, United States v. Mehanna, No. 09-10017-GAO (Nov. 23, 2011), (available on PACER) (testimony of Daniel Genck, Special Agent, FBI). The e-mails recount Mehanna's conversations with three individuals who attempted to go abroad to fight U.S. forces after requesting material from the defendant. One, Ehsanul Sadequee, was subsequently convicted in federal court. Discussing another individual, referred to as Aboo K, an administrator at Tibyan told Mehanna, "[Aboo] told me that he would be going soon. So maybe he made it." Mehanna replied, "I just hope he isn't translating books while he is there. . . . It would be funny in the middle of a battle he remembers that he translated a word wrong." "LOL," the administrator replied. *Id.* at 98. For a summary of related testimony, see Milton J. Valencia, *British Investigator Tells Court of Contact with Terrorists; Still No Evidence Presented to Show Mehanna Acted*, BOS. GLOBE, Nov. 11, 2011, Metro sec. at 3; for a more skeptical view of the danger posed by Internet speech relating to terrorism, see Steven R. Morrison, *Terrorism On-Line: Is Speech the Same As It Ever Was?*, 44 CREIGHTON L. REV. 963 (2011) (concluding that online recruitment does not pose a distinctive threat, and may be a smaller security risk than face-to-face recruitment or other traditional methods). An online debate about the *Mehanna* case between the author and David Cole, a critic of the material support statute, is available at Benjamin Wittes, *Peter Margulies Responds to David Cole,* LAWFARE, April 21, 2012, http://www.lawfareblog.com/2012/04/peter-margulies-responds-to-david-cole/, with follow-up at Benjamin Wittes, *David Cole and Peter Margulies: An Exchange on Tarek Mehanna,* LAWFARE, April 22, 2012, http://www.lawfareblog.com/2012/04/david-cole-and-peter-margulies-an-exchange-on-tarek-mehanna/.

36. *See* Kilburn v. Socialist People's Libyan Arab Jamahiriya, 376 F.3d 1123, 1130 (D.C. Cir. 2004).

Further explanation is useful, since at first blush regulating instruction in nonviolence or international law may seem counterintuitive.[37] Nonetheless, Chief Justice Roberts had a point. As an analogy, consider an author who wants to sell a manuscript to a publisher. Independent praise for the manuscript on a book-lovers' website could be useful; however, it cannot substitute for the efforts of a literary agent who can tailor her campaign to the publisher's likes and dislikes. In the DFTO setting, this tailored relationship gives the organization an advantage not merely in ideas, but also in operational tactics. That is the kind of relationship-based speech that the Court ruled that Congress could prohibit.

To understand why the Court ruled the way it did, it is helpful to consider a fourth hypothetical suggested by the examples given in the *HLP* decision. Suppose a DFTO such as Hamas decided to invite in a speaker on nonviolent techniques. In the past, the Court noted, DFTOs had repeatedly sought to convey a "kinder, gentler" face to the world in order to elicit cash contributions from gullible donors and conceal a renewed military build up. Such groups have repeatedly broken truces, the Court observed, under circumstances showing that they had agreed to the truce only to buy time for rearmament. For example, the Lebanese group Hezbollah has acquired thousands of rockets from Iran, after an attack it launched on Israeli border forces led to a 2006 conflict. Hamas has also rearmed, after rocket attacks on Israel led to a 2008–09 confrontation.

The *HLP* Court ruled that even a speaker who did not intend to aid such ruses could still be deceived by a DFTO into providing cover for the DFTO's rearmament. The difficulty of acquiring information about conduct overseas compounded this problem, according to Chief Justice Roberts. In the domestic sphere, the government can obtain a warrant authorizing surveillance when it has probable cause to believe that the target of an investigation is breaking the law. Overseas, however, the government's ability to engage in surveillance is far more limited, and the United States must rely on other nations who may lack either the ability or the inclination to cooperate. As a result, the Court said that

---

37. *HLP*, incidentally, did not involve an actual prosecution. The plaintiffs in the case never submitted evidence that the government had investigated their activities. Rather, they claimed that section 2339B would chill their lawful speech. While plaintiffs have brought such "preenforcement" challenges previously, these challenges have usually involved statutes that clearly prohibited the plaintiffs' conduct. In those situations, the court has a sufficient record to assess the parties' claims. Justice Stevens at the oral argument in *HLP* said that the *HLP* plaintiffs' efforts were more amorphous and abstract, amounting to an effort to stop "a potential prosecution against somebody for making a potential speech." Courts tend to be more wary of granting claims pervaded by such uncertainty, which may help account for the *HLP* plaintiffs' defeat. By the way, I was cocounsel on an *amicus curiae* brief that asked the Supreme Court to uphold the constitutionality of the federal material support statute and carve out safe harbors for journalists, scholars, human rights groups, and attorneys. *See* Brief of *Amicus Curiae* Scholars, Attorneys, and Former Public Officials with Experience in Terrorism-Related Issues in Support of Petitioners, *HLP*, 130 S. Ct., *available at* http://www.americanbar.org/content/dam/aba/publishing/preview/publiced_preview_briefs_pdfs_09_10_08_1498_PetitionerAmCuTerrorismExperts.authcheckdam.pdf.

the government had advanced a compelling interest in regulating this particular kind of speech.

The Court's decision in *HLP* left many safe harbors for speakers who wished to offer information about topics such as nonviolence or international law. A speaker who acted independently of the DFTO in posting material on a publicly accessible website would be engaged in protected speech. So would a speaker independent of the DFTO who praised the organization's apparent commitment to nonviolence, or for that matter offered abstract praise of the group's violent activities. The decision's discussion of "coordination" between a defendant and a DFTO suggested that conduct that lacked elements of coordination, such as exclusivity or confidentiality, would not be covered by the statute. In other words, an individual could give a speech on nonviolence to a diverse audience that happened to include members of a DFTO, even if the speaker *knew* that members of the DFTO were listening. Moreover, a range of other activities, such as scholarship, journalism, human rights monitoring, legal advocacy, and mediation, would not be subject to substantive restrictions on content.

CRITICISMS OF THE MATERIAL SUPPORT LAW

There are, naturally, several possible criticisms of material support prosecutions.[38] For example, some critics assert that these prosecutions involve stale claims or terrorist wannabes.

Indeed, some of the prosecutions appear at first blush to recycle claims of illegal conduct that occurred 10 or more years ago. In *United States v. El-Mezain*,[39] for example, much of the conduct, involving fundraising for Hamas, happened in the 1990s. However, other factors temper this concern. First, state and federal law pose no obstacle to prosecution of serious crimes such as terrorism, regardless of their vintage. Murder is the most obvious example, but support for terrorism, which helps underwrite murder overseas, is no different in principle. Moreover, in cases like *Holy Land*, the government showed evidence of continued operational contacts between the defendants and Hamas.[40] These substantial contacts suggested that conduct was more recent, even if it had roots in connections made years ago.

One can also argue that many of the people prosecuted under the material support laws were actually terrorist wannabes, ineffectually pursuing an illusion of participation in terrorist plots, but too incompetent to successfully execute such a plan. Here, too, however, countervailing factors are present. Terrorists, after all,

---

38. *See* MARGULIES, LAW'S DETOUR, *supra* note 5, at 112–18.
39. 664 F.3d 467 (5th Cir. 2011).
40. *Id.* at 529–31.

do not need every plan to succeed. They can sponsor a portfolio of plots, hoping that one will work.

The more subtle concern about such prosecutions involves the allocation of law enforcement resources. Prosecuting ineffectual defendants consumes resources and therefore creates opportunity costs. Consider the reliance on informants. Informants can elicit incriminating statements from individuals who specialize in big talk. However, informants may be less successful in identifying disciplined operatives with a knack for staying underneath the radar. Someone like Mohammed Atta, the operational leader for the 9/11 attacks, remained unnoticed in this country for almost two years. Indeed, some dangerous individuals may use informant status to conceal their own terrorist connections.[41] Prosecutors who value the cases such an informant supplies will have little incentive to inquire about the informant's own activities. In this way, material support cases may become low-hanging fruit that distracts government from more substantial targets.

Government also should worry about material support cases producing alienation in communities whose cooperation is vital in counterterrorism efforts. Some spokespersons for Muslim American communities, for example, have warned that communities feel that federal authorities have unfairly targeted them.[42] Prosecutors have to work as diligently as possible to avoid surveillance that is needlessly intrusive, and to acknowledge and respond to community concerns. Proactive prosecutors will meet regularly with community members to establish and maintain trust. Prosecutors must draw a clear line between the vast majority of community members who are committed to following the law and the tiny minority of lawbreakers.

MATERIAL SUPPORT BEYOND CRIMINAL LAW

No discussion of material support would be complete without acknowledgment that it also affects other domains beyond the criminal law. The material support

---

41. *See* Jane Perlez, *American Terror Suspect Traveled Unimpeded*, N.Y. TIMES, Mar. 26, 2010, A1 (reporting that David Headley, who was arrested after allegedly conspiring in the bloody 2008 Mumbai terrorist attacks, had forged contacts with militants in 2002, possibly while he was still an informant for the Drug Enforcement Agency pursuant to a 1990s plea deal); *see also* Annie Sweeney, *Chicago Man Guilty in Danish Terror Plot*, L.A. TIMES, June 10, 2011, A9 (noting that Headley had testified in trial of man accused of participating in Mumbai plot and in plot to retaliate against Danish newspaper for publishing cartoons of the prophet Muhammad; jury, perhaps concerned about Headley's credibility, acquitted defendant of charges involving Mumbai attack but convicted on charges involving retaliation against the newspaper).

42. Aziz Z. Huq, *The Signaling Function of Religious Speech in Domestic Counterterrorism*, 89 TEX. L. REV. 833 (2011); Nina J. Crimm, *High Alert: The Government's War on the Financing of Terrorism and Its Implications for Donors, Domestic Charitable Organizations, and Global Philanthropy*, 45 WM. & MARY L. REV. 1341 (2004).

laws are one element in the latticework of compliance with international obligations regarding terrorist financing. Material support also plays a role in military commission prosecutions and in immigration law.

Since 9/11, the United Nations has moved aggressively to combat terrorist financing. The Security Council has passed resolutions requiring member states to take action. For example, Security Council Resolution 1373 provides that "states are required to prohibit anyone within their personal or territorial jurisdiction from making any funds, resources or financial services available to persons who commit terrorist acts or to entities controlled by them."[43] European courts have held that the "listing process" European nations employ to implement Resolution 1373 lacks adequate procedural safeguards.[44] However, they have not questioned the validity of the substantive provisions banning financing of terrorist groups.

MILITARY COMMISSIONS

Material support is also among the charges that Congress has authorized in military commissions. Under the law, the government can prosecute a noncitizen in a military commission for providing material support to an act of terrorism against the United States or to the Taliban, al-Qaida, and associated forces. While this provision on the surface simply paraphrases the U.S. criminal code, it creates special problems in the military commission context. The Constitution bars what are called ex post facto laws, which criminalize conduct that occurred before the effective date of legislation. Elementary fairness and fundamental conceptions of the rule of law bar criminalizing conduct when the state has not provided notice that such acts are criminal. The rubber meets the road here because all current defendants in military commissions were captured *before* the effective date of the legislation including material support among offenses triable in military commissions.

To view charges against such individuals as constitutional, a court would have to make one of two moves. First, it could hold that military tribunals are not subject to the full force of the ex post facto clause, just as they need not provide a trial by jury equivalent to the trial provided in civilian courts under the Sixth

---

43. U.N. Doc. S/RES/1373, at 1(d) (Sept. 28, 2001); *see also* Security Council Resolution 1267, discussed in S.C. Res. 194, U.N. Doc. S/RES/1904 (Dec. 17, 2009) (imposing sanctions on the Taliban and Al Qaida); FATF steps up fight against money laundering and terrorist financing (Feb. 2012), *available at* http://www.fatf-gafi.org/topics/fatfrecommendations/documents/fatfstepsupthefightagainstmoneylaunderingandterroristfinancing.html (noting importance of international cooperation).

44. *See* Kadi v. Council & Comm'n, 2008 E.C.R. I-6411, I-6502-03 (holding that fundamental principles in customary international law and European Convention on Human Rights required that listed parties have greater access to evidence against them); *cf.* Grant L. Willis, *Security Council Targeted Sanctions, Due Process and the 1267 Ombudsperson*, 42 GEO. J. INT'L L. 673 (2011) (arguing that due process issues continue, mitigated by establishment of independent ombudsperson).

Amendment. On this view, if Congress criminalized material support under the criminal code governing ordinary civilian courts, that would authorize military commission trials, too. However, Congress waited until *after* 9/11 to extend the criminal material support laws' reach in ordinary civilian courts to non-U.S. citizens located abroad. That would make trial problematic for anyone charged with material support that occurred before the attacks.

The second approach also creates problems. In specifying charges triable before military commissions, Congress could have been exercising its power under the Constitution's Article I to "define and punish . . . Offences against the Law of Nations." The law of nations includes the principles, precedents, and practices that constitute international humanitarian law, otherwise known as the law of armed conflict. A court could find that material support was an offense under the common law of armed conflict, just like offenses such as perfidy, which entails flying a "false flag" of surrender to lure in members of opposition forces. The Military Commission Court of Review has taken this approach in the cases of Salim Hamdan (bin Laden's former driver) and al-Qaida propagandist Ali al Bahlul. However, the precedents the court relied on are shaky, at least in Hamdan's case. The closest analog to material support is membership in a criminal organization, which laws adopted by the Nuremberg tribunals criminalized. However, virtually all individuals convicted of membership offenses by Nuremberg and related tribunals were either members of units that played a direct role in killing civilians or were key players in Nazi organizations that provided substantial funding with full knowledge of the organization's murderous activities. None of the cases involved people like Hamdan who provided more generic aid without playing a direct role in killing.

Material support would, however, be an appropriate charge for a defendant who furnished direct and substantial aid to commission of a war crime. Consider Ali al Bahlul, who helped shape al-Qaida's propaganda campaign after the 9/11 attacks. Given the crucial role of propaganda in the planning of al-Qaida's operations, it would be fair to either find a nexus between al Bahlul's conduct and the attacks or classify him as a principal in the organization, like the "Friends of Himmler," whose role in supporting the Nazi SS led to their convictions for membership offenses at Nuremberg.[45]

---

45. *See* United States v. Al Bahlul, 2011 U.S. CMCR Lexis 3, at *116–17 (Ct. Mil. Com. Rev. Sept. 9, 2011) (upholding conviction). To bolster its arguments in both *Hamdan* and *Bahlul*, the government has also recently argued that Congress under its Article I war-making power can authorize trial of material support charges in military commissions. This power, the government has argued, is broader than Congress's power to "define and punish . . . Offences against the Law of Nations." Using its war-making power, the government has asserted, Congress is not limited by the international consensus on the law of armed conflict, but can also draw from the history of the *United States' own* "common law of war." According to the government, this distinctively American body of law authorizes the trial of material support charges before military commissions, even if international principles, precedents, and practice do not. *See* Brief for the United States at 24–46, Hamdan v. United States, No. 11-1257 (D.C. Cir. filed Jan. 17, 2012), *available at* http://www

IMMIGRATION IMPACT

Material support can also have severe consequences in the immigration context. The Patriot Act barred entry to the United States for anyone who provided material support to a terrorist activity, a designated terrorist group, or any other group that the individuals knew or should have known was a terrorist organization. The statute initially did not provide for any exceptions, even if people had provided support under duress. The Bush administration declined to carve out exceptions with congressional authorization, forcing delays on thousands of refugees from Burma, home to one of the world's most oppressive regimes.[46] Because of these hardships, Congress eventually provided for a waiver of some immigration provisions.[47] However, the waiver only applied to undesignated terrorist organizations, leaving many refugees at risk. Moreover, because the Constitution's ex post facto clause does not apply to deportation, which courts have historically distinguished from criminal punishment, the provisions have also been retroactively applied. At least one case involved disqualification from asylum of a Sikh who had provided food and lodging to members of a terrorist group over 10 years before passage of the

---

.lawfareblog.com/wp-content/uploads/2012/01/Hamdan-Brief-for-US-As-Filed.pdf. The government cited examples from the Civil War and other periods of American history in which military commissions tried charges including providing aid and comfort to hostile forces. *Id.* at 32–34 (citing, *inter alia*, G.O. No. 20, HQ, Dep't of the Missouri (Jan. 14, 1862), 1 OR ser. II, at 402–06). Most of these cases, however, involved the trial of individuals who, as American citizens, owed a duty of loyalty to the United States. Neither Hamdan nor al Bahlul had such a duty. Moreover, most of the cases from the crucial Civil War period involved individuals who joined small groups with a more direct link to war crimes than Hamdan's conduct revealed. *See, e.g.*, G.O. No. 20, 1 OR ser. II, *supra*, at 403 (charging that James R.J. Jones did "*by his presence and advice*" assist in bridge-burning) (emphasis added); *id.* at 404 (charging that Thomas R. Smith not only provided "aid and comfort" to group that burned bridges, but both participated in and plotted these acts). In light of these facts, the cases cited by the government are doubtful precedents, at least in Hamdan's case.

Moreover, the Supreme Court has typically viewed the "law of war" as a unitary concept without a separate, distinctively American component. On this view, American experience informs the development of an international body of law. Congress can codify this international corpus through its power under the Define and Punish Clause. *See In re* Yamashita, 327 U.S. 1, 7 (1946) (tracing Congress's power to create military commissions to Define and Punish Clause). The government's recent invocation of a United States "common law of war" would allow Congress to bypass the constraints of the Define and Punish Clause, even though the Constitution's text provides no basis for this interpretive leeway. *See* Peter Margulies, *Defining, Punishing, and Membership in the Community of Nations: Material Support Charges in Military Commissions*, 36 FORDHAM INT'L L.J. __ (forthcoming 2012), *available at* http://ssrn.com/abstract=2129307.

46. *See* James J. Carafano, Brian W. Walsh, J. Kelly Ryan & Paul S. Rosenzweig, *Thwarting Terrorists While Protecting Innocents: The Material Support and Related Provisions of the Immigration and Nationality Act*, HERITAGE FOUND. REPORTS, Jan. 31, 2008.

47. After pressure from Congress and humanitarian groups over a period of years, the administration has begun to grant waivers in some cases involving duress. *See id.*

Patriot Act.[48] While Congress should have the flexibility to modify immigration law when new threats from abroad become apparent, the provisions leave little room for consideration of extenuating circumstances, such as an individual's change of heart after entry into the United States.

EXPERTS

Experts who have questioned the material support statute's constitutionality:

David Cole, Professor, Georgetown Law School; (202) 662-9406; cole@law.georgetown.edu

Wadie Said, Professor, University of South Carolina School of Law; (803) 777-0471; said@law.sc.edu

Experts who support the statute, including the provision of safe harbors for speech:

Norman Abrams, Professor, UCLA School of Law; abrams@law.ucla.edu

Robert Chesney, Professor, University of Texas School of Law; (512) 232-1298; rchesney@law.utexas.edu

Peter Raven-Hansen, Professor, George Washington University Law School; (202) 994-9817; praven@law.gwu.edu

Timothy Zick, Professor, William & Mary Law School; (757) 221-2076; tzick@wm.edu

RESOURCES

Holder v. Humanitarian Law Project, 130 S. Ct. 2705 (2010) (upholding statute).

Robert M. Chesney, *The Sleeper Scenario: Terrorism-Support Laws and the Demands of Prevention*, 42 HARV. J. LEGIS. 1, 12–18 (2005) (providing background on statute).

David Cole, *The First Amendment's Borders: The Place of* Holder v. Humanitarian Law Project *in First Amendment Doctrine*, 6 HARV. L. & POL'Y REV. 147 (2012) (criticizing statute).

---

48. *See* Singh-Kaur v. Ashcroft, 385 F.3d 293 (3d Cir. 2004).

Peter Margulies, *Advising Terrorism: Material Support, Safe Harbors, and Freedom of Speech*, 63 HASTINGS L.J. 455 (2012) (explaining Supreme Court's decision in *HLP*).

Wadie E. Said, Humanitarian Law Project *and the Supreme Court's Construction of Terrorism*, 2011 BYU L. REV. 1455 (2011) (critiquing Court's perspective on terrorism).

Extraterritorial Issues: Investigation and Prosecution of National Security Cases

17

By Jennifer C. Daskal

INTRODUCTION

The past several years have seen an explosion of national security cases involving activities, defendants, and witnesses located overseas. Consider, for example, the case of Somali national Ahmed Abdulkadir Warsame, who was taken into military custody in the Arabian Gulf region in April 2011. Warsame now faces charges in U.S. federal court for, among other things, providing material support to a foreign terrorist organization. All relevant activities took place outside the United States.[1] Or Moroccan national Abdeladim el-Kebir—indicted in federal court in New York for providing material support to al-Qaida based on his activities in Germany and Pakistan.[2] Or the multiple Somali pirates brought

---

1. Press Release, U.S. Att'y for the S. Dist. of N.Y., Accused Al Shabaab Leader Accused of Providing Material Support to Al Shabaab and Al Qaeda in the Arabian Peninsula (July 5, 2011), http://www.justice.gov/usao/nys/pressreleases/July11/-warsameindictmentpr.pdf.

2. Press Release, U.S. Att'y for the E. Dist. of N.Y., Alleged Terrorist Charged with Conspiracy to Provide Material Support to Al Qaeda (Nov. 10, 2011), http://www.justice.gov/usao/nye/pr/2011/2011nov10.html.

to the United States and convicted of crimes occurring far away, in the Gulf of Aden.

Each of these cases raises a number of interesting, complicated, and often contested questions regarding the authority of U.S. courts to prosecute foreign nationals for offenses that take place far from U.S. soil, the constitutional rights of noncitizens apprehended abroad, and the relationship between U.S. and foreign investigatory and prosecutorial services. Among the many questions that arise:

- Under what circumstances can the United States prosecute noncitizens for actions that take place overseas?
- Do *Miranda* rights apply to noncitizens abroad? What about the right to counsel?
- In what circumstances can evidence obtained by foreign governments be introduced into federal court?
- How does the United States secure custody of a suspected terrorist abroad?
- What happens if a foreign national is acquitted or has served his sentence and cannot be returned to his home country?

This chapter will explore each of these issues and more, highlighting areas where the law is settled and where it is unresolved and likely to be the subject of ongoing litigation and controversy. The aim is to identify the key issues that reporters and policy makers may want to know about or focus on, not necessarily to provide clear-cut answers, of which there are often none.

JURISDICTION FOR EXTRATERRITORIAL OFFENSES

In 1909, Supreme Court Justice Oliver Wendell Holmes described the "almost universal rule" that "the character of an act as lawful or unlawful must be determined wholly by the law of the country where the act is done."[3] Holmes's view was consistent with the prevailing (Westphalian) conception of state sovereignty, in which a state exercises exclusive regulatory power over its own territory and not elsewhere.

Since Holmes's time, the United States has increasingly sought to police far-flung criminal activity, chipping away at this once "almost universal rule." The United States has now passed hundreds of criminal laws with express extraterritorial scope.[4] Numerous terrorism and terrorism-related statutes include an explicit

---

3. Am. Banana Co. v. United Fruit Co., 213 U.S. 347, 355 (1909).
4. *See* Chris Doyle, Cong. Research Serv., Extraterritorial Application of United States Criminal Law 37–60 (Mar. 26, 2010) (listing criminal laws with extraterritorial applications).

statement of extraterritorial jurisdiction, including, for example, the prohibitions on providing material support to a terrorist organization;[5] receipt of military-type training from a foreign terrorist organization; financing terrorism;[6] bombing of a public place outside the United States;[7] use of a weapon of mass destruction outside the United States;[8] and acts of terrorism that transcend national boundaries,[9] to name just a few.

Jurisdiction is often limited to specific instances, including, for example, attacks against U.S. persons or property. In other cases, jurisdiction is based on the crime being committed in certain limited and defined spaces, such as aircraft flying to or from the United States. At times, the offender's presence in the United States is deemed sufficient to establish jurisdiction—even if his presence is due solely to the fact that he is being brought to the United States for the purposes of prosecution.[10]

In 2011, for example, Mohamed Ibrahim Ahmed, an Eritrean national and resident of Sweden, was charged in federal court in New York for, among other things, providing material support to and receiving military training from the foreign terrorist organization al-Shabaab, which operates primarily in Somalia. The indictment does not charge that Ahmed engaged in or intended any specific acts within the United States or against U.S. citizens or property. Rather, the sole basis for exercising jurisdiction over him was that he was "brought into" the United States for the purpose of prosecution.[11] Ahmed challenged the jurisdiction of the court to try him and lost, despite the tenuous nature of the link between his actions and the United States.[12]

Challenges such as Ahmed's to the extraterritorial scope of criminal laws raise three interrelated issues:

1. Did Congress intend for the relevant statute to have extraterritorial effect?
2. Does the Constitution permit the extraterritorial application of the statute?
3. Is the extraterritorial application of the statute permitted under international law?

---

5. 18 U.S.C. § 2339B.
6. *Id.* § 2339D.
7. *Id.* § 2332f.
8. *Id.* § 2332a.
9. *Id.* § 2332b.
10. *See, e.g., id.* §§ 2339(B)(d)(1)(C), 2339D(b)(3) (examples of relevant statutory language); United States v. Yousef, 327 F.3d 56 (2d Cir. 2003) (holding that defendant involuntary brought to the United States is "found" there for purposes of asserting jurisdiction); United States v. Rezaq, 134 F.3d 1121 (D.C. Cir. 1998) ("afterward found" requirement permits prosecution even in a case in which the defendant was forcibly brought to the United States to stand trial solely for that offense); United States v. Ahmed, 2011 WL 5041456, at *2–3 (S.D.N.Y. Oct. 21, 2011) (same).
11. *Ahmed*, 2011 WL 5041456, at *2.
12. *Id.* Ahmed subsequently pleaded guilty to one count of conspiring to provide material support to al-Shabaab and one count of conspiring to receive military-type training from al-Shabaab.

Statutory Issues

Congressional intent is key in any analysis of a statute's extraterritorial reach. In Ahmed's case, the relevant statutes expressly state that there is "extraterritorial federal jurisdiction" over the material support for and receipt of military training offenses, and that jurisdiction exists when the "offender is brought . . . into the United States."[13] There is thus no doubt as to Congress's intent that Ahmed could be prosecuted for violating these offenses.[14]

Congressional intent is less clear-cut with respect to other criminal law provisions. At times extraterritorial jurisdiction will be inferred from the statute's aim. Several courts, for example, have concluded that the prohibition on killing U.S. officers or employees applies extraterritorially, given the U.S. government's interest in protecting its personnel from harm wherever they are operating.[15]

Some statutes also employ special terms of art to expand the jurisdiction over certain crimes to areas outside the United States' physical borders. The "special maritime and territorial jurisdiction of the United States" (SMTJ) is defined to include, among other things, the high seas; any aircraft in flight over the high seas or in U.S. airspace; foreign-located U.S. diplomatic, consular, or military installations in cases where the victim or offender is a U.S. national; and places not subject to the jurisdiction of other nations if the victim or offender is a U.S. national.[16] The SMTJ is the primary basis on which the United States has established jurisdiction to prosecute piracy on the high seas.

The scope of the related Military Extraterritorial Jurisdiction Act (MEJA), which is intended to apply substantive criminal law prohibitions to military contractors outside the United States, is a major issue in the prosecution of five Blackwater Worldwide (now Academi) security guards accused of indiscriminately shooting Iraqi civilians in Baghdad's Nisoor Square in September 2007. The guards have argued that their conduct is not covered under MEJA because they were not employed by the Department of Defense and that, therefore, the case must be dismissed. While a district judge rejected the motion to dismiss, he signaled that the issue was a close one. In the event of a conviction, it likely will be the subject of appeal.[17]

---

13. 18 U.S.C. §§ 2339B(d)(1)(C), 2339B(d)(2), 2339(D)(b)(3).
14. See Ahmed, 2011 WL 5041456, at *2 (concluding that the presumption against extraterritoriality was overcome by the clear expression of intent of the lawmakers in this case).
15. See, e.g., United States v. Kassar, 660 F.3d 108, 118 (2d Cir. 2011); United States v. Benitez, 741 F.2d 1312, 1317 (11th Cir. 1984).
16. 18 U.S.C. § 7. This statute purports to define the maritime and territorial jurisdiction of the United States; as a result, crimes subject to this jurisdictional hook are not technically "extraterritorial," even though they take place outside the United States' physical borders.
17. Another special jurisdictional hook includes the "special aircraft jurisdiction" that, among other things, covers U.S. aircrafts in flight, as well as any aircraft over U.S. airspace or with a completed destination in the United States. 49 U.S.C. § 46501.

Constitutional Issues

There are two distinct constitutional law questions: Did Congress have the authority to legislate in this manner? Is the prosecution consistent with due process?

In most cases—including the *Ahmed* case—courts have glossed over the first question and simply assumed that Congress had the constitutional authority to legislate. In general, Congress's power to criminalize extraterritorial conduct derives from its authority to "define and punish . . . Offenses against the Law of Nations"[18] or from an expansive reading of the Foreign Commerce Clause, which authorizes Congress to regulate commerce with foreign nations, and the Necessary and Proper Clause, which authorizes Congress to make laws deemed "necessary and proper" for carrying out the powers vested by the Constitution.[19]

A separate constitutional claim is often made based on an alleged violation of due process rights.[20] Defendants have claimed an insufficient nexus to the United States to justify the prosecution and a lack of fair notice that they could be subject to U.S. prosecution for a crime committed far outside its borders.[21] Although the Supreme Court has yet to weigh in, lower courts—including the *Ahmed* court—have routinely rejected such claims. Courts have, for example, found a "sufficient nexus" between the defendant and the United States to justify prosecution when the intended victims are U.S. nationals or U.S. property (e.g., the piracy cases), or the defendant has knowingly provided support to a foreign terrorist organization that threatens the security of the United States or its nationals (e.g., the *Ahmed*, *Warsame*, and *el-Kebir* cases). Courts have similarly found "fair notice" so long as the defendant would reasonably understand that his conduct was criminal

---

18. U.S. Const. art. I, § 8, cl. 10

19. *Id.* § 8, cl. 3, 18. In *Brehm v. United States*, __ F.3d __, 2012 WL 3243495 (4th Cir. Aug. 10, 2012), the Fourth Circuit concluded that the extraterritorial regulation of military contractors is authorized by a combination of the authority to "raise and support Armies" and the necessary and proper clause (clauses 12 and 18 of Article I, section 8). Moreover, some courts have suggested that the Congress can broadly criminalize extraterritorial conduct based on the federal government's inherent foreign affairs power, although this is a highly contestable assertion when applied to foreign nationals and to conduct that does not fall neatly into traditional foreign affairs powers.

20. *Brehm v. United States*, __ F.3d __, 2012 WL 3243495 (4th Cir. Aug. 10, 2012), is an interesting case in this regard. It involves a South African citizen who, while employed by the military contractor DynCorp in Afghanistan, allegedly assaulted a British national with his knife. Both victim and defendant are noncitizens, and the only contact with the United States is the defendant's employment by a U.S.-based security contractor. The government invoked the Military Extraterritorial Jurisdiction Act to charge him with two counts of assault. Brehm challenged the indictment on due process grounds, arguing that he lacked sufficient nexus with the United States and fair notice to be criminally prosecuted in the United States, but lost. The Fourth Circuit ruled that Brehm's actions affected significant U.S. interests, including the preservation of law and order on the base where the assault took place, and that he had fair notice given that his employment contract explicitly noted the potential liability to criminal prosecution under MEJA. *Id.* at *4–6.

21. There also is a separate, unresolved issue as to whether foreign nationals with no substantial connections to the United States are even protected by the Due Process Clause with respect to actions that take place overseas.

somewhere, even if it was not self-evident that he would be prosecuted in the United States.[22]

International Law Issues

International law has developed its own set of limits on the permissible extraterritorial application of the criminal law. Under customary international law, the extraterritorial application of criminal statutes is permitted in those cases in which the offender or victim is a national of the prosecuting state (known as the "nationality" and "passive personality" principles, respectively); the offense has effects within the prosecuting state, such as a shooting across a border (the "territorial principle"); the offense affects the vital interests of the prosecuting state, such as counterfeiting currency (the "protective principle"); or the offense is universally condemned, such as torture or genocide (the "universality principle"). Treaty provisions also are deemed by many to provide a separate basis for the extraterritorial application of a specific law.

These international law principles guide, but do not dictate, the limits of the United States' extraterritorial jurisdiction. Courts will at times look to these international law principles in evaluating the meaning of an unclear statute. However, a clear statement of congressional intent to apply a statute extraterritorially will trump any international law claim.

In most cases, Congress has legislated consistent with these principles by, for example, requiring injury to a U.S. person or property as a basis for establishing jurisdiction. However, jurisdiction based solely on the fact that the individual is "brought into" the United States, as was the basis for jurisdiction in Ahmed's case, does not seem permissible under international law. There is thus a fair question to be asked about whether the extraterritorial provision of material support to a foreign terrorist organization that operates outside of the United States sufficiently satisfies the protective (or any other) principle to justify the extraterritorial prosecution under international law.[23]

INVESTIGATIONS ABROAD

Prosecutions of extraterritorial offenses raise a number of questions about the applicability of constitutional rights outside the United States, the admissibility

---

22. *See, e.g.*, United States v. Kassar, 660 F.3d 108, 119 (2d Cir. 2011) ("Fair warning does not require that the defendants understand that they could be subject to criminal prosecution *in the United States* so long as they would reasonably understand that their conduct was criminal and would subject them to prosecution somewhere.").

23. A similar question can be asked about the prosecution in *Brehm. See supra* note 20.

of evidence gathered by foreign officials, and the process by which evidence collected by a foreign government is provided to the United States.

The Constitution across National Borders

U.S. citizens, even when abroad, are generally protected by the Constitution's Bill of Rights, although the specific right may apply differently depending on the context.[24] By contrast, the prevailing view is that aliens acting outside the United States are not protected by the Constitution's Bill of Rights unless they have developed "substantial connections" to the United States.[25] Once brought to the United States for trial, aliens are, however, generally considered protected by so-called trial rights, even if they are being prosecuted for actions taken abroad. As a result, the scope of constitutional protections for aliens subject to trial in the United States depends a great deal on whether the right qualifies as a trial right. This is an area of law that is rife with inconsistencies and ambiguities and is likely to be the subject of high-profile litigation in future cases.

- *Fourth Amendment:* In 1990, a plurality of the Supreme Court held that the Fourth Amendment (protecting against unreasonable searches and seizures) is not a trial right, and therefore its protections do not apply to aliens abroad who lack substantial connections to the United States.[26] Evidence obtained as the result of a warrantless—and perhaps even suspicionless[27]—search of an alien's property by U.S. officials outside the United States is thus admissible at trial without violating the Fourth Amendment.
- *Fifth Amendment/Miranda:* Because the Fifth Amendment's protection against self-incrimination is considered a trial right, its protections are deemed to apply to citizens and noncitizens alike. Accordingly, statements made by foreign nationals to U.S. personnel during un-Mirandized overseas interviews are likely to be excluded, unless they fall

---

24. For example, the Second Circuit has held that while U.S. citizens are protected by the Fourth Amendment wherever they are located, the warrant clause does not apply outside the United States' borders due to, among other things, the impracticalities of applying and enforcing the warrant requirement extraterritorially. *In re* Terrorist Bombings of U.S. Embassies in East Africa, 552 F.3d 157, 168–71 (2d Cir. 2008). *See also* United States v. Stokes, 10 F. Supp. 2d 689, 697 (N.D. Ill. 2009); United States v. Flath, 845 F. Supp. 2d 951, 959–61 (E.D. Wis. 2012). Although the Supreme Court has only explicitly addressed the extraterritorial application of the Fifth and Sixth Amendments' jury trial rights to U.S. citizens, *Reid v. Covert*, 354 U.S. 1 (1957), has been interpreted by many as suggesting that the individual rights enumerated in the Constitution protect U.S. citizens wherever they are located, unless impracticable and anomalous.
25. United States v. Verdugo-Urquidez, 494 U.S. 259 (1990).
26. *Id.*
27. The Supreme Court has not yet ruled on this question, and language in the concurring opinions in *Verdugo-Urquidez* suggests that the case might have come out differently had it involved a truly suspicionless search.

within the so-called "public safety" exception to *Miranda*. Any coerced or involuntary testimony—whether made to a U.S. or foreign interrogator—is also likely to be excluded from trial.

There is, however, no violation of the Fifth Amendment's protection against self-incrimination if the government questions the defendant without *Miranda* warnings or otherwise elicits an involuntary statement and does not use the resulting statements in court.[28] There also is an open question as to the scope of the "public·safety" exception (under which un-Mirandized statements are deemed admissible at trial if made in response to questioning reasonably prompted by a concern for the public safety), and the degree to which it or some other exception would cover point-of-capture interrogations on the battlefield and wide-ranging intelligence interviews.[29]

- *Sixth Amendment/Right to Counsel:* The Sixth Amendment right to counsel kicks in at the initiation of adversarial criminal proceedings—whether by way of arraignment, indictment, or other means.[30] Like the Fifth Amendment right against self-incrimination, the Sixth Amendment is a trial right. As a result, aliens and citizens alike are entitled to the right to counsel during criminal proceedings in the United States.

  Unlike the Fifth Amendment, which is violated only when a statement is introduced at trial, the Sixth Amendment is violated at the time the questioning occurred.[31] This, in turn, raises an interesting and unresolved question as to whether the extraterritorial questioning of an indicted foreign national by U.S. personnel violates the Sixth Amendment, even if the statements are never introduced at trial. There is also an unresolved question as to whether, and to what extent, there is a "public safety" or other intelligence-based exception to the Sixth Amendment.

- *Sixth Amendment/Speedy Trial Right:* Also a trial right, the Sixth Amendment's right to a speedy trial protects citizens and noncitizens alike. That said, courts have adopted a flexible view of what counts as an "unreasonable delay" that would violate this right. In *United States v. Ghailani*, for example, a federal district judge in New York concluded

---

28. It is, however, possible that an interrogation could be so abusive as to "shock the conscience," in which case there would likely be a Fifth Amendment due process violation.
29. In September 2011, a district court upheld the most extensive use of the "public safety" exception in a terrorism case to date, concluding that 50 minutes of non-Mirandized questioning about a failed explosive device, the bomb-maker, and other related questions could be admitted at the trial of Umar Farouk Abdulmutullab. Abdulmutullab subsequently pled guilty to a number of terrorism crimes based on his role in the 2009 Christmas Day attempted bombing of an airplane headed to the United States. United States v. Abdulmutallab, 2011 WL 4345243, at *5 (E.D. Mich. Sep. 16, 2011).
30. Interestingly, the filing of a criminal complaint does not trigger the Sixth Amendment right to counsel, but the filing of an indictment does.
31. *See* Kansas v. Ventris, 129 S. Ct. 1841, 1846 (2009).

that a five-year delay between Ghailani's arrest and transfer to federal court, during which time he was held in Central Intelligence Agency and Department of Defense custody, did not violate his Sixth Amendment speedy trial right.[32]

Foreign Investigations and "Joint Ventures"

In many cases, foreign governments will engage in searches, seizures, or interrogations and then turn the information over to the United States for use in federal court. As a general matter, such evidence will not be excluded on constitutional grounds so long as the foreign government complied with its own laws, even if the evidence was gathered in a way that would be impermissible if done by the United States. Thus, foreign governments need not obtain a warrant, issue *Miranda* warnings, or provide access to counsel to indicted persons overseas, even when conducting investigations of U.S. citizens.

If, however, there is a "joint venture" between the United States and the foreign government, based on a finding that the United States participated in or actively directed the relevant search, seizure, or interrogation, then evidence might be excluded absent compliance with the relevant constitutional procedural protections.[33] In addition, coerced or involuntary statements made to foreign officials are likely to be excluded from trial on Fifth Amendment grounds, even if obtained by foreign government officials. Similarly, if the foreign government acts in such a way that "shocks the conscience" by, for example, engaging in torture, evidence may be excluded.

Getting Information to Court

Prosecutions of extraterritorial offenses raise difficult challenges associated with the effort to get information collected by foreign governments to the United States in a form that can be introduced in court. Means by which U.S. prosecutors will seek to obtain admissible information from a foreign government include the following:

- *Direct cooperation:* U.S. law enforcement officials serve in U.S. embassies all over the world, providing a link to foreign law enforcement officials and allowing for more informal types of coordination and communication. These informal relationships are often crucial in

---

32. *See* United States v. Ghailani, 751 F. Supp. 2d 515 (S.D.N.Y. 2010).
33. In practice, it is extremely difficult to prevail on this ground. Tips or limited communications about a specific investigative action, without more, are not deemed to create a joint venture. Even if there is a joint venture, a foreign state's compliance with its own laws will justify a finding of reasonableness under the Fourth Amendment. *See, e.g.*, United States v. Barona, 56 F.3d 1087 (9th Cir. 1995).

gathering relevant evidence, even if it is not always admissible in a criminal case.
- *Mutual legal assistance treaties:* These are generally bilateral treaties that seek to expedite the exchange of evidence and information related to criminal activity. Such treaties include provisions to help ensure that the evidence or information can be admissible in court—for example, by including provisions on authentication of testimony or evidence.
- *Letters rogatory:* An option of last resort (e.g., when there is no executive branch agreement or treaty in place), these are issued by a U.S. court and directed to a foreign government's courts. In practice, these letters are transmitted from the State Department to a foreign government's Ministry of Justice, a process that often takes an extremely long time.

OBTAINING THE DEFENDANT

Once the United States determines it has jurisdiction over an extraterritorial offense and probable cause to arrest, it must find a way to get the defendant into U.S. court. This is often done through a formal extradition process, although it can be achieved by other means as well.[34] While often routine, extradition requests can become tangled in legal challenges and take years to be processed. Among the many prerequisites for extradition, there must be so-called dual criminality, which requires that the act being punished is a crime in both the requesting and receiving state, and the offense may not be a "political offense" such as treason.

At times, extraditing countries have insisted on assurances that the defendant will not be subject to capital punishment or even life in prison. In several instances, extraditing countries have insisted on assurances that the defendant would not be subject to prosecution by military commission. The Netherlands, for example, insisted on a promise that a military commission not try Mahamud Said Omar, who is being prosecuted on charges of recruiting young men from Minneapolis to join al-Shabaab. The United Kingdom insisted on similar assurances before extraditing Syed Hashmi, convicted of providing material support to al-Qaida, as did the Czech Republic before it extradited Oussama Kassir, also convicted of providing material support to al-Qaida.[35] Some countries will refuse to extradite their own nationals for prosecution in a foreign country. (The United

---

34. The United States currently has bilateral extradition treaties with over 100 countries. *See* 18 U.S.C. § 3181 note for a list of the bilateral extradition treaties currently in force.

35. *See* David S. Kris, *Law Enforcement as a Counterterrorism Tool*, 5 J. Nat'l Sec. L. & Pol'y 1, 68 nn.190 & 191 (2011); Robert Chesney, United States v. Mahamud Said Omar: *An Important New Al-Shabaab Case in Federal Court*, Lawfare, Aug. 15, 2011, http://www.lawfareblog.com/2011/08/united-states-v-mahamud-said-omar-an-important-new-al-shabaab-case-in-federal-court/.

States does not take this position and will extradite its own citizens to face foreign prosecution in certain circumstances.)

In other instances, defendants have been seized directly by the United States or transferred to the United States outside of any legal process. In 1987, Fawaz Younis, for example, was lured aboard a ship by U.S. officials in international waters off of Cyprus, taken into U.S. custody, flown to the United States, and convicted of hostage-taking. Warsame was also reportedly captured directly by U.S. personnel in the Arabian Gulf before being flown to the United States to face criminal charges. Even actions that are illegal under international law will not necessarily preclude a trial in U.S. federal court. In 1992, for example, the Supreme Court ruled that the forcible abduction of drug lord Humberto Alvarez-Machain from his office in Guadalajara, Mexico, neither violated the extradition treaty in place between the United States and Mexico nor barred his prosecution in federal court.[36]

Fawaz Younis and Operation "Goldenrod"

On September 13, 1987, Fawaz Younis—the alleged ringleader of an airplane hijacking two years earlier—boarded a small motorboat along with a one-time-friend-turned-informant off the coast of Cyprus. Thinking he was about to engage in a lucrative drug deal, he was lured onto a yacht by several Federal Bureau of Investigation agents purporting to be connected to an international drug dealer named "Joseph." Agents initially greeted him with a routine pat-down and beer, then escorted him to the stern of the ship, tackled him, and arrested him. Younis was then transferred to a naval munitions ship and held there for five days before being flown to the United States and charged in federal court.

Labeled operation "Goldenrod," this was the first time that the United States apprehended an international terrorist overseas and brought him back to the United States for trial. Younis argued that U.S. courts lacked jurisdiction over him for acts that occurred overseas and that the case should be dismissed for outrageous government conduct in his abduction, initial detention, and transfer. Both the trial and appellate court ruled against him, and in October 1989, he was convicted and sentenced to 30 years in prison for aircraft piracy and hostage-taking, among other things.

At times, foreign governments will simply transfer a defendant to U.S. custody without going through the otherwise applicable extradition process, as was reportedly done in the case of Ahmed Ghailani, who is now serving a life sentence for his role in the 1998 embassy bombings in Kenya and Tanzania.

Once in the United States, venue rules generally require that the defendant be tried in the jurisdiction into which he was first brought, unless he was charged

---

36. United States v. Alvarez-Machain, 504 U.S. 655 (1992).

prior to his arrival in the United States.[37] This gives the United States considerable discretion in deciding where to try a suspected terrorist apprehended abroad.[38]

The government also has a reasonable period of time to transport the defendant to the United States before he must be presented before a judge in federal court. (Ordinarily, defendants must be presented to a court within 24 hours of arrest.) At presentment, the judge advises the defendant of the charges against him, the right to remain silent, the right to counsel, and pretrial release procedures. Defendants can and often do waive their presentment rights in order to cooperate with the government in the hopes of obtaining a more lenient sentence.

POSTTRIAL

Foreign nationals who have served their sentence or are acquitted generally are placed into immigration removal proceedings and returned to their home countries. Any alien who is deemed to pose a threat can, and in some cases must, be detained during this process. But what if the alien is stateless or his home country does not want him back? Or what if the alien makes a credible claim that it is likely that he will be tortured upon return, and there is no obvious third-party country to which he can be sent?

The Supreme Court has stated that there is a presumptive six-month limit on post-removal order periods of detention, concluding that continued detention is impermissible once removal is no longer "reasonably foreseeable."[39] It has, however, also stated that extended detention of "particularly dangerous individuals," including terrorists, may be permissible even if removal of those aliens is unlikely. Statutory and regulatory provisions now permit such continued detention of terrorist aliens on security-related grounds, although, as of this writing, these provisions have never been employed or tested before any court.

In some cases, an alien who has been acquitted or who has served his sentence may be a candidate for law of war detention. Such a move would, however, be highly controversial. Both the Ali Saleh Kahlah al-Marri and Jose Padilla cases, in which the United States transferred detainees from civilian court to law of war detention, sparked significant controversy and litigation. Transferring an individual who was acquitted or who has completed his criminal sentence to law of war detention could be even more contentious.

---

37. If, however, the crime involved a continuing offense, such as conspiracy, begun overseas but including acts committed within a state, the applicability of these rules is uncertain; venue rules may require the case to be brought in one of the districts where U.S.-based acts have occurred.

38. Anyone indicted prior to being brought into the United States must be indicted and tried in his last known residence (or the last known residence of a joint offender). If he has no known prior U.S. residence, the indictment must be brought in the District of Columbia.

39. Zadvydas v. Davis, 533 U.S. 678, 701 (2001).

CONCLUSION

Over the past two decades, Congress has steadily expanded the extraterritorial reach of the U.S. criminal law, and U.S. courts are increasingly called upon to prosecute terrorists for crimes that occur outside the borders of the United States. Measured by the conviction rate, such prosecutions have been an overwhelming success. Yet they also raise a host of contested and complex statutory, constitutional, and international law issues. This is an area of law that warrants further attention by scholars, courts, and the media alike.

EXPERTS

Robert Chesney, Professor, University of Texas Law School; (512) 232-1298; rchesney@law.utexas.edu

David Cole, Professor, Georgetown Law Center; (202) 662-9406; cole@law.georgetown.edu

Jennifer Daskal, Georgetown Law Center; (202) 365-3758; jendaskal@gmail.com

Todd Hinnen, former Deputy Assistant Attorney General for National Security, Department of Justice; (202) 654-6259; THinnen@perkinscoie.com

David Kris, former Assistant Attorney General for National Security, Department of Justice; davidskris@aol.com

David Luban, Professor, Georgetown Law Center; (202) 662-9461; luband@law.georgetown.edu

RESOURCES

Articles and Secondary Sources

CHRIS DOYLE, CONG. RESEARCH SERV., EXTRATERRITORIAL APPLICATION OF UNITED STATES CRIMINAL LAW (Mar. 26, 2010).

David S. Kris, *Law Enforcement as a Counterterrorism Tool*, 5 J. NAT'L SEC. L. & POL'Y 1 (2011).

JULIE ROSE O'SULLIVAN, DAVID JAY LUBAN & DAVID P. STEWART, INTERNATIONAL AND TRANSNATIONAL CRIMINAL LAW (Aspen 2010).

Press Release, U.S. Att'y for the S. Dist. of N.Y., Accused Al Shabaab Leader Accused of Providing Material Support to Al Shabaab and Al Qaeda in the Arabian Peninsula (July 5, 2011), http://www.justice.gov/usao/nys/pressreleases/July11/warsameindictmentpr.pdf.

Press Release, U.S. Att'y for the E. Dist. of N.Y., Alleged Terrorist Charged with Conspiracy to Provide Material Support to Al Qaeda (Nov. 10, 2011), http://www.justice.gov/usao/nye/pr/2011/2011nov10.html.

Robert Chesney, United States v. Mahamud Said Omar: An Important New Al-Shabaab Case in Federal Court, LAWFARE, Aug. 15, 2011, http://www.lawfareblog.com/2011/08/united-states-v-mahamud-said-omar-an-important-new-al-shabaab-case-in-federal-court/.

Cases

Am. Banana Co. v. United Fruit Co., 213 U.S. 347, 355 (1909).

Kansas v. Ventris, 129 S. Ct. 1841, 1846 (2009).

Miranda v. Arizona, 384 U.S. 436 (1966).

New York v. Quarles, 467 U.S. 649 (1984).

Reid v. Covert, 354 U.S. 1 (1957).

In re Terrorist Bombings of U.S. Embassies in East Africa, 552 F.3d 157 (2d Cir. 2008).

United States v. Abdulmutallab, 2011 WL 4345243 (E.D. Mich. Sep. 16, 2011).

United States v. Ahmed, 2011 WL 5041456 (S.D.N.Y. Oct. 21, 2011).

United States v. Alvarez-Machain, 504 U.S. 655 (1992).

United States v. Barona, 56 F.3d 1087 (9th Cir. 1995).

United States v. Benitez, 741 F.2d 1312 (11th Cir. 1984).

United States v. Brehm, __ F.3d __, 2012 WL 3243495 (4th Cir. Aug. 10, 2012).

United States v. Flath, 845 F. Supp. 2d 951 (E.D. Wis. 2012).

United States v. Ghailani, 751 F. Supp. 2d 515 (S.D.N.Y. 2010).

United States v. Kassar, 660 F.3d 118 (2d Cir. 2011).

United States v. Rezaq, 134 F.3d 1121 (D.C. Cir. 1998).

United States v. Stokes, 10 F. Supp. 2d 689 (N.D. Ill. 2009).

United States v. Verdugo-Urquidez, 494 U.S. 259 (1990).

United States v. Yousef, 327 F.3d 56 (2d Cir. 2003).

United States v. Yunis, 681 F. Supp. 909 (D.D.C. 1988), *rev'd*, 859 F.2d 53 (D.D.C. 1998).

United States v. Yunis, 924 F.2d 1086 (D.C. Cir. 1991).

Zadvydas v. Davis, 533 U.S. 678, 701 (2001).

Statutes

18 U.S.C. § 7: Special maritime and territorial jurisdiction of the United States defined.

18 U.S.C. § 2332a: Use of weapons of mass destruction.

18 U.S.C. § 2332b: Acts of terrorism transcending national boundaries.

18 U.S.C. § 2332f: Bombings of places of public use, government facilities, public transportation systems, and infrastructure facilities.

18 U.S.C. § 2339A: Providing material support to terrorists.

18 U.S.C. § 2339B: Providing material support or resources to designated foreign terrorist organizations.

18 U.S.C. § 2339C: Prohibitions against the financing of terrorism.

18 U.S.C. § 2339D: Receiving military-type training from a foreign terrorist organization.

18 U.S.C. § 3181 note: Extradition treaties interpretation.

18 U.S.C. ch. 212: Military extraterritorial jurisdiction.

49 U.S.C. §§ 46501 *et seq*: Special aircraft jurisdiction of the United States.

Data Mining: A Primer

By Adam Isles

Public discourse on data mining reflects a larger conversation on how best to leverage technology advances for security purposes while also protecting privacy. In the last half-century, new technologies have developed that allow the recording and storage of vast amounts of information about people's daily lives. As noted in a Congressional Research Service report on data mining, recent times have witnessed dramatic advances in the volume of data collected (some intelligence agency databases reportedly grow at four petabytes a month), the affordability of storage (migration from dollars per megabyte to pennies per megabyte), processing power, and enhanced analytic and interoperability tools.[1]

These information technology advances have, in turn, resulted in significant public discourse on privacy-related implications of the processing and storage of personal data. As early as 1973, a landmark U.S. government report on automated personal data systems—which served as the impetus for the Privacy Act of 1974—warned about the potential for "[q]uick, cheap access to the contents of a very large automated file often [to] prompt an organization or group of organizations to indulge in what might

---

1. *See, e.g.*, JEFFREY W. SEIFERT, CONG. RESEARCH SERV., RL31798, DATA MINING AND HOMELAND SECURITY: AN OVERVIEW 2, 26 (updated Aug. 27, 2008), http://www.lrc.fema.gov/starweb/lrcweb/servlet.starweb?path=lrcweb/STARLibraries1.web&search=R%3D177989. A petabyte constitutes a quadrillion bytes.

be called 'dragnet behavior.'"² Data accuracy—and in particular the fear that decisions would be made based on inaccurate data—was another major concern.

As information technology has advanced, so, too, has the networked nature of the world in which we live, both in terms of IT connectivity and physical connectivity via liberalization of global travel and trade. These changes have introduced asymmetric risks whereby bad acts planned by small cells in faraway places can cause catastrophic consequences to our way of life—either physical, as manifested by the attacks of September 11, 2001, or virtual, as increasingly seen in the cyber domain.³ The drive to *prevent* such attacks has focused attention, in part, on how recent IT advances, in particular data mining techniques, can be applied to identify relationships that are not obvious (e.g., between known and heretofore unknown members of a terror cell) and generate other insights that human investigators, manually sifting through records and evidence, could not.

So where does this leave us? As Supreme Court Justice Samuel Alito recently noted: "Dramatic technological change may lead to periods in which popular expectations are in flux and may ultimately produce significant changes in popular attitudes."⁴ This chapter offers a primer on data mining by first defining the term and attempting to explain what makes data mining controversial. It then frames data mining within the broader context of privacy law and policy to explain both history and what may be changing. A discussion of the underlying technology is also offered both to explain the impetus behind various government research programs and to outline the limits of the technology. Finally, several widely publicized cases with perceived data mining implications are described within a definitional, historical, and technological context.

---

2. *See* U.S. DEP'T OF HEALTH, EDUC. & WELFARE, RECORDS, COMPUTERS AND THE RIGHTS OF CITIZENS: REPORT OF THE SECRETARY'S ADVISORY COMMITTEE ON AUTOMATED PERSONAL DATA SYSTEMS ch. II (July 1973), http://aspe.hhs.gov/datacncl/1973privacy/tocprefacemembers.htm#preface [hereinafter SEC'Y'S ADVISORY COMM. ON AUTOMATED PERSONAL DATA SYSTEMS REPORT].

3. *See* Office of the Dir. of Nat'l Intelligence, Annual Threat Assessment of the U.S. Intelligence Community for the House Permanent Select Committee on Intelligence 2 (Feb. 3, 2010), http://www.dni.gov/index.php/newsroom/testimonies/104-congressional-testimonies-2010http://www.dni.gov/index.php/newsroom/testimonies/104-congressional-testimonies-2010 ("According to the DNI, 'We cannot be certain that our cyberspace infrastructure will remain available and reliable during a time of crisis.'").

4. *See, e.g.*, United States v. Jones, 132 S. Ct. 945 (2012) (Alito, J., concurring), http://www.supremecourt.gov/opinions/11pdf/10-1259.pdf.

> Recent years have seen the emergence of many new devices that permit the monitoring of a person's movements. In some locales, closed-circuit television video monitoring is becoming ubiquitous. On toll roads, automatic toll collection systems create a precise record of the movements of motorists who choose to make use of that convenience. Many motorists purchase cars that are equipped with devices that permit a central station to ascertain the car's location at any time so that roadside assistance may be provided if needed and the car may be found if it is stolen.

Id. at 963.

WHAT IS DATA MINING?

Wikipedia tells us simply that data mining "is the process of discovering new patterns from large data sets involving methods at the intersection of artificial intelligence, machine learning, statistics and database systems."[5] By contrast, the Government Accountability Office (GAO) offers the following definition: "Data-mining systems . . . apply database technology and associated techniques—such as queries, statistical analysis, and modeling—[to personal information] in order to discover information in massive databases, uncover hidden patterns, find subtle relationships in existing data, and predict future results."[6] The two most common types of data mining are, according to the GAO, pattern-based queries and subject-based queries.

> Pattern-based queries search for data elements that match or depart from a pre-determined pattern, such as unusual travel patterns that might indicate a terrorist threat. Subject-based queries search for any available information on a predetermined subject using a specific identifier. This identifier could be linked to an individual (such as a person's name or Social Security number) or an object (such as a bar code or registration number). For example, one could initiate a search for information related to an automobile license plate number.[7]

In terms of governmental data mining activities, such techniques are widely used in the defense and intelligence communities. In addition, the Federal IT Dashboard (which describes itself as a "website enabling federal agencies, industry, the general public and other stakeholders to view details of federal information technology investments") indicates that seven federal civilian agencies planned to spend more than $140 million on data mining tools in fiscal year 2012.[8] Regarding the GAO definition, "subject-based queries" could apply to a significant amount of criminal investigative activity that occurs today—e.g., agents looking through transactional data such as phone records, travel records, and financial data for patterns of criminal activity and mapping out the hubs and spokes of an organized crime group. Looking at this data allows both a clearer picture of a target's actions over time and the discovery of links to other associates that can help map out a

---

5. *See* "Data mining," http://en.wikipedia.org/wiki/Data_mining.
6. *See* U.S. Gov't Accountability Office, GAO-11-742, Data Mining: DHS Needs to Improve Executive Oversight of Systems Supporting Counterterrorism 6 (2011), http://www.gao.gov/new.items/d11742.pdf.
7. *Id.*
8. *See* Federal IT Dashboard, Portfolio Overview—Services, http://www.itdashboard.gov/portfolios/service_group=592.

criminal network. For example, a simple analysis of contact phone numbers in airline passenger name records linked Mohamed Atta and five of the 9/11 hijackers.[9]

Nonetheless, this activity has sometimes aroused public debate. Scrutiny is usually triggered either as the size and scope of databases expand[10] or when the government is alleged to have violated some policy related to the management of this data—either by failing to comply with statutory procedural requirements to provide notice to the public when new systematic collection of personal data occurs[11] or by exceeding its authority to collect information in the first place.[12]

That said, law enforcement mostly considers only the second type—pattern-based queries—as "true" data mining. And, in fact, the definition of "data mining" in the Data Mining Reporting Act aligns to this policy view.[13] Pattern-based queries can involve looking at historical events (fraud cases, terrorism cases), identifying commonalities in the underlying circumstances (e.g., typical demographics, locations), creating rule sets that turn these commonalities into database search criteria, and then applying these rules against all of the underlying data to identify new risks. Such queries can also entail identifying "normal" behavior for individuals in question, and then flagging deviations from that norm as "anomalies."

---

9. *See* Superseding Indictment, United States v. Zacarias Moussaoui, Criminal No. 01-455-A (E.D. Va. July 2002), http://fl1.findlaw.com/news.findlaw.com/wsj/docs/moussaoui/usmouss71602spind.pdf.

10. *See, e.g.,* Electronic Frontier Found., Report on Investigative Data Warehouse (Apr. 2009), https://www.eff.org/issues/foia/investigative-data-warehouse-report.

11. *See* U.S. Gov't Accountability Office, Letter to Cong. Committees, Aviation Security: Transportation Security Administration Did Not Fully Disclose Uses of Personal Information During Secure Flight Program Testing in Initial Privacy Notices, but Has Recently Taken Steps to More Fully Inform the Public (July 22, 2005), http://www.gao.gov/new.items/d05864r.pdf.

12. *See, e.g.,* U.S. Dep't of Justice, Office of Inspector Gen., A Review of the Federal Bureau of Investigation's Use of Exigent Letters and Other Informal Requests for Telephone Records (Jan. 2010), http://www.justice.gov/oig/special/s1001r.pdf.

13. The Data Mining Reporting Act, which requires DHS to report annually on activities deemed "data mining," defines data mining as:

> a program involving pattern-based queries, searches, or other analyses of 1 or more electronic databases, where—
>
> (A) a department or agency of the Federal Government, or a non-Federal entity acting on behalf of the Federal Government, is conducting the queries, searches, or other analyses to discover or locate a predictive pattern or anomaly indicative of terrorist or criminal activity on the part of any individual or individuals;
>
> (B) the queries, searches, or other analyses are not subject-based and do not use personal identifiers of a specific individual, or inputs associated with a specific individual or group of individuals, to retrieve information from the database or databases; and
>
> (C) the purpose of the queries, searches, or other analyses is not solely—
>
> > (i) the detection of fraud, waste, or abuse in a Government agency or program; or
> >
> > (ii) the security of a Government computer system.

42 U.S.C. § 2000ee-3(b)(1).

What Is Data Mining?

Data mining is not limited in use to governmental authorities. The payment card industry mines the massive amounts of payment card transaction data to improve fraud detection and prevention activities. For example, certain factors have been identified as indicators pointing to future likely fraud cases—larger-than-normal orders; orders consisting of several of the same item; orders made up of big ticket items; orders shipped "rushed" or "overnight"; orders from Internet addresses at free e-mail services; orders shipped to an international address; and multiple orders using different names, addresses, and card numbers, but coming from the same IP address.[14]

As a practical matter, governmental data mining generates the greatest attention when applied to innocent persons' data without being based on a specific basis for examination (what law enforcement calls "predication"). Key factors to consider include the following:

- *Use of personally identifying information, or PII.* As noted above, is personally identifying information actually used? A number of systems entail data mining, but not with respect to PII.
- *Likelihood of positive findings—the credibility of the "pattern."* The National Research Council authored a major study on the use of data mining tools in counterterrorism investigations, and the study in part distinguished between the use of data mining in fraud-related versus counterterrorism activities. "Such techniques often work well in commercial settings, for example for fraud detection, where they are applied to highly structured databases and are honed through constant use and learning," said the report, which went on to warn that the problems confronting counterterrorism analysts are "vastly more difficult."[15]
- *Consequences of a hit.* In a commercial payment card context, some transactions result in manual review by the credit card company, some result in follow-up questions to the customer over the phone, and some result in declined transactions.[16] In a governmental context, most data mining programs require some manual, human intervention and decision-making before further action is taken.
- *Use of commercial data and context.* The use of commercial data—data collected about individuals by commercial entities (e.g., airlines, credit card companies, credit bureaus)—has engendered controversy for two

---

14. *See, e.g.*, VISA E-COMMERCE MERCHANTS GUIDE TO RISK MANAGEMENT: TOOLS AND BEST PRACTICES FOR BUILDING A SECURE INTERNET BUSINESS 47 (2008), http://usa.visa.com/download/merchants/visa_risk_management_guide_ecommerce.pdf [hereinafter VISA E-COMMERCE GUIDE].

15. *See* NAT'L RESEARCH COUNCIL, PROTECTING INDIVIDUAL PRIVACY IN THE STRUGGLE AGAINST TERRORISTS: A FRAMEWORK FOR PROGRAM ASSESSMENT 3 (2008), http://www.nap.edu/openbook.php?record_id=12452 [hereinafter NAT'L RESEARCH COUNCIL PRIVACY REPORT]. The report warned that "even in well-managed programs [data mining] tools are likely to return significant rates of false positives, especially if the tools are highly automated."

16. *See, e.g.*, VISA E-COMMERCE GUIDE, *supra* note 14, at 49–50.

reasons: questionable accuracy[17] and questionable effectiveness as a tool for identifying terrorism-related risk factors.[18] But context matters—the use of commercial data for fraud detection is much more widely accepted.

- The GAO found that in the wake of Hurricanes Katrina and Rita in 2005, the Federal Emergency Management Agency (FEMA) made millions of dollars in payments to thousands of registrants who submitted Social Security numbers that had not been issued or belonged to deceased individuals. The GAO review also detected that FEMA made tens of thousands of payments to registrants who provided other false or duplicate information on their registrations.[19] The GAO recommended that FEMA utilize commercial data to scrutinize disaster applications, and FEMA now subjects applications to automatic address and occupancy electronic verification—i.e., to confirm that the address is deliverable and is not high risk (e.g., tattoo parlor, pawn shop) and, through an electronic check of property, that an applicant actually lives at the property.[20]
- Likewise, the GAO has highlighted the value of commercial data as an immigration fraud reduction tool. For example, regarding permanent residence applications, a December 2008 GAO report found that commercially available databases such as AutoTrack, ChoicePoint, and LexisNexis could help confirm whether, in marriage-based petitions, the petitioner and spouse live at the same address and whether, in employment-based petitions, the employer appears to be a legitimate firm.[21]
- *Predication and context.* Applying data mining techniques to records about innocent persons arouses more controversy than applying them to

---

17. *See, e.g.*, U.S. Gov't Accountability Office, GAO 04-385, Computer-Assisted Passenger Prescreening Program Faces Significant Implementation Challenges (2004), http://www.gao.gov/assets/250/241425.pdf.

18. *See, e.g.*, Seifert, *supra* note 1, at 3 ("For example, an application may identify that a pattern of behavior, such as the propensity to purchase airline tickets just shortly before the flight is scheduled to depart, is related to characteristics such as income, level of education, and Internet use. However, that does not necessarily indicate that the ticket purchasing behavior is caused by one or more of these variables.").

19. *See* U.S. Gov't Accountability Office, GAO-06-403T, Expedited Assistance for Victims of Hurricanes Katrina and Rita: FEMA's Control Weaknesses Exposed the Government to Significant Fraud and Abuse 4, 5 (2006), http://www.gao.gov/new.items/d06403t.pdf.

20. *See* U.S. Gov't Accountability Office, GAO 09-671, Hurricanes Gustav and Ike Disaster Assistance: FEMA Strengthened Its Fraud Prevention Controls, but Customer Service Needs Improvement 5 (2009), http://www.gao.gov/new.items/d09671.pdf.

21. *See* U.S. Gov't Accountability Office, GAO 09-55, Immigration Benefits: Actions Needed to Address Vulnerabilities in Process for Granting Permanent Residency 30 (2008), http://www.gao.gov/new.items/d0955.pdf.

law enforcement records about subjects of active criminal and terrorist investigations.[22] These concerns apply even more so in the international context; for example, the European Data Protection Supervisor released a 2010 report critical of the U.S. approach to air passenger screening (described below), concluding "that the bulk transfer of data about innocent people for risk assessment purposes raises serious proportionality issues."[23]

More generally, in both subject-based and pattern-based data mining, various factors can limit the ability of the analyst to arrive at the correct analytical conclusion. Misidentifications can result in individuals being erroneously associated with terrorism, fraud, or other crime. Even with good data, lack of analytical training and tools can result in both missed connections and suspicion that turns out to be without merit (for example, relationships between identified terrorists and other individuals, or behavior that fits a suspicious pattern, may well have an entirely innocent explanation).[24] Among the GAO's key recommendations for data mining systems is having both strong organizational capacity to manage data mining programs and procedures to evaluate both data quality and system effectiveness.[25]

HISTORICAL CONTEXT

The federal government has, at least to date, had considerable constitutional latitude to conduct data mining activities, assuming the data was lawfully collected, although statute and policy do impose notable limitations. In the United States, the most basic privacy-related rights for citizens, foreigners present in the United States, and certain other categories of people are enshrined in the Fourth Amendment to the Constitution, which provides that "[t]he right of the people to be secure in their persons, houses, papers, and effects, against unreasonable searches and seizures, shall not be violated, and no warrants shall issue, but upon probable

---

22. *See* NAT'L RESEARCH COUNCIL PRIVACY REPORT, *supra* note 15, at 2 ("Because the data being analyzed are primarily about ordinary, law-abiding citizens and businesses, false positives can result in invasion of their privacy.").

23. *See* Opinion of the European Data Protection Supervisor on the Communication from the Commission on the Global Approach to Transfers of Passenger Name Record (PNR) Data to Third Countries (Oct. 19, 2010), http://www.edps.europa.eu/EDPSWEB/webdav/site/mySite/shared/Documents/Consultation/Opinions/2010/10-10-18_PNR_EN.pdf.

24. *See, e.g.*, SEIFERT, *supra* note 1, at 3.

25. *See* U.S. GOV'T ACCOUNTABILITY OFFICE, GAO-11-742, DATA MINING: DHS NEEDS TO IMPROVE EXECUTIVE OVERSIGHT OF SYSTEMS SUPPORTING COUNTERTERRORISM 17–21 (2011), http://www.gao.gov/new.items/d11742.pdf. Other key elements include evaluation of privacy impact, executive review of investments, and transparency and external oversight.

cause." Government access to data in which a person has a "reasonable expectation of privacy" is prohibited without a judicially approved warrant.[26]

That said, courts have, in interpreting "reasonable," limited the application of the warrant requirement of the Fourth Amendment in a number of circumstances. For example, in the area of searches at international borders, the Supreme Court held in *United States v. Flores-Montano* that individuals have a reduced expectation of privacy given the government's compelling interest in controlling who and what comes in and out of the country: "The Government's interest in preventing the entry of unwanted persons and effects is at its zenith at the international border. Time and again, we have stated that 'searches made at the border, pursuant to the longstanding right of the sovereign to protect itself by stopping and examining persons and property crossing into this country, are reasonable simply by virtue of the fact that they occur at the border.'"[27]

The Supreme Court has also concluded that individuals generally have no reasonable expectation of privacy, for Fourth Amendment purposes, in records they share with third parties. Thus, business records and personal data collected by banks and telecommunications providers have, for the most part, been deemed unprotected by the Fourth Amendment,[28] although scholarly debate has arisen over whether this exception should continue to apply, given the above-described advances in data storage and integration.[29] Moreover, personal data submitted to the government—for example, as part of a visa or benefits application—has to date generally fallen outside of Fourth Amendment protections since it has been consensually shared with the government.

The Fourth Amendment is, however, a "floor," and Congress can, by statute, establish additional privacy protections. Indeed, Congress has chosen to do so repeatedly, imposing both substantive restrictions on the government's ability to collect certain data—such as communications and financial information—absent certain evidentiary thresholds, and process requirements for personal data collected by the government (e.g., with whom it may be shared and how long it may be stored). For example, in the United States, financial data is protected by the

---

26. Other constitutional limitations theoretically apply. For example, the First Amendment restricts the government from activity that could somehow impinge on an individual's right to free exercise of religion; abridge freedom of speech, or of the press; or impinge on the right to assemble peaceably or to petition for redress of grievances. The Fifth Amendment prohibits deprivation of life, liberty, or property, without due process of law.

27. United States v. Flores-Montano, 541 U.S. 149 (2004), http://www.law.cornell.edu/supct/html/02-1794.ZO.html.

28. *See, e.g.*, United States v. Miller, 425 U.S. 435 (1973) (bank records), http://caselaw.lp.findlaw.com/scripts/getcase.pl?court=us&vol=425&invol=435; Smith v. Maryland, 442 U.S. 735 (1979) (telephone toll records), http://caselaw.lp.findlaw.com/scripts/getcase.pl?court=us&vol=442&invol=735. Communications content, however, is generally protected by the Fourth Amendment.

29. *See, e.g.*, THE CONSTITUTION PROJECT, PRINCIPLES FOR GOVERNMENT DATA MINING: PRESERVING CIVIL LIBERTIES IN THE INFORMATION AGE 16 (2010), http://www.constitutionproject.org/pdf/DataMiningPublication.pdf.

Historical Context

Right to Financial Privacy Act (RFPA) and other statutes.[30] Under RFPA, a financial institution generally may not release financial data unless the government secures a valid subpoena or search warrant for the information.[31] That said, once collected, the government has latitude on how to leverage the data in question as long as subsequent uses are consistent with the government's underlying authority to collect and use it.

In the early 1970s, the secretary of the Department of Health, Education, and Welfare (HEW) grew concerned that the law afforded little protection for data subjects (that is, the people about whom information was being collected). He convened an advisory committee on automated personal data systems to recommend a course of action that would strike a balance between government efficiency and privacy interests.[32] The advisory committee established a set of principles that served as the basis for the Privacy Act of 1974, passed in the immediate wake of the Watergate scandal.

The Privacy Act regulates the collection, maintenance, use, and dissemination of personal information by federal executive branch agencies—and penalizes improper disclosure.[33] With respect to collection and maintenance, the act requires that each agency "maintain in its records only such information about an individual as is relevant and necessary to accomplish a purpose of the agency required to be accomplished by statute or by executive order of the president."[34] The Privacy Act does, however, create an exception for law enforcement and intelligence-related records systems. The Privacy Act also requires that each agency generally provide individuals notice of each new system that collects personal data, called system of records notices, or SORNs.[35]

Moreover, the E-Government Act of 2002 requires agencies to conduct privacy impact assessments (PIAs) when developing or procuring information technology systems that collect, maintain, or disseminate personally identifying

---

30. Codified at 12 U.S.C. §§ 3401 *et seq.*

31. In the context of a national security investigation, the records may also be obtained through use of an administrative order known as a National Security Letter. 18 U.S.C. § 3511.

32. *See* SEC'Y'S ADVISORY COMM. ON AUTOMATED PERSONAL DATA SYSTEMS REPORT, *supra* note 2. The secretary who commissioned the report was Elliott Richardson, before he became attorney general. His replacement, Caspar Weinberger (who became secretary of defense in the Reagan administration) received the report.

33. The Privacy Act applies only to U.S. citizens and lawful permanent residents, and not to visitors or other aliens. As a matter of policy, the Department of Homeland Security has determined that it will treat "mixed systems" (that is, those containing personally identifiable information (PII) about both U.S. nationals and aliens, such as border-control records) as if they were subject to the Privacy Act. *See* Memorandum from Hugo Teufel, Chief Privacy Officer, Privacy Policy Guidance Memorandum No. 2007-01 (as amended Jan. 17, 2007).

34. *See* U.S. DEP'T OF JUSTICE, OFFICE OF PRIVACY & CIVIL LIBERTIES, OVERVIEW OF THE PRIVACY ACT OF 1974 (2010 ed.), http://www.justice.gov/opcl/1974privacyact-overview.htm

35. 5 U.S.C. § 552a(e)(4).

information.[36] The act requires, in part, that PIAs analyze what information is being collected, why it is being collected, how long it will be kept, and how it will be used, applying a privacy perspective.

The HEW advisory committee's work spawned international efforts to define privacy guidelines, first in the form of guidelines at the Organization for Economic Cooperation & Development, then in the form of an international convention drafted by the Council of Europe, and then as binding European Union law in the form of the 1995 EU Data Protection Directive (Directive 95/46/EC). This work was also in part the basis for a set of Fair Information Practice Principles (FIPPs) that have since been formally designated as the foundational principles for privacy policy at the Department of Homeland Security (DHS) by that agency's chief privacy officer.[37] Among other provisions, the FIPPs state that DHS should collect only PII that is directly relevant and necessary to accomplish the specified purposes; retain PII only for as long as necessary to fulfill the specified purposes; and use PII solely for the purposes specified in prior public notices. Sharing PII outside the department should be for a purpose compatible with the purpose for which the PII was collected.[38]

What, then, are the implications for governmental data mining? Assuming the underlying data is lawfully collected, the government has considerable latitude on how to leverage it, subject to statutory notice requirements and self-imposed policy limitations such as the FIPPs. That said, two notable developments may affect that landscape.

First, in January 2012, the European Commission proposed to update the 1995 data protection directive, adding a number of new privacy protections.[39] Of relevance to data mining, a key feature of the proposal was the "right to be forgotten,"[40] and the proposal also strengthens existing EU law that allows

---

36. *See* Office of Mgmt. & Budget, Guidance for Implementing the Privacy Provisions of the E-Government Act of 2002 (Sept. 26, 2003), http://www.whitehouse.gov/omb/memoranda_m03-22/. While the E-Government Act excludes both human resource databases for federal employees and defined national security systems from PIA requirements, DHS has nevertheless chosen to conduct PIAs on these systems too. *See* Memorandum from Hugo Teufel, Chief Privacy Officer, DHS Policy Regarding Privacy Impact Assessments (Dec. 30, 2008).

37. *See* Memorandum from Hugo Teufel, Chief Privacy Officer, The Fair Information Practice Principles: Framework for Privacy Policy at the Department of Homeland Security (Dec. 29, 2008).

38. *Id.*

39. European Comm'n, *Proposal for a Regulation of the European Parliament and of the Council on the Protection of Individuals with Regard to the Processing of Personal Data and on the Free Movement of Such Data (General Data Protection Regulation)*, COM (2012) 11 final (Jan. 25, 2012), http://ec.europa.eu/justice/data-protection/document/review2012/com_2012_11_en.pdf.

40. *Id.* art. 17, at 51.

Historical Context

individuals to object to certain data mining activities.[41] To the extent that such restrictions are imposed on data transfers to non-EU member states, this development could conceivably affect U.S. use of data obtained from EU entities.

Second, notwithstanding earlier Supreme Court doctrine, concerns about privacy-related implications of technological advances are finding voice in recent judicial rulings—either directly or indirectly by encouraging Congress to act. In *United States v. Maynard*, the D.C. Circuit Court of Appeals established a sort of "mosaic theory" test in distinguishing between use of a beeper to track a vehicle's single journey (lawful because the suspect "by driving on public roads 'voluntarily conveyed to anyone who wanted to look' his progress and route" and thus had no reasonable expectation of privacy in his destination) and use of a GPS device to track a vehicle's movements 24 hours a day for four weeks (unlawful because "the likelihood that anyone will observe all these movements is effectively nil").[42] In *Maynard*, even though each individual movement is exposed to the public, the whole of these movements was *not* constructively exposed because the "whole reveals more—sometimes a great deal more—than the sum of the parts."[43]

The Supreme Court upheld the D.C. Circuit Court of Appeals ruling 9–0, although with sharply divided reasoning. While five justices based their decision, at least in part, on narrow trespass grounds, four others, led by Samuel Alito, supported the thrust of the appeals court's reasoning and called at least implicitly for a congressional updating of statutorily created privacy protections to address new technology:

> In the pre-computer age, the greatest protections of privacy were neither constitutional nor statutory, but practical. Traditional surveillance for any extended period of time was difficult and costly and therefore rarely undertaken. The surveillance at issue in this case—constant monitoring of the location of a vehicle for four weeks—would have required a large team of agents, multiple vehicles, and perhaps aerial assistance. Only an

---

41. *Id.* art. 20, at 55. Per Article 20, an individual "shall have the right not to be subject to a measure which produces legal effects concerning this natural person or significantly affects this natural person, and which is based solely on automated processing intended to evaluate certain personal aspects relating to this natural person or to analyse or predict in particular the natural person's performance at work, economic situation, location, health, personal preferences, reliability or behaviour."
42. United States v. Maynard, 615 F.3d 544, 558 (D.C. Cir. 2010), *aff'd sub nom*, United States v. Jones, 132 S. Ct. 945 (2012).
43. *Id.* The court added:

> Repeated visits to a church, a gym, a bar, or a bookie tell a story not told by any single visit, as does one's not visiting any of these places over the course of a month. The sequence of a person's movements can reveal still more; a single trip to a gynecologist's office tells little about a woman, but that trip followed a few weeks later by a visit to a baby supply store tells a different story. A person who knows all of another's travels can deduce whether he is a weekly church goer, a heavy drinker, a regular at the gym, an unfaithful husband, an outpatient receiving medical treatment, an associate of particular individuals or political groups—and not just one such fact about a person, but all such facts.

Id. at 562.

investigation of unusual importance could have justified such an expenditure of law enforcement resources. Devices like the one used in the present case, however, make long-term monitoring relatively easy and cheap. In circumstances involving dramatic technological change, the best solution to privacy concerns may be legislative.[44]

GPS tracker data and third-party transactional data are two very different forms of data, and in the latter case an individual has consented to the transfer of his or her data to a third party. That said, the underlying call for congressional action might also generate interest in addressing the broader "mosaic" question and in the ability of the government or a third-party aggregator to draw multiple different streams of records together to paint a "mosaic" of the individual's daily life.[45]

UNDERSTANDING THE RELATIONSHIP OF TECHNOLOGY TO POLICY

To understand the nuances of data mining, it is important to consider some of the underlying challenges in managing data flow. It is said that people are "drowning in data but starving for knowledge."[46] Thus, the government has devoted significant energy toward solutions that can help agencies become more effective in utilizing the data they are collecting and sharing. Some of the discussion around data mining has related to how such technology, once developed, would be utilized. Examples include the following:

- *Discoverability.* For data to be useful, it has to be discoverable. Data ideally is indexed at the point of ingest by the type of data it represents (person, place, thing, event, etc.). The Markle Foundation has produced seminal work on information sharing, and its reports emphasize the

---

44. United States v. Jones, 132 S. Ct. 945, 963–64 (2012) (Alito, J., concurring), http://www.supremecourt.gov/opinions/11pdf/10-1259.pdf. The concurrence also noted that previous Supreme Court jurisprudence, which depended heavily on notions of "reasonable expectation of privacy," may be hard to apply in eras of rapidly changing technology, when reasonable expectations are being upended:

> [T]he *Katz* test rests on the assumption that this hypothetical reasonable person has a well-developed and stable set of privacy expectations. But technology can change those expectations. Dramatic technological change may lead to periods in which popular expectations are in flux and may ultimately produce significant changes in popular attitudes. New technology may provide increased convenience or security at the expense of privacy, and many people may find the tradeoff worthwhile. And even if the public does not welcome the diminution of privacy that new technology entails, they may eventually reconcile themselves to this development as inevitable.

Concurring opinion at 962.

45. *See also* Kerr, *The Fourth Amendment and New Technologies: Constitutional Myths and the Case for Caution,* 102 MICH. L. REV. 801, 850–51 (2004) (*cited in Jones* (Alito, J., concurring)).
46. *See* NAT'L RESEARCH COUNCIL PRIVACY REPORT, *supra* note 15, at 186.

critical importance of discoverability. "Just as a card catalogue in a library serves as a central index, directing users to relevant books—but doesn't provide the book itself—these 'data indices' point users to data holders and documents, depending on the search criteria used."[47]

- *Identity/entity resolution.* Part of the challenge of "discoverability" is ensuring that the card catalogue is assembled accurately. As noted previously, data quality challenges are one of the main sources of data mining concern. When multiple records are collected, it is important to identify which records resolve to the same person. This process can be "surprisingly difficult."[48] Challenges can include data entry errors (misspellings); natural name variations (nicknames, name change upon marriage); variances in cultural naming practices (the use of "bin" in Arabic names, the use of the mother's family name in Spanish cultures); and multiple name variations resulting from translation from non-Latin character sets (Cyrillic, Arabic, and Chinese character sets).[49] Moreover, multiple different individuals may hold the same name, which can be a problem when name is the only identifier. Name-based matching efforts have produced well-known examples of innocent travelers impeded and high-risk travelers allowed to proceed undetected.[50] Thus, for example, under the Secure Flight program, the Transportation Security Administration (TSA) collects not only a passenger's full name, but also birth date, gender, and passport information (for international flights). The TSA justifies the additional data sets on the grounds that they reduce the number of mismatches and associated delays.[51]

- *Analytics.* It is not enough simply to have data. To generate the value, analysts must gain "operationally relevant" insight from the information. Analysts can process and remember only a limited amount of data. Technology can be leveraged to enhance what analysts can do rather than burden them—it "frees humans to do what they do well: think,

---

47. *See* MARKLE FOUND. ISSUE BRIEF, DISCOVERABILITY (Sept. 1, 2009), http://www.markle.org/sites/default/files/MTFBrief_Discoverability.pdf.
48. NAT'L RESEARCH COUNCIL PRIVACY REPORT, *supra* note 15, at 189.
49. *See, e.g.,* WCC Group's description of the challenges of multicultural name-matching, http://www.wcc-group.com/ (under Downloads, select Multi-Cultural Name Matching).
50. Both the late Sen. Ted Kennedy and Rep. John Lewis, of civil rights–era fame, reported being identified for enhanced screening based upon a mistaken match to a watchlist. *See* Barrett, *Kennedy Has Company on Airline Watchlist,* CNN.COM, Aug. 20, 2004, http://edition.cnn.com/2004/ALLPOLITICS/08/20/lewis.watchlist/index.html.
51. *See* U.S. DEP'T OF HOMELAND SEC., PRIVACY IMPACT ASSESSMENT FOR THE SECURE FLIGHT PROGRAM 10–11 (Oct. 21, 2008), http://www.dhs.gov/xlibrary/assets/privacy/privacy_pia_secureflight2008.pdf

ask questions and make judgments about complex situations."[52] One important example is "persistent query," or the ability to command a system to alert an analyst automatically when new records appear that match the query criteria.[53] For example, imagine if, in the 2009 Christmas bombing plot, analysts had set a persistent query for new records where "nationality = Nigerian" and "location = Yemen" (so that a question that an analyst asked based on reports of Nigerians traveling to Yemen to receive terrorist training persists in databases and is automatically linked to a report of a Nigerian father's warning about his son's travel to Yemen).

- *Interoperability.* When multiple record sets are involved, it can also be a challenge to match data across these sets—put another way, to make these record sets interoperable. Semantic interoperability standards allow two databases to talk to each other. For example, an automobile may be called a "car" in one database and a "vehicle" in another. Technical interoperability know-how is needed to map one data set to another, particularly at scale. Both are necessary so that information can flow easily from one system to another and be understood.
- *Scalability.* The sheer volume of data collected today poses challenges in the ability of governmental authorities to store and process that data.[54] Significant governmental effort has been focused on how to build systems to manage rapidly growing volumes of data, both in terms of storage and processing.
- *Privacy-enhancing technology.* Considerable discussion has also developed concerning whether privacy considerations can be built into technology design principles so that systems are built to limit *ex ante* the collection or availability of nonrelevant data. For example, the Markle Foundation Task Force has called for such measures as anonymization, using a decentralized network pointer-system structure and aligning access not just to a security clearance, but to whether a user's specific

---

52. *See* U.S. Dep't of Homeland Sec., Enabling Distributed Security in Cyberspace: Building a Healthy and Resilient Cyber Ecosystem with Automated Collective Action 8 (Mar. 23, 2011), http://www.dhs.gov/xlibrary/assets/nppd-cyber-ecosystem-white-paper-03-23-2011.pdf.
53. *See, e.g.*, Paul Rosenzweig, *Connecting the Dots and the Christmas Plot*, Nat'l Sec. L.J., Jan. 25, 2010, http://harvardnsj.org/2010/01/connecting-the-dots-and-the-christmas-plot/.
54. *See, e.g.*, Janet Napolitano, Sec'y of Homeland Security, Remarks at the Massachusetts Institute of Technology: The Future of Science as Public Service, Mar. 14, 2011, http://www.dhs.gov/ynews/speeches/sp_1300130988072.shtm.

At the same time, DHS is part of the nation's Intelligence Community, which receives more terabytes of data each day than the entire text holdings of the Library of Congress. The National Counterterrorism Center's 24-hour Operations Center receives 8,000 to 10,000 pieces of counterterrorist information every day.

role necessitates access, through an "authorized use" policy.[55] Moreover, according to the proposed new EU data protection directive, "'privacy by design' and 'privacy by default' will also become essential principles in EU data protection rules—this means that data protection safeguards should be built into products and services from the earliest stage of development."[56]

IN THE NEWS

Significant public attention on data mining has focused on a number of government programs.

Computer-Assisted Passenger Prescreening System (CAPPS II)

CAPPS II was a TSA prescreening system intended to assess the likelihood that travelers are who they claim to be and perform a risk assessment to detect individuals who may pose an aviation security threat. CAPPS II was canceled in name and replaced by the now-operational (and more narrowly scoped) Secure Flight program. CAPPS II would have collected basic passenger information, similar to what is collected by the Secure Flight program today (it would have collected name, date of birth, address, and phone number; Secure Flight mandates the collection of name, date of birth, and gender), and run that information against several preexisting databases. Although the thinking behind CAPPS II evolved over time, particularly with respect to assessing a traveler's "roots in the community," the final version described in the government's *Federal Register* notice was not intended as a pattern-based data mining program. It endeavored to accomplish two objectives: verify that a traveler was who he or she claimed to be, and determine whether that passenger was on a lookout list. It was to have verified identity by using commercial data. The use of commercial data was not, in final form, aimed at detecting patterns (e.g., patterns of travel or residential history patterns). It was aimed at verifying that the address given to the airline was, in fact, probably the traveler's address, and the underlying commercial data was not to be transferred to the government.[57]

---

55. *See* MARKLE FOUND. REPORT, MOBILIZING INFORMATION TO PREVENT TERRORISM: ACCELERATING DEVELOPMENT OF A TRUSTED INFORMATION SHARING ENVIRONMENT (July 1, 2006), http://www.markle.org/publications/556-mobilizing-information-prevent-terrorism. MARKLE FOUND. BRIEF, MEETING THE THREAT OF TERRORISM: AUTHORIZED USE (Aug. 1, 2009), http://www.markle.org/downloadable_assets/20090825_authusestndrd.pdf.

56. *See* European Comm'n, How Does the Data Protection Reform Strengthen Citizens' Rights? (2011), http://ec.europa.eu/justice/data-protection/document/review2012/factsheets/2_en.pdf.

57. *See* 68 Fed. Reg. 45,266 (Aug. 1, 2003), *available at* http://www.gpo.gov/fdsys/pkg/FR-2003-08-01/pdf/03-19574.pdf.

- Regarding lookouts, the record is confusing. In one press statement, DHS stated that CAPPS II would have checked against terrorist watchlists and criminal databases, in the latter case to determine whether the passenger was subject to an outstanding warrant for a crime of violence.[58] However, a separate *Federal Register* notice describing the program could have been interpreted, whether correctly or not, to include nonviolent serious crimes and immigration concerns as within the scope of the program.[59]
- Critics might raise a number of concerns with CAPPS II—for example, whether the underlying commercial data used to verify address was accurate; whether it is appropriate to run criminal as well as terrorist checks against the traveling public; and whether there was a danger of "mission creep," where checks for lesser, nonviolent offenses might eventually be run.

CAPPS II did not, at least in final form, entail pattern-based mining. CAPPS I, an earlier program regulated by TSA but administered by the airlines, was pattern based. CAPPS I applied predefined patterns against passenger reservations to flag travelers who fit those patterns for additional scrutiny.[60] Moreover, this pattern analysis automatically led to physical consequences—to wit, more intensive physical screening at the TSA checkpoint. In the case of CAPPS I, the government did not, however, ingest the underlying data itself.

Total Information Awareness

The Total Information Awareness (TIA) program launched by the Defense Advanced Research Projects Agency, an agency of the Department of Defense, also attracted controversy. Unlike CAPPS II, TIA did not appear to involve any new *collection* of personal information. Instead, TIA was intended to allow agencies to better "share, analyze, understand and make decisions based on whatever data they already had legally collected."[61] TIA's objective was to help agencies "connect the dots" through three broad functions: advanced collaboration and decision support tools, language translation, and data search and pattern recognition. Full implementation of TIA was blocked by Congress, although some of the underlying technology research has continued.

---

58. *See* Press Release, Dep't of Homeland Sec., CAPPS II: Myth and Facts (Feb. 13, 2003). DHS has since deleted this press release from its website. A similar press release, dated Feb 12, 2004, is available at http://www.techlawjournal.com/agencies/dhs/capps/20040212b.asp.

59. *See* 68 Fed. Reg. 45,266 (Aug. 1, 2003).

60. *See* TSA Paperwork Reduction Act Notice on Secure Flight (Sept. 21, 2004), http://www.tsa.gov/assets/pdf/Secure_Flight_PRA_Notice_9.21.04.pdf (describing CAPPS I).

61. *See*, Hearing Before the Subcomm. on Terrorism, Threats and Unconventional Capabilities, House Armed Servs. Comm. (Mar. 27, 2003), www.darpa.mil/WorkArea/DownloadAsset.aspx?id=1778 (statement of Dr. Tony Tether, Director, Defense Advanced Research Projects Agency).

These tools in development are theoretically not as controversial. Had TIA been fully implemented, what was most controversial was the transfer of TIA tools to operational agencies that could use their stored data to marry together innocent person data to identify unspecified patterns without guidelines.

Automated Targeting System

Customs and Border Protection (CBP) utilizes its Automated Targeting System (ATS) to focus agency efforts on international "travelers, conveyances and cargo shipments that most warrant greater scrutiny."[62] One of the ATS modules, ATS-P, collects and maintains passenger name record (PNR) data, which is data provided to airlines and travel agents by or on behalf of air passengers seeking to book travel.[63] Having collected this data, CBP then runs a series of analytics against the PNR data, including comparison with derogatory data sets (e.g., terrorist watchlists and wants and warrants lists) and against analytic "rules" (basically algorithms) that CBP has developed based on "investigatory and law enforcement data, intelligence, and past case experience."[64] It is these latter rules-based analytics that, when run against general traveling public data, generate the most classic use of data mining.

Importantly, the results of data mining do not automatically generate any adverse action against an individual: "As part of CBP's inspection policies and procedures no adverse action is taken by CBP with respect to an individual, cargo or conveyance until the relevant information is reviewed by a well-trained CBP officer."[65]

As noted earlier, the acceptability of data mining is context dependent. In the ATS example, the government's interest in preventing the entry of unwanted persons and effects is at its zenith at the international border. Moreover, ports of entry have threshold processing times that, when exceeded (due to security checks or otherwise), can result in massive delays and service interruption. Particularly given increasing volumes of international trade and travel, the United States has relied on risk assessment of travelers and cargo, both of which are already subject

---

62. *See* U.S. Dep't of Homeland Sec., Privacy Impact Assessment for the Automated Targeting System 2 (Aug. 3, 2007), http://www.dhs.gov/xlibrary/assets/privacy/privacy_pia_cbp_ats_updated_fr.pdf.

63. *Id.* at 3 ("CBP began receiving PNR data voluntarily from air carriers in 1997. Currently, CBP collects this information as part of its border enforcement mission and pursuant to the Aviation and Transportation Security Act of 2001 (ATSA).").

64. *Id.* at 4. According to CBP: "A large number of rules are included in the ATS modules, which encapsulate sophisticated concepts of business activity that help identify suspicious or unusual behavior. The ATS rules are constantly evolving to both meet new threats and refine existing rules."

65. *Id.* at 10.

to inspection, to make the inspection process more efficient. And the government has also been able to demonstrate tangible successes as a result.[66]

That said, a significant portion of passenger data originates with air carriers domiciled in European Union member states. U.S. authorities have negotiated a series of agreements with EU officials to ensure continued access to that data. The latest of these agreements was recently approved by the European Parliament after a significant debate based on privacy concerns from select members of Parliament.[67]

Terrorist Finance Tracking Program

The U.S. government believes that transactional financial information can be extremely valuable in identifying links between the various nodes of a terrorist enterprise, and it has utilized the Department of the Treasury's subpoena power to collect such information from financial institutions. One program that attracted significant attention was the use of this subpoena power to collect financial information from the Society for Worldwide Interbank Financial Telecommunication, or SWIFT, an international member-owned cooperative providing communications services to financial institutions.

Unlike ATS, where passengers have at least implicitly consented to the sharing of their PNR with CBP by virtue of their decision to travel, individuals utilizing the global financial system presumably do not expect that their data will be subject to such scrutiny.

That said, the U.S. government maintains that its activities under the Terrorist Finance Tracking Program (TFTP) do not equate to data mining, and expressly proscribes "algorithmic or automated profiling or computer filtering."[68] Moreover, a search of SWIFT data must be predicated on the requestor providing "preexisting information demonstrating a nexus between the subject of the search and terrorism or its financing."[69] In other words, in contrast to ATS and CAPPS II, some level of predication is required before financial records can be accessed for

---

66. For examples, see Letter from Michael Chertoff, Sec'y of Homeland Sec., to Members of the European Parliament (May 14, 2007), http://useu.usmission.gov/media/pdfs/may1407_chertoff_ep_letter.pdf.

67. *See* Press Release, Alliance of Liberals and Democrats for Europe, EP Rapporteur In 't Veld set to reject new EU-US Passenger Name Records Agreement (PNR) (Feb. 1, 2012), http://www.alde.eu/nc/key-priorities/civil-liberties/single-news/article/ep-rapporteur-in-t-veld-set-to-reject-new-eu-us-passenger-name-records-agreement-pnr-37871/.

68. *See* U.S. Dep't of Treas., Terrorist Finance Tracking Programs: Questions and Answers 4 (2011), http://www.treasury.gov/resource-center/terrorist-illicit-finance/Terrorist-Finance-Tracking/Documents/Final%20Updated%20TFTP%20Brochure%20(8-5-11).pdf ("The TFTP may not be used for data mining or any other type of algorithmic or automated profiling or computer filtering.").

69. *Id.* at 4.

TFTP purposes. Retention of data is limited to five years, and third-party overseers can review and audit searches.[70]

EXPERTS

Bryan Cunningham, Principal, Cunningham Partners LLC; (303) 743-0003; bryan@cunninghampartners.com

Jim Dempsey, Center for Democracy and Technology; (415) 814-1710; jdempsey@cdt.org

Jim Harper, CATO Institute; (202) 789-5200; jharper@cato.org

Adam Isles, Director, Strategy & Policy Consulting, Raytheon Co.; (703) 284-4256; adam.isles@raytheon.com

John Kropf, Deputy Counsel, Privacy & Information Governance, Reed Elsevier; (202) 785-3550; john.kropf@reedelsevier.com

Paul Rosenzweig, Former Deputy Assistant Secretary for Policy, Department of Homeland Security; (202) 547-0660; paul.rosenzweig@redbranchconsulting.com

Marc Rotenberg, Electronic Privacy Information Center; (202) 483-1140; rotenberg@epic.org

RESOURCES

Jeffrey W. Seifert, Cong. Research Serv., RL31798, Data Mining and Homeland Security: An Overview (updated Aug. 27, 2008), http://www.lrc.fema.gov/starweb/lrcweb/servlet.starweb?path=lrcweb/STARLibraries1.web&search=R%3D177989. A petabyte constitutes a quadrillion bytes.

U.S. Dep't of Homeland Sec., Privacy Impact Assessment for the Automated Targeting System 2 (Aug. 3, 2007), http://www.dhs.gov/xlibrary/assets/privacy/privacy_pia_cbp_ats_updated_fr.pdf.

U.S. Gov't Accountability Office, GAO-11-742, Data Mining: DHS Needs to Improve Executive Oversight of Systems Supporting Counterterrorism (2011), http://www.gao.gov/new.items/d11742.pdf.

Markle Found. Report, Mobilizing Information to Prevent Terrorism: Accelerating Development of a Trusted Information

---

70. *Id.*

SHARING ENVIRONMENT (July 1, 2006), http://www.markle.org/publications/556-mobilizing-information-prevent-terrorism.

NAT'L RESEARCH COUNCIL, PROTECTING INDIVIDUAL PRIVACY IN THE STRUGGLE AGAINST TERRORISTS: A FRAMEWORK FOR PROGRAM ASSESSMENT (2008), http://www.nap.edu/openbook.php?record_id=12452.

U.S. DEP'T OF JUSTICE, OFFICE OF PRIVACY & CIVIL LIBERTIES, OVERVIEW OF THE PRIVACY ACT OF 1974 (2010 ed.), http://www.justice.gov/opcl/1974privacyact-overview.htm.

U.S. DEP'T OF HEALTH, EDUC. & WELFARE, RECORDS, COMPUTERS AND THE RIGHTS OF CITIZENS: REPORT OF THE SECRETARY'S ADVISORY COMMITTEE ON AUTOMATED PERSONAL DATA SYSTEMS (July 1973), http://aspe.hhs.gov/datacncl/1973privacy/tocprefacemembers.htm#preface.

Exports of Surveillance Technology to Repressive Regimes

19

By Michael T. Gershberg

After years of assuming that the Internet spelled the end of authoritarian regimes, we have been shaken awake from our dreams of technologically determined democratization. We now realize that information technology cuts both ways.

Information technology can actually be quite useful to authoritarian governments that want to monitor and suppress their own citizens. Much of this technology is produced by firms in Western countries. In fact, laws like the Communications Assistance for Law Enforcement Act[1] and the Wiretap Act[2] have created a significant market in the West for equipment to intercept communications for lawful purposes. These products are important tools in fighting crime, but in the West their use is regulated by civil rights laws and a robust legal compliance culture intended to protect citizens from unwarranted surveillance. But these protections disappear once the technology crosses the border into an authoritarian country.

It's an interesting story, and in recent years, it has proven evergreen. Human rights groups, reporters, bloggers, and politicians have begun to focus attention on American and European tech firms accused of helping authoritarian governments to crack down on dissent. Some examples:

---

1. 47 U.S.C. §§ 1001–1010.
2. 18 U.S.C. § 2512(2).

- In 2006 and 2007, Yahoo! faced a human rights lawsuit and grilling before a congressional committee when reports surfaced that the company provided Chinese authorities with information relating to a local prodemocracy journalist's e-mail account that resulted in the journalist's conviction and sentencing to a 10-year prison term.[3]
- In 2006 and 2008, Google faced a public relations backlash and congressional hearing following accusations from human rights groups that it was filtering Internet content as mandated by the Chinese government.[4]
- In early 2011, as the "Arab Spring" was beginning, Narus, a wholly owned subsidiary of Boeing, was accused of selling deep packet inspection technology to Egypt Telecom that could be used to monitor Internet traffic and cell phone calls.[5]

These stories have natural public appeal, and plenty of groups are eager to reinforce the narrative in the hope of restricting such sales. My firm has been counsel to several companies accused of improper sales to authoritarian regimes and has had a ringside seat as journalists have struggled to report the legal issues that surround these stories.

One problem is that the relevant laws are complex and deeply dependent on the facts of the specific case, making it difficult even for experienced lawyers to quickly evaluate whether a company's conduct has crossed the line into illegality. Another problem is that, procedurally, the constraints placed on companies by the need to provide accurate and consistent information to government regulators (and, in some cases, prosecutors) means that the reporting cycle for corporate internal investigative efforts will be much slower than the news cycle. As a result, reporters may get daily input from the sources that know the least about the facts, while having to wait weeks or months to get fact-based responses from the companies accused of misconduct. In this chapter, I outline the major substantive and procedural issues that shape the legal outcome of these stories.

---

3. *Yahoo Plea over China Rights Case*, BBC NEWS, Aug. 28 2007, http://news.bbc.co.uk/2/hi/6966116.stm; *Yahoo Accused of Misleading Congress About Chinese Journalist*, CNN.COM, Oct. 16, 2007, http://articles.cnn.com/2007-10-16/us/yahoo.congress_1_shi-tao-yahoo-spokeswoman-tracy-schmaler-general-counsel-michael-callahan?_s=PM:US.

4. Leo Tallay, *Google in China: Do No Evil?*, AMNESTY INT'L, May 16, 2008, http://www.amnesty.org.au/china/comments/13407/; *Human Rights Watch Berates Google over China Censorship*, NATURALNEWS.COM, Aug. 15, 2006, http://www.naturalnews.com/019990_internet_censorship_human_rights.html.

5. Timothy Karr, *One U.S. Corporation's Role in Egypt's Brutal Crackdown*, HUFFINGTON POST, Jan. 28, 2011, http://www.huffingtonpost.com/timothy-karr/one-us-corporations-role-_b_815281.html.

SUBSTANTIVE LAW—A PATCHWORK OF RULES

Let's start with substantive law. Reporters contemplating stories about the use of Western surveillance technology by repressive regimes will very quickly confront the question of whether targeted companies actually did something illegal—and they will often find that there is not a simple answer. This is so for two reasons.

First, even conduct that sounds questionable may nonetheless be legal under the law of the jurisdiction where the company resides. For example, there are periodic news reports that U.S. software products have been found in use in countries such as Iran and Syria. However, most of the time, there is no evidence that the software was illegally exported by a U.S. company. Diversion of products from lawful customers to barred countries is common, especially after the goods have been delivered. And while it is easy to say in such cases that *someone* violated U.S. law, the U.S. manufacturer itself may well have committed no violation.

For example, a review of Commerce Department export violation orders since 2007 shows only two enforcement cases apparently involving monitoring or telecommunications equipment. Several other enforcement cases involved more general items, such as computer equipment and electronic components, although there is no evidence on the public record that these were intended for surveillance. To take a more recent example, when Chinese telecommunications equipment vendor ZTE Corp. sold a surveillance system to Iran in March 2012, the sale reportedly included hardware and software from U.S. companies such as Microsoft, Hewlett-Packard, Oracle, Cisco Systems, Dell, Juniper Networks, and Symantec. Apparently, however, none of the U.S. companies had knowledge of this deal.[6] A month later, reports surfaced that ZTE planned a second sale of computer equipment to Iran that included products made by IBM, Cisco, Brocade Communications, Oracle, Juniper, and Symantec.[7] While ZTE says it has abandoned the sale, this episode shows how easily U.S. products can be diverted to restricted destinations without the manufacturer's involvement.

Second, the laws that do exist are often nuanced, and the ultimate legality of conduct may depend on facts that cannot be determined without extensive investigation. For example, the applicability of U.S. export control laws to technology products manufactured abroad may depend on the specific amount of U.S.-origin content in the product.[8] Another example is that obligations under the Electronic Communications Privacy Act and under European data protection laws can depend greatly on the vagaries of where data has traveled or is physically stored. Even where U.S. law applies, some rules impose strict liability for prohibited activity, while others require certain knowledge or intent.

---

6. Steve Stecklow, *Special Report: Chinese Firm Helps Iran Spy on Citizens*, REUTERS, Mar. 22, 2012, http://www.reuters.com/article/2012/03/22/us-iran-telecoms-idUSBRE82L0B820120322.

7. Steve Stecklow, *China's ZTE Planned U.S. Computer Sale to Iran*, REUTERS, Apr. 10, 2012, http://www.reuters.com/article/2012/04/10/us-zte-iran-aryacell-idUSBRE8390T720120410.

8. *See* 15 C.F.R. §§ 734.3–734.4.

There are several sources of laws of which reporters should be aware. The main ones are described next.

Export Controls and Economic Sanctions

The United States maintains a comprehensive system of export controls that regulates the sale of almost all U.S.-origin items for national security and foreign policy reasons. The two main frameworks related to surveillance technology are the export controls regulations administered by the Commerce Department and the economic sanctions laws administered by the Treasury Department.

The United States controls the export of certain commercial, "dual use" items (items with both a commercial and a military use). Different controls apply depending on the type of product, the destination, and the end use or end user. Surveillance products have among the strictest controls, requiring an export license for sales to almost every destination and end user, and the Commerce Department has a general policy for these products.[9] Crime control and detection items also require an export license for most destinations. The export rules state that license applications for these items will generally be "considered favorably on a case-by-case basis unless there is civil disorder in the country or region or unless there is evidence that the government of the importing country may have violated internationally recognized human rights."[10]

U.S. economic sanctions regulations are usually directed at countries that are hostile to the U.S. government. The regulations typically are issued pursuant to either the Trading with the Enemy Act[11] or the International Emergency Economic Powers Act.[12] The Treasury Department currently imposes comprehensive trade embargoes against Cuba, Iran, and Sudan, while both Treasury and Commerce have export restrictions against Burma, Syria, and North Korea. Treasury's country-specific sanctions may include bans on exports, imports, providing or receiving services, financial transactions, business-related travel, and many other types of activities. Treasury also imposes sanctions on the handmaidens to current and past authoritarian regimes—such as former and current government officials, government agencies, and political parties.

In addition, U.S. economic sanctions prohibit U.S. persons from doing business with so-called Specially Designated Nationals, or SDNs. These are persons, entities, organizations, and vessels that the U.S. government has identified as engaging in narcotics trafficking, proliferation of weapons of mass destruction, terrorism or support for terrorist activities, destabilizing behavior in regions important to U.S. interests, corruption, or acting on the behalf of governments identified above to the detriment of U.S. interests. These SDNs are identified in

---

9. 15 C.F.R. § 742.13.
10. 15 C.F.R. § 742.7(b).
11. 50 U.S.C. app. §§ 1–44.
12. 50 U.S.C. §§ 1701–1706.

a list published by the Office of Foreign Assets Control.[13] There are thousands of such SDNs; many of them are located in countries friendly to the United States.

Iran and Syria Sanctions Related to Surveillance Technology

After allegations that U.S. companies helped Iran squelch election protests, Congress passed the Comprehensive Iran Sanctions, Accountability, and Divestment Act of 2010. CISADA enacted strict new U.S. sanctions against Iran, including a provision specifically targeted at surveillance technology. Section 106 of CISADA prohibits the federal government from entering into a procurement contract with any company that exports "sensitive technology" to Iran, including any equipment that restricts the free flow of information in Iran or that monitors, disrupts, or restricts free speech in Iran.[14] Similar legislation was later introduced with respect to Syria.[15]

Under regulations recently promulgated by the Defense Department, the General Services Administration, and NASA to implement Section 106 of CISADA, U.S. government contractors must now certify that they do not provide Iran with "sensitive technology," as described above.[16] Persons determined to be exporters of restricted items will also be listed on the Excluded Parties List, a comprehensive list of parties barred from receiving federal contracts and other federal assistance. As of June 2012, no exporter has yet been listed under this provision. But, in January 2012, the State Department began an investigation of the Chinese company Huawei Technologies for allegedly providing censorship and mobile phone tracking technology to Iran.[17] The investigation was in response to a request from six congressmen, who—relying at least in part on an article published in *The Wall Street Journal*[18]—expressed concern that Huawei was exporting mobile telecommunications surveillance and tracking technology to Iran for use in disrupting, monitoring, or suppressing communications.

Maintaining the pressure on Iran, and in light of the continued crackdown in Syria, President Obama recently issued an executive order authorizing the imposition of sanctions on entities that help these two governments use surveillance technologies to commit human rights abuses.[19] The order allows the U.S. government

---

13. U.S. Dep't of Treasury, Specially Designated Nationals List (SDN), http://www.treas.gov/offices/enforcement/ofac/sdn/.

14. CISADA § 106(a), (c), Pub. L. No. 111-195 (2010).

15. Iran Threat Reduction and Syria Human Rights Act of 2012, S 703, Pub L. 112-158 (2012).

16. 48 C.F.R. § 25.1103(e); Federal Acquisition Regulation; Certification Requirement and Procurement Prohibition Relating to Iran Sanctions, 76 Fed. Reg. 68,027 (DoD, GSA, NASA Nov. 2, 2011), *as amended in final rule*, 77 Fed. Reg. 23,368 (Apr. 18, 2012); 48 C.F.R. § 52.225-25(c)(1).

17. *See, e.g.*, Michael Kan, *U.S. State Department Investigating Huawei on Iran Concerns*, IDG News, Jan. 5, 2012.

18. Steve Stecklow et al., *Chinese Tech Giant Aids Iran*, Wall St. J., Oct. 27, 2011, http://online.wsj.com/article/SB10001424052970204644504576651503577823210.html.

19. Exec. Order 13,606, Blocking the Property and Suspending Entry Into the United States of Certain Persons With Respect to Grave Human Rights Abuses by the Governments of Iran and Syria via Information Technology (Apr. 22, 2012).

to freeze the assets of companies and individuals responsible for providing the governments of Iran and Syria with goods, services, or technology "likely to be used to facilitate computer or network disruption, monitoring, or tracking that could assist in or enable serious human rights abuses." The order also targets entities that operate such technologies. Although the order is aimed primarily at Iranian and Syrian entities—and in fact, the first named parties hit with these sanctions were Iranian and Syrian governmental and telecommunications entities—the treasury secretary has broad power to impose sanctions on companies and people from any country, including the United States.

Human Rights Litigation

Another legal tool that has become more prominent in recent years is civil litigation, brought by victims of human rights violations, under the Alien Tort Statute.[20] The Alien Tort Statute is a very old law that has been revived in recent decades. It provides federal courts with jurisdiction over civil lawsuits brought by aliens for acts "in violation of the law of nations"—wherever on the globe those violations may occur. Therefore, the statute allows aliens from anywhere in the world to file suit in the United States against a company[21] that is implicated in a "violation of the law of nations"—including such international human rights violations as torture, extrajudicial killing, prolonged arbitrary detention or arrest, forced disappearances, denial of rights of association, and cruel, inhuman, or degrading treatment.

Lawsuits under the Alien Tort Statute have been brought by both advocacy groups and more profit-oriented plaintiffs' law firms. The typical lawsuit is brought in the name of citizens of a developing country who have been mistreated by their government—arbitrarily arrested, tortured, or killed. But instead of suing their government, the plaintiffs sue a corporation that they believe helped the government engage in these activities. This "aiding and abetting" theory may succeed if the facts show that the company (1) provided assistance or encouragement to the government that "has a substantial effect on the perpetration" of the harm or provided "the means by which a violation of the law is carried out," and (2) was aware or should have known that its assistance would aid the government.[22]

Securities Law

The Securities and Exchange Commission's (SEC's) Office of Global Security Risk[23] was established to ensure that companies (domestic or foreign) trading

---

20. 28 U.S.C. § 1350.
21. The Supreme Court is currently considering the issue of whether the Alien Tort Statute applies to companies, or just individuals. *See* Kiobel v. Royal Dutch Petroleum Co., No. 10-1491.
22. *In re* South African Apartheid Litigation, 617 F. Supp. 2d 228 (S.D.N.Y. 2009).
23. *See* U.S. Securities & Exch. Comm'n, Office of Global Security Risk, http://www.sec.gov/divisions/corpfin/globalsecrisk.htm.

on U.S. exchanges disclose business activities in or involving states designated by the State Department as sponsoring terrorism—currently Cuba, Iran, Sudan, and Syria. The Office of Global Security Risk's mandate has generally been to seek information on corporate activities in terrorist-sponsoring countries, obtain disclosure if appropriate, and share the information across government agencies.

Because other agencies actually enforce export and sanctions rules, the SEC's role is somewhat redundant, and its inquiries sometimes have a perfunctory air. For example, if a company's website states that it does business in Latin America, or if it has a drop-down "address" menu for requesting information that includes every country in the world, the SEC may send a letter asking whether the company does business in Cuba. While the likelihood of finding a violation of law with such techniques is remote, for journalists the correspondence has one big advantage: the responses usually become a matter of public record.

EU Restrictions

The United States is not the only country concerned about the use of surveillance technology by repressive regimes. In December 2011, in response to the continued violence in Syria, the European Union banned the export of surveillance technology and software to Syria. Specifically, the EU sanctions prohibit the supply of "equipment or software intended primarily for use in the monitoring or interception by the Syrian regime" of voice or Internet communications, as well as any assistance to install, operate, or update such equipment or software.[24] This rule was part of a broad set of EU sanctions on Syria for its repression of internal dissent. (The United States had already banned the supply of such technology to Syria because U.S. sanctions had long prohibited almost all exports to Syria.)

Wiretap Law

The federal wiretap statute contains detailed restrictions on surveillance activities as well as provisions on the sale and distribution of surveillance technology. In particular, the wiretap statute provides for criminal penalties for any person who intentionally sends in "foreign commerce" (i.e., exports) "any electronic, mechanical, or other device, knowing or having reason to know that the design of such device renders it primarily useful for the purpose of the surreptitious interception of wire, oral or electronic communications."[25] There are certain exceptions for communications service providers acting in the normal course of business, governmental entities, and governmental officers, employees, and contractors.[26]

---

24. Council Decision 2011/782/CFSP of 1 December 2011 Concerning Restrictive Measures Against Syria and Repealing Decision 2011/273/CFSP, O.J. (L 319), 0056–0070 (Dec. 2, 2011).
25. 18 U.S.C. § 2512(1)(a).
26. *See* 18 U.S.C. § 2512(2).

However, as a general rule, it is a criminal violation to export such surveillance technology from the United States.

PROCEDURE—VASTLY DIFFERING TIME HORIZONS BETWEEN NEWS AND INVESTIGATION CYCLES

Determining the basic legality of a company's conduct is hard enough, but the task for reporters writing about this topic is further complicated by the fact that these stories develop essentially on two separate time horizons. On the one hand, there is the news cycle, which develops over days and weeks. As initial facts emerge, various parties respond to those facts, and new stories develop out of those parties' responses. The news cycle is quick, and it feeds off of public interest in the story. Some of the actors—human rights groups and plaintiffs' lawyers among them—can respond quickly and have an interest in doing so.

Others—government officials and companies accused of wrongdoing—must follow a far slower timetable. Companies cannot say much about the incident in question until they have nailed down all the facts. First reports from the battlefront, the saying goes, are always wrong, and companies that rush to put out statements based on their first reports often have to make corrections that cost them credibility later. As a result, well-advised companies often say very little until they are absolutely sure of their facts. This makes it hard for reporters, who often get one side of the story quickly and then have to write stories with only minimal input from the companies in question.

A hypothetical case study may help illustrate the problem. Let's assume for the sake of this case study that we are talking about a responsible American company—one that generally makes a good-faith effort to comply with the law. And let's also assume that this company stands accused of providing some key piece of technology that a foreign government has used to track dissidents' use of social media.

The news cycle begins first, because that's how the accusations come out:

1. First, a report surfaces, either directly to a reporter or from a watchdog group indicating that technology from our hypothetical company (Hypo Co.) is being used by an authoritarian government's intelligence services.
2. Next, the story gets picked up more broadly by human rights groups, journalists, and bloggers, and the story really gains momentum.
3. If sufficient public attention is drawn to an issue, politicians will weigh in, condemning the provision of U.S. technology to repressive regimes and demanding an investigation. Sometimes they will also use the incident as a reason to introduce legislation or hold hearings.
4. As the story develops further, plaintiffs' lawyers may get involved, filing a human rights suit on behalf of dissidents harmed by the

Procedure—Vastly Differing Time Horizons

authoritarian government's surveillance activities and alleging facts reported by the media. Note that plaintiffs need only *allege* facts against Hypo Co. to file a complaint. They do not, at the initial stages of a suit, need to make any evidentiary showing. But there is always a risk that the public, not familiar with the details of American civil procedure, will take these allegations as the truth.
5. With each reaction to the story, new stories may be published or aired (e.g., "Congressman Calls for Hearings into the Sale of Hypo Co. Technology to Authoritarian Regime," "Human Rights Activists Sue Hypo Co.").

For the company in question, the cycle is very different:

1. The company's investigation cycle begins either the day the story comes out, or a few days or weeks earlier, when a reporter or human rights group comes to Hypo Co. asking for comment on the report.
2. If the news reports suggest a violation of U.S. law, Hypo Co.'s management typically gets in touch with relevant government regulators, promises to cooperate, and then launches an internal investigation. (Most U.S. regulators encourage self-investigating and self-reporting as a way of saving government resources.) Internal investigations usually include seizure of electronic records such as e-mails and memos, followed by interviews with any employees involved in the matter. This kind of detailed, quasi-prosecutorial review will almost always turn up some new facts, and sometimes it will show that employees at some level knew or should have known of a likely violation of law. The purpose of the investigation is, in part, to double-check and question the reports first sent to headquarters. With such a detailed effort underway, it would be unwise for the company to rely publicly on those first reports, which have not yet been corroborated by investigators.
3. If litigation is reasonably anticipated, perhaps under the Alien Tort Statute, additional constraints may operate, as Hypo Co. is required to freeze all relevant records so the plaintiff's attorney can seek evidence through the discovery process. This too can take time, and it introduces the possibility that the plaintiff's attorney will seek to discredit the company by seizing on records that contradict any public statements made during the early press coverage. To avoid this, the lawyers handling the litigation will try to throttle public statements until they have reviewed all the files subject to discovery.
4. Then comes the long haul, as all of the interested parties wait for the results of the investigation or the litigation. It can take weeks to locate relevant evidence (e.g., documents, witnesses, e-mails). It can take still longer to sift through all of the documents, interview possible errant

employees, and reach a conclusion. When investigation results are filed with regulators, it can often take additional years for the regulators to reach a decision on how to handle the matter. In the case of civil suits, it can also take years to get a trial date, and, in most cases, the facts are never actually tested in court because these types of suits often settle well in advance of trial.

At the end of the investigations and the litigation, months or years after the initial press reports, it may turn out that the facts were quite different from those first reported. For reporters, the risk is that, unable to immediately obtain the company's side of the story, they rely too much on accusations or advocacy groups' self-interested interpretations of facts. This risk cannot be eliminated, but an understanding of the processes followed by companies and regulators should at least help the reporter not to equate silence with guilt in the early stages of a story. Likewise, a better understanding of reporters' needs for timely information should motivate companies to develop strategies to increase transparency in getting information to the public.

CONCLUSION

The popular uprisings of 2011, occurring around the world, have brought into focus like never before the power of technology for mobilizing political action as well as the opportunities it creates for government surveillance. Add to this rising concerns in the West about the privacy implications of new technology, and there is little doubt that cooperation by Western tech companies with foreign governments will be a fixture of reporting in years to come. While the legal aspects of these stories may not be what draws the public's interest, reporters need to understand the legal realities—both substantive and procedural—because, at a minimum, these realities will determine the information that companies are willing to provide.

EXPERTS

Cindy Cohn, Legal Director, Electronic Frontier Foundation; (415) 436-9333; cindy@eff.org

Sue E. Eckert, Former Assistant Secretary of Commerce for Export Administration and Senior Fellow, Watson Institute for International Studies, Brown University; (401) 863-3928; sue_eckert@brown.edu

Edward J. Krauland, Partner (Export Controls, International Regulation, and Compliance), Steptoe & Johnson LLP; (202) 429-8083; ekrauland@steptoe.com

Michael Vatis, Partner (Data Security and Privacy, National and Homeland Security), Steptoe & Johnson LLP; (212) 506-3927; mvatis@steptoe.com

Juan Zarate, Former Deputy Assistant to the President and Deputy National Security Adviser for Combating Terrorism, Former Assistant Secretary of the Treasury for Terrorist Financing and Financial Crimes, Senior Adviser, Transnational Threats Project and Homeland Security and Counterterrorism Program at the Center for Strategic and International Studies; Media Contact: H. Andrew Schwartz, (202) 775-3242, aschwartz@csis.org

RESOURCES

Statutes and Regulations

Communications Assistance for Law Enforcement Act, 47 U.S.C. §§ 1001–1010 (sets requirements for telecommunications carriers' ability to carry out surveillance for law enforcement purposes).

Wiretap Act, as amended by the Electronic Communications Privacy Act, 18 U.S.C. §§ 2510–2522 (regulates the interception, use, and disclosure of wire, oral, and electronic communications).

International Emergency Economic Powers Act, 50 U.S.C. §§ 1701–1706 (authorizes economic sanctions and export control regulations).

Trading with the Enemy Act, 50 U.S.C. app. §§ 1–44 (prohibits trade with enemy countries; authorizes certain economic sanctions against Cuba and North Korea).

Export Administration Regulations, 15 C.F.R. §§ 730 *et seq.* (Commerce Department regulations implementing export controls on commercial and dual-use items).

Comprehensive Iran Sanctions, Accountability, and Divestment Act of 2010, Pub. L. No. 111-195, 124 Stat. 1312 (Iran sanctions legislation, including restrictions related to provision of sensitive technology to Iran).

Alien Tort Statute, 28 U.S.C. § 1350 (authorizes lawsuits by aliens in the United States for human rights violations anywhere in the world).

Publications and Government Web Pages

U.S. Commerce Dep't, Regional Considerations, http://www.bis.doc.gov/policiesandregulations/regionalconsiderations.htm (summaries of export control requirements for sensitive destinations).

U.S. Treas. Dep't, Sanctions Programs and Country Information, http://www.treasury.gov/resource-center/sanctions/Programs/Pages/Programs.aspx (summaries of Treasury Department sanctions programs).

U.S. Commerce Dep't, Export Violations, http://efoia.bis.doc.gov/ExportControlViolations/TOCExportViolations.htm (copies of export violation orders, settlement agreements, and charging letters).

U.S. Treas. Dep't, Civil Penalties and Enforcement Information, http://www.treasury.gov/resource-center/sanctions/CivPen/Pages/civpen-index2.aspx (economic sanctions enforcement settlement agreements and penalty data).

Jonathan C. Drimmer & Sarah R. Lamoree, *Think Globally, Sue Locally: Trends and Out-of-Court Tactics in Transnational Tort Actions*, 29.2 BERKELEY J. INT'L L. 456 (2011) (history and trends in Alien Tort Statute litigation).

European Comm'n, Dual-Use Export Controls, http://ec.europa.eu/trade/creating-opportunities/trade-topics/dual-use/.

Part IV

Homeland Security Issues

The Use of the Military in the Homeland

20

By Kurt Johnson

One of the most important and sensitive concerns of our time is how to properly use the military in the homeland, especially in a representative democracy such as the United States. We are engaged in an ongoing struggle to strike the right balance between maintaining national security and protecting civil liberties against a backdrop of suspicion fueled by perceived and actual abuses of the past, both in our country and in those from which our founders, early settlers, and later immigrants all emigrated.

Thomas Jefferson saw the dangers of a standing army in a free society: "There are instruments so dangerous to the rights of the nation and which place them so totally at the mercy of their governors that those governors, whether legislative or executive, should be restrained from keeping such instruments on foot but in well-defined cases. Such an instrument is a standing army."[1]

Perhaps, however, the danger is not so much the military threat to domestic civilian government, as Jefferson mused, but rather the overreliance on the military to solve all of our problems.

That concern has more current echoes for Gene Healey and Benjamin Friedman of the Cato Institute: "[C]reeping militarization continues, and few in the media or Congress object. The militarized future to fear isn't one that ends in a dictatorship or martial law. Our troops' commitment to civilian rule prevents that. The danger we face is one in which the public embraces the

---

1. *Thomas Jefferson to David Humphreys, March 18, 1789, in* THE WORKS OF THOMAS JEFFERSON IN TWELVE VOLUMES (Paul Leicester Ford ed., Federal Ed. 1904).

notion that civilian institutions are weak and messy, and that when you want the job done, you call in the boys in green. That approach will make us no safer—only less free."[2]

Yet, properly restrained and guided by law, a free press, and watchful citizens, the military can be a valuable "force multiplier" in support of civilian disaster management and first responder entities. This chapter discusses the key authorities and restraints under which our military operates in the homeland to achieve that objective.

MILITARY ROLES IN THE HOMELAND

The military has two primary roles in the homeland. The first is military defense of the country, the traditional overseas war-fighting mission applied to the homeland. In response to the September 11, 2001, attacks, the Department of Defense established U.S. Northern Command, known as USNORTHCOM, to provide command and control of Department of Defense homeland defense efforts under a single geographic combatant command. Additionally, the North American Aerospace Defense Command, or NORAD, is a U.S. and Canadian organization charged with the missions of aerospace warning and aerospace control for North America. NORAD accomplishes its missions by responding to unknown, unwanted, and unauthorized air activity approaching and operating within the two countries' airspaces.

The second major role for the military in the homeland is to provide defense support to civil authorities in addressing those threats that pose the greatest risk to the security of the country, including acts of terrorism, cyberattacks, pandemics, and catastrophic natural disasters.[3] "Defense Support of Civil Authorities" is the second of USNORTHCOM's two primary missions. Military support to civil authorities could be provided at any or all of the phases of preventing, protecting against, responding to, and recovering from those threats (see figure).

The Continuum of Defense Support to Civil Authorities

---

2. *Be Wary of Using Military as Police*, ORANGE CNTY. REGISTER, Dec. 26, 2008, at Local 17.
3. *See* Presidential Policy Directive/PPD-8: National Preparedness (Mar. 30, 2011), http://www.dhs.gov/xabout/laws/gc_1215444247124.shtm.

314

Although the military's routine, day-to-day role in the homeland is to support civil authorities, certain scenarios, particularly those involving large-scale terrorism, present challenges in determining whether the military should operate in its normal civil support role or in a defense role.

CIVILIAN CONTROL OF THE MILITARY

The framers of our Constitution planned for complete civilian control of the military, giving Congress the powers to "declare War," "raise and support Armies," and "provide and maintain a Navy."[4] The Constitution also designates the president as "Commander in Chief of the Army and Navy of the United States, and of the Militia of the several States when called into the actual Service of the United States."[5] This concept is so deeply ingrained in American government and tradition that it has led to high-profile events such as President Harry Truman's firing of Gen. Douglas MacArthur in 1951 over policy differences in the conduct of the Korean War. Truman later wrote in his memoirs:

> If there is one basic element in our Constitution, it is civilian control of the military. Policies are to be made by the elected political officials, not by generals or admirals. Yet time and again General MacArthur had shown that he was unwilling to accept the policies of the administration. By his repeated public statements he was not only confusing our allies as to the true course of our policies but, in fact, was also setting his policy against the President's. . . . If I allowed him to defy the civil authorities in this manner, I myself would be violating my oath to uphold and defend the Constitution.[6]

FEDERAL VERSUS STATE POWERS AND THE TENTH AMENDMENT TO THE U.S. CONSTITUTION

A mere 28 words of the Constitution powerfully limit the authority of the federal government and the use of the military in the homeland. Fearing an overbearing federal government, the framers of the Constitution limited its powers with the Tenth Amendment: "The powers not delegated to the United States by the Constitution, nor prohibited by it to the States, are reserved to the States respectively, or to the people."

---

4. U.S. CONST. art I, § 8.
5. U.S. CONST. art II, § 2.
6. HARRY S. TRUMAN, MEMOIRS BY HARRY S. TRUMAN: YEARS OF TRIAL AND HOPE 444 (Doubleday 1955).

Their intent was to establish a federal government with "limited and enumerated powers" and to reserve to the individual states all other authorities and powers. James Madison wrote:

> The powers delegated by the proposed Constitution to the federal government are few and defined. Those which are to remain in the State governments are numerous and indefinite. The former will be exercised principally on external objects, as war, peace, negotiation, and foreign commerce; with which last the power of taxation will, for the most part, be connected. The powers reserved to the several States will extend to all the objects which, in the ordinary course of affairs, concern the lives, liberties, and properties of the people, and the internal order, improvement, and prosperity of the State.[7]

This general authority of a state to govern the health, welfare, and safety of its citizens, also known as the "police power," limits federal—including military—intervention in a state in nearly every circumstance until and unless its governor so requests. Accordingly, the Stafford Act, discussed later in this chapter, and several similar federal assistance statutes are triggered only by a request from a governor to the president. For example, federal assistance, including more than 20,000 federal troops, began flowing to Louisiana in the wake of Hurricane Katrina only after Gov. Kathleen Blanco made a formal request to President George W. Bush.

THE "MILITARY"

What precisely constitutes the "military" is a surprisingly complex matter. When military forces are called out after major disasters such as Hurricane Katrina, few citizens understand that two or more distinct forces are helping them. Although they wear identical uniforms, those forces have different chains of command, different authorities, and different weapons policies. Citizens are most familiar with Title 10[8] active duty federal forces—our traditional war-fighting troops whose chain of command runs to the president, via the geographic combatant command, which is USNORTHCOM for the homeland. They are less knowledgeable about forces making up the "reserve component," which includes both Title 10 federal reserve forces and National Guard forces. Complicating matters further, the National Guard forces may be in one of three possible statuses: Title 10, reporting to the president and paid with federal funds; Title 32, reporting to their state's governor but paid with federal funds; or State Active Duty, reporting to the governor and paid with state funds (see table).

---

7. THE FEDERALIST NO. 45 (James Madison).
8. Title 10 of the U.S. Code contains statutes governing the U.S. military.

Title 10, Title 32, and the Chain of Command

Force	Chain of Command	Pay	Authority
Title 10 Active Duty	President	Federal	Title 10 U.S. Code
Title 10 Reserves	President	Federal	Title 10 U.S. Code
National Guard in Title 10 Status	President	Federal	Title 10 U.S. Code
National Guard in Title 32 Status	Governor	Federal	Title 32 U.S. Code
National Guard in State Active Duty Status	Governor	State	State Law

Same uniform, but different statuses

UNITY OF COMMAND VERSUS UNITY OF EFFORT AND THE DUAL STATUS COMMANDER

Addressing widespread criticism of the Department of Defense response to Hurricane Katrina, a senior DoD official testified that "[t]he Constitution is lots of things, but it's not a model of efficiency"[9] in a disaster. That is due in large part to the constitutional division of power between the federal government and individual state governments.

In its traditional overseas war-fighting role, the U.S. military is accustomed to a clear and crisp chain of command that runs from the individual soldier to the president. When soldiers with different chains of command operate side by side in the homeland, however, that unity of command is not possible. The Constitution prohibits Title 10 forces from exercising command and control over State Active Duty status National Guard forces, and vice versa. Nevertheless, these forces must operate together through unity of *effort* to achieve a common objective. In some situations, particularly preplanned events such as the Democratic and Republican National Conventions, that unity of effort can best be accomplished through designation of a "dual status commander."

---

9. *Hurricane Katrina: The Defense Department's Role in the Response: Hearing Before the Senate Comm. on Homeland Security and Governmental Affairs*, 109th Cong. 29 (2006) (statement of Paul McHale, Assistant Secretary of Defense for Homeland Defense).

If both the president and the affected governor agree, a single military officer may hold both a state and a federal commission.[10] That officer may then command all of the military forces—both federal and state—in a mutually exclusive manner. His chain of command runs to the president in his command of Title 10 forces, and to the governor in his command of Title 32 and State Active Duty forces (see figure).

The Dual Status Commander

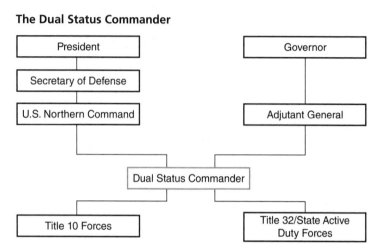

WHO IS IN CHARGE? THE CIVIL SUPPORT/HOMELAND DEFENSE CONTINUUM

Military performing a civil support mission in the homeland will never, by definition, be in charge of the operation. When it comes to the murky divide between criminal activity and terrorism, however, it becomes far less clear whether the military should always remain in a civil support role or, under extreme circumstances, shift to a homeland defense role.

To illustrate this conundrum, it is useful to imagine a civil support/homeland defense continuum (see figure). At one extreme of the continuum, a lone-wolf terrorist crosses the U.S. land border with an AK-47 rifle, intent on killing as many Americans as he can before he is killed or captured. It is likely that most Americans would agree that this terrorist is the primary responsibility of civilian law enforcement agencies and not the military, although the civilian law enforcement agencies might request and use certain unique military assets in support of their efforts. At the other end of the continuum, a nation-state crosses the U.S. air and land borders with military jets, tanks, and troops, intent on bringing down the American government and claiming American territory as its own. It is likely that

---

10. 32 U.S.C. §§ 315, 325 (2006).

The Civil Support/Homeland Defense Continuum

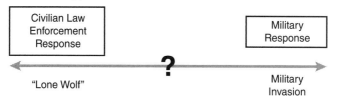

most Americans would agree that this situation is the primary responsibility of the military, perhaps with civilian agencies in support.

Determining whether civilian law enforcement or the military should lead the response becomes much more difficult as we inch closer to the middle of the continuum. Instead of one lone wolf, suppose we had 10? 100? 1,000? Or suppose the lone wolf was carrying a dirty bomb instead of an AK-47? A nuclear weapon? At some point along the continuum, each of us will reach our individual tipping point where we believe that the situation calls for the military to lead the response. At that point we no longer sense a criminal threat calling for a law enforcement response, but a threat to the national security of the United States calling for a military response. Some will reach their tipping point based on their assessment that the threat has exceeded the capabilities of law enforcement, while others will make their determination based on the nature of the weapon and the extent of physical and psychological harm it will cause.

Recent real-world events in the United States, such as the Christmas Day 2009 attempted suicide bombing aboard a plane by the "Underwear Bomber," Umar Farouk Abdulmutallab, and the 2009 Fort Hood massacre by Army Maj. Nidal Malik Hasan, have generated a spirited debate about the nature of the threats and whether they represent mere criminal actions or actual threats to the national security.

Because there is nothing in law that clearly articulates the tipping point, most who have studied this question agree that the point would be determined in any given situation by the president, using his constitutional commander-in-chief authority. The National Defense Authorization Act for fiscal year 2012 suggests that Congress is tilting to the right of the tipping point, requiring that those individuals, perhaps even U.S. citizens, who act in coordination with or pursuant to the direction of al-Qaida be held in military custody pending disposition under the law of war.[11]

The president's determination has considerable legal and operational consequences for use of the military in the homeland.

To the left of the tipping point, normally the Department of Homeland Security or the Department of Justice has the lead role for any federal response, and the Department of Defense operates in *support*, underpinned by several statutory authorities permitting certain limited military support to civilian law enforcement[12]

---

11. *See* National Defense Authorization Act for Fiscal Year 2012, H.R. 1540, 112th Cong. §§ 1021, 1022 (2011).
12. 10 U.S.C. ch. 18, Military Support for Civilian Law Enforcement Agencies (2006).

and disaster consequence management pursuant to the Stafford Act.[13] Under the Stafford Act, the president, pursuant to a request by a governor, declares a major disaster or emergency, which triggers federal assistance to state and local efforts. That assistance may include Department of Defense assets.

To the right of the tipping point, the Department of Defense has the lead role, operating under the president's constitutional commander-in-chief authority. NORAD forces routinely operate in the homeland to the right of the tipping point in the air domain. It is conceivable that maritime forces would operate to the right of the tipping point in certain situations, such as an offshore vessel launching cruise missile strikes against the homeland. It is also possible that a land-based terrorist threat or attack would be of such magnitude that a president would choose, at least in the short term, to respond with military force.

In that situation, the military would likely operate in both a support and a lead role simultaneously in different parts of the homeland. The president could choose to give a portion of the military the lead in a certain discreet operation—defending critical infrastructure, for example—while leaving the rest of the military in its traditional civil support role for other threats around the country.

To the left of the tipping point, attackers would be treated as criminals and prosecuted under the criminal justice system, with *Miranda* rights, habeas corpus, rules of evidence, attorneys, trials, and jail sentences. To the right of the tipping point, attackers would be treated as enemy combatants under the law of war, defined as "[t]hat part of international law that regulates the conduct of armed hostilities. It is often called the 'law of armed conflict,'"[14] and is based primarily on the Geneva Conventions of 1949 and their Additional Protocols.[15] The attackers would not be entitled to *Miranda* rights or habeas corpus on that side of the tipping point. They could be killed or captured and, if captured, would be held as prisoners of war until the end of the conflict. During their detention, they could be tried for war crimes under some relaxed rules of evidence.

THE POSSE COMITATUS ACT AND THE INSURRECTION ACT

The Posse Comitatus Act[16] of 1878 prohibits the direct, active participation of federal military forces to execute civilian law. Although it was enacted in response to the perceived misuse of Army troops in the South after the Civil War, there is

---

13. Robert T. Stafford Disaster Relief and Emergency Assistance Act, 43 U.S.C. §§ 5121 *et seq.* (2006).

14. U.S. Dep't of Def., Dir. 2311.01E, DoD Law of War Program (May 9, 2006, incorporating Change 1, Nov. 15, 2010).

15. The International Committee of the Red Cross provides an excellent overview of the Geneva Conventions of 1949 and Their Additional Protocols, http://www.icrc.org/eng/war-and-law/treaties-customary-law/geneva-conventions/index.jsp.

16. 18 U.S.C. § 1385 (2006).

a very good argument that its principles are rooted in the country's foundational documents. The Act provides:

> Whoever, except in cases and under circumstances expressly authorized by the Constitution or Act of Congress, willfully uses any part of the Army or the Air Force as a posse comitatus or otherwise to execute the laws shall be fined under this title or imprisoned not more than two years, or both.[17]

Although the statute applies only to the Army and Air Force, Department of Defense policy extends its prohibitions to the Navy and Marine Corps.[18] The Act applies to the National Guard only when units are in Title 10 status. When in either Title 32 or State Active Duty status, the National Guard may be used in a law enforcement role to perform such functions as preventing looting after a natural disaster. The Act does not apply to the Coast Guard during peacetime when it is operating as part of the Department of Homeland Security, but does apply when it is operating as part of the Navy in time of war or pursuant to orders of the president.[19] It is important to note that the Act's restrictions apply only to the military's civil support mission, which includes support to law enforcement. They do not apply to the military's homeland defense mission, which by definition does not constitute support to law enforcement.

There are several exceptions to the Posse Comitatus Act that allow federal troops to assist civilian law enforcement officials with certain specified training, use of military equipment, and expert advice.[20] A key exception is the Insurrection Act,[21] which authorizes the president to use federal military forces in a law enforcement capacity in three situations:

1. *To assist a state government at the request of the state's legislature or governor if the legislature cannot be convened.* This was the authority used by President George H.W. Bush to assist in quelling the 1992 Los Angeles riots.
2. *To enforce federal authority.* This was the authority used by three presidents to enforce public school desegregation between 1957 and 1963.
3. *To protect constitutional rights.* This was the authority used by President John F. Kennedy in response to the 1963 civil rights protests in Alabama.

---

17. *Id.*
18. U.S. Dep't of Def., Dir. 5525.5, DoD Cooperation with Civilian Law Enforcement Officials (Jan. 15, 1986, incorporating Change 1 of Dec. 20, 1989, pursuant to 10 U.S.C. § 375).
19. 14 U.S.C. § 3 (2006).
20. 10 U.S.C. §§ 371–382 (2006).
21. 10 U.S.C. §§ 331–333 (2006).

THE USE OF THE MILITARY IN THE HOMELAND

Left to right: Navy Capt. Kurt Johnson, senior legal adviser to commander of NORAD and U.S. Northern Command; Navy Adm. Timothy Keating, commander of NORAD and U.S. Northern Command; President George W. Bush. This discussion centered on whether the Insurrection Act could be used in the aftermath of Hurricane Katrina.

The Insurrection Act most recently came to national attention in 2006, with a debate on whether it afforded President George W. Bush the authority to deploy federal troops in a law enforcement capacity to New Orleans to deal with the lawlessness in the immediate aftermath of Hurricane Katrina.

Most legal experts agreed that none of the Insurrection Act's three sections triggered authority for the president in this situation, in large part because the drafters of the Act had contemplated rebellion against government and not natural-disaster-induced lawlessness. Congress subsequently amended the third section of the Act[22] to provide modest additional authority to the president in situations such as natural disasters, terrorist acts, epidemics, and serious public health emergencies. Those changes were repealed entirely[23] one year later at the behest of numerous state governors and others who resisted expansion of presidential authority at the expense of individual state authority. *To this day, there is no clear authority in a natural disaster for the president to deploy federal troops to a state in a law enforcement capacity without the governor's consent.*

---

22. John Warner National Defense Authorization Act for Fiscal Year 2007, Pub. L. No. 109-364, 120 Stat. 2083.
23. National Defense Authorization Act for Fiscal Year 2008, Pub. L. No. 110-181, 122 Stat. 3.

IMMEDIATE RESPONSE AUTHORITY

Lives are at risk and valuable property is threatened in the critical hours and days following an earthquake, hurricane, or other disaster, whether natural or man-made. In addition to the state's National Guard forces, federal military forces in the area possess crucial life-saving assets and skills. Military forces are normally not deployed, however, without an order from the secretary of defense via the chain of command to individual units.

Nevertheless, certain serious conditions demand immediate action, and time does not always permit gaining prior approval from the chain of command. Local military commanders are therefore authorized to provide immediate assistance to save lives, prevent human suffering, and mitigate great property damage.

This "Immediate Response Authority" is derived from the president's authority as commander in chief and implemented through Department of Defense policy.[24] Immediate Response Authority is triggered by a request from civilian authorities and is generally provided on a cost-reimbursable basis. Because Immediate Response Authority is not an exception to the Posse Comitatus Act, federal troops may not engage in law enforcement activities or provide direct support to civilian law enforcement agencies. Although there are no specific time[25] or geographic limitations on providing this type of assistance, it will normally end quickly as USNORTHCOM takes command of the situation. Such was the case in Hurricane Katrina, multiple California wildfires, and other USNORTHCOM natural disaster recovery support operations.

INTELLIGENCE OVERSIGHT

Jefferson wrote that "[i]t is probable . . . that not knowing how to use the military as a civil weapon, [the civil authority] will do too much or too little with it."[26] Doing "too much" with the military in the homeland, coupled with the military's

---

24. U.S. Dep't of Def., Dir. 3025.18, Defense Support of Civil Authorities (DSCA) (Dec. 29, 2010).

25.
> An immediate response shall end when the necessity giving rise to the response is no longer present (e.g., when there are sufficient resources available from State, local, and other federal agencies to respond adequately and that agency or department has initiated response activities) or when the initiating DoD official or a higher authority directs an end to the response. The DoD official directing a response under immediate response authority shall reassess whether there remains a necessity for the Department of Defense to respond under this authority as soon as practicable but, if immediate response activities have not yet ended, not later than 72 hours after the request for assistance was received.

Id. at 5.

26. *Thomas Jefferson to William Carmichael, 1789, in* THE JEFFERSON CYCLOPEDIA (John P. Foley ed., 1900).

enormous appetite for intelligence information, could significantly compromise civil liberties.

Military intelligence collection in the homeland is regulated by a series of presidential executive orders and Department of Defense directives[27] that are designed to protect the constitutional rights and privacy of "U.S. persons" and allow intelligence collection entities to protect national security. Those regulations grew out of a series of domestic intelligence abuses in the 1960s and 1970s, like the FBI's infamous surveillance of domestic political groups. The broadly protected category of "U.S. persons" includes U.S. citizens, permanent resident aliens, groups substantially composed of U.S. persons, and U.S. corporations.

In order for a federal military intelligence unit to collect information on U.S. persons, it must show, first, that collection of such information is necessary to accomplish its mission and, second, that there is a foreign nexus—a foreign intelligence or counterintelligence tie to the U.S. person. Purely domestic threats to national security with no foreign nexus, such as criminal gangs and militia groups, are the business of the FBI and other law enforcement agencies, not the military, and the military is prohibited from retaining, analyzing, or disseminating information concerning them. The foreign nexus has traditionally been based on some kind of direct foreign link to the U.S. person, such as foreign travel, funding, and communication.

The foreign nexus requirement raises a debate about whether the military should be able to collect intelligence on "homegrown terrorists" to whom there is no traditional direct foreign link, but the U.S. person is inspired by, acts in conformity with, and follows the teachings and directions of a foreign terrorist group. The homegrown terrorist is often self-radicalized simply through material he absorbs from websites.

For example, of the six men who plotted to kill soldiers at Fort Dix in New Jersey in 2007, two were U.S. persons who were inspired by the al-Qaida call for jihad against America. If such threats multiply, the military anticipates playing a support role to law enforcement or, in the most extreme case, being called out by the president in a limited war-fighting role. Without prior intelligence enabling it to "know thy enemy,"[28] the military is unable to conduct the planning and training it needs to be successful in either role. The military lives by President Dwight D. Eisenhower's observation that "plans are nothing; planning is everything." Solid, actionable intelligence is an integral part of good planning. These regulations apply to the military's intelligence agencies and entities.

---

27. Exec. Order No. 12,333, United States Intelligence Activities, 46 Fed. Reg. 59,941, 3 C.F.R. 1981 Comp., at 200; U.S. Dep't of Def., Dir. 5240.01, DOD Intelligence Activities (Aug. 27, 2007); U.S. Dep't of Def., Dir. 5240.1-R, Procedures Governing the Activities of DOD Intelligence Components That Affect U.S. Persons (Dec. 1982).

28. SUN TZU, THE ART OF WAR (6th c. B.C.) ("It is said that if you know your enemies and know yourself, you will not be imperiled in a hundred battles; if you do not know your enemies but do know yourself, you will win one and lose one; if you do not know your enemies nor yourself, you will be imperiled in every single battle.").

The rest of the U.S. military is governed by the Privacy Act[29] and Department of Defense regulations[30] concerning collection of U.S. person information. Such information may be collected only if it pertains to direct threats to Department of Defense personnel, facilities, or operations. The military is not entitled to collect information, for example, on peaceful protesters exercising their right to free speech outside of a military installation.

Any information on criminal activity that does not represent a direct threat may be passed to federal, state, and local law enforcement agencies, and then must be purged from all Department of Defense data systems. As the military gets more heavily involved in domestic support operations following hurricanes, floods, wildfires, and other disasters, it is increasingly using intelligence assets for non-intelligence-gathering missions. For example, military aircraft, both manned and unmanned, are frequently used to assess damage and search for survivors in support of the Federal Emergency Management Agency. In performing such missions, any intentional collection of criminal activity information would likely constitute direct support to law enforcement and violate the Posse Comitatus Act, but any incidental collection of such information in performing an otherwise lawful mission could be passed to law enforcement agencies before it is purged.

CONCLUSION

American taxpayers annually spend approximately $600 billion to $700 billion on the Department of Defense, primarily to equip and train the military to defend U.S. citizens and interests around the world. We have built perhaps the most capable, best trained, and best equipped government entity in the history of humankind. Accordingly, as former Defense Secretary Donald Rumsfeld said, "It's reasonable for [American taxpayers] to expect the military to step in to support other missions as it's able"[31] to protect Americans in the homeland and assist them in recovering from man-made and natural disasters. The overarching challenge, particularly as we encounter new threats not contemplated in current law, is doing so in ways that zealously guard American civil liberties, shield our federalist system and protect states' rights, preserve civilian control of the military, and honor our traditions as reflected in the Posse Comitatus Act.

Although the law evolves slowly, the basic system is in place today to appropriately guide military operations in the homeland. If we continue to adhere to our historic national tradition that "[g]overnment . . . is the empire of laws and not of men,"[32] if we insist on transparent government and an informed citizenry, and if

---

29. Privacy Act of 1974, 5 U.S.C. § 552a (2006).
30. U.S. Dep't of Def., Dir. 5200.27, Acquisition of Information Concerning Persons and Organizations Not Affiliated with the Department of Defense (Jan. 7, 1980).
31. Donald Rumsfeld, Sec'y of Def., Address at a Pentagon Town Hall Meeting (May 19, 2006).
32. JAMES HARRINGTON, THE COMMONWEALTH OF OCEANA (John Streater pr., 1656).

we aggressively defend our free press, then we will have little to fear and much to benefit from use of the military in the homeland.

EXPERTS

Duncan Aukland, Staff Judge Advocate and General Counsel, Ohio National Guard; Colonel, JAG Corps, Ohio Army National Guard; (614) 336-7022; Duncan.aukland@us.army.mil

Kevin Cieply, Associate Dean for Academic Affairs, John Marshall Law School, Colonel (ret.) JAG Corps, Wyoming Army National Guard; (404) 872-3593; kcieply@johnmarshall.edu

Geoffrey Corn, Professor of Law, South Texas College of Law, Lieutenant Colonel (ret.), JAG Corps, U.S. Army; (713) 646-2973; gcorn@stcl.edu

Kurt Johnson, Director, Center for Homeland Security, University of Colorado; Senior Legal Advisor to Commander of NORAD and U.S. Northern Command (2005–2008); Captain (ret.), JAG Corps, U.S. Navy; (719) 255-3132; kjohnso9@uccs.edu

Gary Walsh, Chief, International/Operations Law Branch Headquarters, NORAD and U.S. Northern Command; Lieutenant Colonel (ret.), JAG Corps, U.S. Army; (719) 554-8098; Gary.Walsh@northcom.mil

RESOURCES

John Norton Moore & Robert Turner, Legal Issues in the Struggle Against Terror (Carolina Academic Press 2010).

Col. John T. Gereski & Lt. Col. Christopher R. Brown, *Two Hats Are Better Than One: The Dual-Status Commander in Domestic Operations*, Army Law. (DA PAM 27-50-445, 2010).

Richard H. Kohn, *An Essay on Civilian Control of the Military*, 1997 Am. Diplomacy.

Steve Bowman, Cong. Research Serv., Homeland Security: The Department of Defense's Role (May 14, 2003).

Kathleen Gereski, *The Department of Defense as Lead Federal Agency*, II (3) Homeland Sec. Affairs (October 2006).

CONG. RESEARCH SERV., ANNOTATED CONSTITUTION: TENTH AMENDMENT RESERVED POWERS (1992; supp. 1994, 1996, 1998 & 2000).

Michael Greenberger & Arianne Spaccarelli, *The Posse Comitatus Act and Disaster Response*, in HOMELAND SECURITY AND EMERGENCY MANAGEMENT: A LEGAL GUIDE FOR STATE AND LOCAL GOVERNMENTS (ABA 2010).

Border Security and the Law

21

By Susan Ginsburg

Is border security about security breaches, as when the Detroit "Underwear Bomber" was able to obtain a visa, or is it about stopping illegal immigration from Mexico and patrolling the border with Canada? Perhaps surprisingly, border security is not a term of art in contemporary national security strategy or in statute or case law. Instead its meaning is informal and elastic, and can refer to a broad range of problems that give rise to newsworthy incidents and legal controversies. Prominent among these practical and legal topics are

- terrorist mobility and the use of intelligence laws to defeat it
- the use of immigration laws in counterterrorism
- traveler screening and the visa process
- illegal immigration and related border control and immigration enforcement
- military homeland defense

Excluded from these for present purposes is an even longer list of border-security-related issues: criminal trafficking and smuggling (of weapons of mass destruction, people, illegal drugs, or cash); air and maritime interdiction; transnational pandemics and food poisonings; cross-border pollutants; the migratory impact of natural disasters, political crises, and global warming; and global cyber flows. The point here is that, given globalized economies and communications, most contemporary security problems have a cross-border dimension.

In the interest of narrowing the scope to manageable proportions, this chapter sticks closely to border security as it relates to more traditional national security matters and to the border security topic of greatest controversy: immigration enforcement.

BACKGROUND

Today's national security law developed in response to military and strategic nuclear threats, primarily from the former Soviet Union. These threats did not include the possibility of a full-scale invasion by land from Canada or Mexico or by sea. National security law, therefore, all but excluded the subject of border security, understood as including the control of land and coastal borders and immigration law. National security law is primarily embodied in the National Security Act of 1947, intelligence law, State Department and military defense statutes and regulations, and the law of war, or humanitarian law, based on international treaties and international common law. Oriented toward foreign policy, it is constitutionally grounded in the president's executive authorities.

Border security law, by contrast, is found primarily in the Immigration and Nationality Act and in the trade, customs, and regulatory and criminal laws that govern U.S. coastal and land borders for immigration, customs, agricultural and public health issues, drug and human trafficking, and other criminal purposes. Environmental and other regulatory laws, and laws governing tribal lands, also play a role in a complex mix of federal, state, and local laws that apply along the nation's borders. Banking and cyber laws address cross-border financial flows. Oriented toward domestic policy, border security matters constitutionally have been primarily the purview of Congress.

National security and border security, however, have gradually become intertwined in the public perception. The conflation began when unauthorized migration across the southwest border became a public concern during the 1990s, and the Immigration and Naturalization Service (INS) began building a fence as a deterrent to illegal entry. During the same period, beginning with the creation of the first terrorist watchlist in 1990, senior government officials began to exploit immigration, customs, and border-related criminal laws as elements of the response to terrorist threats, trafficking in dangerous materials and people, and other criminal risks arising from globalized legal and illegal markets. The September 11, 2001, attacks precipitated a more comprehensive look at long-term risks posed by individuals. The Homeland Security Act of 2002 represented a strategic turning point because it established a homeland security organization to address the gap that these enhanced security risks opened up between immigration and national security practice, while deepening and accelerating the legal changes already underway.

Homeland security law is composed of original requirements (such as the establishment of the Department of Homeland Security) combined with inherited and adapted aspects of traditional national security and criminal, civil liberties, and immigration laws. No consensus exists on the definitions and scope of national security, homeland security, and criminal law as they confront cross-border terrorism, cybersecurity, organized crime, and other new or elevated risks and threats. While border security is an aspect of homeland security, the issues it raises cut across multiple legal fields.

BORDER SECURITY INTELLIGENCE AUTHORITIES

Terrorist movement is the border security risk most closely linked to national security. This includes U.S. citizen terrorists' ability to travel to and from foreign countries as well as alien terrorists' ability to gain access to or residence in the United States. It encompasses clandestine border crossing, fraudulent travel documents or fraudulent acquisition of travel documents, or violating the terms of a visa. Because intelligence is the most important tool in counterterrorism, the legal basis for intelligence practices relating to countering terrorist mobility is a key concern.

Intelligence resources potentially useful in countering terrorist mobility include reports on terrorist plans to violate U.S. borders; terrorist travel intelligence collection and analysis;[1] the National Counterterrorism Center's Terrorist Identification Data Environment, which is an amalgam of disparate watchlists; and surveillance relating to transport of weapons of mass destruction.

As with other national security arenas, border-security-related intelligence practice is governed by the National Security Act of 1947 as amended and Executive Order 12,333, United States Intelligence Agencies, as amended,[2] and other statutes such as the Foreign Intelligence Surveillance Act of 1978 and the USA PATRIOT Act.[3] But because the intelligence laws were designed principally to support collection of intelligence relating to foreign governments and not intelligence about transnational terrorist groups operating quasi-independently or security problems related to border crossing, adapting these laws to border security needs is an ongoing challenge.

Border security is not a term of art in intelligence law, and there is no statute focused on border security intelligence per se. Rather, there is a patchwork of laws

---

1. THE 9/11 COMMISSION REPORT, FINAL REPORT OF THE NATIONAL COMMISSION ON TERRORIST ATTACKS UPON THE UNITED STATES 385 (Norton 2004).
2. Amendments are published in Executive Orders 13,284 (2003), 13,355 (2004), and 13,470 (2008).
3. Pub. L. No. 107-56.

leaving much to interpretation. First, the intelligence community collects and analyzes foreign intelligence that self-evidently includes foreign terrorist efforts to breach U.S. borders.[4] Second, Congress made counternarcotics efforts a subject for intelligence agencies in the 1980s,[5] as well as human trafficking and smuggling, all of which may be linked to terrorist travel. Further, Congress defined intelligence related to national security as including matters "bearing on national or homeland security."[6] As border security is considered homeland security, this broader formulation could be read to allow for an unspecified expansion of intelligence activities. Given this statutory invitation, barriers to specific border-security-related intelligence activities are likely to be constitutional, bureaucratic, prudential, and political in relation to congressional members and committees.

The ambiguous scope of border security intelligence is reflected institutionally. The intelligence community as defined by Congress includes, in addition to the six major intelligence agencies, the Drug Enforcement Administration's Office of National Security Intelligence, the Department of Homeland Security's Office of Intelligence and Analysis, and the Coast Guard in DHS. The intelligence community, however, excludes the intelligence or national security offices of DHS's Customs and Border Protection (CBP), Immigration and Customs Enforcement (ICE), and Citizenship and Immigration Services. Yet these agencies screen for and investigate terrorists among aliens crossing the borders clandestinely, entering through ports of entry, and seeking change in their immigration status. The intelligence community also includes the State Department's Office of Intelligence and Research, but not the elements within the State Department's Bureau of Consular Affairs and Diplomatic Security that screen for terrorists in visa applications or investigate passport and visa forgery, manipulation, and illegal distribution, including to terrorists.[7]

These definitional and institutional ambiguities play out in two areas: overhead surveillance and information-sharing. Overhead surveillance from reconnaissance satellites to detect clandestine routes and movements of people spanning national borders potentially affects terrorists, traffickers, illegal aliens, and U.S. citizens living in the vicinity of a smuggling tunnel's U.S. endpoint; distinctions between authorized targets and others are not easy to maintain. While satellite usage to assist in managing natural disasters is well accepted, Congress has been uneasy with the potential for capturing citizen activities in carrying out other overhead homeland-security-related surveillance at borders, declining to expand DHS authorities in this arena.

Congress's view is shifting under pressure from federal and state law enforcement agencies that want to use surveillance drones, some for border security purposes. The unarmed vehicles can carry video equipment, infrared thermal imagery

---

4. 50 U.S.C. § 401a(3).
5. Anti-Drug Abuse Act of 1988, Pub. L. No. 100-690, § 4801.
6. 50 U.S.C. § 401a(5)(iii).
7. 50 U.S.C. § 401a(4).

instruments, and radiation and wireless network detectors. Currently several hundred organizations, including police departments in Miami-Dade, Houston, and Seattle, are certified to use drones. CBP's growing number of Predator drones patrol the southwest border, and the agency has plans to maintain two dozen unmanned aerial vehicles, or UAVs, by 2016 to gain nationwide coverage. Congress in February 2012 passed a bill requiring the Federal Aviation Administration to draft a plan for permitting drones to operate in airspace hitherto reserved for manned airplanes.[8]

Congress's privacy caucus has expressed concern. The privacy ramifications of these authorities have yet to be plumbed fully. The Supreme Court in 1986 held that because overflights capture information exposed to the public, the practice does not implicate privacy rights.[9] But it has suggested some limits, at least where something other than regular visual surveillance is involved.[10] The Supreme Court decision in *United States v. Jones*, barring the government's use of GPS tracking devices on motor vehicles on Fourth Amendment grounds, suggests stronger protections against new forms of surveillance.[11]

The extent to which border agencies may share, retain, and use information—especially operational or administrative—remains contentious. DHS and State Department operational entities collect and analyze operational information about the movement of people and goods—visa application information, airline passenger data, cargo manifests, and immigration records. The border, transport, and travel agencies compile the information they produce about suspected terrorists, sometimes combining it with intelligence information, feed it into the National Counterterrorism Center's terrorist database, and use it for border screening and law enforcement investigations. A variety of federal and state fusion centers, such as the El Paso Intelligence Center, the Human Smuggling and Trafficking Center, and the Coast Guard's Joint Interagency Task Force-South, bring together information on border security matters from law enforcement, immigration, and border agencies as well as intelligence and military entities. Operational, investigative, and intelligence-sharing agreements with Canada, Mexico, and other mobility security partners globally add a layer of legal complexity.

Underlying the contradictory and ambiguous organizational and legal arrangements are the same legal challenges that pervade counterterrorism generally: how to share information and support secure border functions and related law enforcement to the degree necessary and appropriate, relative to other demands on intelligence resources, without carrying out prohibited domestic surveillance or privacy intrusions or otherwise infringing on fundamental rights and liberties, while providing adequate processes for correcting errors and redressing problems. Attorney General Eric Holder has promulgated guidelines on the collection and

---

8. The FAA Modernization and Reform Act (Feb. 14, 2012).
9. Dow Chem. v. United States, 476 U.S. 227 (1986).
10. Kyllo v. United States, 533 U.S. 27 (2001).
11. United States v. Jones, 132 S. Ct. 945 (2012).

use of various agencies' information for counterterrorism purposes, including citizen and noncitizen travel and flight records, immigration benefit files, and passport and visa databases.[12] Under the attorney general's guidelines, the National Counterterrorism Center may retain the information for five years, an increase over the initial limit of 180 days set in 2008 for retention of information when there is no suspicion that an individual has a tie to terrorism. Each new terrorist incident that catches government authorities by surprise can be expected to result in a reexamination of these guidelines. The complex information-sharing arrangements increase the problems for individuals if they are mistakenly associated with a terrorist risk. How to resolve the rights of individuals while maintaining a terrorist deterrent and defense is likely to give rise to litigation and statutory proposals.

USE OF IMMIGRATION LAW IN COUNTERTERRORISM

The federal government made extensive use of immigration law as a counterterrorism tool immediately following the 9/11 attacks, and immigration law remains an important tool for addressing known or suspected foreign terrorists. But due in part to abuses that occurred in 2001, the legal intersection of immigration law and counterterrorism is the subject of continuing debate. Four areas draw media attention: (1) the terrorism grounds of inadmissibility and deportability, (2) alien registration laws, (3) immigration detention, and (4) immigration legal proceedings.[13]

Inadmissibility and Deportability Grounds

Controversy continues to surround the questions of the standards to be applied to determine when a visitor, refugee, or asylum applicant should be excluded or denied admission on terrorism grounds, or when terrorism-related factors should be the basis for deporting a legal permanent resident (green card holder). The fundamental dispute is whether the terrorism-related immigration laws fail to admit too many innocent visitors, refugees, and asylees, and make lawful permanent residents overly vulnerable to removal without adequate cause. The focal point for this discussion is the "material support" provisions of terrorism laws, which describe what conduct other than terrorist activities may be grounds for prosecution or immigration law action.

Congress in 1990 gave the secretary of state discretion to bar any noncitizen who had engaged in a terrorist activity or was reasonably believed to be likely to do

---

12. U.S. DEP'T OF JUSTICE, GUIDELINES FOR ACCESS, RETENTION, USE, AND DISSEMINATION BY THE NATIONAL COUNTERTERRORISM CENTER (NCTC) OF INFORMATION IN DATASETS CONTAINING NON-TERRORISM INFORMATION (effective Mar. 22, 2012).

13. David A. Martin, *Refining Immigration Law's Role in Counterterrorism, in* LEGISLATING THE WAR ON TERROR: AN AGENDA FOR REFORM (Ben Wittes ed., Brookings Inst. Press 2009).

so.[14] In response to the 1993 attack on the World Trade Center and the 1995 Oklahoma City bombing, Congress in 1996 directed the secretary of state to designate and publish a list of terrorist organizations and to exclude noncitizens based on their membership in or representation of these groups. Providing material support that would assist a terrorist in carrying out terrorist acts also became grounds for exclusion, if the person knew or should have known of this usage.[15] Organizations on this list later became known as Tier I organizations. There is a fairly elaborate procedure for designating a Tier 1 group, since material support to such a group is also a crime for which everyone, including U.S. citizens, is subject to prosecution.

In response to the 9/11 attacks, Congress, through the USA PATRIOT Act[16] and the REAL ID Act,[17] greatly broadened the definition of terrorist activities for immigration purposes. It made it easier for the secretary of state to designate organizations as terrorist, resulting in a new list of what are known as Tier II organizations. Congress also provided that a terrorist organization could be any group composed of two or more people if the group engages in terrorist activity; such potentially minimal groups are known as Tier III organizations. Immigration officials make findings about Tier III groups in individual adjudications; no official list is required.

The term "terrorist" now encompasses those who incite, prepare, or plan terrorist activities and gather information on potential targets; those who use a position of prominence to endorse terrorism; representatives of groups that support terrorist organizations; and spouses or children of persons inadmissible on terrorism grounds unless they either did not know of the activity or renounced it.[18] Regardless of group affiliation, the attorney general, a consular officer, or the secretary of homeland security may deem someone inadmissible for having engaged in terrorist activity.

Because of the combined impact of the loose nature of the Tier III category, the expanded definition of terrorist activity, the executive branch interpretation of the term "material" to include minor acts, and the heavy burden of proof now imposed on any individual who claims that the support was unwitting, the successive statutes have made it much easier to exclude or remove anyone who provides material support to a terrorist organization.[19]

The terrorism grounds do not distinguish between someone who faces deportation after many years of living in the United States as a lawful permanent resident and a tourist who is applying for a visa before being admitted to the United States. Nonimmigrant visa applicants have varying degrees of interest at stake, from losing out on a vacation to being prevented from joining a fiancé, accepting a scholarship, or pursuing a significant work opportunity. But the individual already

---

14. Immigration Act of 1990, Pub. L. No. 101-649, 104 Stat. 4978.
15. 8 U.S.C. § 1189 (2008).
16. *Id.*
17. Pub. L. No. 109-13, 119 Stat. 302 (2005).
18. 8 U.S.C. § 236A(a)(1).
19. Immigration and Nationality Act (INA) §§ 212(a)(3)(b), 212(a)(3)(B)(iv)(VI)(dd).

permanently residing in the United States has an even greater stake. For that reason there are calls to differentiate the terrorism grounds that apply for exclusion and for deportation.

The attenuated nature of the terrorism grounds has also led to some extremely distorted consequences for refugees and asylum seekers. Refugees of groups who directly aided the United States, like the Hmong people who supported the United States in Vietnam, were barred on the grounds of their participation in armed resistance, which placed them within the expanded definition of Tier III groups. Asylum seekers who paid money to ransom a child have been barred because the executive branch interpreted the statute to apply even to material support provided under duress. Such cases provoked political controversy, and Congress responded in 2005, not by narrowing the material support bar or excluding from its coverage those who acted under duress, but by giving the secretary of state and the secretary of homeland security the power to exempt either groups or individuals. Use of the exemption power is discretionary and not subject to judicial review. The Hmong and several other groups have been exempted, and the secretary of homeland security has authorized Citizenship and Immigration Services officers to provide individual exemptions to those who can establish they acted under duress. Nonetheless, the process for issuing and applying exemptions is cumbersome. The material support provisions are likely to be the source of debate for a long time to come.

Alien Registration Laws

Alien registration became controversial when the government in 2002 required Muslims and Arabs from designated countries to register with INS upon entry to the United States or, if already present, through a special registration system. The idea of being required to register one's presence with the government as a member of a specific alien minority group did not sit well with some citizens because of its facially discriminatory quality. On the other hand, many solid democracies have registration provisions for all aliens, and even national identification cards for citizens and noncitizens alike, whereas the United States historically has limited the practice to people who were perceived to pose security risks. The Immigration and Nationality Act's alien registration provisions[20] had their origins in the Alien Registration Act of 1940, also known as the Smith Act, which was passed as the United States was gearing up to fight fascism. Amended in 1952 and used against Communists during the Cold War, it was later invoked to register Iranian students after the 1978 hostage-taking in Tehran.

The registration program instituted in response to the 9/11 attacks was called the National Security Entry-Exit Registration System (NSEERS). Border authorities mandated detailed questioning for males ages 16 to 45 from a specified group

---

20. INA ch. 7, §§ 261–266.

of predominantly Muslim and Arab countries and North Korea, and required those individuals who were admitted from this group to report in after 30 days in the United States and annually from then on and to leave the country through one of a few designated airports where they were again interviewed in detail. Adult male aliens from the designated countries who were already in the United States (with short-term visas) were required to register, be fingerprinted and questioned, and provide notification of change of address on a continuing basis. Courts across the country rejected a range of constitutional challenges to NSEERS, from equal protection claims to those under the Fourth, Fifth, and Sixth amendments, recognizing the government's broad powers to design such programs.[21]

The components of the program requiring ongoing check-ins and change-of-address notifications ended in 2003, and the program was otherwise largely folded into DHS's 2003 initiation of US VISIT, which fingerprints and photographs virtually all entering nonimmigrant visa holders, although the requirement to depart only through certain airports remained. Homeland Security Secretary Janet Napolitano ended NSEERS entirely in 2011 on the grounds of redundancy. Although any future application of the registration law is likely to be challenged on constitutional grounds, constitutional judicial precedents permitting such programs are strong.

Immigration Detention

Detention law relating to border security is one aspect of a legally complicated detention picture that encompasses issues of military versus civilian authority to detain suspected alien terrorists. Setting aside military law, Congress has not fully separated detention rules applicable to non-U.S. persons who *are* suspected on terrorism grounds from rules applicable to visitors and lawful permanent residents *not* believed to be associated with terrorism. In the absence of a detention regime specifically designed for terrorist suspects, the Department of Justice exploited standard immigration law authorities to arrest and detain more than 700 "special interest" aliens after 9/11. The practice led to considerable abuses and no clear information about apprehension of genuine terrorists. Some detainees were held a year or more in poor and even abusive conditions awaiting an FBI clearance, even after they had been ordered removed because they had chosen not to contest the deportation charges.

Detention is a well-established practice in immigration law. Rules govern the duration of detention during the period before charges are filed, after charges are filed but before an immigration hearing takes place, and after a hearing has taken place and a removal order issued. But how much better immigrants would fare in the aftermath of a future terrorist attack is uncertain. While Congress has taken a

---

21. *See, e.g.*, Kandamar v. Gonzales, 464 F.3d 65 (1st Cir. 2006) (rejecting constitutional claims and noting the government's broad powers to design such programs) (citing Narenji v. Civiletti, 1980 U.S. App. LEXIS 20952 (D.C. Cir. Jan. 31, 1980) (upholding Iranian student registration)).

stab at detention rules governing terrorist suspects, how these laws relate to standard immigration law rules remains unclear.

Until shortly after the September 11 attacks, a Department of Justice regulation required initial procedures to be held within 24 hours after an individual's arrest on immigration charges to review the validity of the charges and to consider release pending a full hearing, based on criteria of flight risk and dangerousness. (These involve review by another immigration officer.) An interim rulemaking on September 17, 2001, amended that provision to permit 48 hours for these decisions and to allow an exceptional additional "reasonable period of time" to hold a noncitizen without charges in case of "an emergency or other extraordinary circumstance."[22] The rule change provoked immediate controversy, and Congress responded with a more confined provision in the USA PATRIOT Act. Enacted in October 2011, the law authorized immigration officials to detain any noncitizen suspected of terrorist activity upon certification by the attorney general or the deputy attorney general. Congress set a limit of seven days of detention under this provision in the absence of filing charges against the suspected terrorist under immigration law or the criminal code.[23] Although the regulation theoretically allows for a longer period of detention based on a proper finding of an emergency, INS and then DHS have not found such an emergency since 2001.

Once a noncitizen is charged with immigration violations, the due process clause of the Constitution does not entitle the individual to be released pending a removal hearing; even lawful permanent residents may be held "for the brief period necessary for their removal proceedings."[24] Nonetheless, aliens have long had a right under regulations to a hearing on a case-by-case basis to decide whether they should be detained prior to a removal hearing. Congress made an exception in 1996, requiring aliens subject to removal for aggravated felonies and certain other crimes to be detained until their hearing; the Supreme Court upheld this mandatory detention provision.[25] Also, arriving asylum seekers are subject to mandatory detention until they have established a credible fear of persecution, after which they may be released until their hearing.[26]

There are more constraints on indefinite detention based on immigration violations once hearings have been held and a removal order issued. The Supreme Court has held that immigration authorities may not hold indefinitely either inadmissible noncitizens ordered removed or removable criminal aliens. (The circumstance of indefinite detention that the Supreme Court addressed arises when an individual ordered to be removed cannot be returned to his home country, either because the government refuses to accept him or due to the political or security

---

22. 66 Fed. Reg. 48,334–01.
23. INA § 236A.
24. Demore v. Kim, 538 U.S. 510 (2003).
25. Antiterrorism and Effective Death Penalty Act, Pub. L. No. 104-132, 110 Stat. 1214 (1996); Illegal Immigration Reform and Immigrant Responsibility Act, Pub. L. No. 104-208, div. C, 110 Stat. 3009-546 (1996); *Demore*, 538 U.S. 510.
26. INA § 235(b)(1)(B)(iii)(IV).

situation in the country.) The Court noted constitutional concerns, but did not squarely decide whether the Constitution requires a time limit. (It also suggested a possible exception for terrorist cases.) The Court found a presumptive six-month limit on detention in the Immigration and Naturalization Act, after which noncitizens must be released if their removal does not appear likely in the reasonably foreseeable future.[27]

Rules following the Supreme Court reading of the law allow supervised release after six months of detention for noncitizens for whom there is no significant likelihood of removal, but they permit continued detention of individuals in limited circumstances—for example, if their release would be adverse to U.S. foreign policy or present a threat to national security or if the noncitizens are determined to be especially dangerous based on mental illness plus conviction of a crime.[28] Congress in the USA PATRIOT Act, though, permits a suspected noncitizen terrorist to be detained until finally removed or cleared of the charge only upon initial certification by the attorney general or deputy attorney general personally, plus review by the attorney general every six months, and subject to habeas corpus review in the federal courts.[29]

The net result of this mix of provisions is that counterterrorism authorities appear to have limited flexibility in addressing suspected alien terrorists on immigration grounds. Although in a future emergency, they theoretically could apply immigration law to stretch out the period of detention before charging by invoking an emergency, or other extraordinary circumstances, simply filing the immigration charge is likely. In circumstances where a removal order has been issued, authorities may avoid the six-month limitation on detention found by the Supreme Court by invoking either the regulations setting forth limited exceptions to release or the USA PATRIOT Act's provisions for six-month reviews by the attorney general. In the future, Congress may need to reconsider this area because there is a limited range of circumstances where extended detention by the federal government may make sense when the person cannot be removed.

Immigration Proceedings

Procedural issues concerning government secrecy during the immigration hearing process always provoke debate. The Department of Justice's blanket decision in 2001 to close more than 700 hearings of special-interest alien detainees contradicted the normal expectation that hearings would be open or, at most, closed on a case-by-case basis. DoJ ended the practice before the Supreme Court could address the issue; it remains an unresolved procedural question for the future.

Classified information may be used in immigration proceedings, but the scope of due process protections for the noncitizen in these circumstances is not settled

---

27. Zadvydas v. Davis, 533 U.S. 678 (2001); Clark v. Martinez, 543 U.S. 371 (2005).
28. 8 C.F.R. §§ 241.4, 13.
29. INA § 236A(a)(1).

law.[30] Problems concerning the use of classified information may arise throughout the spectrum of adjudications, from visitor visa determinations to decisions on the deportability of a permanent resident. In the visa context, when an individual is overseas, investigative information is generally unavailable to the applicant, who also has no opportunity for review other than by refiling at a future date.[31] The absolute nature of consular authority, which is not even subject to reversal by a superior, has often been questioned. The use of classified sources provides another reason that arguments are likely to continue to be made for creating more checks in the visa system.

Seeking to set ground rules for using classified information, Congress in 1996 provided for an Alien Terrorist Removal Court, in effect a national security court for aliens. It permits use of classified evidence against permanent residents in deportation proceedings, but with protections, including the availability of counsel with high-level clearances. This court's protections, however, are not available to aliens with less than permanent resident status, even if they have lived in the United States for a considerable time or have close family ties here. In such cases, courts usually request summaries of classified evidence to be provided and may conduct an in camera review of classified evidence, the use of which is subject to fairly rigorous internal controls by immigration authorities. But both of these precautions are discretionary and depend on a judge's willingness to use them. Litigation and reform efforts are likely to focus on making this type of protection mandatory, on expanding the jurisdiction of the Alien Terrorist Removal Court to assist aliens with a significant stake in American life who face deportation on terrorism grounds, and ultimately perhaps on establishing a terrorism court with jurisdiction covering domestic as well as foreign terrorists. The debate about the type of court best suited for terrorism trials is far from finished.

TRAVELER SCREENING AND THE VISA PROCESS

As any American traveling since 9/11 knows, sovereign governments—which have the right to protect themselves—still control borders.[32] For citizens and legal permanent residents (included as "U.S. persons") living near the border with Canada or Mexico or traveling in the Caribbean, counterterrorism at the borders has meant the end of easy back-and-forth movement. The State Department under amendments to the Immigration and Nationality Act now requires U.S. persons

---

30. INA § 235(c).
31. Bustamonte v. Mukasey, 531 F.3d 1059 (9th Cir. 2008); Kleindienst v. Mandel, 408 U.S. 753 (1972).
32. "[S]earches made at the border, pursuant to the longstanding right of the sovereign to protect itself by stopping and examining persons and property crossing into this country, are reasonable simply by virtue of the fact that they occur at the border." United States v. Ramsey, 431 U.S. 606, 616 (1977).

to show a passport or other state and federally approved specialized identification as a condition of reentering the United States. Congress also required security enhancements to U.S. passports and other specialized identification, and gave CBP officers increased access to terrorism-related databases for screening purposes. A legal debate about the extent to which U.S. persons must supply biometrics including fingerprints to be able to travel is likely to occur in the future as the European Union begins including fingerprints in its passports.

The tightening of border security has given new impetus to disputes over the scope of permissible border searches of people and property and over allowable constraints on the individual's exercise of the right to movement. The Fourth Amendment's normal requirement that officials must obtain a warrant based on probable cause from a judge in order to perform a search of a person or property (absent exigent circumstances) is subject to a border exception. Officials need not have a warrant or probable cause for routine physical searching of a traveler at international borders and airports. The search need not be based on a suspicion, unless it goes beyond a pat-down, in which case it is considered nonroutine and CBP must have a "reasonable suspicion" that contraband is present in order to conduct the search.[33]

Property is even less protected. Travelers have not prevailed in challenging border searches of electronic media, such as computers. While the Supreme Court has not ruled on the question, two appellate courts have upheld DHS's view that such searches are permissible under the Fourth Amendment's border exception and do not violate First Amendment rights.[34] Limitations on such searches at the border, even of U.S. persons, have yet to be declared.

The scope of a citizen's right to movement, which exists under international law, including in the International Bill of Human Rights but not explicitly in the Constitution, is becoming a more prominent legal issue. In some cases, counterterrorism officials have sought to prevent U.S. citizens from returning to the United States after travel to foreign countries based on their placement on a terrorist watchlist. That is, while U.S. officials could not say that a citizen is barred from returning, they asserted their authority to protect airline safety by barring dangerous individuals from airplanes. These cases have resulted in agreements in which the Transportation Security Administration allowed the return of the individuals on a flight with an air marshal or the individual was permitted to return by other means. Constitutional right-to-travel cases historically reached the Supreme Court in the context of limiting the travel of those associated with Communist influence; the right remains to be tested in the context of counterterrorism.

Foreigners, of course, are subject to many more requirements than U.S. persons in order to enter the United States. Requirements differ according to the type of travel involved—whether the individual is a tourist, working person, student or

---

33. United States v. Cotterman, 637 F.3d 1068, 1079–80 (9th Cir. 2011).
34. United States v. Arnold, 523 F.3d 941 (9th Cir. 2008); United States v. Ickes, 393 F.3d 501, 504 (4th Cir. 2005).

other visitor, or an intending immigrant. An alphabet soup of visa types is adjudicated by DHS's Citizenship and Immigration Services and by the Department of State's Bureau of Consular Affairs. Upon a foreigner's arrival at a port of entry, CBP issues the actual permission to enter for a specified period of time.

Some countries' tourists are exempt from visa requirements, usually reciprocally with the United States. Congress sets the standards for the U.S. visa waiver program, and since 9/11, visa cooperation has been tied to other countries' security practices and prospects. As globalization intensifies, access to a country is increasingly an economic concern—tourism, education, and business depend on the flow of people into the United States. Thus, there is a tension that continually needs to be resolved in visa policy between minimizing risk and enlarging economic prosperity and freedom of the individual.

Newsworthy issues that tend to arise in this arena are

- a breach of security in the visa process, such as granting a visa to a terrorist
- a perceived unfairness or even abuse of the applicant or a group of applicants in the visa process
- untoward delays and backlogs
- complaints by a country that it is not accorded visa waiver status

Except for the issue of unfairness and abuse relating to visa applicants, these issues are largely matters of policy priorities, management, bureaucratic cultures, and politics. Who is or is not granted a visa, placed on a watchlist, or permitted to enter the United States raises important questions of constitutional and immigration law. The core question is the scope of rights to be accorded non-U.S. persons who seek to enter the United States. The baseline assumption is that as a constitutional matter Congress has plenary power to determine who enters, and that therefore a watchlisted visa applicant or one denied a visa for any other reason has little recourse to challenge the determination. As the movement of people becomes more critical to families and businesses, however, this long-standing assumption, and the extremely limited options available to a traveler denied a visa, is likely to be challenged. Some countries already permit certain classes of visa applicants to challenge denials of visas administratively.

ILLEGAL IMMIGRATION AND BORDER SECURITY

There is debate over whether illegal immigration in general is a national security problem. But certainly terrorist access, border crossing by members of violent criminal organizations, and unauthorized entry to work or reside in the United States are all to varying degrees homeland security problems, at a minimum because Americans must be confident that laws will be implemented constitutionally, citizens and communities protected effectively, and the U.S. economy supported successfully.

Illegal entry, work, and residence, primarily by Mexicans and Central Americans, rather than terrorist threats dominate public discourse about border security. Especially hot topics are how to stop migrants from crossing the border illegally and how to handle the approximately 11 million migrants working and residing illegally within the United States, the border fence, and the degree to which local governments can participate in enforcing immigration laws.

The Border Fence

The border fence clearly has an impact on local residents, the environment, and relations with Mexico. But the main legal theme of the fence saga is DHS's ever-increasing control over the border area. It is worth getting a sense of Congress's meandering pursuit of its construction as a good example of the often-convoluted development of immigration and border-related laws.

The Immigration and Nationality Act gave the attorney general broad powers to control and guard the U.S. border, powers transferred to the DHS secretary under the Homeland Security Act of 2002.[35] The U.S. Border Patrol invoked that authority to implement a policy of "prevention through deterrence" by building the first solid steel barrier in 1990, seeking to deter illegal entries and drug smuggling in the San Diego Border Patrol Sector. It completed the 14-mile, 10-foot-high barrier in 1993.

When migrants entering from Mexico found ways around the barrier, Congress authorized construction of a triple-layer fence in the Illegal Immigration Reform and Immigrant Responsibility Act of 1996 (IIRAIRA).[36] In this law, Congress also took what was in retrospect an initial step to expand executive authority to provide for homeland security by giving the attorney general the authority to purchase land in connection with the mandated 14-mile reinforced fence.[37]

Five years later, Congress granted the DHS secretary the "sole discretion" to waive "all legal requirements" (such as environmental laws) as necessary to ensure expeditious construction, merely by publishing the decision in the Federal Register. In effect, Congress gave the executive branch legislative authority to pick and choose which statutes would continue to apply in areas where the fence was to be built, an unusual bending of the constitutional separation of powers.[38] Congress simultaneously severely circumscribed judicial review of the secretary's actions by, among other steps, permitting lower court review only of constitutional challenges in federal courts and appeal only upon writ of certiorari to the

---

35. INA, 8 U.S.C. § 1103(a)(5), Pub. L. No. 104-208, §§ 102(a), 441, 1512, 1517.
36. Pub. L. No. 104-208, div. C, 110 Stat. 3009-546, part of the Omnibus Consolidated Appropriations Act of 1997.
37. Pub. L. No. 107-203, § 201(a) (2002).
38. Pub. L. No. 13, Emergency Supplemental Appropriations for Defense, the Global War on Terror, and Tsunami Relief, for the fiscal year ending Sept. 30, 2005, Div. B, tit. 1, REAL ID Act, § 102.

Supreme Court. The Supreme Court declined to review the statute, refusing to take the one case brought before it.[39]

In 2006, Congress expressly changed the tactical purpose of the fence from one of deterrence to one of "achiev[ing] operational control on the border," meaning "the prevention of all unlawful entries into the U.S., including entries by terrorists, unlawful aliens, instruments of terrorism, narcotics, and other contraband."[40] Congress also directed 700 miles of at least two layers of reinforced fencing, additional physical barriers, roads, lighting, cameras, and sensors, extending through five designated zones in California, New Mexico, and Texas.

Along with construction of the fence, DHS in 2006 initiated its SBInet program to construct an ambitious integrated border security infrastructure referred to as a "virtual fence." Although canceled by Secretary Janet Napolitano in 2011 on the grounds of ineffectiveness and cost overruns, DHS continues to support research and development of improved border protection technology.

Congress gave DHS more flexibility in implementing border security in 2007, stating in the 2008 omnibus budget bill that "nothing in this [fence mandate] shall require the Secretary of Homeland Security to install fencing, physical barriers, roads, lighting, cameras, and sensors in a particular location along an international border of the United States, if the Secretary determines that the use or placement of such resources is not the most appropriate means to achieve and maintain operational control over the international border at such location."

With this flexibility, DHS has finished approximately 650 miles of fence, including about 300 miles of vehicle barriers and just over 36 miles of double-layered fencing. The legal background of the southwest border fence built thus far shows how the evolution from traditional immigration law to homeland security law is enhancing executive authority as against congressional, state, local, and tribal authorities. With the fence continuing to draw political fire—from proponents, opponents, and local authorities seeking more say in the process—the law governing it can be expected to develop further.

Canada

The legal background for security measures along the border with Canada differs significantly from that for the southwest border fence. Congress in 2006 mandated, as part of the Secure Fence Act, a Northern Border Study "on the construction of a state-of-the-art barrier system along the northern international land and maritime border." Rather than building a fence along the northern border, however, the United States has entered into increasingly comprehensive agreements with Canada involving intelligence-sharing, joint investigations, and joint

---

39. Cnty. of El Paso v. Chertoff, 2008 U.S. Dist. LEXIS 83045 (W.D. Tex. 2008), *cert. denied*, 129 S. Ct. 2789 (2009).

40. Secure Fence Act of 2006, Pub. L. No. 109-367, § 2.

maritime patrols, among other collaborative measures.[41] Because these agreements are not cast as treaties, the Senate has not exercised its advice and consent role. While similar agreements exist between the United States and Mexico, they are not set forth in public documents, and they exist in addition to, rather than instead of, a major border barrier program.

The different approaches to the southwest and northern borders illustrate the lack of a single paradigm for border security and the executive branch's growing discretion in developing and implementing homeland security strategy and law with respect to the nation's territorial borders.

ALLOCATION OF FEDERAL, STATE, AND LOCAL IMMIGRATION AUTHORITY

In contrast to DHS's increasingly centralized powers with respect to physical border security measures, the trend is toward greater state and local government participation in immigration enforcement. A debate about federalism is taking place in two contexts: the federal-state enforcement partnership, and state and local legislative actions. New laws are being adopted and Supreme Court jurisprudence in this arena is evolving rapidly, so the discussion here describes the legal issues at stake in these situations rather than the latest statutes and decisions.

Federal-State Enforcement Partnership

Federal immigration authorities have long seen local authorities as potential force multipliers in addressing an illegal resident population, historically seeking various kinds of informal cooperation. Since the mid-1990s, the federal government has solicited the formal help of state and local law enforcement through a program to train officers in specific immigration functions—investigation, apprehension, and detention. IIRAIRA established the statutory basis for these federal-state enforcement partnerships, often referred to by the statutory section 287(g). The specific functions allowed under the partnerships initially followed an internal Department of Justice opinion that kept the state and local authorities out of civil enforcement. When the policy orientation of the Department of Justice shifted by 2002, a later and still-controversial opinion stated that state and local law enforcement agencies could engage in both civil and criminal enforcement.

Through ICE programs such as the Criminal Alien Program or Secure Communities, federal-local partnerships enable local officials to determine the immigration status of individuals in jails or encountered during local police operations.

---

41. U.S. Dep't of Homeland Sec., Beyond the Border Action Plan (Dec. 7, 2011); U.S. Dep't of Homeland Sec., Beyond the Border: A Shared Vision for Perimeter Security and Economic Competitiveness (Feb. 4, 2011).

DHS retains the discretion to decide whether there is a potential deportable violation and whether to request that the individual be detained for eventual transfer to ICE or removal. ICE and other law enforcement authorities also cooperate in apprehending noncitizens who have been ordered removed on criminal grounds but have not left the country. Because DHS retains discretion in individual cases and also may revise the terms of 287(g) programs, these partnerships do not raise any federalism concerns.

State Legislative Actions Relating to Enforcement

Some cities, for economic, humanitarian, or political reasons, have enacted or promulgated sanctuary laws, which prohibit investigation of immigration status except under narrow circumstances, while three states issue drivers' licenses to residents without regard to immigration status. At least one appellate court has restricted the scope of a sanctuary law on the grounds that it is preempted by federal law.

Some states, notably Arizona, not satisfied that the DHS-led partnerships reduce the illegal population sufficiently, have passed laws authorizing their own immigration enforcement practices, outside of the 287(g) partnerships. In 2002, DoJ reversed its earlier opinion and stated in a still-controversial substitute opinion that it is constitutionally permissible for state police to arrest noncitizens based on civil deportability alone. A variety of related statutes and ordinances have been enacted. State laws may include, for example, penalizing businesses for hiring illegal aliens; requiring police to verify the immigration status of anyone they stop, detain, or arrest on suspicion of being in the country illegally, before the person is released; criminalizing noncitizens' failure to apply for or carry federally authorized alien registration papers; barring unauthorized aliens from soliciting, applying for, or performing work; and authorizing warrantless arrest of a noncitizen if there is probable cause to believe the person has committed a deportable offense.

The core constitutional question raised by such laws is whether under the supremacy clause of the Constitution federal immigration law preempts the state or local law at issue. The central issue is whether the local enactment stands in conflict with federal laws, executive priorities, or international concerns, or instead is a mere augmentation of enforcement in a manner that is harmonious with federal statutes.

It is easy to see, at least in theory, how laws would be impermissible that actually conflict with federal immigration laws and federal immigration policy or conflict with U.S. foreign policy. Provisions that ignore humanitarian protections for noncitizens entitled to asylum or protection from the consequences of a natural disaster, for example, conflict with clear federal laws. However, where there is less direct conflict the courts have more latitude to refine long-standing preemption doctrine, and some state immigration-enforcement-related statutes have been upheld.

Numerous challenges to state laws relating to immigration enforcement have invoked the Constitution's equal protection, due process, and privileges and immunities clauses as well as the First and Fourth Amendments or a state's constitution. A number of state laws have been blocked on constitutional grounds. A recent Supreme Court case, *Arizona v. United States*, involving Arizona's Support Our Law Enforcement and Safe Neighborhoods Act, addresses some of these issues and, broadly speaking, tends to support federal supremacy in immigration matters.[42] It likely represents the first salvo in an ongoing struggle between states and the federal government over immigration controls.

MILITARY HOMELAND DEFENSE

The subject of the military's role in border security brings to the fore all the incongruities inherent in the terminology of border security. On the one hand, many people have the conviction that the United States must be able to defend its borders in a traditional sense. On the other hand, the national security community does not view U.S. borders as a source of military threat; neither illegal migration nor drug trafficking rises to the level of military invasion. Although border security does not fit into the traditional box of national security as exercised by the military, the potential for terrorist access and cross-border movement of weapons of mass destruction, as well as the large scale of illegal migration, drug smuggling, and human trafficking, all make border security a significant homeland security challenge. While the military still remains largely excluded from exercising authority at U.S. borders, the mix of statutory and regulatory provisions that address this subject authorize more military involvement than civilian leaders permit as a matter of policy. The basics are as follows.

First, the secretary of homeland security is responsible for preventing the entry of terrorists, weapons of mass destruction, and other prohibited goods and for implementing immigration law, including its enforcement at the nation's borders.

Second, the Posse Comitatus Act and related statutes prohibit military forces from executing domestic laws except where the Constitution or Congress explicitly authorizes particular actions.[43] The Constitution empowers Congress to call forth the militia, now the National Guard, to execute the laws of the Union.[44] Congress has also expressly authorized use of the military to execute domestic law through general rules of assistance to civilian authorities and to suppress insurrections.[45] The most significant ongoing involvement of the military in domestic law

---
42. Arizona v. United States, 567 U.S. __, No. 11-182 (June 25, 2012).
43. 18 U.S.C. 1385.
44. U.S. CONST. art. I, § 8, cl. 15.
45. *Id.*

is Congress's granting of law enforcement authority to the Coast Guard. A little known fact is that this agency, while it operates under the Department of Homeland Security, is a branch of the U.S. Armed Forces; the president and Congress have the authority to transfer it to the Department of the Navy.

Third, there are the exceptions to DHS authority and action and to the Posse Comitatus restrictions. The Department of Defense is authorized to provide *support* to DHS and other federal, state, and local law enforcement authorities when requested, in particular for counterdrug and certain other countertrafficking and counterterrorism activities.[46] The Department of Defense in 2002 established the U.S. Northern Command, or USNORTHCOM, to provide command and control of DoD's homeland defense efforts and to coordinate military support to civilian authorities.[47]

The National Guard is a military force that is shared by the federal government and the states. A Guard unit may be called to active duty in a state status under the control of state and territorial governors (Title 32) or in federal status under the control of the president (Title 10). Congress in 2004 authorized the secretary of defense to provide federal funding to a state for use of National Guard forces in the event of a "homeland defense activity," which is defined as "an activity undertaken for the military protection of territory or domestic population of the United States . . . from a threat or aggression against the United States."[48]

The language does not associate military authorities with efforts to reduce illegal migration, but Congress has authorized the National Guard to provide administrative support to CBP in its border functions. Nevertheless, the rhetoric of border security, if not the reality of actual threats, likely will lead to further discussion of what constitutes a threat sufficient to engage the military further at the nation's borders. The appropriate scope of the Posse Comitatus Act, which is less of a barrier to military involvement in domestic affairs than might be assumed, will also inevitably become a subject of further debate as the population faces new emergencies.

CONCLUSION

Homeland security occupies the intersection of border security and national security, and most legal issues connected to border security as commonly understood arise from homeland security law and related constitutional law. Because homeland security law is a new field, the legal framework for a specific issue can be hard to nail down. Some elements of homeland security law, like intelligence law,

---

46. 10 U.S.C. ch. 18, Military Support to Civilian Authorities.
47. Chairman, Joint Chiefs of Staff, Joint Publication 3-26, Homeland Security, Aug. 2, 2005, at II-7.
48. Defense Authorization Act for Fiscal Year 2005, Pub. L. No. 108-375, div. A, tit. V, subtit. B, §§ 901–908.

remain closely tied to their traditional contexts, and not clearly adapted to the new context of homeland security law. Only a few homeland security intelligence lawyers have comprehensive expertise in this arena. Other elements of homeland security law, such as immigration law relating to security issues, are exceedingly complex, in terms of the statutory provisions and constitutional arguments. These legal problems require considerable expertise to pinpoint and explain in a simple fashion. A sizable community of immigration lawyers is available, however, to unpack these issues. Any legal doctrine relating to border security is guaranteed to be evolving, often in a direction hard to forecast.

EXPERTS

Stewart Baker, former DHS Assistant Secretary for Policy (2005–2009); Partner, Steptoe & Johnson, LLP; (202) 429-6402; sbaker@steptoe.com

Muzaffar Chishti, Director, Migration Policy Institute Office at New York University School of Law; (212) 992-8844; muzaffar.chishti@nyu.edu

Robert P. Deasy, Director of Liaison and Information, American Immigration Lawyers Association; (202) 507-7612; rdeasy@aila.org

Susan Ginsburg, Non-Resident Fellow, Migration Policy Institute, Washington; (202) 550-0025; SGinsburg@USCivilSecurity.com

Donald Kerwin, Executive Director, Center for Migration Studies, New York City; (212) 337-3080; DKerwin@cmsny.org

David A. Martin, former Principal Deputy General Counsel, DHS (2009–2010); Warner-Booker Distinguished Professor of International Law, University of Virginia School of Law; (434) 924-3144; dam3r@virginia.edu

Denyse Sabagh, Partner, Duane Morris, LLP; (202) 776-7817; DSabagh@duanemorris.com

Margaret Stock, Counsel, Lane Powell, LLP; (907) 264-3323; StockM@lanepowell.com

C. Stewart Verdery, Jr., former DHS Assistant Secretary for Border and Transportation Security Policy (2003–2005); Partner and Founder, Monument Policy Group; (202) 719-9999 ext. 6; Stewart@MonumentPolicy.com

Kathleen Campbell Walker, Partner, Cox Smith; (915) 541-9360 or (915) 433-5563; kwalker@coxsmith.com

James W. Ziglar, former INS Commissioner (2001–2002); Senior Counsel, VanNess Feldman; (202) 288-8747; jwz@ziglargroup.com

RESOURCES

IMMIGRATION AND AMERICA'S FUTURE: A NEW CHAPTER: REPORT OF THE INDEPENDENT TASK FORCE ON IMMIGRATION AND AMERICA'S FUTURE (Spencer Abraham & Lee H. Hamilton cochairs, 2006) http://www.migrationpolicy.org/ITFIAF/finalreport.pdf.

The Canada-U.S. Border: Balancing Trade, Security and Migrant Rights in the Post-9-11 Era, 19 GEO. IMMIGR. L.J. 199 (Winter 2005).

THE 9/11 COMMISSION REPORT, FINAL REPORT OF THE NATIONAL COMMISSION ON TERRORIST ATTACKS UPON THE UNITED STATES (Norton 2004).

9/11 AND TERRORIST TRAVEL: A STAFF REPORT OF THE NATIONAL COMMISSION ON TERRORIST ATTACKS UPON THE UNITED STATES (Hillsboro 2004).

SUSAN GINSBURG, SECURING HUMAN MOBILITY IN THE AGE OF RISK (Migration Policy Inst. 2010).

STEWART BAKER, SKATING ON STILTS: WHY WE AREN'T STOPPING TOMORROW'S TERRORISM (Hoover Inst. Press 2010).

Muzaffar Chishti, Policy Beat, MIGRATION INFORMATION SOURCE, http://migrationinformation.org/archive.cfm?Cat=policy.

Airport Screening and Scanning

22

By J. Bennet Waters and Paul Rosenzweig*

INTRODUCTION

Until 2001, aviation security regimes were largely designed to counter two types of threats: terrorists using guns or knives to hijack airplanes to use them and the passengers as negotiating tools and those attempting to destroy the planes with bombs. On September 11, 2001, 19 hijackers aboard four aircraft used crude weapons not only to take control of their planes but also to use the aircraft themselves as destructive missiles. Following those attacks, the Transportation Security Administration (TSA) was created to protect against future terrorist activities focused on transportation.

In the last decade, the TSA has taken a number of steps to mitigate the potential consequences of terrorist plots, including increasing the layers of security, hardening the structural integrity of aircraft cockpit doors, and significantly increasing the number of armed federal air marshals on domestic and international

---

*In 2009, the Chertoff Group (of which Dr. Waters is a Managing Director) provided strategic advisory services to Rapiscan, which manufactures backscatter AIT machines. The Chertoff Group's services did not involve work related to aviation security, advanced imaging technology, or government representation or lobbying of any type. The Chertoff Group did not and has not had any role in AIT procurement by TSA or other U.S. government agencies. Mr. Rosenzweig became a Senior Advisor to the Chertoff Group in 2012.

flights. As a result, terrorists shifted their tactics, techniques, and procedures away from simply trying to take control of aircraft with the goal of using them as weapons in favor of blowing them up in flight. They have also displayed a propensity to use items that traditional checkpoint screening equipment cannot identify; in particular, they have focused on the use of liquid, plastic, and powdered explosives.

These changes in terrorist tactics place in context the TSA's screening efforts. These range from the use of data analytics and behavioral profiling (a common practice in Israel and elsewhere), to the Secure Flight regulations in the United States that require individuals to provide some additional identifying information like date of birth and gender when making airline reservations and, ultimately, to the current controversy over the use of advanced imaging technology (AIT, or so-called body scanners). In this chapter we focus on the legality of this governmental scrutiny, an analysis that takes place principally under the Fourth Amendment and implicates citizens' expectations of privacy. These questions—of the legality of airport screening—have been the subject of legal analysis for nearly 40 years.

We should note at the outset that many of the issues of concern to citizens and journalists involve not the legal rules themselves but the alleged misapplication of those rules in individual cases—the reports of subjecting grandmothers and babies to inappropriate scrutiny, for example. While certainly a suitable subject of journalistic concern, those incidents typically do not involve questions of legality or even of policy, but rather involve poor judgment or overzealousness. Likewise, we have not addressed allegations that scanners are being used to display genitalia or that the TSA is saving images in contravention of law and policy because, as far as we are aware (and we both have firsthand experience from government service), these concerns are speculation with no factual basis. To the extent they were true, they would be readily acknowledged as violations of law.[1]

THE LEGAL ENVIRONMENT

One argument made about airport scanners in general (and most recently about AIT) is that they violate the Fourth Amendment's prohibition on unreasonable searches. The general paradigm is that searches by the government may, in some cases, require a warrant and probable cause to believe that a crime has been committed. Plainly, the searches that occur when a scanner is used or when an individual is subject to a pat-down in secondary screening do not fit into this model—no warrants are issued and the searchers do not have probable cause to believe that the individuals are committing or have committed criminal acts.

---

1. Finally, we note that we have also not considered one aspect of TSA airport screening with significant legal and policy implications: the use of behavioral analysis by behavior detection officers to identify potential subjects of enhanced scrutiny. That issue, while quite substantial, is beyond the scope of this chapter.

Instead, airport inspections using scanners have been analyzed under a separate aspect of the Fourth Amendment—one that permits administrative searches without a warrant or probable cause provided that they are not "unreasonable." In the case of scanners, the argument turns on the question of whether the use of the scanners is "reasonable" in this context.

Many in the public would say not. After all, for example, AIT scanners are by anyone's judgment more intrusive than simple observation. And they reveal things that have not been voluntarily exposed to public view by the traveler. The argument then is that this level of intrusiveness is unreasonable, in part because it is unnecessary.

So far, the courts have said otherwise. As a general matter the Supreme Court has said that whether an administrative search is "unreasonable" within the condemnation of the Fourth Amendment "is determined by assessing, on the one hand, the degree to which it intrudes upon an individual's privacy and, on the other, the degree to which it is needed for the promotion of legitimate governmental interests."[2]

For airport screening, the "reasonableness" analysis began back in the 1970s, when airport screening started. Early on, the screening used simple magnetometers to detect metal objects like guns. Later, bomb detection technology was developed. At that time, many of the same arguments were made as are being advanced today. Opponents argued that the screening was unnecessary and intrusive, and impermissibly treated all travelers as suspects.

Yet when confronted with these early technologies, the courts held that using screening technology was constitutional: "To meet the test of reasonableness, an administrative screening search must be as limited in its intrusiveness as is consistent with satisfaction of the administrative need that justifies it. It follows that airport screening searches are valid only if they recognize the right of a person to avoid search by electing not to board the aircraft."[3]

Here we see two interrelated, but distinct, aspects of the legal analysis at play. First, the administrative screening must have been based on a justified need (to prevent hijacking) and must have been limited in intrusiveness to the degree necessary to achieve the administrative objective. Second, because air travel is not mandated, those who flew had a choice not to board the plane. By choosing to do so, they effectively consented to the search prior to boarding.

Nearly identical arguments have played out in more recent times, though today the courts no longer care about the question of consent—all that is required is that the administrative screening be reasonable and that the passenger elect to enter the process. Thus, one court approved X-ray detection machines, using these words: "The search procedures used in this case were neither more extensive nor more intensive than necessary under the circumstances to rule out the presence of weapons or explosives."[4]

---

2. United States v. Knights, 534 U.S. 112, 118–19 (2001).
3. United States v. Davis, 482 F.2d 893, 910 (9th Cir. 1973).
4. United States v. Aukai, 497 F.3d 955, 962 (9th Cir. 2007) (en banc).

If the past is any guide, it is likely that when the federal courts are presented with cases involving newer scanning technology (like AIT), they will reach the same conclusion. Indeed, as the language of one court of appeals demonstrates, the courts can be somewhat dismissive of the constitutional privacy claim: "Th[e] balance clearly favors the Government here. The need to search airline passengers 'to ensure public safety can be particularly acute,' . . . and, crucially, an AIT scanner, unlike a magnetometer, is capable of detecting, and therefore of deterring, attempts to carry aboard airplanes explosives in liquid or powder form. On the other side of the balance, we must acknowledge the steps the TSA has already taken to protect passenger privacy, in particular distorting the image created using AIT and deleting it as soon as the passenger has been cleared. More telling, any passenger may opt-out of AIT screening in favor of a pat-down, which allows him to decide which of the two options for detecting a concealed, nonmetallic weapon or explosive is least invasive."[5] Though it seems strange to outside observers, the prospects for a successful Fourth Amendment challenge to any airport scanning program, like AIT use, appear quite limited.

ADVANCED IMAGING TECHNOLOGY: UNDERSTANDING THE TECHNOLOGY

Though the concept of nonmetallic explosives is not new—there were nearly successful attacks originating in Asia in 1996[6] and Europe in 2001[7]—recent events and threat reporting suggest a deliberate and continued shift away from metallic weapons to those that are not readily identified by traditional walk-through magnetometers. In the past six years alone, counterterrorism officials have disrupted plots in London,[8] in the skies over Detroit,[9] and in cargo shipped from Yemen.[10] Each plot is tangible evidence of terrorists' commitment to developing innovative weapons and tactics to evade TSA screening technologies. Indeed, overt actions involving liquid (London), plastic (Detroit), and powdered (Yemen) explosives are stark examples of how terrorists are trying new and different ways to exploit nonmetallic

---

5. EPIC v. DHS, 653 F.3d 1, 10–12 (D.C. Cir. 2011) (citation omitted).

6. Raymond Bonner & Benjamin Weiser, *Echoes of Early Design to Use Chemicals to Blow Up Airliners*. N.Y. TIMES, Aug. 11, 2006, http://www.nytimes.com/2006/08/11/world/europe/11manila.html?_r=1&ref=bojinkajetlinersbombplot.

7. Michael Elliott, *The Shoe Bomber's World*, TIME, Feb. 16, 2002, http://www.time.com/time/world/article/0,8599,203478,00.html.

8. Dominic Casciani, *Liquid Bomb Plot: What Happened?* BBC NEWS, Sept. 9, 2008, http://news.bbc.co.uk/2/hi/uk_news/7564184.stm.

9. CBS News Online Archive, The Christmas Day Terror Attack, http://www.cbsnews.com/2718-201_162-445.html.

10. *Source: Explosives Found in Suspicious Packages Packed Powerful Punch.* CNN, Oct. 29, 2010, http://articles.cnn.com/2010-10-29/us/security.concern_1_suspicious-packages-petn-explosive-material?_s=PM:US.

explosives to bring down airplanes. Recently, the international intelligence community uncovered yet another "upgraded" version of the underwear bomb. In each case, the perpetrators specifically designed and developed weapons that would not be detected by TSA's standard screening equipment. Based on knowledge of these perpetrators and their concepts of operation for carrying out terrorist attacks, the TSA began research and development for new technologies with better capabilities.

The TSA executes its mission through a risk-based, layered approach that combines actionable intelligence with technologies to ensure that passengers are not attempting to bring prohibited items aboard aircraft. In the past, magnetometers that detected specific amounts of metal were the primary tools for physical passenger screening. In the wake of plots specifically focused on the use of nonmetallic weapons, and in recognition of the inherent limitations of magnetometers against nonmetallic threats, the TSA faced a new challenge: fielding cost-effective, efficient technologies that find nontraditional weapons hidden in nontraditional places on passengers' bodies without taking too much time to do so in order to avoid increasing passengers' wait times. The TSA thus issued requirements for equipment capable of locating objects hidden within or beneath travelers' clothing. In response to these requirements, the aviation security industry developed several novel approaches to passenger screening. Known collectively as advanced imaging technology, or AIT, two types of devices are in use today: those that rely on backscatter X-ray and those that use millimeter wave. Backscatter machines work by emitting very small amounts of nonpenetrating ionizing radiation, which is reflected off of a person's body and captured in the form of an image. Millimeter wave machines, on the other hand, rely on nonionizing electromagnetic waves that generate images as those waves are reflected off of passengers' bodies. In both cases, the machines identify nonorganic items located within or beneath travelers' clothing. Images of AIT scans are viewed on computer screens by trained TSA officers, and anomalies are reported to the checkpoint via two-way radio transmission. Additional screening—including pat-downs or physical inspection—is then used to determine whether the anomalous object poses a threat to aviation security. By 2012, there were more than 640 machines in use at 165 airports across the United States.[11]

LIMITATIONS AND CONCERNS

While AIT machines represent significant advances over traditional magnetometers, they are not the panacea of aviation security screening for several reasons. First, legitimate concerns have been raised about privacy and individual liberties associated with the use of AIT; second, there are limitations to AIT capabilities

---

11. Transp. Sec. Admin., Advanced Imaging Technology (AIT), http://www.tsa.gov/approach/tech/ait/index.shtm.

themselves; third, first-generation AIT machines relied almost exclusively on human eyes to interpret images correctly, leading to concerns over the fallibility of human observation when viewing lower-quality images without computerized tools; and, finally, given that both backscatter and millimeter wave rely on energy to generate images (nonpenetrating ionizing radiation in the former; electromagnetic waves in the latter), there are safety issues that merit careful and ongoing attention.

Privacy

Privacy advocates and civil libertarians have raised appropriate concerns about the importance of striking the right balance between security and the need to respect privacy and individual liberties. The TSA has taken a number of steps to recognize and protect travelers' privacy and dignity in the screening process. Foremost, AIT is optional; those who opt out of AIT can elect to have a physical search conducted in private. In addition, facial features on images used by TSA screeners are blurred; genitalia are obscured by electronic filters; screeners viewing the images in a remote location never see the passengers; and the machines TSA uses in airports do not store, transmit, or copy images. Sometimes these privacy concerns are expressed as an argument that the use of AITs violates the law, a topic discussed in more detail below.

Technological Capability

Current generation AIT machines do not use penetrating radiation and thus are only able to identify substances or devices that are secreted *on* the body, but not *within* the body (as was the case in the attempt on the life of Saudi Interior Minister Mohamed bin Nayef).[12] However, they are capable of identifying a wide range of objects—both metallic and nonmetallic—with a high degree of sensitivity. In this regard, AIT machines represent a significant advance over traditional magnetometers, which are incapable of identifying nonmetallic objects at any level.

Accuracy

First-generation AIT machines relied exclusively on TSA officers to view images of screened passengers. Given the subtleties with which some objects were depicted on grainy, black-and-white images, some raised concerns about the "human factor" associated with accurately interpreting the outputs of AIT machines. In February 2011, the TSA began field-testing Automated Target Recognition (ATR) software, which uses computerized algorithms to determine the presence or absence of

---

12. Sheila MacVicar, *Al Qaeda Bombers Learn from Drug Smugglers*, CBS EVENING NEWS, Sept. 28, 2009, http://www.cbsnews.com/2100-18563_162-5347847.html.

anomalies on each AIT image. Instead of generating a raw image of each screened passenger, ATR superimposes an electronic marker on an avatar to isolate anomalies and target secondary screening directly to the affected area.

Concerns over Safety

Some critics have argued that backscatter machines are not safe due to the ionizing radiation on which they rely. In a 32-page report issued in February 2012, the Department of Homeland Security Office of the Inspector General (OIG) evaluated the safety testing of 247 backscatter units deployed in 39 airports. The OIG concluded that the TSA has conducted sufficient and validated testing, all of which deemed TSA's use of backscatter AIT to be safe and well within published standards.[13] Further, according to the TSA:

> Advanced imaging technology is safe and meets national health and safety standards. Backscatter technology was evaluated by the Food and Drug Administration's (FDA) Center for Devices and Radiological Health (CDRH), the National Institute for Standards and Technology (NIST), and the Johns Hopkins University Applied Physics Laboratory (APL). All results confirmed that the radiation doses for the individuals being screened, operators, and bystanders were well below the dose limits specified by the American National Standards Institute (ANSI). For comparison, the energy projected by millimeter wave technology is thousands of times less than a cell phone transmission. A single scan using backscatter technology produces exposure equivalent to two minutes of flying on an airplane.[14]

NECESSITY AND JUSTIFICATION: THE ADMINISTRATIVE PROCEDURES ACT

Even if AITs are considered safe and accurate, those determinations do not, as a matter of law, necessarily justify their deployment. As with any new regulatory system, the governmental agency advancing the new program must demonstrate that its decision to begin the program is consistent with existing law and grounded in reason. TSA has yet to fully make that case for AITs.

When the TSA first began deploying AIT, it did so in the immediate aftermath of the notorious Christmas Day 2009 "Underwear Bomber" case. The TSA has

---

13. U.S. Dep't of Homeland Sec., Office of the Inspector Gen., OIG-12-38, Transportation Security Administration's Use of Backscatter (Feb. 2012), http://www.oig.dhs.gov/assets/Mgmt/2012/OIG_12-38_Feb12.pdf.

14. Transp. Sec. Admin., TSA Contact Center Frequently Asked Questions: Is AIT Safe?, http://www.tsa.gov/travelers/customer/editorial_1029.shtm#2.

argued that in deploying the AIT, it was not changing any rules but merely modifying its security procedures in light of need. If, in fact, the use of AITs was just a procedural change, rather than a substantive one, the TSA would not be obliged to provide the public with notice of the change and an opportunity to comment. The Administrative Procedures Act (APA) requires, however, that when new substantive rules (sometimes called "legislative rules") are promulgated, the public must have an opportunity to have input.

Certainly, the line between procedural changes and substantive ones is often fuzzy. But the same D.C. appeals court that rejected the Fourth Amendment challenge has also concluded that using AITs is a substantive change. The judges noted that the use of AIT has perhaps a broader effect on the American public than almost any other rule of government operation. And the court noted as well that issues of efficacy, privacy, and safety have proven to be of broad public concern and comment.[15] And so in September 2011, the court concluded that the TSA must open up a public "notice and comment" period for discussion and justification of the need for AITs. Though the court instructed TSA to begin the process "promptly," as of late September 2012 it has not yet done so.

This appeals court order is a step in the process of determining whether AITs are lawful. In making judgments about substantive rules, federal agencies traditionally have wide latitude and their decisions are commonly accorded significant deference by the courts, especially when security is at issue. Thus, the challenge to use of AIT under the APA is probably a long shot to forcing the TSA to change its policy. But, as the matter is ongoing, the final outcome has yet to be determined.

EXPERTS

Thomas Bossert, former Deputy Assistant to the President for Homeland Security and Counterterrorism; (202) 689-5117

Frank Cillufo, Homeland Security Policy Institute, The George Washington University; (202) 994-2437; cilluffo@gwu.edu

James Harper, Cato Institute; (202) 789-5200; jharper@cato.org

Robert Jamison, former Deputy Administrator, Transportation Security Administration; (703) 413-8899; Robert.d.jamison@gmail.com

Morris "Mo" McGowan, former Assistant Administrator, Office of Security Operations, TSA; (202) 207-2930

Rick "Ozzie" Nelson, Center for Strategic and International Studies; (202) 775-3128; aschwartz@csis.org

---

15. EPIC v. DHS, 653 F.3d 1, 5–6 (D.C. Cir. 2011).

Michael Restovich, former Assistant Administrator, Office of Security Operations, TSA; (202) 207-2930; mrestovich@gmail.com

Marc Rotenberg, Electronic Privacy Information Center; (202) 483-1140; rotenberg@epic.org

RESOURCES

U.S. DEP'T OF HOMELAND SEC., FY 2013 BUDGET IN BRIEF (Feb. 2012), http://www.dhs.gov/xlibrary/assets/mgmt/dhs-budget-in-brief-fy2013.pdf.

U.S. DEP'T OF HOMELAND SEC., TRANSP. SEC. ADMIN., PRIVACY IMPACT ASSESSMENT FOR WHOLE BODY IMAGING (Oct. 17, 2008), http://www.dhs.gov/xlibrary/assets/privacy/privacy_pia_tsa_wbi.pdf.

U.S. DEP'T OF HOMELAND SEC., OFFICE OF INSPECTOR GEN., OIG-12-06, TSA PENETRATION TESTING OF ADVANCED IMAGING TECHNOLOGY (Nov. 2011), http://www.oig.dhs.gov/assets/Mgmt/OIG_SLR_12-06_Nov11.pdf.

U.S. DEP'T OF HOMELAND SEC., OFFICE OF THE INSPECTOR GEN., OIG-12-38, TRANSPORTATION SECURITY ADMINISTRATION'S USE OF BACKSCATTER (Feb. 2012), http://www.oig.dhs.gov/assets/Mgmt/2012/OIG_12-38_Feb12.pdf.

EPIC v. DHS, 653 F.3d 1 (D.C. Cir. 2011).

Andrew Welch, *Full-Body Scanners: Full Protection from Terrorist Attacks or Full-On Violation of the Constitution?*, 37 TRANSP. L.J. 167, *available at* http://law.du.edu/documents/transportation-law-journal/past-issues/v37-03/Welch-Body-Scanners.pdf.

Responding to Biological Attacks

23

By Barry Kellman*

In 2001, powdered anthrax in envelopes disrupted the U.S. government, cost billions to clean up, and killed five people. Terrorist groups such as Aum Shinrikyo (which released sarin gas in the Tokyo subway in 1995) experimented with biological weapons. Al-Qaida built an anthrax lab in Afghanistan in the 1990s. Experts are concerned that future biological attacks could cause consequences substantially exceeding anything other than perhaps those of nuclear weapons—hundreds of thousands of casualties, trillions of dollars of losses, and exceptional levels of panic. The Commission on Prevention of Weapons of Mass Destruction Proliferation and Terrorism asserted in 2008 that bio-attacks are the most likely catastrophic threat.[1]

How should the government be ready to respond to a catastrophic bioattack given that no one knows when, where, or even whether it will occur? It is useful to break this question into three principle components. First, how can responders quickly and accurately know what agent has been used so that they can respond effectively? Second, how can responders have sufficient medicines to treat affected populations against whichever agent has been used? Third, how can responders effectively limit the damage and restore order? Literally dozens of U.S. government agencies and programs have relevant and often overlapping responsibilities without centralized oversight—a bureaucratic condition that

---

*Robert Hoekstra, DePaul '12, contributed to this discussion.

1. COMM'N ON THE PREVENTION OF WEAPONS OF MASS DESTRUCTION PROLIFERATION AND TERRORISM, WORLD AT RISK (2008).

makes it difficult for people inside and outside government to understand what is exactly going on.

DETECTION AND DIAGNOSIS

Each specific bioagent demands a uniquely specific response. The proper response to an anthrax attack is very different from the proper response to a smallpox or plague attack. Moreover, decisions must be made quickly to stanch a pandemic's spread. Being able to accurately and quickly detect and diagnose a bioattack depends on having sophisticated capacities in place to gather, transmit, and analyze health and environmental data.

Detection

The earlier that a bioattack is detected, the better. Yet unlike an explosion or other conventional attack, a bioattack will not be immediately obvious until disease symptoms are overwhelming. Even then, there will likely be confusion about which disease is causing those symptoms. The challenge, therefore, is to get accurate data quickly enough to mobilize an effective response. Programs managed by the departments of Homeland Security (DHS) and Health and Human Services (HHS) are responsible for detection of a bioattack.

BioWatch for Sensing Pathogens

Experts believe that bioattack agents will likely be released in the air within highly trafficked indoor sites such as arenas, airports, or subway stations. To detect unusual releases, DHS's Office of Health Affairs (OHA) BioWatch program places biosensors in major American cities that are connected to a national 24/7 early warning system.[2] Although DHS has not confirmed the exact number of cities engaged in the BioWatch program or the exact location of sensors, at least 31 cities are part of the program—including Philadelphia, New York, D.C., San Diego, Boston, Chicago, Miami, Atlanta, Detroit, Denver, San Francisco, Seattle, St. Louis, Houston, and Los Angeles—with a goal of expanding to as many as 120 cities.

The sensors test for anthrax, smallpox, plague, the infectious disease tularemia, and perhaps other agents, although the exact list is undisclosed. Testing for bioagents in the air is extremely difficult. If the sensor is too specific, it might neglect a dangerous release. If the sensor is too broad, it might falsely react to

---

2. http://www.dhs.gov/xabout/structure/gc_1296249066184.shtm. *See generally* DEP'T OF HOMELAND SEC., OFFICE OF INSPECTOR GEN., DHS; MANAGEMENT OF BIOWATCH PROGRAM, http://www.oig.dhs.gov/assets/Mgmt/OIG_07-22_Jan07.pdf.

something natural and benign. DHS officials, therefore, are continuously trying to improve sensor capacities.

Programs for Reporting Unusual Diseases

Other than via sensors, a bioattack can be detected through reports of unusual disease outbreaks. By accumulating reports of often-disparate symptoms, public health officials can identify a pattern that might suggest an epidemic. "Biosurveillance" refers to a continuous process for monitoring the environment for markers of disease. The key to biosurveillance is systematic collection and analysis of data that can usefully characterize an event as well as support outbreak investigation. For example, the 2009 swine flu outbreak was initially signaled by a sudden increase in worker and student absenteeism in Veracruz, Mexico, along with elevated purchases of over-the-counter flu remedies. In 2007, the 9/11 Commission Act required the development of the National Biosurveillance Integration Center (NBIC) to identify, characterize, localize, and track biological events. The Health Incident Surveillance Branch within the Health Threats Resilience Division of the DHS-OHA supervises the NBIC in coordination with 11 federal agencies.[3]

The BioSense program is an important component of biosurveillance. BioSense was initiated in 2003 as an integrated public health surveillance program managed by the Centers for Disease Control and Prevention (CDC).[4] Patient-anonymous data is collected from electronic health record systems, school absentee data, pharmacy data, food-borne outbreaks, and other information sources for syndromic analysis. State and local public health authorities have access to this secure data to aid in analysis; public health authorities may now designate BioSense for receiving syndromic surveillance test messages.

The CDC promotes disease reporting through the Public Health Information Network (PHIN), a network of information systems that optimizes electronic disease reporting with a common lexicon and technical requirements, and by promulgating an overall health information exchange architecture.[5] The National Electronic Disease Surveillance System is an Internet-based exchange architecture designed to enhance the PHIN by transferring appropriate public health, laboratory, and clinical data efficiently and securely over the Internet to public health departments. Notably, increased resources are being devoted to standards-based electronic messaging between stakeholders at multiple levels (providers, labs, local and state public health authorities, and the CDC).[6]

---

3. http://www.dhs.gov/xabout/structure/oha-national-biosurveillance-integration-center.shtm.
4. http://www.cdc.gov/biosense.
5. http://www.cdc.gov/phin/about.html.
6. http://www.cdc.gov/phin/library/documents/pdf/111759_NEDSS.pdf.

The CDC's BioIntelligence Center (BIC) provides situational awareness of potential threats to local and state governments.[7] BIC analysts examine health data regarding 11 outbreak syndromes such as fever, rash, and gastrointestinal distress in order to detect unusual concentrations that might indicate a significant threat to public health. When appropriate, the CDC director's Emergency Operations Center[8] monitors the situation and coordinates data and analysis with the BIC. The CDC also works to identify outbreaks with local and international partners. The CDC Center for Global Health maintains regular relationships with the World Health Organization and numerous other national health departments and ministries.[9]

Diagnosis

Whether a pandemic is natural or intentional, it is imperative to accurately diagnose its cause in order to dispense effective countermeasures, to track its origin and spread, and to investigate potential perpetrators. Diagnosis of pathogens is coordinated by the CDC through the national Laboratory Response Network.[10] The LRN is a nationwide network composed primarily of local, state, and federal government laboratories that provide confirmatory testing of potential bioterrorism pathogens in all 50 state public health labs and in additional locations.[11] Consensus protocols for testing were developed by the CDC, the FBI, and the Association of Public Health Laboratories prior to the anthrax mailings of 2001.

In addition, the National Bioforensics Analysis Center (NBFAC), part of the National Biodefense Analysis and Countermeasures Center operated by the DHS in partnership with the FBI, is a central facility for analyzing biological samples to identify and attribute the use of biological weapons.[12] NBFAC has implemented a multifaceted research and development program, established a stand-alone Safety and Biosurety Program and Quality/Accreditation Program, and received select agent handling certification from the CDC for all laboratory staff and facilities. The NBFAC has also established a National Bioforensic Repository Collection

---

7. http://www.cdc.gov/biosense/files/BIC.pdf.
8. http://www.cdc.gov/phpr/eoc.htm.
9. *See* http://www.cdc.gov/maso/pdf/CGHfs.pdf.
10. http://www.bt.cdc.gov/lrn/.
11. *See* M. J. R. Gilchrist, *A National Laboratory Network for Bioterrorism: Evolution from a Prototype Network of Laboratories Performing Routine Surveillance*, 165 MILITARY MEDICINE supp. 2 (2000); A.P. Perkins, T. Popovic & K. Yeskey, *Public Health in the Time of Bioterrorism*, 8 EMERGING INFECTIOUS DISEASES (Oct. 2002), http://www.cdc.gov/ncidod/EID/vol8no10/02-0444.htm. *See also* Dep't of Health & Human Servs., Public Health Emergency Preparedness: Transforming America's Capacity to Respond, Fact Sheet, Sept. 11, 2003.
12. http://www.dhs.gov/files/labs/gc_1166211221830.shtm. *See* John Vitko Jr., Director of Dep't of Homeland Sec., National Biodefense Strategy, Congressional Testimony (July 28, 2005).

with a comprehensive management plan and acquisition strategy to provide reference microbiological material against which suspect samples can be compared.[13]

MEDICAL COUNTERMEASURES

Unlike most other disasters, which require generic treatment of injuries due to blast and fire, treating victims of bioattacks requires rapid and targeted application of specific medical countermeasures, or MCMs, such as vaccines and antidotes. Doing this effectively poses two challenges:

1. Many MCMs need to be developed or improved, entailing substantial research and testing.
2. MCMs need to be securely stockpiled, distributed to attack sites, and disseminated to victims under conditions of extreme stress.

MCM Development

Producing MCMs against bioattacks is a risky business. Developing MCMs against many different pathogens is scientifically challenging; the market for useful products is extremely uncertain; and large research and development investments might never bring a fair return.

Project BioShield, the comprehensive system for MCM preparedness,[14] is organized around three main aspects:

1. Funding and procurement;
2. Facilitation of research and development; and
3. Facilitation of countermeasure use in an emergency.

A complex bureaucracy, administered by HHS through the Office of the Assistant Secretary for Preparedness and Response (ASPR), is responsible for incentivizing MCM preparedness. The National Institutes of Health and the National Institute of Allergy and Infectious Diseases have primary responsibility to see that promising drug candidates are awarded contracts through Project BioShield's funds. The institutes' approach is known as the "push" incentive because it tries to set in motion the wheels of research and expedite reviews of promising biodefense drugs through the application process.[15]

---

13. *See* Dep't of Homeland Sec. Nat'l Bioforensic Analysis Ctr. (NBFAC), http://www.dhs.gov/xres/labs/gc_1166211221830.shtm.
14. http://www.hhs.gov/open/contacts/aspr.html.
15. *See HHS Implementation of Project Bioshield: Hearing Before the Subcommittee on Health of the House Committee on Energy and Commerce* (Apr. 6, 2006), http://www.hhs.gov/asl/testify/t060406.html (testimony of Alex M. Azar II, Deputy Secretary, Dep't of Homeland Security).

Within ASPR, the Biomedical Advanced Research and Development Authority (BARDA) oversees and coordinates research and acquisition of MCMs and is primarily responsible for facilitating communication between the federal government and the biomedical industry.[16] For MCMs at an advanced level of development, the BioShield Special Reserve Fund enables BARDA to purchase and stockpile MCMs while simultaneously providing funding for their research and development and providing the manufacturer with a guaranteed purchaser—the U.S. government. The Medical Countermeasure Development Fund, separate and in addition to the BioShield Special Reserve Fund, allows BARDA authorities to sponsor innovative research to improve MCMs.

When a promising MCM is developed, the Public Health Emergency Medical Countermeasures Enterprise (PHEMCE), overseen by BARDA as a multi-agency collaboration, determines its requirements and prioritizes development and acquisition programs.[17] Through the use of milestone contracts that allow companies to receive payments prior to final delivery of the goods, BARDA/PHEMCE can review the progress and determine whether the work is satisfactory so that promising drugs may be appropriately transitioned for additional funding.

The Department of Defense (DoD) has complementary programs. For example, the Defense Advanced Research Projects Agency's Accelerated Manufacture of Pharmaceuticals program is authorized to create a system for producing 3 million doses of vaccines or monoclonal antibodies within 12 weeks.[18]

Project BioShield was initially funded with $5.6 billion, but some of that funding has since been transferred to basic research and to development of antiviral medications against flu. One reason for these transfers is that BioShield has had very limited success, generating only a handful of useful MCMs. Most experts give BioShield credit for alleviating some bureaucratic and financial impediments to developing MCMs and attribute its lack of success to the scientific complexity of discovering safe and effective medicines against threatening scourges.[19]

---

16. U.S. Dep't of Health & Human Servs., Pub. Health Emergency Med. Countermeasures Enter. & Biomedical Advanced Research & Dev. Auth., BARDA Strategic Plan, 2011–2016, http://www.phe.gov/about/barda/Documents/barda-strategic-plan.pdf.

17. U.S. Dep't of Health & Human Servs., Pub. Health Emergency Med. Countermeasures Enter. (PHEMCE) Implementation Plan, https://www.medicalcountermeasures.gov/BARDA/documents/phemce_implplan_041607final.pdf.

18. http://www.darpa.mil/Our_Work/DSO/Programs/Accelerated_Manufacture_of_Pharmaceuticals_(AMP).aspx. *See* Gronvall et al., *Flexible Defenses Roundtable Meeting: Promoting the Strategic Innovation of Medical Countermeasures*, 5(3) Biosecurity & Bioterrorism (2007).

19. *See* Wil S. Hylton, *Warning: There's Not Nearly Enough of This Vaccine to Go Around*, N.Y. Times, Oct. 30, 2011, at 26.

New Vaccine Production Capacities

The government's efforts to increase medical countermeasures' production have had some success. A recently opened vaccine production facility in North Carolina is owned and managed by Novartis; the Department of Health and Human Services contributed 49 percent toward the facility's total investment of nearly $1 billion. The facility produces vaccines using cultured canine kidney cells (instead of the traditional chicken eggs) to grow flu vaccine—as much as 50 million doses. Use of tissue culture instead of eggs reduces the danger of contamination and increases capacities for rapid mass production of vaccine. The new facility might reduce production times from five months to four, although there is dispute among experts if the new facility will in fact reduce production times by that much. There is also some disagreement about the impact of the time savings, with proponents emphasizing the ability to incorporate new data about the disease into the vaccine while other experts point out that, even at four months, a sudden and acute pandemic would already be in its second stage. (*See* Mitchel L. Zoler, *Flu Vaccine Facility May Not Speed Production*, Skin & AllergyNews, Feb. 1, 2012, at 34.)

In addition, Medicago, with a $21 million contract from the Defense Advanced Research Projects Agency, recently opened a new vaccine production facility in Research Triangle Park, North Carolina, which makes flu vaccine from virus-like particles from tobacco leaves. In this process, only 30 days are required to develop vaccine. This process is claimed to also have the advantage of reducing the cost as well as the timing of vaccine production. (*See* Frank Vinluan, *Medicago's RTP Vaccine Facility Opens to Address Pandemics*, MedCity News, Nov. 14, 2011, http://www.medcitynews.com/2011/11/medicagos-rtp-vaccine-facility-opens-to-address-pandemics/.) In any event, the next stage in vaccine production involves use of recombinant technology that is forecast to reduce production times to 12 weeks, but this capability is at least two years away.

Stockpile Planning, Distribution, and Dispensation

There does not exist surge capacity to produce MCMs when a bioattack happens. Therefore, MCMs must be produced in advance and stored in the Strategic National Stockpile (SNS)—a network of warehouses holding stores of medicines and equipment for distribution during emergencies. Locations and contents of specific countermeasures are kept secret for security reasons, but these certainly include countermeasures to common bioterrorism threats such as anthrax, smallpox, and tularemia.[20] Because MCMs must be maintained under strict temperature and other constraints, elaborate plans for the SNS have been developed by BARDA; the CDC manages the stockpile with the support of BARDA, DHS, and DoD.

---

20. https://www.medicalcountermeasures.gov/BARDA/BARDA.aspx.

When a disease emergency is declared, an affected state's governor must request delivery of MCMs, although in cases of national emergency the president can assume this responsibility. CDC officials, in coordination with officials of the Federal Emergency Management Agency as well as state and local officials, are authorized to evaluate the situation, determine the most prudent action, and prioritize MCM dispensation. Under current plans, supplies from the SNS will be distributed to affected areas rapidly through push packages—government-owned caches of supplies and medications—within 12 hours via either trucks or commercial cargo aircraft. Concurrently, the SNS Program will deploy its Stockpile Service Advance Group to coordinate with state and local officials so that the SNS assets can be efficiently received and distributed upon arrival at the site.[21]

There is ongoing debate over the best method of dispensing MCMs to the public. Until relatively recently, plans have called for dispensation from central locations such as schools and community centers. This has the advantage of putting the MCMs into the hands of state and local health departments whose staffs have been trained on the reception, protection, and dispensation of these supplies. There are, however, disadvantages, especially for people with challenged mobility or who live far from urban centers. Moreover, central dispensation assumes that emergency responders are able to work and that there is a command and control system to effectively guide the process. In a dire emergency, these assumptions might not be realistic.[22]

For some MCMs—especially those that can be self-administered—an alternative to centralized dispensation is to get them to each household, typically through postal delivery. This is far more convenient for housebound citizens. Moreover, inducing people to stay in their homes is important to reduce the spread of contagious disease; it obviously makes sense to avoid having them come to a central site to get their medicine. However, not all medicines can be self-administered, and even effective delivery of medicines to each household does not ensure that they will be taken correctly. Advance delivery of medicine along with substantial information on proper use can alleviate some of these problems, but some medicines have a short shelf life, so delivering them in advance of an emergency might not be effective. Officials are weighing different options, none of which is perfect.

RESPONSE AND RESTORATION OF ORDER

In many respects, response to bioattacks will be similar to any catastrophe. For example, as part of the normal National Response Framework, a governor can

---

21. *See* http://www.cdc.gov/phpr/stockpile/stockpile.htm.
22. *See* MIRIAM DAVIS ET AL., DISPENSING MEDICAL COUNTERMEASURES FOR PUBLIC HEALTH EMERGENCIES: WORKSHOP SUMMARY (Inst. of Medicine of Nat'l Acads. 2008), http://books.nap.edu/openbook.php?record_id=12221.

request the president to declare a state of emergency, which triggers the Federal Emergency Management Agency's authority under the Federal Emergency Response Plan pursuant to the National Incident Management System[23] to provide technical and advisory assistance, funds, and supplies. Yet bioattacks pose a unique threat that cannot be addressed adequately with normal emergency declaration process because of the intensive need for specialized response. In connection with bioattacks, three aspects of consequence mitigation and restoration of order deserve special attention.

Use of Military Forces

Generally, emergency response does not involve the direct use of military forces because of restrictions in the Posse Comitatus Act[24] and the Stafford Act.[25] National Guard units may be used under the direction of their state's governor because as state militias they are not bound generally by the Posse Comitatus Act. In response to bioattacks, however, the U.S. attorney general may request assistance from the defense secretary because of the immediate need for specialized materials and training. The U.S. attorney general and the defense secretary must jointly determine that the biological weapon poses "a serious threat to the interest of the United States" and that three factors exist:

1. Civilian expertise and capabilities cannot immediately counter the threat;
2. The Defense Department's capabilities are necessary to counter the threat; and
3. Enforcement of the laws against weapons of mass destruction would be impaired if the Defense Department was not allowed to act.[26]

Public Health Mobilization

While the CDC has a great role in sharing information and providing both resources and expertise, primary responsibility for much of a public health response will rest upon the individual state public health departments. These departments, through the governor's authority, can implement restrictions after an emergency is declared and can do a large portion of laboratory testing. Finally, state public health departments will likely coordinate mass casualty treatment and care.

Local public health departments have a critical role in public messaging, the operation of local clinics, and information sharing among medical institutions. Public messaging will likely include best practices for limiting the spread of

---

23. http://www.fema.gov/emergency/nims/.
24. 18 U.S.C. § 1385.
25. 42 U.S.C. §§ 5121–5207.
26. 10 U.S.C. § 382.

disease and other advisories. Local departments may be the first to identify local public health impacts, and they have a responsibility to notify state and federal agencies.

In the case of a biological attack, the traditional command and control under the National Incident Management System mentioned earlier will remain in place. Public health authorization is required for movement restrictions at the state level and for stockpile distribution at the federal level, and offers other protections. Because other agencies may not have the same specialized knowledge about protection from pathogens or treatment protocols, or a technical understanding of disease spread, public health departments are likely to take the lead in response priorities and will likely encounter great deference.

Restricting Movement

If a contagious agent is used in a bioattack, the need to stanch the spread of disease may call for quarantine, restrictions on travel, curfews, closing of borders, or cancellation of public gatherings. Most states authorize the governor to declare martial law during an emergency and to take personal property subject to constitutional guarantees of fair compensation. Governors also have broad authority to reallocate the use of publicly owned facilities. It may be necessary, for example, to convert public schools into sheltering, triage, or command and control centers. Typically, there is a defined statutory period during which the governor may act in consultation with the state's public health department but without legislative approval.

Although federal authority requires more statutory certainty, various executive authorities have similarly broad powers in the correct conditions. The surgeon general may, with the approval of the secretary of the Department of Health and Human Services, make rules to prevent interstate and international transmission of disease, including issuing orders to apprehend and detain those believed to be infected by disease.[27] This authority does not extend to local quarantines, but the HHS secretary may aid local officials in setting up their quarantines.[28]

Whenever a restriction such as a quarantine or evacuation is ordered, there will be some noncompliance. Judgment must be made to determine the amount of force allowed to enforce the restriction. The force allowable for a precautionary quarantine versus preventing the spread of a disease that could result in the deaths of hundreds of millions will be dramatically different. With the societal stress, traditional crimes such as looting and robbery will become more likely. Responders who must use force are held liable only if their actions constituted unreasonably excessive force given what the responder was aware of at the time.

---

27. 42 U.S.C. §§ 264 *et seq.*
28. 42 U.S.C. § 243.

CONCLUSION

Bioattack response planning must address the risk that an attacker can commit a huge catastrophe using any of various attack agents and multiple ways to release them. Yet a U.S. bioattack has happened only once—the 2001 anthrax attacks. There is scant experience on which to predict how a response to such potentially distinctive high-consequence events will unfold on a large scale. Moreover, the maze of bureaucratic responsibility for responding to bioattacks means that no centralized authority (short of the president) will exercise overarching command and control. Indeed, federal responsibilities are spread among various offices in DHS and HHS with support from the attorney general, surgeon general, and Defense Department; state and local officials also have critical roles in response. On top of all this is the likely unprecedented panic that a bioattack will provoke. All these factors—lack of experience, mass consequences and panic, variable conditions and attack modes, overlapping responsibilities—will make it difficult to sort out the facts of a bioattack. For journalists, as with other response communities, the key to success is preparedness.

EXPERTS

Phyllis Arthur, Biotechnology Industry Organization, Director Health & Regulatory Affairs; (202) 962-6664; parthur@bio.org

Ronald Atlas, Co-Director of the Center for the Deterrence of Biowarfare and Bioterrorism, University of Louisville; (502) 852-3957; r.atlas@louisville.edu

Gerald Epstein, Deputy Assistant Secretary for Chemical, Biological, Radiological, and Nuclear Policy, Department of Homeland Security; (202) 282-0615; Gerald.epstein@hq.dhs.gov

Julie Fischer, Senior Associate, Global Health Security, Stimson Center; (202) 223-5956; jfischer@stimson.org

Jo Husbands, National Academy of Sciences; (202) 334-2816; jusband@nas.edu

Leonard Spector, Director, James Martin Center for Nonproliferation Studies; (202) 842-3100; Leonard.spector@miis.edu

Terence Taylor, President, International Council for the Life Sciences; (202) 659-8058; taylor@iclscharter.org

Tevi Troy, Visiting Senior Fellow, Hudson Institute; (202) 974-2400; ttroy@hudson.org

Paul Walker, Director, Security and Sustainability Program, Global Green USA; (202) 222-0700; pwalker@globalgreen.org

RESOURCES

Government Reports

Nat'l Sec. Council, National Strategy for Countering Biological Threats (Nov. 2009), http://geneva.usmission.gov/wp-content/uploads/2009/12/Natl-Strategy-for-Countering-BioThreats.pdf.

Comm'n on the Prevention of Weapons of Mass Destruction Proliferation and Terrorism, World at Risk (2008), http://a.abcnews.go.com/images/TheLaw/WMD-report.pdf#http://a.abcnews.go.com/images/TheLaw/WMD-report.pdf.

2012 Public Health Emergency Medical Countermeasures (PHEMCE) Strategy, http://www.phe.gov/Preparedness/mcm/phemce/Documents/2012-PHEMCE-Strategy.pdf.

Ctrs. for Disease Control & Prevention, Strategic National Stockpile (Mar. 31, 2009), http://www.bt.cdc.gov/stockpile/.

Ctrs. for Disease Control & Prevention, Smallpox Response Plan and Guidelines (2002), http://www.bt.cdc.gov/agent/smallpox/response-plan/.

Ctrs. for Disease Control & Prevention, Annex 5: Suggested prevention Planning Activities for State and Local Public Health Authorities (draft 2003), http://www.bt.cdc.gov/agent/smallpox/response-plan/files/annex-5.pdf.

Dep't of Homeland Sec., National Infrastructure Protection Plan (2009), http://www.dhs.gov/xlibrary/assets/NIPP_Plan.pdf.

Dep't of Homeland Sec., National Response Plan (2004), http://permanent.access.gpo.gov/lps56895/NRP_FullText.pdf.

Nat'l Research Council, Globalization, Biosecurity, and the Future of the Life Sciences (2006), http://www.nap.edu/catalog.php?record_id=11567.

Frank Gottron, Cong. Research Serv., RL 33907, Project BioShield: Appropriations, Acquisitions, and Policy Implementation Issues for Congress (2007), http://www.fas.org/sgp/crs/terror/RL33907.pdf.

Frank Gottron & Dana A. Shea, Cong. Research Serv., R411232, Federal Efforts to Address The Threat of Bioterrorism (2010), http://www.fas.org/sgp/crs/terror/R41123.pdf.

U.S. Gov't Accountability Office, GAO-08-180, First Responders' Ability to Detect and Model Hazardous Releases (2008), http://www.gao.gov/new.items/d08180.pdf.

RAND Health, Recommended Infrastructure Standards for Mass Antibiotic Dispensing (2008), http://www.rand.org/pubs/technical_reports/2008/RAND_TR553.pdf.

Books

Anne L. Clunan, Peter Rene Lavoy & Susan B. Martin, Terrorism, War, or Disease?: Unraveling the Use of Biological Weapons (Stanford Univ. Press 2008).

Barry Kellman, Bioviolence—Preventing Biological Terror and Crime (Cambridge Univ. Press 2007).

Gary D. Koblentz, Living Weapons: Biological Warfare and International Security (Cornell Univ. Press 2009).

Pandemics and Bioterrorism: Transdisciplinary Information Sharing for Decision-Making Against Biological Threats (Andrey Trufanov ed., IOS Press 2010).

Jonathan B. Tucker, Chemical-Biological Terrorism—Threats and Responses (IOS Press 2009).

Articles

D.A. Ashford, R.M. Kaiser & M.E. Bales, *Planning Against Biological Terrorism: Lessons from Outbreak Investigations*, Emerging Infectious Disease (2003), http://www.ncbi.nlm.nih.gov/pubmed/12737732.

J.C. Butler et al., *Collaboration Between Public Health and Law Enforcement: New Paradigms and Partnerships for Bioterrorism Planning and Response*, Emerging Infectious Disease (2002), http://www.cdc.gov/ncidod/EID/vol8no10/02-0400.htm.

Michael Chertoff, *Confronting Biological Threats to the Homeland*, 2008 Joint Force Quarterly 8.

Lea Ann Fracasso, *Developing Immunity: The Challenges in Mandating Vaccinations in the Wake of a Biological Terrorist Attack*, 13 DePaul J. Health Care L. 1 (2010).

David R. Franz, *Biological Terrorism: Understanding the Threat, Preparation, and Medical Response*, 46 Disease-a-Month 127–90 (Feb. 2000).

D.M. Hartley et al., *Landscape of International Event-Based Biosurveillance*, J. Emerging Health Threats (2010), http://www.ncbi.nlm.nih.gov/pmc/articles/PMC3167659/.

Barry Kellman, *The Biological Weapons Convention and the Democratization of Mass Violence*, 2(2) GLOBAL POLICY 210–16 (May 2011).

Barry Kellman, *A Global Architecture for Medical Counter-Measure Preparedness Against Bioviolence*, 2011 U. ST. THOMAS L.J. 500.

Taiwo A. Oriola, *Against the Plague: Exemption of Pharmaceutical Patent Rights as a Biosecurity Strategy*, 7 U. ILL. J.L. TECH. & POL'Y 287, 329–30 (2007).

Vladan Radosavlijevic & Goran Belojevic, *A New Model of Bioterrorism Risk Assessment*, BIOSECURITY AND BIOTERRORISM, Dec. 1, 2009, at 443.

Lisa D. Rotz et al., *Public Health Assessment of Potential Biological Terrorism Agents*, EMERGING INFECTIOUS DISEASE (2002), http://www.ncbi.nlm.nih.gov/pmc/articles/PMC2732458/.

Alfred J. Sciarrino, *The Grapes of Wrath and the Speckled Monster, Part III: Epidemics, Natural Disasters and Biological Terrorism—The Federal Response*, 10 MICH. ST. U. J. MED. & L.430 (2006).

Willy A. Valvdivia-Granda, *Bioinformatics for Biodefense: Challenges and Opportunities*, BIOSECURITY AND BIOTERRORISM, Mar. 1, 2010, at 69.

L.M. Wein, D.L. Craft & E.H. Kaplan, *Emergency Response to an Anthrax Attack*, 100(7) PROC. NAT'L ACAD. SCI. 4346–51 (2003).

About the Editors

Timothy J. McNulty is a veteran journalist whose career in national and foreign news coverage includes roles as both a war correspondent and White House correspondent. He is a Lecturer at Northwestern University's Medill School of Journalism, is Co-Director of the school's National Security Journalism Initiative, and serves on the adjunct faculty of the University of Chicago's Graham School, where he teaches literary nonfiction writing.

McNulty was the *Chicago Tribune*'s Public Editor and, earlier, Associate Managing Editor for Foreign News. During a long career at the newspaper, including posts as National Editor and Foreign Editor, McNulty helped direct the newspaper's coverage of the September 11 tragedy, the American strike into Afghanistan, and the invasion of Iraq.

Earlier, he was a national correspondent based in Atlanta. Following the reestablishment of diplomatic relations with China, McNulty was one of the first eight American journalists allowed to reside in and report from Beijing. Later as a foreign correspondent, he worked in Beirut and Jerusalem and reported throughout the Middle East.

In Washington for more than a decade, McNulty focused on social and political policymaking, including five years as a White House correspondent. In 1992, McNulty won the White House Correspondents' Association award for journalistic excellence for a series on the impact of satellite television on presidential decision-making and diplomacy. McNulty was the National Reporter for the *Tribune*'s 1985 series on the emergence of an urban underclass, which won the Robert F. Kennedy Journalism Award and the Sidney Hillman Foundation Award. He won the *Tribune*'s Beck Award three times, for his contribution to reporting on Tiananmen Square, for his coverage of the Israeli siege of Beirut, and for his distinguished reporting on the suicide/killing of more than 900 cult followers in Guyana.

ABOUT THE EDITORS

McNulty holds a bachelor's degree from Wayne State University in Detroit and a master's degree from Georgetown University.

Paul Rosenzweig is the founder of Red Branch Consulting PLLC, a homeland security consulting company, and a Senior Adviser to the Chertoff Group. Rosenzweig formerly served as Deputy Assistant Secretary for Policy and twice as Acting Assistant Secretary for International Affairs in the Department of Homeland Security, where his responsibilities ranged from aviation security, border control, and visa policy to international data sharing, biological threats, and international relations. He is currently a Distinguished Visiting Fellow at the Homeland Security Studies and Analysis Institute, a federally funded research and development center.

Rosenzweig also serves as a Professorial Lecturer in Law at George Washington University, where he teaches a class on cybersecurity law and policy. He is a Senior Editor of the *Journal of National Security Law & Policy* and a Visiting Fellow at The Heritage Foundation. In 2011 he was a Carnegie Fellow in National Security Journalism at the Medill School of Journalism at Northwestern University. He is also a member of the American Bar Association Standing Committee on Law and National Security.

Rosenzweig is a cum laude graduate of the University of Chicago Law School, has a master of science degree in chemical oceanography from the Scripps Institution of Oceanography, University of California at San Diego, and a bachelor's degree from Haverford College. Following graduation from law school he served as a law clerk to Judge R. Lanier Anderson III of the U.S. Court of Appeals for the Eleventh Circuit.

He is the co-author (with James Jay Carafano) of the book *Winning the Long War: Lessons from the Cold War for Defeating Terrorism and Preserving Freedom* and author of the forthcoming book *Cyber Warfare: How Conflicts in Cyberspace Are Challenging America and Changing the World.*

Ellen Shearer is the William F. Thomas Professor of Journalism in the Medill School of Journalism at Northwestern University, based in the school's Washington Program bureau, and is co-director of the Medill National Security Journalism Initiative. She is President of the Washington Press Club Foundation. She was a leader in the News21 project on privacy and civil liberties post-9/11; those stories won a special National Press Foundation citation and were picked up by hundreds of newspapers and TV stations. Prior to the start of the war in Iraq, she created, with funding from the McCormick Foundation, a new course called Covering Conflicts, Terrorism, and National Security, which educated graduate students as well as working journalists on military strategy, conflicts, crimes of war, terrorism, and other national security issues and which also provided hazardous environmental training to help journalists protect themselves during dangerous reporting assignments.

About the Editors

Shearer was the conference coordinator for the Reuters Foundation/Medill Washington Conference, which addressed the quality of information Americans receive from the U.S. news media concerning Russia; she was curator for the Mongerson Prize for Investigative Reporting on the News and is the Medill liaison with the Crimes of War Project and Military Reporters and Editors. She regularly serves as an accreditor for the Accrediting Council on Education in Journalism and Mass Communications. Since 1999 she has coordinated judging for the White House Correspondents' Association's annual awards.

She is co-author of the book *Nonvoters: America's No-Shows* and has written chapters in six other books. Before joining the Medill faculty, Shearer, who has more than 20 years of experience in the news industry, was a senior editor at *New York Newsday*, a consulting editor at Newhouse News Service, and a marketing executive at Reuters, and held positions as senior executive, bureau chief, and reporter during a 10-year stint at United Press International.

About the Contributors

Julia Atcherley is an Associate at Levine Sullivan Koch & Schulz in New York City. She received her LL.M. from Columbia University School of Law, where she concentrated on media litigation, intellectual property, and national security law. While studying at Columbia, Atcherley interned in the United Nations' International Justice Program with Human Rights Watch. She previously worked as a Solicitor at the Australian-based law firm Mallesons Stephen Jaques in Sydney, where she was a member of the firm's Intellectual Property and Media law group.

Laurie R. Blank is the Director of the International Humanitarian Law Clinic at Emory University School of Law, where she teaches international humanitarian law and works directly with students to provide assistance to international tribunals, nongovernmental organizations, and law firms around the world on cutting edge issues in humanitarian law and human rights. Blank is the co-director of a multiyear project on military training programs in the law of war and the co-author of "Law of War Training: Resources for Military and Civilian Leaders." She is a member of the American Bar Association's Advisory Committee to the Standing Committee on Law and National Security. Before joining Emory, Blank was a Program Officer in the Rule of Law Program at the United States Institute of Peace. Blank received a master of arts degree in international relations from The Paul H. Nitze School of Advanced International Studies at The Johns Hopkins University, and a J.D. from New York University School of Law.

Andrew M. Borene is Editor-in-Chief of *The U.S. Intelligence Community Law Sourcebook* (American Bar Association). He is Executive Director of Robotics Alley (www.roboticsalley.org) and Assistant General Counsel at ReconRobotics (www.reconrobotics.com). Borene is a former Associate Deputy General Counsel with the Department of Defense and has taught at the Humphrey Institute of Public Affairs. He served as a Marine intelligence officer with the 1st Marine Division in Iraq. During law school, he was a judicial extern in the chambers of U.S. District Judge John Tunheim. In 2009, he was awarded a State Department fellowship as an Emerging American Leader for the study of postconflict peace-building in Northern Ireland. Borene holds a J.D. from the University of Minnesota Law School and a B.A. in economics from Macalester College. He serves as Director of Special Projects for the ABA Standing Committee on Law and National Security.

Geoffrey S. Corn joined the South Texas University faculty in 2005, where he has taught national security law, law of armed conflict, criminal law, criminal procedure, comparative terrorism law, international law, ethics for prosecutors, and military law for civilian practitioners. Corn spent 22 years as an Army officer and civilian employee. He served as the Army's Senior Law of War Expert in the Office of the Judge Advocate General and Chief of the Law of War Branch in the International Law Division. His military career also included service as a Tactical Intelligence Officer in Panama, Chief Prosecutor for the 101st Airborne Division, Chief of International Law for United States Army Europe, Regional Defense Counsel for the Western United States, and Professor of International and National Security Law at the Army Judge Advocate General's School. Corn is the Faculty Adviser to the National Security Law Society at South Texas. Corn earned his J.D. from George Washington University and his LL.M. from the Army Judge Advocate General's School. He is also a graduate of the Army Command and Staff College.

Jennifer C. Daskal is a Fellow at Georgetown University's Center on National Security and the Law. From 2009 to 2011, she was Counsel to the Assistant Attorney General for National Security at the Department of Justice. During that time, she served on the Detention Policy Task Force and provided legal advice on a range of national security matters, including intelligence oversight, immigration policy, and detention and interrogation practice. Prior to joining the Justice Department, she worked as Senior Counterterrorism Counsel at Human Rights Watch. She previously practiced criminal law as a staff attorney for the Public Defender Service for the District of Columbia. Daskal has a J.D. from Harvard Law School and a master of arts degree in economics from Cambridge University. She is a Term Member of the Council on Foreign Relations.

James X. Dempsey is Vice President for Public Policy at the Center for Democracy & Technology, a nonprofit public policy organization focused on privacy and other issues affecting the future of the Internet. Dempsey joined CDT in 1997 and served as Executive Director from 2003 to 2005. He currently heads CDT's West Coast office in San Francisco. At CDT, Dempsey has concentrated on Internet privacy and government surveillance. He coordinates the Digital Due Process coalition, a diverse group of companies, advocacy groups, and think tanks working to update the Electronic Communications Privacy Act of 1986. Prior to joining CDT, Dempsey was Deputy Director of the nonprofit Center for National Security Studies. From 1985 to 1995, Dempsey was Assistant Counsel to the House Judiciary Committee's Subcommittee on Civil and Constitutional Rights.

W. Renn Gade, a Colonel in the U.S. Army, is detailed from U.S. Special Operations Command as a legal adviser to the Office of the Director of National Intelligence, National Counterintelligence Executive. Previously, he has served as Staff Judge Advocate (senior legal adviser) to a number of joint and Army commands, including U.S. Special Operations Command, Multinational Force-Iraq, Multinational Corps-Iraq, XVIII Airborne Corps, and 82d Airborne Division. He also has served as the Military Assistant to the Department of Defense General Counsel, Deputy Legal Counsel to the Chairman of the Joint Chiefs of Staff, and Chief, International and Operational Law, Office of the Judge Advocate General. Gade's career includes wide-ranging experience in international and operational law issues as well as extensive criminal and civil trial work.

Michael T. Gershberg is Of Counsel in the Washington office of Steptoe & Johnson LLP, where he is a member of the International Department. Gershberg advises foreign and domestic clients regarding the application of export control and economic sanctions statutes and regulations administered by the Bureau of Industry and Security at the Commerce Department, the Directorate of Defense Trade Controls at the State Department, and the Department of Treasury's Office of Foreign Assets Control. Gershberg's practice also involves matters of data protection and cybersecurity. He advises companies regarding their rights and obligations under the surveillance provisions of the Electronic Communications Privacy Act, the Communications Assistance for Law Enforcement Act, the Federal Wiretap Act, and federal and state privacy laws. He also counsels companies regarding encryption import, export, and use rules in the United States and jurisdictions around the world. His experience with encryption items includes product classification, encryption licensing, and related compliance and enforcement issues.

Susan Ginsburg is a Nonresident Fellow of the Migration Policy Institute and a policy analyst, and has served on two Department of Homeland Security advisory committees. As a Senior Counsel on the 9/11 Commission, she was the team leader for its examination and recommendations concerning terrorist tactics for travel, visa acquisition, entry, and maintaining status in the United States. She served as Chief of Staff and Senior Advisor and Coordinator of Firearms Policy to the Undersecretary for Enforcement at the Department of the Treasury from

1994 to 2001. A lawyer, she practiced civil litigation and clerked for Judge A. Leon Higginbotham of the U.S. Court of Appeals for the Third Circuit. She is the author of *Securing Human Mobility in the Age of Risk: New Challenges for Travel, Borders, and Migration* (Migration Policy Institute 2010). Her publications also include "Securing Human Mobility at the US-Canada Border," *National Strategy Forum Review* (Summer 2010), and *Countering Terrorist Mobility: Shaping an Operational Strategy* (Migration Policy Institute 2006).

David W. Glazier is a Professor of Law and the Lloyd Tevis Fellow at Loyola Law School Los Angeles, where he teaches and researches in the area of international law. His scholarship focuses on law of war issues in the so-called War on Terror, with particular emphasis on the current and historical use of military commissions. Glazier served 21 years as a U.S. Navy Surface Warfare Officer before retiring from command of a guided missile frigate, the USS George Philip, to attend law school. He earned his J.D. from the University of Virginia School of Law, where he served on the editorial board of the Virginia Law Review and earned the Best Note award for his original foray into military commission scholarship, "Kangaroo Court or Competent Tribunal?: Judging the 21st Century Military Commission." Following law school he remained at the University of Virginia for two years as a Research Fellow at the Center for National Security Law and an Adjunct Professor before moving to Loyola. Glazier also earned a master of science degree from Georgetown University in government/national security studies, a diploma from the Naval War College, and a bachelor's degree in history from Amherst College.

Amos N. Guiora is a Professor of Law at the S.J. Quinney College of Law, the University of Utah. Guiora, who teaches criminal procedure, international law, global perspectives on counterterrorism, and religion and terrorism, incorporates innovative scenario-based instruction to address national and international security issues and dilemmas. He is a member of the American Bar Association's Law and National Security Advisory Committee. Guiora is the author of *Global Perspectives on Counterterrorism, Fundamentals of Counterterrorism, Constitutional Limits on Coercive Interrogation, Homeland Security: What Is It and Where Are We Going?*, and *Freedom from Religion: Rights and National Security*. He served for 19 years in the Israel Defense Forces as Lieutenant Colonel, and held a number of senior command positions, including Commander of the IDF School of Military Law and Legal Advisor to the Gaza Strip.

Todd Hinnen is a Partner at Perkins Coie law firm in Washington. From 2009 to 2011, Hinnen served as Acting Assistant Attorney General and as a Deputy Assistant Attorney General in the Department of Justice's National Security Division. He also served as Chief Counsel to then-Sen. Joseph R. Biden, Jr., as a Director in the National Security Council's Combating Terrorism Directorate, and as

About the Contributors

a prosecutor in the Department of Justice's Computer Crime & Intellectual Property Section. Hinnen graduated from Amherst College and Harvard Law School, and clerked for Judge Richard C. Tallman of the U.S. Court of Appeals for the Ninth Circuit.

Adam Isles is Director for Strategy and Policy Consulting on homeland security at Raytheon Co. Previously, he was Deputy Chief of Staff for Secretary Michael Chertoff at the Department of Homeland Security. He first joined the federal government in 1997 as a career lawyer in the Criminal Division of the Department of Justice. He received his J.D. from Harvard Law School and his B.A. from Yale University. He also serves as a Senior Associate in the Counterterrorism and Homeland Security Program at the Center for Strategic and International Studies.

Kurt Johnson is the Director of the Center for Homeland Security at the University of Colorado at Colorado Springs. CHS is one of four centers composing the National Institute of Science, Space, and Security Centers. The University selected Johnson in 2009 to spearhead the CHS domestic and international homeland defense, and homeland security education and training programs. Johnson retired from the Navy in 2008 with the rank of Captain. His final assignment was as the Senior Legal Advisor to the Commander of NORAD and U.S. Northern Command from 2005 to 2008. From 2001 to 2003, he served as the senior U.S. Navy/U.S. Marine Corps Legal Advisor in the Middle East during Operations Enduring Freedom and Iraqi Freedom. Other assignments included two command tours and Deputy Staff Judge Advocate for U.S. Pacific Command.

Barry Kellman, President of the International Security & Biopolicy Institute, is Professor of International Law at the DePaul University College of Law in Chicago. Kellman's work for the past decade has focused primarily on countering security dangers associated with intentionally inflicted disease. His most recent book, *Bioviolence: Preventing Biological Terror and Crime*, is a comprehensive strategy for law enforcers, scientists, and public health officials to prevent the intentional infliction of disease. Kellman served as Special Advisor to the Interpol Program on Prevention of Biological Terrorism, on the National Academies of Sciences Committee on Research Standards and Practices to Prevent the Destructive Application of Biotechnology, and as Legal Adviser to the National Commission on Terrorism. Kellman has published widely on weapons proliferation and smuggling, the laws of armed conflict, Middle East weapons control, global biopreparedness, and nuclear nonproliferation.

Eugene Kontorovich is a Professor of Law at Northwestern University. His research spans the fields of constitutional and international law. He is a leading expert on maritime piracy, universal jurisdiction, and international criminal law. He has been called on to advise lawyers in historic piracy trials around the world, as well as journalists at *The New York Times*, *The Wall Street Journal*, and many other media organizations. His scholarship has been often relied on in federal court opinions, including several landmark piracy cases. He went to college and law school at the University of Chicago, where he also later taught. He clerked for Judge Richard Posner on the U.S. Court of Appeals for the Seventh Circuit. He has been honored with a membership at the Institute for Advanced Study in Princeton and the Bator Award from the Federalist Society. He is the author of *Justice at Sea: Piracy and the Limits of International Criminal Law*, forthcoming from Harvard University Press.

Lee Levine is a Founding Partner at Levine Sullivan Koch & Schulz in Washington and has represented media clients in libel, invasion of privacy, reporters' privilege, copyright, and related First Amendment cases for more than three decades. Levine has litigated in the courts of more than 20 states and the District of Columbia and has appeared in most federal courts of appeal and in the highest courts of 10 states. He is the lead author of the treatise *Newsgathering and the Law*, is a co-author of the casebook *Media and the Law*, and has written extensively on newsgathering, the First Amendment, and other media law topics. Levine is also an Adjunct Professor of Law at the Georgetown University Law Center, where he teaches media law.

Peter Margulies teaches national security law, human rights, immigration law, and professional responsibility at Roger Williams University and wrote *Law's Detour: Justice Displaced in the Bush Administration*, a critique of the Bush administration's approach to national security. A contributor to the Lawfare blog, Margulies advocates a third way that reconciles counterterrorism and individual rights. Margulies has participated in a number of Supreme Court cases, including *Holder v. Humanitarian Law Project* and *Padilla v. Kentucky*. Recent articles include "True Believers at Law: Legal Ethics, National Security Agendas, and the Separation of Powers" and "The Fog of War Reform: Change and Structure in the Law of Armed Conflict after September 11" for the Marquette Law Review, and "Advising Terrorism: Material Support, Safe Harbors" and "Freedom of Speech" for the Hastings Law Journal.

Jim McPherson is the Executive Director of the National Association of Attorneys General, one of the oldest legal associations in the country. He is also the current Chair of the American Bar Association Standing Committee on Law and National Security. Prior to joining NAAG, McPherson served as the General Counsel for the Department of Defense Counterintelligence Field Activity. In 2006, McPherson completed a career in the Navy, retiring as the 39th Judge Advocate General of the Navy. McPherson graduated from San Diego State University with a degree in public administration. He obtained his J.D. from the University of San Diego School of Law, and was awarded a master of laws degree in military law from The Judge Advocate General's School. During his military career, McPherson received the Distinguished Service Medal, the Legion of Merit (two awards), and the Meritorious Service Medal (four awards).

Vijay M. Padmanabhan is an Assistant Professor at Vanderbilt University Law School. From 2003 to 2008 he served as an Attorney-Adviser in the Office of Legal Adviser at the Department of State. While there he served as the agency's Chief Counsel on Guantanamo and Iraq detainee litigation, and advised the department on law of war and human rights law questions. He also coordinated public diplomacy regarding detainee issues. From 2008 to 2011 he was a Visiting Assistant Professor at the Benjamin N. Cardozo School of Law. Padmanabhan's areas of research are international humanitarian law, international human rights law, and international criminal law.

Deborah Pearlstein is an Assistant Professor of Law at Cardozo Law School, where she teaches courses in U.S. constitutional law, international law, and national security. From 2003 to 2007, Pearlstein served as the Founding Director of the Law and Security Program at Human Rights First, where she led the organization's efforts in research, litigation, and advocacy surrounding U.S. detention and interrogation operations. Among other projects, Pearlstein led the organization's first monitoring mission to the U.S. Naval Base at Guantanamo Bay, Cuba; prepared a series of briefs *amicus curiae* to the Supreme Court; and co-authored multiple reports on the human rights impact of U.S. national security policy, including *Command's Responsibility*, which provided the first comprehensive accounting of detainee deaths in U.S. military custody since 2002. Pearlstein also worked closely with members of the military and intelligence communities, including in launching a series of off-the-record workshops to address key policy challenges in U.S. counterterrorism efforts. Pearlstein was appointed in 2009 to the American Bar Association's Advisory Committee on Law and National Security. A magna cum laude graduate of Harvard Law School, Pearlstein clerked for Judge Michael Boudin of the U.S. Court of Appeals for the First Circuit, then for Justice John Paul Stevens of the Supreme Court.

Benjamin Powell is a partner with the law firm WilmerHale. Powell served as General Counsel to the first three Directors of National Intelligence from 2006 until March 2009. Powell worked with leaders across the Intelligence Community and in Congress to modernize the Foreign Intelligence Surveillance Act in 2008. He previously served from 2002 to 2006 as Special Assistant to the President and Associate White House Counsel, where he was extensively involved in work on intelligence legislation and intelligence transformation initiatives. Powell clerked on the Supreme Court for Justices John Paul Stevens and Byron White, and the

ABOUT THE CONTRIBUTORS

U.S. Court of Appeals for the Second Circuit for Judge John M. Walker Jr. Prior to law school, Powell served in the U.S. Air Force and also worked for the Federal Bureau of Investigation. In the Air Force, Powell led one of the largest Department of Defense computer network development programs for the Intelligence Community and worked in support of the U.S. Space Command Joint Space Intelligence Center, U.S. Navy Fleet Intelligence Centers, U.S. Central Command, and Air Combat Command. In May 2009, he received the National Security Agency's Intelligence Under Law Award for his commitment to the conduct of intelligence activities under the rule of law. He is a recipient of the Central Intelligence Agency Seal Medallion and the National Security Agency Bronze Medallion.

Harvey Rishikof is Professor of Law at the iUniversity at Drexel University, Chair of the American Bar Association Advisory Standing Committee on Law and National Security, Co-Chair of the ABA Taskforce on Cyber and Security, and on the Board of Visitors of the National Intelligence University. He is a lifetime member of the Council on Foreign Relations and the American Law Institute. Rishikof is the former Senior Policy Advisor to the Director of National Counterintelligence at the Office of the Director of National Intelligence and Chair of the American Bar Association Advisory Standing Committee on Law and National Security. He was a Professor of Law and National Security Studies at the National War College, where he also was Chair of the Department of National Security Strategy. Rishikof is a former member of the law firm Hale and Dorr, is a former Dean of the Law School at Rhode Island, and has been a consultant to the World Bank and USAID on law reform. He also served as Legal Counsel to the Deputy Director of the FBI (1997–99) and as liaison to the Office of the Attorney General at the Department of Justice. He was Administrative Assistant to the Chief Justice of the Supreme Court (1994–96) and a Law Clerk in the Third Circuit Court of Appeals for Judge Leonard I. Garth. Rishikof has been a Tutor in Social Studies at Harvard University. His most recent book, co-edited with Roger George, is *The National Security Enterprise—Navigating the Enterprise*.

David Scharia is the Legal and Criminal Justice Coordinator at the Counter Terrorism Executive Directorate of the United Nations Security Council. Scharia provides legal advice to the Security Council's Counter Terrorism Committee on States' implementation of relevant Security Council resolutions. From 1996 to 2005, Scharia was a First Senior Deputy at the Supreme Court division in the Attorney General office in Israel. In that role, he was the Lead Attorney in major counterterrorism cases before the Supreme Court of Israel and the Chair of the Inter-Ministerial Counter-Terrorism Committee. Scharia is on the international advisory board of several research institutions. Currently Scharia is a Visiting Scholar at the New York University Center for Global Affairs and a Scholar in Residence at Columbia Law School. He is a frequent lecturer on these issues in international forums. Scharia is the author of *The Supreme Court of Israel and*

About the Contributors

the Fight Against Terrorism: From PM Rabin's Assassination to Operation Cast Shield and *Wiretaps, Informants, and Secret Agents: Maintaining the Rule of Law in the Prosecution of Terrorism.*

Glenn M. Sulmasy is the Chair of the Law Faculty, Professor of Law, and a member of the U.S. Coast Guard Academy's Permanent Commissioned Teaching Staff. He coordinates and teaches international law and constitutional law in the Humanities Department. He also teaches criminal justice and is the Director of the Homeland Security Law Lecture Series. Sulmasy received his bachelor's degree in government from the U.S. Coast Guard Academy in 1988, earned his J.D. cum laude from the University of Baltimore School of Law and an LL.M from Berkeley School of Law, and attended the Harvard Kennedy School. He is co-editor of *International Law Challenges: Homeland Security and Combating Terrorism* and author of *The National Security Court—A Natural Evolution of Justice in an Age of Terror.* Sulmasy is a captain in the Coast Guard.

Chris Tribolet is an Assistant Professor of Law at the U.S. Coast Guard Academy. He teaches courses on military justice and maritime law enforcement. Prior to teaching at the Coast Guard Academy, Tribolet served as a line attorney for the Coast Guard, prosecuting courts-martial, assisting the Department of Justice in federal trials, and providing legal advice on maritime operations to Coast Guard units. His operational experience includes two years of sea duty and four years at Marine Safety Office San Francisco Bay. He is a 1997 graduate of the U.S. Coast Guard Academy and a 2006 graduate of U.C. Hastings College of Law. Tribolet is a lieutenant commander in the Coast Guard.

John R. Tunheim has served as a United States District Judge since 1995. Tunheim served as the Chairman of the U.S. Assassination Records Review Board, an independent federal agency responsible for reviewing and facilitating public disclosure of previously classified government records related to the assassination of President John F. Kennedy. He led negotiations with intelligence officials from Russia, Belarus, Cuba, and Mexico for release of foreign records. To declassify intelligence and law enforcement records, he was frequently called upon to review current classified operations to determine whether release of older records was appropriate. Tunheim is actively involved with the United States Judicial Conference. He worked as the principal outside adviser to the process that developed the Kosovo Constitution. He has worked on rule of law development projects in Kosovo, Uzbekistan, Georgia, Russia, Montenegro, Jordan, Hungary, Bulgaria, Kazakhstan, Kyrgyzstan, Moldova, and Lithuania. He has taught as an Adjunct Professor of Law at the University of Minnesota Law School. Tunheim served as Chief Deputy Attorney General and as Minnesota Solicitor General. He was a Staff Assistant to U.S. Sen. Hubert H. Humphrey, and Law Clerk to Senior District Judge Earl Larson. He is a graduate of the University of Minnesota Law

School and Concordia College. A former Chair of the Council of the American Bar Association Division on Government and Public Sector Lawyers, he serves on the American Bar Association Standing Committee on Law and National Security.

J. Bennet Waters is a Member and Managing Director of the Chertoff Group, LLC, where his work is focused on counterterrorism, critical infrastructure protection, and strategic advice on mergers, acquisitions, and private equity investments in intelligence and homeland security technologies. Waters served from 2005 to 2009 at the Department of Homeland Security, where he was Counselor to two Deputy Secretaries; Deputy Assistant Administrator at the Transportation Security Administration; and Chief of Staff for the Office of Health Affairs. Prior to entering government, he spent more than a decade in the private sector, where he held strategic, financial, and operations roles in early-stage organizations and turnaround situations. He is a frequent speaker and author on counterterrorism, transportation security, emergency preparedness, and disaster management.

Index

A
Abbottabad compound, 124–125
Abdulmutallab, Umar Farouk, 218, 319
Academi, 266
Accelerated Manufacture of Pharmaceuticals program, 366
Achille Lauro, 136
ACLU v. National Security Agency, 10
Actionable intelligence, 168
Adams, John, 14
Administrative personnel proceedings
   administrative punishment, 185–186
   common proceedings, 184
   more serious charge and proceeding, 184–185
   overview of, 183–184
Administrative Procedures Act (APA), 358
Administrative punishment, 185–186
Advanced imaging technology (AIT)
   accuracy, 356–357
   concerns over safety, 357
   Fourth Amendment and, 358
   legal environment, 352–354
   limitations and concerns, 355–357
   necessity and justification for use, 357–358
   overview of, 354–355
   privacy issues, 356
   technological capability, 356
   types of devices, 355

Afghanistan, 99, 101, 115, 125
Agents of foreign powers, 199, 230, 233
Ahmed, Mohamed Ibrahim, 265
Airport screening
   advanced imaging technology, 352, 354–355
   experts, 358–359
   legal environment, 352–354
   limitations and concerns, 355–357
   necessity and justification, 357–358
   overview of, 351–352
   resources, 359
   and scanning, 351–359
AIT. *See* Advanced imaging technology
al-Awlaki, Anwar, 161
al Bahlul, Ali Hamza, 178, 259
al-Marri, Ali Saleh Kahlah, 274
al-Nashiri, Abd al-Rahim, 179
al-Qaida
   Abdeladim el-Kebir and, 263
   anthrax lab in Afghanistan, 361
   designated as foreign terrorist organization, 251
   detention, interrogation, and trial of, 5
   detention of operatives of, 115
   drone strikes against, 99
   inapplicability of prisoner of war status to captured operatives of, 106
   military commissions and, 258
   Oussama Kassir and, 272

INDEX

al-Qaida, *continued*
  recognized as armed conflict, 179
  rise of the threat of international terrorism and, 217–218
  role of propaganda in, 259
  Somali piracy and, 137
  Syed Hashmi and, 272
  testimony of experts on, 249
  Title 10, U.S. Code and operations against, 125
  U.N. Security Council Resolution 1267 and, 85
  United States v. Mehanna and, 253
  warrantless wiretapping of, 3
al-Shabaab, 137, 265, 272
al-Zawahiri, Ayman, 253
Alien Registration Act of 1940, 336
Alien registration laws, 336–337
Alien Terrorist Removal Court, 339
Alien Tort Statute, 71, 304
Alito, Samuel, 280, 289
Alvarez-Machain, Humberto, 273
Ambos, Kai, 91, 91n37
American Civil Liberties Union, 241
American-Israel Public Affairs Committee, 17
American National Standards Institute (ANSI), 357
American Revolution, 174
Amnesty International, 166
Amnesty Int'l USA v. McConnell, 241n21
Analytics, 291–292
Angolan Civil War, 127
Annan, Kofi, 83
ANSI. *See* American National Standards Institute
Anthrax, 361
  attacks, 201
AORs. *See* Areas of responsibility
APA. *See* Administrative Procedures Act
Arab Spring, 300
Araunah, 155
Archipelagic states, 152
Arctic, 151
Areas of responsibility (AORs), 207

Armed attacks
  constitution of, 101–102
  requirement of immediacy, 103–104
  requirement of necessity, 102
  requirement of proportionality, 103
  responding to, 102–104
Article 2(4), Charter of the United Nations, 99
Article 15, Uniform Code of Military Justice, 184
Article 41, Charter of the United Nations, 100
Article 51, Charter of the United Nations, 100
Article I, U.S. Constitution, 3–4, 135, 259
Article II, U.S. Constitution, 4
Article III, U.S. Constitution, 4
Article VI, U.S. Constitution, 74
Articles of War, 174
Ashcroft, John, 221
Ashcroft v. al-Kidd, 7
ASPR. *See* Office of the Assistant Secretary for Preparedness and Response
Association of Public Health Laboratories, 364
ATF. *See* Bureau of Alcohol, Tobacco, Firearms, and Explosives
Atlanta Olympics bombing of 1996, 201
ATR. *See* Automated Target Recognition
Atta, Mohammed, 257
Attorney General Guidelines for Domestic FBI Operations, 215
Attorney General Guidelines for FBI National Security Investigations and Foreign Intelligence Collection, 221
Augustine of Hippo, 164
Aum Shinrikyo, 361
Authorization for Use of Military Force, 6, 72, 106n15, 239
Automated Target Recognition (ATR), 356
Automated Targeting System (ATS), 295–296
AutoTrack, 284

B

B-2 Spirit bomber program, 30
Backscatter X-ray machines, xii, 355, 357
Bank Secrecy Act, 209
Barbary Pirates, 136
BARDA. *See* Biomedical Advanced Research and Development Authority
Baring, Alexander (Lord Ashburton), 101
Bartnicki v. Vopper, 16
Baselines, 149
Bering Sea, 155
Beslan terrorist attacks, 88
BIC. *See* BioIntelligence Center
Biddle, Francis, 176
bin Laden, Osama
   in al-Qaida's network, 253
   plan to capture, 129
   raid on Abbottabad compound, 124–125, 130
   religious proclamation of, 217
   U.N. Security Council Resolution 1267 and, 85
BioIntelligence Center (BIC), 364
Biological attacks
   articles, 373–374
   BioWatch program, 362–363
   books, 373
   detection, 362
   diagnosis, 364–365
   experts, 371
   government reports, 372–373
   medical countermeasure, 365–368
   overview of, 361–362
   programs for reporting unusual diseases, 363–364
   public health mobilization, 369–370
   resources, 372–374
   response and restoration of order, 368–370
   restricting movement, 370
   use of military forces, 369
Biomedical Advanced Research and Development Authority (BARDA), 366, 367
BioSense program, 363
BioShield Special Reserve Fund, 366
BioWatch program, 362–363
Black, Hugo, 15
Blackwater Worldwide, 266
Blanco, Kathleen, 316
Body scanners, 352
Boeing Company, 300
Border fence, 343–344
Border Patrol, 202
Border searches, 341
Border security
   allocation of federal, state, and local immigration authority, 345–347
   background, 330–331
   experts, 349
   illegal immigration and, 342–345
   intelligence authorities, 331–334
   journalist use of phrase, xi
   law, 330
   resources, 350
   role of military in, 347–348
   traveler screening and, 340–342
   use of immigration law in counterterrorism and, 334–340
Boumediene v. Bush, 7, 181
Bradbury, Steven G., 131
Branzburg v. Hayes, 19
Brennan, William J., 14
Brinkema, Leonie, 20
Bureau of Alcohol, Tobacco, Firearms, and Explosives (ATF), 204
Bureau of Consular Affairs, 332, 342
Bureau of Diplomatic Security, 332
Burma, 260, 302
Bush administration
   Iraq war and, 4
   military commissions and, 71, 177–178
   National Security Strategy, 104
   USA PATRIOT ACT and, 260
   Justice Department official in, 4
Bush, George H.W., 158
Bush, George W.
   creation of National Security Service within FBI, 206
   drone policy, 161
   International Court of Justice ruling and, 73

INDEX

Bush, George W., *continued*
  issuing of order for use of military commissions, 173–174
  response to Hurricane Katrina, 316
  United Nations Convention on Law of the Sea ratification and, 158
  warrantless foreign intelligence surveillance and, 6
  wartime authority of, 3, 4

C

Cameron, David, 139
Canada, 340, 344–345
CAPPS I, 294
CAPPS II. *See* Computer-Assisted Passenger Prescreening System
Caroline Doctrine, 164
Caroline Incident, 100–101, 164
Carter, Jimmy, 6
Cash assistance, ban on, 252
Cassese, Antonio, 89, 90, 90–91n34
Caterpillar Inc., 10
CBP. *See* U.S. Customs and Border Protection
CDC. *See* Centers for Disease Control and Prevention
CDRH. *See* Center for Devices and Radiological Health
CE. *See* Counterespionage
Center for Devices and Radiological Health (CDRH), 357
Center for Global Health, 364
Center for Security Policy, 158
Centers for Disease Control and Prevention (CDC), 363–364, 367, 369
Central Intelligence Agency (CIA)
  creation of, 127, 198
  interrogation practices of, 180–181
  Legacy of Ashes (Weiner), 217
  secret operations and Title 50, 123–133
Charter of the United Nations
  Article 2(4), 99, 157–158
  Article 41, 100
  Article 51, 100, 101, 163, 164, 170
  Chapter VII, 85, 99, 100
  international law and, 68, 83
  role of the U.N. Security Council in, 84–85

Cheney, Richard, 20
Chile, 127, 147
China, 149
ChoicePoint, 284
Church Committee, 198, 216–217
CI. *See* Counterintelligence
CI Division, 206
CIA. *See* Central Intelligence Agency
CIL. *See* Customary international law
CISADA. *See* Comprehensive Iran Sanctions, Accountability, and Divestment Act of 2010
Cisco Systems, Inc., 301
City of Ontario v. Quon, 236
Civil support/homeland defense continuum, 318–319
Civil War, 175, 198
Clapper v. Amnesty Int'l USA, 241n21
Classification
  ban on use of, 31
  definition, 31
  Executive Orders governing, 27–28
  experts, 36
  "For Official Use Only" designation and, 34–35
  glossary, 31–33
  legal consequences for violating rules, 35–36
  modern categories of, 28–29
  resources, 36
  sensitive compartmented information controls of, 29–30
  special access programs and, 30
  U.S government secrecy and, 25–37
  in U.S. history, 25–26
Classified information
  access to, 33–34
  definition, 26, 31
  ground rules for using, 340
  use in immigration proceedings, 339–340
Classified Information Procedures Act, 178
Classified National Security Information, 27–28, 41–65
Clearance, 31

Index

Clinton administration, 158
Clinton, Bill, 146
CLS. *See* Commission on the Limits of the Continental Shelf
Cold War, 217
Colombia, 102, 106
Columbus, Christopher, 146
Colvin, John, 13n1
Combatants
  immunity, 114
  lawful status and privileges, 113–114
Commercial data, 283–284
Commission on Prevention of Weapons of Mass Destruction Proliferation and Terrorism, 361
Commission on the Intelligence Capabilities of the United States Regarding Weapons of Mass Destruction, 206, 230
Commission on the Limits of the Continental Shelf (CLS), 151, 152
Communications Assistance for Law Enforcement Act, 299
Comprehensive Iran Sanctions, Accountability, and Divestment Act of 2010 (CISADA), 303
Computer-Assisted Passenger Prescreening System (CAPPS II), 293–294
Confidential source, 31
Consent
  of the flag state, 154
  by foreign coastal state, 155
  of vessel's master, 154
Conspiracy, 245–246
Constructive presence, 155–156
Content interception, 231–234
Contiguous zone (CZ), 151, 153
Continental Congress, 174
Convention against Torture, 71
Convention for the Suppression of Terrorist Financing, 82
Convention for the Suppression of Unlawful Acts against the Safety of Maritime Navigation, 136
Corrie v. Caterpillar, 10
Council of Europe, 288
Counter-Terrorism Committee (CTC), 87
Counterespionage (CE), 204

Counterespionage Section, 205
Counterintelligence (CI), 204
Counterintelligence Section, 205
Counterterrorism
  international instruments, 82–83, 87
  provisions under 18 U.S.C. § 956, 248
  provisions under 18 U.S.C. § 2339A, 248
  role of consent in, 99
  targeted killings, 104, 161–172
  United Nations Global Counter-Terrorism Strategy, 81
  United Nations policy, 81, 91
  U.S.-based intelligence and, 199
  use of immigration law in, 334–340
Court-martial
  hypothetical case, 186–192
  investigation and prosecution, 187
  military commissions and, 175, 176
  proceedings, 186–192
  prosecutorial discretion, 188n12
Court of Criminal Appeals, 192
Courts. *See also* U.S. Court of Appeals; U.S. Supreme Court
  Article III of U.S. Constitution and, 4
  disputes regarding the exercise of wartime authority and, 9–10
  international, 70
  questions of international law in U.S., 71–75
  upholding designation as foreign terrorist organization, 251–252
Covert action
  definition, 127
  exclusions from definition of, 128
  experts, 132–133
  resources, 133
  under Title 50 of the U.S. Code, 126–127
  traditional military activities and, 129–132
Criteria-based decision-making, 167
CT Division, 206
CTC. *See* Counter-Terrorism Committee
Cuba, 246, 302, 305
Customary international law (CIL)
  constructive presence, 155–156
  overview of, 69–70
  terrorism as a crime under, 90–91

INDEX

Cybersecurity, xi, 241–242
CZ. *See* Contiguous zone
Czech Republic, 272

D

Damage to the national security, 28n11, 31
Dames & Moore v. Regan, 6
Data mining
 Automated Targeting System, 295–296
 Computer-Assisted Passenger Prescreening System, 293–294
 defined by Data Mining Reporting Act, 282n13
 definition, 281
 experts, 297
 factors to consider in use, 283–284
 GAO recommendations, 285
 government programs, 293–297
 historical context, 285–290
 overview of, 279–280
 relationship of technology to policy, 290–293
 resources, 297–298
 Terrorist Finance Tracking Program (TFTP), 296–297
 Total Information Awareness, 294–295
 types of, 281
 use of commercial data for fraud detection in, 284
Data Mining Reporting Act, 282
Data Mining Statute, 210
Data protection laws, 286–290, 301
Declassification, 31
Defense Advanced Research Projects Agency, 294, 366, 367
Defense Intelligence Agency, 208
Defense Support of Civil Authorities, 314
Delayed-notice searches, 234
Dell Inc., 301
Deportability grounds, 334–336
Designated as foreign terrorist organizations (DFTOs), 246, 247, 251
Detainee Treatment Act of 2005 (DTA), 6
Detention, 115–116, 274, 337–339
DFTOs. *See* Designated as foreign terrorist organizations

DHS. *See* U.S. Department of Homeland Security
DI. *See* Directorate of Intelligence
Direct cooperation, 271–272
Directive 95/46/EC, 288
Director of National Intelligence (DNI), 203–204
Directorate of Intelligence (DI), 206
Discoverability, 290–291
Dispensation, medical countermeasure, 367–368
Distribution, medical countermeasure, 367–368
Document, 31
DoD. *See* U.S. Department of Defense
Domestic intelligence, 197–198
Domestic Investigations and Operations Guide, 215, 222, 224
Domestic law, 69
Domestic wiretapping, 3, 9, 230, 239–241
Draft Comprehensive Convention on International Terrorism, 84
Drones
 border security and, 333
 journalist use of phrase, xi
 policy, 161
 strikes, 99
Drug Enforcement Administration, 204
DTA. *See* Detainee Treatment Act of 2005
Dual Status Commander, 317–318
Due process clause, 165–166, 338

E

E-Government Act of 2002, 287
E-mail, 236
ECHR. *See* European Court of Human Rights
Economic sanctions, 302–303
ECPA. *See* Electronic Communications Privacy Act
EEZ. *See* Exclusive economic zone
18 U.S.C. § 956, 248
18 U.S.C. § 2339A, 246, 247–249
18 U.S.C. § 2339B, 246, 250–254
Eisenhower, Dwight D., 324
el-Kebir, Abdeladim, 263, 267
El Paso Intelligence Center, 333

Electronic Communications Privacy Act (ECPA), 231, 235, 237, 241, 301
Electronic surveillance
  access to stored communications, 235–237
  agents of foreign powers, 230
  constitutional origins, 227–228
  content interception, 231–234
  content vs. noncontent, 228–229
  cybersecurity and, 241–242
  definition, 233–234
  experts, 242
  Foreign Intelligence Surveillance Amendments Act and, 239–241
  physical searches and, 234–235
  resources, 242
  rules for conducting, 199
  statutes regulating, 231–241
  transactional data, 237–238
  warrantless surveillance program, 239–241
Ellis, Thomas S., 18
Emergency Operations Center, 364
Espionage Act of 1917, 16–17, 20–21, 22
EU. *See* European Union
European Commission, 288
European Court of Human Rights (ECHR), 70
European Union (EU)
  data protection laws, 288–289, 301
  passenger data, 296
  sanctions against Syria, 305
Ex parte Quirin, 115, 176
Excluded Parties List, 303
Exclusive economic zone (EEZ), 152–153, 157
Executive Orders
  8381, 26
  12333, 32, 199, 218–219
  13526, 27–28, 34, 35, 41–65
  basics of, 27
  governing classification, 27–28
Executive oversight, national security investigations, 224
Exemption power, 336
Export controls, 302–303
Extrajudicial killing, 166

Extraterritorial offenses
  cases, 276–277
  Constitution across national borders and, 269–271
  constitutional issues, 267–268
  experts, 275
  foreign investigations, 271
  getting information to court and, 271–272
  international law issues, 268
  investigations abroad, 268–272
  joint ventures, 271
  jurisdiction for, 264–268
  obtaining the defendant, 272–274
  posttrial, 274
  resources, 275–276
  statutes, 277
  statutory issues, 266

F

F-117A Nighthawk "stealth fighter," 30
Faina, 135
Fair Information Practice Principles (FIPPs), 288
Farabundo Martí National Liberation Front (FMLN), 101
FDA. *See* U.S. Food and Drug Administration
Federal Bureau of Investigation (FBI)
  diagnosis of pathogens and, 364
  Domestic Investigations and Operations Guide, 215, 222
  national security investigations and, 215
  Office of Integrity and Compliance, 224
  Office of the General Counsel, 224
  stored communications obtained by, 236
  U.S.-based intelligence and, 198, 204–207
  use of National Security Letters, 237
Federal Emergency Management Administration, 202
Federal Emergency Management Agency (FEMA), 284, 325, 368, 369
Federal Emergency Response Plan, 369
Federal Register, 293, 294
FEMA. *See* Federal Emergency Management Agency

INDEX

Field Intelligence Group (FIG), 206
Fifth Amendment, U.S. Constitution, 269–270
50 U.S.C.
§ 413b, 128–129
covert action under, 126–127
definition, 124
raid on Abbottabad compound and, 130
statutory framework for, 130
FIG. *See* Field Intelligence Group
Final Report of the National Commission on Terrorist Attacks Upon the United States, 129, 129n24
Findings, 128–129
FIPPs. *See* Fair Information Practice Principles
First Amendment, U.S. Constitution
border searches and, 341
criminal prosecution of journalists and, 16–18
experts, 21
foreign intelligence investigations and, 238
legislation and, 22
material support laws and, 246
national security and, 13–23
Pentagon Papers and, 14–16
publications, 22–23
reporter's privilege and, 18–21
resources, 22–23
Sedition Act and, 14
United States v. Mehanna and, 253
FISA. *See* Foreign Intelligence Surveillance Act
FISC. *See* Foreign Intelligence Surveillance Court
FISCR. *See* Foreign Intelligence Surveillance Court of Review
Fisheries conservation zones, 147
Flag-state consent, 154
FMLN. *See* Farabundo Martí National Liberation Front
FOIA. *See* Freedom of Information Act
"For Official Use Only" (FOUO), 32, 34–35
Foreign coastal state consent, 155

Foreign intelligence
collection activities and national security investigations, 215, 220
collection activities and preliminary investigations, 223
definition, 200, 231
role of Federal Bureau of Investigation in collection of, 219
surveillance activity and the Fourth Amendment, 229
U.S.-based collection of, 199
Foreign Intelligence Surveillance Act (FISA)
the ""wall" and purpose requirement of, 235
agents of foreign powers and, 230
border security and, 331
definition electronic surveillance in, 233–234
electronic surveillance and, 227
national security investigations and, 215
oversight of national security investigations and, 225
overview of, 219–220
passage of legislation, 199
pen/trap devices and, 238
preliminary investigations and, 223
stored communications and, 236
Terrorist Surveillance Program and, 9
Title III, The Omnibus Crime Control and Safe Streets Act and, 232–233
USA PATRIOT ACT and, 209
Foreign Intelligence Surveillance Amendments Act of 2008, 223, 239–241
Foreign Intelligence Surveillance Court (FISC), 199, 219, 230, 234, 240
Foreign Intelligence Surveillance Court of Review (FISCR), 219–220, 229–230, 234
Foreign investigations, 271
Foreign nexus requirement, 324
Foreign power, 233
Fort Hood massacre, 218, 319
FOUO. *See* "For Official Use Only"

Fourth Amendment, U.S. Constitution
  across national borders, 269
  advanced imaging technology and, 358
  airport screening and scanning, 352–353
  border searches and, 341
  content interception and, 232
  physical searches and, 234
  on privacy of records shared with third parties, 286
  question of exception to warrant requirement, 229–230
  remote data storage and, 236
  searches, 227–228
Fourth Geneva Convention, 115
Frankfurter, Felix, 7
Franklin, Larry, 17
Freedom of Information Act (FOIA)
  categories for exemption from mandatory release under, 34–35
  executive branch classification authority and, 26
  exemptions, 28, 34–35
  "For Official Use Only" designation and, 32
Friedman, Benjamin, 313

G
Gang of Eight, 129
GAO, 281, 284
Gates, Robert, 217
General Intelligence Division (GID), 198
General Services Administration, 303
Geneva Conventions
  in civil support/homeland defense continuum, 320
  Common Article 2, 105
  Common Article 3, 106, 109
  international law and, 68, 83
  military commissions and, 177, 179
  principle of humanity in, 109, 109n23
  purpose of, 107
Germany, 142
Ghailani, Ahmed, 273
GID. *See* General Intelligence Division
Global Counter-Terrorism Strategy, 81
Gonzales, Alberto, 206
Goodman, Bobby, 105

Google Inc., 300
Grotius, Hugo, 68
Guantanamo Bay detention facility, xii, 3, 6, 75, 115–116
Guantanamo Bay military commission issues, 179–181
Guantanamo Bay trials, 178–179
Gulf of Aden, 135
Gulf of Guinea, 137
Gulf of Mexico, 147

H
Habeas corpus, 13n1, 175, 320
Habeas Corpus Act, 198
Hague Convention IV (1899), 107
Hamas, 246, 247, 251, 255
Hamdan, Salim, 74–75, 178, 259
Hamdan v. Rumsfeld, 6, 7, 8, 73, 106n15
Hamdan v. United States, 259–260n45
Hamdi v. Rumsfeld, 8, 73, 115
Hamdi, Yaser, 72
Hariri, Rafiq, 90
Hasan, Nidal, 218, 319
Hashmi, Syed, 272
Healey, Gene, 313
Health Incident Surveillance Branch, 363
Health Threats Resilience Division, 363
Heritage Foundation, 158
HEW. *See* U.S. Department of Health, Education, and Welfare
Hewlett-Packard Company, 301
Hezbollah, 102
HHS. *See* U.S. Department of Health & Human Services
Hicks, David, 177
HIG. *See* High-Value Detainee Interrogation Group
High-Value Detainee Interrogation Group (HIG), 206
Hmong people, 336
Holder, Eric, 333
Holder v. Humanitarian Law Project, 7, 245n4, 247, 250, 254–256
Holmes, Oliver Wendell, 264
Holy Land Foundation v. Ashcroft, 251, 256

INDEX

Homegrown terrorists, 324
Homegrown violent extremists (HVEs), 209
Homeland Security Act of 2002, 202, 330, 343
Hoover, J. Edgar, 198
Hostis humani generis, 135
Hot pursuit, 155
House Permanent Select Committee on Intelligence, 199
House Permanent Select Committee on Intelligence (HPSCI), 131
HPSCI. *See* House Permanent Select Committee on Intelligence
Huawei Technologies Co. Ltd., 303
Human intelligence (HUMINT), 167
Human rights litigation, 304
Human Smuggling and Trafficking Center, 333
Human trafficking, 156
HUMINT. *See* Human intelligence
Hurricane Katrina, 284, 316, 323
Hurricane Rita, 284
Hussein, Saddam, 98
HVEs. *See* Homegrown violent extremists

I

IC. *See* Intelligence community
ICC. *See* International Criminal Court
ICCPR. *See* International Covenant on Civil and Political Rights
ICE. *See* U.S. Immigration and Customs Enforcement
ICJ. *See* International Court of Justice
Identity/entity resolution, 291
IIRAIRA. *See* Illegal Immigration Reform and Immigrant Responsibility Act
Illegal immigration, 342–345
Illegal Immigration Reform and Immigrant Responsibility Act of 1996 (IIRAIRA), 343, 345
Immediacy, 103–104
Immediate Response Authority, 323
Immigration
   allocation of federal, state, and local authority, 345–347
   illegal, 342–345

material support of terrorism and, 260–261
use of immigration law in counterterrorism, 334–340
Immigration and Nationality Act
   alien registration provisions of, 336
   border fence and, 343
   border security law in, 330
   INS v. Chadha and, 8
   traveler screening and, 340
   USA PATRIOT ACT and, 209
Immigration and Naturalization Service (INS), 330
Immigration laws
   alien registration laws, 336–337
   detention, 337–339
   exemptions, 336
   federal-state enforcement partnership, 345–346
   immigration proceedings and, 339–340
   inadmissibility and deportability grounds, 334–336
   material support provisions of terrorism laws and, 334–336
   state legislative actions relating to enforcement, 346–347
   use in counterterrorism, 334–340
Immigrations and Customs Enforcement, 202
Imminence, 168
In re Grand Jury Subpoena, Judith Miller, 20
In re Sealed Case, 219
Inadmissibility grounds, 334–336
Informants, 250
Information, 32
Innocent passage, 148
INS. *See* Immigration and Naturalization Service
INS v. Chadha, 8
Insurrection Act, 321–322
Intelligence activities, 32
Intelligence Authorization Act of 2012, 131
Intelligence community (IC), 32, 198
Intelligence Identities Protection Act of 1982, 22

Index

Intelligence oversight, 323–325
Intelligence Reform and Terrorism Prevention Act (IRTPA), 203
Intelligence, U.S.-based
  background, 197–199
  definition, 200
  director of national intelligence, 203–204
  experts, 210
  Federal Bureau of Investigation and, 204–207
  future challenges with, 208–210
  law and organizational structure, 197–213
  post-9/11 changes and the structure of enterprise, 201–202
  resources, 210–213
  U.S. Department of Defense and, 207–208
  U.S. Department of Homeland Security and, 202–203
  U.S. Department of Justice and, 204–207
Internal Security Act of 1950, 26, 27
International Bill of Human Rights, 341
International counterterrorism instruments, 82–83
International Court of Justice (ICJ), 70, 73, 101
International courts, 70
International Covenant on Civil and Political Rights (ICCPR), 72
International Criminal Court (ICC), 68, 70, 88–89
International Emergency Economic Powers Act, 302
International law
  customary, 69–70, 90–91
  defining terrorism under, 79–93
  experts, 75–76, 92
  extraterritorial offenses, 268
  jus ad bellum, 98–104
  jus in bello, 105–118
  proportionality test, 169–170
  recent cases, 73
  resources, 76–77, 92–93
  right to movement, 341
  role in domestic courts, 67–77
  role of International Criminal Court, 88–89
  sources of, 68
  targeted killings and, 161–172
  treaties, 68–69
  in U.S. courts, 71–75
International Security Assistance Force, 99
Internet, 131
Interoperability, 292
Iran, 6, 246, 302, 305
IRTPA. *See* Intelligence Reform and Terrorism Prevention Act
Israel, 80, 102
IT Dashboard, 281

J

Jackson, Robert, 6
Jane's Defence Weekly, 17
Jefferson, Thomas, 13n1, 313, 323
JIATF-South. *See* Joint Interagency Task Force-South
JIATF-West. *See* Joint Interagency Task Force-West
JITF-CT. *See* Joint Intelligence Task Force for Combating Terrorism
Johns Hopkins University Applied Physics Laboratory, 357
Johnson, Lyndon, 149
Joint Intelligence Task Force for Combating Terrorism (JITF-CT), 208
Joint Interagency Task Force-South (JIATF-South), 207, 333
Joint Interagency Task Force-West (JIATF-West), 207
Joint ventures, 271
Journalists
  criminal prosecution of, 16–18
  privilege, 18–21
Judicial oversight, national security investigations, 225
Juniper Networks Inc., 301
Jurisdiction, for extraterritorial offenses, 264–268
Jus ad bellum
  armed attacks, 101–102
  consent, 99

INDEX

Jus ad bellum, continued
  definition, 98–99
  experts, 119–120
  immediacy, 103–104
  international legal basis for the use of force, 98–104
  necessity, 102
  proportionality, 103
  resources, 120–121
  responding to an armed attack, 102–104
  self-defense, 100–104
  targeted killings and, 104
  U.N. authorizations, 99–100
Jus in bello
  combatant immunity, 114–115
  core principles, 107–113
  definition, 105
  detention, 115–116
  distinction, 110–112
  experts, 119–120
  humanity, 109–110
  lawful combatant status and privileges, 113–114
  military necessity, 108
  proportionality, 112–113
  regulating the conduct of hostilities, 105–118
  resources, 120–121
  rules of engagement, 116–118
  triggering the law of armed conflict, 105–107

K
Kassir, Oussama, 272
Katz test, 290n44
Keith case, 230
Kenya, 142
Kerry, John F., 158
Khobar Towers bombing of 1996, 201
Koh, Harold, 11
Korean War, 6
Kriegsraison, 108
Kris, David, 216
Kurdistan Workers' Party (PKK), 102, 252
Kuwait, 98, 101

L
Laboratory Response Network, 364
Law of armed conflict (LOAC)
  combatant immunity, 114
  core principles, 107–113
  definition, 105
  detention, 115–116
  distinction, 110–112
  humanity, 109–110
  lawful combatant status and privileges, 113–114
  military necessity, 108
  Nuremberg Tribunal ruling on, 98
  proportionality, 112–113
  rules of engagement, 116–118
  triggering the law of, 105–106
Law of the Sea Tribunal, 158
Law of war, 259–260n45
Leahy, Patrick, 236
Legacy of Ashes (Weiner), 217
Legal attaché offices (LEGATs), 207
LEGATs. *See* Legal attaché offices
Legislative oversight, national security investigations, 225
Legitimate targets, 167–168
Letters rogatory, 272
LexisNexis, 284
Libby, Lewis "Scooter," 20
Liberation movements, 80
Liberation Tigers of Tamil Eelam (LTTE), 251, 252–253
Libya, 3, 11, 85, 99, 106
Lincoln, Abraham, 13n1
LOAC. *See* Law of armed conflict
Lockerbie plane bombing, 85
Lod Airport massacre, 80
Lone wolf, 233
Lord Ashburton (Alexander Baring), 101
LTTE. *See* Liberation Tigers of Tamil Eelam
Lugar, Richard, 158, 159

M
Madison, James, 316
Madrid Address, 83–84
Maersk Alabama, 138

Index

Manual for Courts-Martial (MCM), 183, 186, 191
Mare liberum, 146–147
Marine scientific research, 157
Markle Foundation, 290, 292
Martens clause, 107
Martins, Mark J., 97
Material support laws
   conspiracy law and, 245–246
   criticisms of, 256–257
   history of, 246–247
   hypothetical cases regarding, 243–245
   immigration impact, 260–261
   immigration laws and, 334–336
   material support beyond criminal law, 257–258
   material support of designated organizations, 250–256
   military commissions and, 258–259
   prosecutions for aiding terrorist activity under section 2339a, 247–249
   use of informants, 250
MCM. *See* Medical countermeasures
Medellin, Jose, 72–73
Medellin v. Texas, 72–73
Medicago, 367
Medical countermeasure (MCM)
   development, 365–366
   new vaccine production capacities, 367
   stockpile planning, distribution, and dispensation, 367–368
Mehanna, Tarek, 253–254
MEJA. *See* Military Extraterritorial Jurisdiction Act
Mexican War of 1846–48, 174
Mexico, 340, 345
Microsoft Corporation, 301
Military
   civil support/homeland defense continuum, 318–319
   civilian control of, 315
   experts, 326
   Immediate Response Authority, 323
   Insurrection Act and, 321–322
   intelligence collection, 324
   intelligence oversight, 323–325
   limits on use of, 315–316
   Posse Comitatus Act and, 321
   reserve component of, 316
   resources, 326–327
   roles, 314–315
   Title 10 forces, 316–318
   Title 32 forces, 316–318
   unity of command vs. unity of effort and the Dual Status Commander, 317–318
   use of, 313–327
Military activities
   covert action and traditional, 129–132
   experts, 132–133
   resources, 133
   under Title 10 of the U.S. Code, 125–126, 316–318, 321, 348
Military Commission Convening Authority, 180
Military Commission Court of Review, 259
Military commissions
   Bush administration, 6, 7, 177–178
   experts, 182
   trials under Military Commissions Act, 178–179
   historical background of, 174–176
   issuing of military order by George W. Bush, 173–174
   journalist use of phrase, xi
   material support laws and, 258–259
   resources, 182
Military Commissions Act of 2006, 177, 178
Military Commissions Act of 2009, 174, 178, 181
Military contractors, 266
Military Extraterritorial Jurisdiction Act (MEJA), 266
Military justice
   administrative personnel proceedings, 183–186
   court-martial proceedings, 186–192
   foundations of, 183
   posttrial proceedings, 192
Military necessity, 108
Military Rules of Evidence (MRE), 183, 190
Miller, Judith, 19–20

INDEX

Milligan, Lambdin P., 175
Millimeter wave machines, 355
Miranda rights, 320
Miranda warnings, 269–270
Mohamed v. Jeppesen Dataplan, 10
Money Laundering Control Act of 1986, 209
Morgan, Henry, 136
Mosaic theory test, 289
MRE. *See* Military Rules of Evidence
Mubarak, Hosni, 85
Mueller, Robert, 205
Mukasey, Michael, 222
Munaf v. Geren, 8
Munich Olympics massacre, 80
Mutual legal assistance treaties, 272

N

Napolitano, Janet, 337
Narus, Inc., 300
NASA. *See* National Aeronautics and Space Administration
National Aeronautics and Space Administration (NASA), 303
National Biodefense Analysis and countermeasure Center, 364
National Bioforensic Repository Collection, 364
National Bioforensics Analysis Center (NBFAC), 364
National Biosurveillance Integration Center (NBIC), 363
National Counterterrorism Center (NCTC), 203–204, 331, 333, 334
National Defense Authorization Act of 2012, 131–132, 319
National Electronic Disease Surveillance System, 363
National Guard, 316–317, 321, 323, 347–348, 369
National Incident Management System, 370
National Institute for Standards and Technology (NIST), 357
National Institutes of Health, 365
National Joint Terrorism Task Force (NJTTF), 206
National of Allergy and Infectious Diseases, 365

National Operations Center (NOC), 202
National Research Council, 283
National Response Framework, 368
National security
   allocation of powers to branches of government, 3–4
   border security and, 329–350
   classification levels and, 28–29
   criminal prosecution of journalists and, 16–18
   definition, 32
   experts, 12
   First Amendment and, 13–23
   investigations abroad, 268–272
   jurisdiction for extraterritorial offenses, 264–268
   law, 330
   legislation, 22
   publications, 22–23
   resources, 12, 22–23
   separation of powers and, 3–12
National Security Act of 1947
   border-security-related intelligence practice and, 331
   creation of Central Intelligence Agency and, 127, 198
   Executive Order 13526 and, 28
   foreign intelligence as defined by, 200
   intelligence community as defined by, 32
   national security law and, 330
   responsibilities of director of central intelligence and, 26
National Security Agency (NSA), 208, 241
National Security Branch, 206
National Security Council, 127
National Security Division (NSD), 204, 220–221, 223
National Security Entry-Exit Registration System (NSEERS), 336–337
National Security Investigations and Prosecutions (Kris & Wilson), 216
National security investigations (NSIs)
   collapse of the Soviet Union and the end of the Cold War, 217
   early abuses and the Church Committee, 216–217
   emergence of a legal framework for, 218–224

Executive Order 12333 and, 218–219
executive oversight, 224
experts, 226
Foreign Intelligence Surveillance Act and, 219–220
historical foundations of modern, 216–218
institutional reform and creation of National Security Division, 220–221
judicial oversight, 225
legislative oversight, 225
oversight of, 224–225
overview of, 215–216, 225–226
resources, 226
rise of the threat of international terrorism, 217–218
National Security Letters (NSLs), 215, 225, 237
NBFAC. *See* National Bioforensics Analysis Center
NBIC. *See* National Biosurveillance Integration Center
NCTC. *See* National Counterterrorism Center
NDA. *See* Nondisclosure agreement
Necessary and Proper Clause, 267
Necessity, 102
"Need to know," 32
Netherlands, 272
New York Times, 15, 19, 239
New York Times Co. v. Gonzales, 20
New York Times Co. v. Sullivan, 14
New York Times Co. v. United States, 15
9/11 Commission Act of 2007, 363
The 9/11 Commission Report: Final Report of the National Commission on Terrorist Attacks Upon the United States, 129, 129n24, 199, 201–202
Nisoor Square, 266
NIST. *See* National Institute for Standards and Technology
Nixon, Richard M., 11, 145, 149
NJTTF. *See* National Joint Terrorism Task Force
NOC. *See* National Operations Center
Non-refoulement, 140
Non-U.S. persons, 232
Nondisclosure agreement (NDA), 33

Noninternational armed conflict, 106–107
Nonmetallic explosives, 354–355
NORAD. *See* North American Aerospace Defense Command
North American Aerospace Defense Command (NORAD), 314, 320
North Atlantic Council, 102
North Atlantic Treaty, 102
North Korea, 302, 337
Norway, 149
Novartis, 367
NSD. *See* National Security Division
NSEERS. *See* National Security Entry-Exit Registration System
NSI Guidelines. *See* Attorney General Guidelines for FBI National Security Investigations and Foreign Intelligence Collection
NSIs. *See* National Security Investigations
NSLs. *See* National Security Letters
Nuremberg Tribunal, 98

O

Obama administration, rationale for the al-Awlaki killing, 162
Obama, Barack
  drone policy, 161
  Executive Order 13526, 27–28, 34, 35, 41–65
  Executive Order 13606, 303n19
  military commissions and, 178
  NATO mission in Libya and, xii, 11
  wartime authority of, 3
Office Hours, 184
Office of Foreign Assets Control, 303
Office of Global Security Risk, 304
Office of Health Affairs, 362
Office of Integrity and Compliance, 224
Office of Intelligence and Analysis, 332
Office of Intelligence and Research, 332
Office of Justice for Victims of Overseas Terrorism, 205
Office of Law and Policy, 205
Office of Legal Counsel, 4, 7, 8–9, 131
Office of Military Commissions, 180
Office of National Security Intelligence, 332
Office of Strategic Services (OSS), 127

INDEX

Office of the Assistant Secretary for Preparedness and Response (ASPR), 365–366
Office of the General Counsel (OGC), 224
Office of the Inspector General (OIG), 357
OGC. *See* Office of the General Counsel
OIG. *See* Office of the Inspector General
Oklahoma City bombing of 1995, 201, 246, 335
Omar, Mahamud Said, 272
Operation "Goldenrod," 273
Oracle Corporation, 301
Organization for Economic Cooperation & Development, 288
Organization of American States, 102
OSS. *See* Office of Strategic Services

P

Padilla, Jose, 247–249, 274
Pakistan, 124–125
Palestinian terrorists, 136
Palmer, Mitchell, 198
Pan Am Flight 103 disaster, 85
Passenger name record (PNR), 295
Passports, 341
Pattern-based queries, 281
Pen Register Act, 238
Pen registers, 238
Pentagon Papers, 15
Personal data, protection of, 288
Personally identifying information (PII), 283, 288
Petraeus, David, 97
PHEMCE. *See* Public Health Emergency Medical Countermeasures Enterprise
Philippine Insurrection of 1899, 176
PHIN. *See* Public Health Information Network
Physical searches, 234
PI. *See* Preliminary investigation
PIAs. *See* Privacy impact assessments
PII. *See* Personally identifying information
Pike Committee, 198
Piracy
   background, 135–137
   causes of Somali, 137–138
   difficulties in prosecution, 140–141
   experts, 142–143
   in history, 136
   law experts, 142
   political science experts, 142
   private military contractors and rules of engagement, 138–140
   resources, 143
   security experts, 142
   Somali, 135
   transfers for trial, 141–142
   unauthorized broadcasting, 156
   as universal crime, 156
Pirate radio, 156
PKK. *See* Kurdistan Workers' Party
Plame, Valerie, 19
PNR. *See* Passenger name record
Posse Comitatus Act, 320–322, 325, 347–348, 369
Posttrial proceedings, 192
Powell, Lewis, 19
Predator drones, 333
Predicated investigations, 223
Predication, 283, 284–285
Preliminary investigation (PI), 223
Presentment Clause, U.S. Constitution, 8
President
   Article II of U.S. Constitution and, 4
   national security crises and, 4
   separation of powers and, 3–12
   use of force and authority of, 4–7
Pretrial agreements (PTAs), 192n21
Privacy, 356
Privacy Act, 325
Privacy Act of 1974, 28, 210, 279, 287
Privacy-enhancing technology, 292
Privacy impact assessments (PIAs), 287–288
Privacy test, 228
Private military contractors, 138–140
Privilege, 18–21
Probable cause, 232
Project BioShield, 365, 366
Propaganda, 253
Proportionality, 103, 112–113
Proportionality test, 169–170
Prosecutorial discretion, 188n12

Index

Public Health Emergency Medical countermeasure Enterprise (PHEMCE), 366
Public Health Information Network (PHIN), 363
Purpose requirement, 235
Pursuit Group, 204

R
RCM. *See* Rules for Courts-Martial
Reagan administration, 146, 157
Reagan, Ronald, 146, 158
REAL ID Act, 335
Refugees, 336
Remote data storage, 236
Report of the Secretary-General's High-Level Panel on Threats, Challenges and Changes, 83
Republic of Vietnam, 99, 149
Revolutionary Armed Forces, 102
RFPA. *See* Right to Financial Privacy Act
Rice, Condoleezza, 197
Right of approach, 153–154
Right of self-defense, 101–102
Right of visit, 153–154
Right to counsel, 270–271
Right to Financial Privacy Act (RFPA), 237, 287
Right to movement, 341
Right to privacy, 236, 286
Right to speedy trial, 270–271
Risen, James, 20–21
Roberts, John, 177
Roberts, John G., Jr., 254, 255
Robertson, James, 177
ROE. *See* Rules of engagement
Rome Statute of the International Criminal Court, 68, 83
Roosevelt, Franklin D., 26, 176
Roper v. Simmons, 70
Rosen, Steven J., 17–18
Royall, Kenneth C., 176
Rules for Courts-Martial (RCM), 183
Rules of engagement (ROE)
 law of armed conflict and, 116–118
 private military contractors and, 138–140

Rumsfeld, Donald, 325
Rumsfeld v. Padilla, 249

S
Sack, Robert, 20
Safeguarding, 32
Safety and Biosurety Program and Quality/Accreditation Program, 364
Santiago Declaration, 147
SAPs. *See* Special access programs
Saul, Ben, 91, 91n37
SBInet program, 344
SCA. *See* Stored Communications Act
Scalability, 292
SCI. *See* Sensitive compartmented information
Scott, Winfield, 174, 175
SDNs. *See* Specially Designated Nationals
Searches and seizures, 227–228, 234–235, 341, 352
SEC. *See* U.S. Securities and Exchange Commission
Secure Fence Act, 344
Secure Flight program, 291, 293, 352
Securities law, 304
Security clearance, 32
Security countermeasure, 32
Security manager, 32
Sedition Act of 1798, 14
Self-defense
 historical background of, 163–166
 right of, 101–102
 targeted killings and, 161–172
Senate Foreign Relations Committee, 158
Senate Select Committee on Intelligence, 131, 199
Sensitive compartmented information (SCI), 29–30, 32
Separation of powers
 claims settlement agreements and, 6–7
 commander-in-chief authority of President, 4, 5–6
 congressional infringement on president's authority, 8
 disputes regarding the exercise of wartime authority and courts, 9–10

405

INDEX

Separation of powers, *continued*
  exercise of wartime authority and congressional restrictions, 9
  military commissions and, 6, 7
  national security and, 3–12
  powers of the courts, 4
  Terrorist Surveillance Program and, 6, 9
  torture memo and, 8–9
  wartime authorities of Congress, 3–4
September 11, 2001 terrorist attacks
  airport screening and scanning after, 351–359
  alien registration laws after, 336–337
  border security and, 330
  court rulings on foreign intelligence exception to warrant requirement since, 230
  establishment of U.S. Northern Command, 314
  immigration detention after, 338
  immigration law after, 334–340
  inflection point in American law and policy, xi
  legal authorities governing secret operations following, 123–133
  material support laws after, 243, 246
  Mohammed Atta and, 257
  national security investigations and, 218
  planning of, 280
  right of self-defense against nonstate actors, 101–102
  role of al-Qaida in, 217
  targeted killings and, 165
  triggering the law of armed conflict and, 106n15
  U.N. Security Council resolutions, 86–87
  United Nations counterterrorism policy and, 81
  U.S.-based intelligence enterprise following, 201
7 July 2005 London bombings, 87
Seychelles, 141, 142
Sherman, William T., 108
SIGINT. *See* Signal intelligence
Signal intelligence (SIGINT), 167
Six-Day War, 104

Sixth Amendment, U.S. Constitution, 270–271
SJA. *See* Staff judge advocate
Slave trading, 156
Smith Act, 336
SMTJ. *See* Special maritime and territorial jurisdiction of the United States
SNS. *See* Strategic National Stockpile
Society for Worldwide Interbank Financial Telecommunication (SWIFT), 296
Somali piracy, 135, 137–138
Somalia, 106
SORNs. *See* System of records notices
Sosa v. Alvarez-Machain, 73
Sotomayor, Sonia, 208
Soviet Union, 217
Special access programs (SAPs), 30, 33
Special maritime and territorial jurisdiction (SMTJ), 266
Special security officer (SSO), 33
Special Tribunal for Lebanon (STL), 90–91, 91n37
Specially Designated Nationals (SDNs), 302–303
SSO. *See* Special security officer
Staff judge advocate (SJA), 192
Stafford Act, 316, 369
State Active Duty forces, 316–318
State of War (Risen), 20
State terrorism, 83
Steel Seizure Case, 5, 7
Sterling, Jeffrey, 20
Stewart, Potter, 19
STL. *See* Special Tribunal for Lebanon
Stockpile planning, medical countermeasure, 367–368
Stockpile Service Advance Group, 368
Stored communications, 235–237
Stored Communications Act (SCA), 231, 235–237
Strait of Gibraltar, 151
Strait of Hormuz, 151
Straits of Malacca, 137
Strategic National Stockpile (SNS), 367–368
Subject-based queries, 281–282
Sudan, 302, 305

Index

Suicide bomber infrastructure, 167–168
Supremacy Clause, 74
Surratt, Mary, 175
Surveillance technology
  economic sanctions, 302–303
  experts, 308–309
  export controls, 302–303
  exports to repressive regimes, 299–310
  government web pages, 309–310
  human rights litigation and, 304
  Iran and Syria sanctions related to, 303–304
  publications, 309–310
  regulations, 309
  resources, 309–310
  securities law and, 304–305
  statutes, 309–310
  use by repressive regimes and news and investigation cycles, 306–308
  use by repressive regimes and substantive law, 301–306
  wiretap laws and, 305–306
SWIFT. *See* Society for Worldwide Interbank Financial Telecommunication
Symantec Corporation, 301
Syria, xii, 105, 302, 305
System of records notices (SORNs), 287

T

Taliban, 3, 85, 106, 258
Tamil Tigers. *See* Liberation Tigers of Tamil Eelam
Tanzania, 141
Targeted killings
  actionable intelligence, 168
  core principles, 163
  as counterterrorism measure, 104
  decision-making process, 166–170
  differentiating extrajudicial killing from, 166
  experts, 170–171
  historical background of self-defense, 163–166
  issues, 162–163
  journalist use of phrase, xi
  law and, 161–172
  legitimate targets, 167–168
  proportionality test, 169–170
  resources, 171–172
Taylor, Telford, 114
Teach, Edward (Blackbeard), 136
Telecom Egypt, 300
10 U.S.C.
  definition, 124
  military activities under, 125–126, 316–318, 321, 348
  statutory framework for, 130
Tenth Amendment, U.S. Constitution, 315–316
Territorial sea, 148, 149–151
Terrorism
  as a crime under international customary law, 90–91
  defining at United Nations, 80–84
  defining under international law, 79–93
  experts, 92
  immigration law and, 335–336
  international counterterrorism instruments, 82–83
  as an international crime, 88–89
  material support of, 243–262
  noninternational armed conflict and, 106–107
  recent debates at the United Nations to define, 84
  resources, 92–93
  rise of the threat of international, 217–218
  September 11, 2001 terrorist attacks, 86–87
  U.N. resolutions to take measures against, 86–88
  U.N. Security Council and the definition of, 84–86
Terrorist, as defined by 8 U.S.C. § 236A(a)(1), 335
Terrorist Finance Tracking Program (TFTP), 296–297
Terrorist Identification Data Environment, 331
Terrorist Identities Datamart Environment (TIDE), 204
Terrorist Screening Center (TSC), 206

INDEX

Terrorist Surveillance Program (TSP), 6, 9
Test prong table, 169
TFTP. *See* Terrorist Finance Tracking Program
Third Geneva Convention, 113, 115
32 U.S.C, 316–318, 321, 348
TIA. *See* Total Information Awareness
Tibyan Publications, 253
TIDE. *See* Terrorist Identities Datamart Environment
Tier II organizations, 335
Title 10, U.S. Code
  definition, 124
  military activities under, 125–126, 316–318, 321, 348
  statutory framework for, 130
Title 32, U.S. Code, 316–317, 321, 348
Title 50, U.S. Code
  covert action under, 126–127
  definition, 124
  raid on Abbottabad compound and, 130
  section 413b, 128–129
  statutory framework for, 130
Title III, The Omnibus Crime Control and Safe Streets Act of 1968, 231–234
Torture, 71
Torture memo, 8–9
Total Information Awareness (TIA), 294–295
Trace devices, 238
Trade embargoes, 302
Trading with the Enemy Act, 302
Transactional data, 237–238
Transit passage, 151–152
Transportation Security Administration (TSA)
  airport screening and scanning, xii, 351–358
  Homeland Security Act and, 202
  right to movement and, 341
  Secure Flight program, 291, 293, 352
  use of advanced imaging technology by, 354–355
Traveler screening
  airport screening and scanning, 351–359
  Automated Targeting System, 295–296
  border security and, 340–342

Computer-Assisted Passenger Prescreening System, 293–294
  Secure Flight program, 291, 293
Treaties, 68–69
Treaty of Westphalia, 68
Truman, Harry, 6, 147
TSC. *See* Terrorist Screening Center
TSP. *See* Terrorist Surveillance Program
Turkey, 102
21 July 2005 London bombings, 87

U

Unabomber, 201
Unauthorized broadcasting, 156
Unauthorized disclosure, 33
UNCLOS. *See* United Nations Convention on Law of the Sea
UNCLOS I, 148
UNCLOS II, 148
UNCLOS III. *See* United Nations Convention on Law of the Sea
"Underwear Bomber," 319, 329, 357
Uniform Code of Military Justice (UCMJ)
  Article 15, 184
  Article 32 Investigation, 188
  Article 36, 177
  Article 86, 189
  Article 92, 189
  Article 121, 189
  Article 122, 189
  in court-martial proceedings, 186
  as foundation of military justice, 183
  mandate of "equal" access to evidence in, 180
  military commissions and, 7, 71
United Kingdom, 272
United Nations. *See also* Charter of the United Nations
  Ad Hoc Committee, 84
  Charter, 83, 84–85, 99
  combating terrorist financing and, 258
  defining terrorism at, 80–84
  Global Counter-Terrorism Strategy, 81
  Maersk Alabama and, 138
  recent debates to define terrorism at, 84
  resolutions to take measures against, 86–88

408

Index

Sixth Committee, 84
treaties and, 68
United Nations Convention on Law of the Sea (UNCLOS)
　Arctic and, 151
　Article 22, 154
　Article 101(a)(1), 136
　Article 105, 141–142
　Article 111, 155
　Article 301, 157
　background, 145–146
　consent by a foreign coastal state, 155
　consent of vessel's master, 154
　constructive presence, 155–156
　conventions on the law of the sea and, 148
　definition of piracy in, 136
　early development of the law of the sea, 146–147
　exceptions to Article 92, 153–157
　experts, 159
　hot pursuit, 155
　jurisdiction creep, 147
　parts of, 149–153
　principles in, 145
　push for comprehensive law of the sea treaty, 148–149
　resources, 159–160
　right of visit and right of approach, 153–154
　status in U.S. Law, 158–159
　universal crimes, 156–158
　universal jurisdiction status of piracy in, 141–142
United Nations Security Council Resolutions
　748, 85
　1189, 85
　1267, 85
　1368, 102
　1373, 86–87, 86–87n15, 258
　1540, 87
　1566, 88
　1624, 87
　1970, 99
　1973, 99
　on piracy, 137

United Nations Security Council (UNSC)
　Counter-Terrorism Committee, 87
　definition of terrorism and, 84–86
　Special Tribunal for Lebanon, 90
United States v. Ahmed, 265, 267
United States v. Al Bahlul, 259–260n45
United States v. El-Mezain, 256
United States v. Flores-Montano, 286
United States v. Ghailani, 270–271
United States v. Jones, 208, 229, 280n4, 290n44, 333
United States v. Maynard, 289
United States v. Mehanna, 253–254
United States v. Morison, 17
United States v. Rosen, 17–18
United States v. U.S. District Court, 230
Universal crimes, 156–158
UNSC. *See* United Nations Security Council
U.S. Air Force, 183, 184, 321
U.S. Army, 174, 184, 321
U.S. Citizenship and Immigration Services, 332, 336, 341
U.S. Coast Guard
　administrative personnel proceedings in, 184
　border security and, 332, 333
　granting of law enforcement authority to, 348
　Homeland Security Act and, 202
　Posse Comitatus Act and, 321
　use of doctrine of right of visit to board, 154
U.S. Congress
　Article I of U.S. Constitution and, 3–4
　authority over covert actions by, 127
　Authorization for Use of Military Force, 6, 72, 125
　border security and, 332
　customary international law and, 71
　exclusions from definition of covert action by, 128
　jurisdiction for extraterritorial offenses, 268
　material support legislation, 247
　military commissions and, 6, 176
　national security crises and, 4

INDEX

U.S. Congress, *continued*
  oversight of national security investigations, 225
  on placement of border fence, 343–344
  power to criminalize extraterritorial conduct, 267
  resources on U.S.-based intelligence, 213
  role in use of force, 10–11
  separation of powers and, 3–12
  Total Information Awareness program and, 294
  use of military forces and, 347–348
  visa applicants and, 342
  wartime authorities of, 3–4
U.S. Constitution
  across national borders, 269–271
  Article I, 3–4, 135, 259
  Article II, 4, 125
  Article III, 3
  Article VI, 74
  Attorney General Guidelines and, 222
  classification authority and, 26
  Domestic Investigations and Operations Guide and, 222
  due process clause, 165–166, 338
  Executive Order 13526 and, 28
  Fifth Amendment, 165
  First Amendment, 13, 341
  Fourteenth Amendment, 165
  Fourth Amendment, 227–228, 229–230, 232, 341, 352–353, 358
  Necessary and Proper Clause, 267
  on piracy, 135
  Presentment Clause, 8
  Supremacy Clause, 74
  Tenth Amendment, 315–316
  use of military forces and, 347
U.S. Court of Appeals
  D.C. Circuit, 19, 177, 289
  Fourth Circuit, 17, 21, 141
  Ninth Circuit, 236
  Second Circuit, 10, 20, 241
  Sixth Circuit, 10, 236
U.S. Court of Appeals for the Armed Forces, 192
U.S. Customs and Border Protection (CBP), 295, 332, 333, 348

U.S. Department of Commerce, 302
U.S. Department of Defense (DoD)
  budget, 325
  in civil support/homeland defense continuum, 319–320
  Defense Advanced Research Projects Agency, 294, 366, 367
  establishment of U.S. Northern Command, 314
  Immediate Response Authority and, 323
  intelligence oversight, 324
  Iran sanctions and, 303
  law of armed conflict characterization and, 105
  medical countermeasure programs, 366
  military defense and, 348
  Office of Military Commissions, 180
  Posse Comitatus Act and, 321
  Privacy Act and, 325
  regulations on collection of U.S. person information, 325
  response to bioattacks, 370
  response to Hurricane Katrina, 317
  secret operations and Title 10, 123–133
  Strategic National Stockpile and, 367
  U.S.-based intelligence and, 207–208
  use of "For Official Use Only" designation, 34
U.S. Department of Health & Human Services (HHS), 365, 367, 370
U.S. Department of Health, Education, and Welfare (HEW), 287, 288
U.S. Department of Homeland Security (DHS)
  BioWatch program, 362–363
  border fence, 343–344
  border security intelligence and, 332
  in civil support/homeland defense continuum, 319
  Computer-Assisted Passenger Prescreening System and, 293
  Fair Information Practice Principles at, 288
  Office of Intelligence and Analysis, 332
  Office of the Inspector General, 357
  Posse Comitatus Act and, 321
  response to bioattacks, 370

Index

SBInet program, 344
Strategic National Stockpile and, 367
U.S.-based intelligence and, 202
use of "For Official Use Only" designation, 34
U.S. Department of Justice
   Attorney General Guidelines and the FBI Guide, 221–224
   in civil support/homeland defense continuum, 319
   Foreign Intelligence Surveillance Act and, 239
   General Intelligence Division, 198
   immigration detention, 337–338, 339
   National Security Division, 220–221, 223
   Office of Information Policy, 37
   Office of Legal Counsel, 4, 7, 8–9, 131
   resources on U.S.-based intelligence, 213
   torture memo, 8–9
   United States v. Rosen, 17
   U.S.-based intelligence and, 204–207
U.S. Department of State, 305, 332, 341
U.S. Department of the Treasury, 302
U.S. Drug Enforcement Administration, 332
U.S. embassy bombings in Africa of 1998, 201, 217, 273
U.S. entity, 33
U.S. Food and Drug Administration (FDA), 357
U.S. Government Accountability Office, 284
U.S. Immigration and Customs Enforcement (ICE), 332
U.S. Marine Corps, 184, 321
U.S. Marshals Service, 204
U.S. Navy, 184, 321
U.S. Navy SEALS, 138
U.S. Northern Command (USNORTHCOM), 207, 314, 316, 323, 348
U.S. persons, 232, 233, 324, 340–341
U.S. Securities and Exchange Commission (SEC), 304
U.S. State Department, 137
U.S. Supreme Court
   Ashcroft v. al-Kidd, 7
   Bartnicki v. Vopper, 16
   Boumediene v. Bush, 7, 181
   court-martial convictions and, 192
   customary international law and, 69–70
   on detention periods, 274
   Hamdan v. Rumsfeld, 6, 7, 8, 73, 106n15
   Hamdi v. Rumsfeld, 8, 73,
   Holder v. Humanitarian Law Project, 7, 245n4, 247, 250, 254–256
   on immigration detention, 338–339
   INS v. Chadha, 8
   on law of war, 259–260n45
   Medellin v. Texas, 72–73
   military commissions and, 175, 176, 177
   Munaf v. Geren, 8
   national security decisions, 7–8
   New York Times Co. v. Sullivan, 14
   New York Times Co. v. United States, 15
   on reasonable expectation of privacy, 289–290
   Roper v. Simmons, 70
   ruling on "special needs" exception to warrant requirement, 229–230
   on seizures, 228
   Sosa v. Alvarez-Machain, 73
   two-prong test for what constitutes a search, 227–228
   United States v. Flores-Montano, 286
   United States v. Jones, 208, 229, 333
   United States v. U.S. District Court, 230
   on wiretapping, 228
   Youngstown Sheet & Tube Co. v. Sawyer, 5
US VISIT (United States Visitor and Immigrant Status Indicator Technology), 337
USA PATRIOT ACT (Uniting and Strengthening America by Providing Appropriate Tools Required to Intercept and Obstruct Terrorism Act of 2001)
   border security and, 331
   creation of National Security Division, 204–205
   FISA's purpose requirement and, 235

INDEX

USA PATRIOT ACT, *continued*
   Foreign Intelligence Surveillance Act and, 209, 220, 230
   immigration detention and, 338, 339
   immigration law and, 335
   material support laws and, 247
   pen/trap devices and, 238
   physical searches and, 234
USA PATRIOT Reauthorization and Improvement Act of 2001, 199
Use of force
   Congressional regulation on, 10–11
   international legal basis for, 98–104
   liberation movements and, 80
   president's constitutional authority for, 4–7
   role of consent in, 99
   rules of engagement and, 116–118
   self-defense and, 100–104
   U.N. authorizations for, 99–100
USNORTHCOM. *See* U.S. Northern Command
USPACOM, 207
USS *Cole* attack, 179, 201
USSOUTHCOM, 207

V

Vessel's master consent, 154
Vienna Convention on Consular Relations, 73
Vietnam War, 10, 127
Violation, 33
Visas, 340–342
Voicemail, 236

W

Wall Street Journal, 303
War of Spanish Succession, 136
War Powers Resolution (WPR), 10–11
Warrantless surveillance programs, 3, 9, 230, 239–241
Warrants, 9, 230, 236
Warsame, Ahmed Abdulkadir, 263, 267, 273
Washington Post, 15
Weapons of Mass Destruction Directorate, 206
Webster, Daniel, 101, 164
Weiner, Tim, 217
Weissman, Keith, 17–18
Wikipedia, 281
Wilson, Douglas, 216
Wiretap Act, 223, 231–234, 299
Wiretapping
   Fourth Amendment and, 228
   Keith case, 230
   laws, 305–306
   provisions under Foreign Intelligence Surveillance Ac, 233–234
   Title III, The Omnibus Crime Control and Safe Streets Act and, 232–233
   warrantless, 3, 9, 230, 239–241
WMD Commission. *See* Commission on the Intelligence Capabilities of the United States Regarding Weapons of Mass Destruction
World Trade Center bombing of 1993, xi, 201, 335
World War I, 198
WPR. *See* War Powers Resolution

Y

Yahoo! Inc., 300
Yemen, 99
Yoo, John C., 4
Youngstown Sheet & Tube Co. v. Sawyer, 5
Younis, Fawaz, 273

Z

ZTE Corporation, 301